21st CENTURY
GODDESS

The modern girl's guide to the universe

JESSICA ADAMS ✳ **JELENA GLISIC** ✧ **ANTHEA PAUL**

CORGI BOOKS

21st CENTURY GODDESS
A CORGI BOOK: 0 552 15071 1

Originally published in Australia by Allen & Unwin
First publication in Great Britain

PRINTING HISTORY
Corgi edition published 2004

1 3 5 7 9 10 8 6 4 2

Copyright © Jessica Adams 2002
Copyright © Jelena Glisic 2002
Copyright © Anthea Paul 2002

Designed and set in Futura Book by Julia Lloyd.

Corgi Books are published by Transworld Publishers,
61-63 Uxbridge Road, London W5 5SA,
a division of The Random House Group Ltd,
in Australia by Random House Australia (Pty) Ltd,
20 Alfred Street, Milsons Point, Sydney, NSW 2061, Australia,
in New Zealand by Random House New Zealand Ltd,
18 Poland Road, Glenfield, Auckland 10, New Zealand
and in South Africa by Random House (Pty) Ltd,
Endulini, 5a Jubilee Road, Parktown 2193, South Africa.

Printed and bound in Great Britain by
Mackays of Chatham plc, Chatham, Kent.

Papers used by Transworld Publishers are natural, recyclable products made from wood grown in sustainable forests. The manufacturing processes conform to the environmental regulations of the country of origin.

Contents

When a woman has owned her passionate nature, allowing love to flood her heart, her thoughts grow wild and fierce and beautiful. Her juices flow. Her heart expands. She has thrown off crutch and compromise. She has glimpsed the enchanted kingdom, the vast and magical realms of the Goddess within her. Here, all things are transformed.

Marianne Williamson, *A Woman's Worth*

Welcome God

You have just entered the quintessential feminine zone – the realms of the 21st Century Goddess – where a new world is waiting. Know who you are and want to go to the next level? You're in the right place. It's time to get on with it in the most powerful time for women since witches were the true and revered healers on the planet, and women in general were the custodians of all that was sacred in cultures throughout the world. Because you are connected to all of those who went before, you have stardust in your DNA from those earliest stars that exploded millennia ago – you have the Goddess within you and . . . she wants out! Your original natural purpose contains the promise and power of the ages past and is ultimately magical. However, for many of us that purpose has been dormant for too long. Unleash your personal Goddess and tap into your true essence through gaining a full understanding of your ancient roots, and reap the benefits of living more fully now.

We hope you'll be learning even more about yourself and your eternal connection to the Goddess of centuries past with our guide to the deeply mystical. We cover the most important topics of interest to aspiring Goddesses and these are presented for the first time as a comprehensive overview. The subjects covered in each chapter are usually written about or presented in isolation, but as you'll soon see, when viewed together they make for a very compelling – and bewitching – combination. From the more whimsical aspects of angels to the weightier facts of astrology, numerology and magic, here are our best tips for uncovering and discovering the Goddess within. We have the lowdown on crystals, potions and remedies, rituals to invoke and unblock healing universal energies, mantras to manifest your heart's true desires, and much more.

A portion of the proceeds of 21st Century Goddess will go towards charities that support the Tibetan cause. A Buddhist culture, Tibet has the Goddess Green Tara – 'She who liberates' – as its most revered female deity. With the deep-seated belief in non-violence and compassion at the core of its culture, Tibet is a more than worthy recipient of the support it continues to receive worldwide in its quest for a peaceful coexistence with its neighbours. We honour Green Tara and we support His Holiness, the Dalai Lama of Tibet and the Tibetan people in their ongoing struggle for liberation and the full restoration of their independence.

Ultimately we hope that this book will be a guide to bring you all the joys in life that you desire. We want to bring enchantment and beauty into all facets of your journey. And we hope that you'll find many new ways to do so within these pages. it's the beginning of a whole new spiritual period for women and we, your Goddesses-in-waiting, are proud to be your hostesses for what will undoubtedly be a magical, sensuous and wondrous journey.

Wishing you well . . .

Jessica, Jelena and Anthea
21st century Goddesses

Goddess

In order to be a Goddess in the new millennium—a true 21st Century Goddess – you need a working knowledge of the ancient roots of the archetypal Goddesses of civilizations and cultures past. If you missed that particular history (er, herstory) class then we've got just the ticket for you! In this chapter you'll scrub up on your mythology, add a smidgen of psychology, a dash of metaphysics, and while you're at it get a bit of dirt under your fingernails.

Teachers open the door, but you must enter by yourself.

[Chinese Proverb]

Now, we know you're a modern woman of the world – just by the fact that you're reading this. You've probably got a mobile phone, high-speed internet access, and more than likely you do your shopping on the net. You're technologically plugged in to the 21st century and the fact that you've still got more things to do than is humanly possible is a given! We know you know life is more than high-tech gadgets and deadlines though, and we want to help you to go to the next level in order to get the most out of it. Now to do that, we'd really like you to grab a cup of tea, sit quietly for just a minute or three, and devote some serious consideration to one major question: Who are you . . . really? Some of you may be able to roll off some confident answers to that, but if you're like most of us the answer(s) is probably a bit of a mystery grab bag and certainly can't be done in fifteen words or less. We hope we can help you to unravel at least a good part of the mystery. Put it this way, by the end of the book we hope you'll have a greater understanding of the complex being that is you.

To begin, we want to take you back, way back in time, to the territory of the original spiritual warrior, the Goddess. It is ancient land indeed and we're going there! To uncover this heartland of our collective female heritage, we need to check out the roots for they are covered in moss, clay, earth, and salt water, and they are the critical starting point for all that is to come. Think of it like this: You can assess the present only if you have a firm grip on what went down in the past. And the way we see it, everything is derivative and you can put it in perspective far more readily if you have a good grounding in the classic originators of it. For instance, to appreciate and understand the current popular and dance music scene you need to know where its roots lie. The Beatles, Elvis Presley, Aretha Franklin, and jazz greats such as Miles Davis, Charlie Parker, and John Coltrane lead you all the way to modern Goddesses such as Madonna and Britney Spears! Ditto all the famous artists throughout the ages, and accordingly the ancient and mythical Goddesses of the past. The thing is, no matter what area you look at in our world today, we very much need the past to anchor any new experiences we may have in the future. The past lends the necessary framework from which to view them. This is how we learn.

The new Goddess

So, what is a 21st Century Goddess – and what (on earth!) is wrong with the old version? Well . . . there's nothing actually wrong with the old version but it seemed to us that the time had come to spruce it up a bit. We decided it was time, in fact, to take the concept of the Goddess out for a bit of a run and some much-needed fresh air. She needed to be dusted off and revamped for an era that calls for a new attitude and a new and substantive approach to life, not just lifestyle. You could say it was "a calling" of sorts that, once heard, we had no option but to heed. As well, there ensued many dinner discussions, phone calls, and glasses of champagne, which led us to it. Well, that's our excuse anyway! We felt strongly that the concept of what a Goddess is (and why it's still relevant) needed a bit of re-invention for this new era that finds the planet – and everyone on it – facing more problems than in its entire history. We are staring down a barrel that is loaded with the collective sins of the past, and this critical moment demands new solutions, new connections and, most importantly, new ideas and information. We're trying to do our bit to build a better society and a more tuned in one at that. However, the work begins at home – and frequently alone. Remember: It's personal first.

The re-invention of yourself is an ongoing quest that is emotional, physical, and spiritual. For us, that's what the definition of what being a modern Goddess is all about. It's about being committed to yourself, first and foremost, and this means being committed to your own spiritual and personal growth, living with intention and passion while striving to contribute to your immediate world and the world at large in a positive, meaningful way. Your life is your vision quest, and so it's up to you how you design it, how you conduct and carry yourself on the path you've selected and, most of all, how you follow through. We've given you our very best to support you and help you tackle all of that and more by defining and working with the ultimate spiritual warrior energy source of the ancient Goddess.

The Goddess defined

A Goddess is formally defined as a female deity, traditionally worshipped and revered for certain qualities most often found in nature. A Goddess is said to be "divine in character or nature" and is therefore composed of the essence of The Supreme Being. All Goddesses are representative of the universal (and truly cosmic) female energy principle that revolves around the physical creation of nature and the processes of life. Worshipped as such, the Goddess is symbolic of that most divine part within each of us, male or female. Well, we assume you already knew you were divine, but maybe you never knew just how much! The answer is . . . infinitely! Certainly we believe you should be worshipped anyway . . . and the best method that we know to bring in worship from others is to start with yourself. Our definition goes a bit beyond this as we believe a Goddess in the 21st Century needs to have a full arsenal of energy-raising and healing tools, and a range of channels to aid her journey towards conscious awareness. She salutes the Goddesses of the past whilst seeking new knowledge to augment her own spiritual path. It's not passive – it's active – and that's why we begin with the Goddess as a source of energy-raising and healing, and we then cover other areas which have the same intention, such as astrology, numerology, crystals, oils, and remedies, creative visualization, and so forth. All of these can assist you to raise the Goddess energy within you. They are individually and complementary support mechanisms whether or not they are used in their totality.

But we're getting ahead of ourselves. To set the scene for you in this chapter, we take a look at many different Goddesses from a variety of historic and contemporary cultures. Then (to avoid confusion) we have whittled this list down to the six Goddesses we classify as the "major" Goddesses. These constitute the shortlist we felt represented the most relevant and powerful Goddess archetypes. We explain and explore what an archetype is and how it is relevant to general Goddess energy. Once you have examined and understood each of the Goddess archetypes, you can then apply the energy principles at work in your current life experience. We should state from the outset that you may be "doing" a particular Goddess archetype which can change at any time, so you can experience different Goddess energies at different times in your life – it's a dynamic and ongoing process. It's also a more than fascinating exercise which, when undertaken seriously and with passion and commitment, can bring about massive change in outlook, choices, actions and, ultimately, personal power.

Each chapter within this book is but one thread in a much wider web, which is still being woven. In our search for the meaning of this web, we must delve into our personal, inner worlds to bring light to its deepest aspects. The gauntlet has been thrown down and the challenge for each of us in this new age is to see if we are truly willing to let go of outdated belief systems and conditioned responses. Only then can we be aware of our full potential and, accordingly, our life's purpose. With this in mind, we delve into topics in the rest of the book that we felt all women (a.k.a all Goddesses) would definitely benefit from having some sort of a handle on. These other areas serve as a complement to the basic framework of what we believe being a Goddess is all about. Well, surprise, surprise . . . 'cos baby: it's all about YOU!

The perfect Goddess

Unless you were force-fed the entire Encyclopaedia Britannica by hot-housing parents in childhood, you probably heard, like most of us, about the Gods and Goddesses of Ancient Greek and Egyptian mythology first in (yawn) history lessons at school. As the tragedies, travesties, and triumphs of these spectacular entities of the heavens and underworld were revealed to us in those classrooms, something else happened . . . we were hooked!

Most of us can remember at least the basic storyline of Aphrodite, Goddess of Love, or of Icarus who burned his wings flying too close to the sun, or poor old Narcissus who drowned in the reflection of his own beauty. In our wonder and amazement of these other-worldly stories, we were taking our rightful place as the successors to a mystical and magical world where miracles happened and nothing was impossible. This is our real inheritance.

As children we understood this implicitly and we related to the Gods and Goddesses, in all their various manifestations. How exotic and beautiful the Greek Goddesses seemed to us! They were usually possessed of a radiant beauty and/or an ethereal nature, or just of unusual qualities that were beyond the reach (and comprehension) of mere mortals. But still we related to them ... and with good reason, for they are in reality a part of us, that part from which we have separated, the part of us which is divine – that part that possesses God-like qualities. The Goddess is that part of us which is total and absolute perfection: right here and right now.

Accepting the notion of innate perfection may well be a tall order (and it doesn't have to be an ego trip); however, regarding yourself as infinite and perfect in this moment is exactly what we're going to persuade you to do! The thing is, as a human being having the evolutionary experience of being a woman in this lifetime, you are exactly and perfectly positioned for your individual destiny. You've been given this incarnation to realize your own innate perfection and to also recognize the same quality in all living things. That is why you're here – because you are a Goddess!

The Goddess within

The concept of being a Goddess is often used fairly loosely but as a "concept" and as an energy form the Goddess is still relevant today. The Goddesses of Ancient Greece were the main characters in stories designed to highlight qualities or energies we are each capable of having, experiencing, and revealing. While you are obviously in a different physical form to those in the myths, you are a Goddess nonetheless – you have Goddess energy and that's all there is to it! To fully serve your own unique purpose on the planet, however, you need to truly (madly, deeply) feel it and know it. To feel it means to reconnect with your intrinsic and ancient Goddess energy and to know it means to then work with it, to achieve all that you can while you're here. So, while you're thinking about your personal, individual destiny and what that may or may not encompass, let's drill down to the nuts and bolts of what the Goddess is all about and get to work on raising that energy.

"AWAKEN, O SLEEPING GODDESS"

The herstory of the Goddess (so far!)

The Goddess has many facets, names and faces – she is the moon, she is the earth, and she is the stars. Goddess worship dates back to Palaeolithic times, coinciding with ancient creation myths and beliefs. Throughout the centuries the Goddess has acquired a thousand names but she has always been represented as Mother Nature. The Goddess religion is a nature-based religion and those worshipping the Goddess therefore worship nature.

Goddess-oriented cultures were the oldest form of religious worship as communities (led by the female elders and healers) worshipped the "Great Mother" until newer, male-dominated cultures overran them. Goddess worship was by far the predominant ritual but over time this gradually changed to the worship of male God figures. Due to this, Goddess worship sharply declined, although it never fully died out. Indeed, the remnants of it remained within the hearts of the people, and the rituals that honour her have survived by being handed down quietly through the centuries. Evidence appears to indicate most ancient tribes and cultures worshipped a Goddess in some form, and from every land across the globe there is a Goddess represented in every culture. She is Artemis, Aphrodite, Athena, Isis, Lakshmi, and Diana among others.

Now things are starting to come full circle, with formal religions taking more of a complementary role to alternative modes of spirituality. There's a lot more experimentation going on, which actually makes life a lot more interesting. If you're familiar with the current trend of mix-and-match fashion, you know how to throw on a piece of designer clothing, add to that something vintage or maybe something from a discount store, then you create a truly individual fashion look. Well, in the same way, many of us are now investigating new forms of spirituality to add to or substitute for those more formal religious ideas. From this comes the confidence to create one's own belief systems. This is probably why the Goddess is still relevant. It's time to really tap into female energy – it's time to heal.

Girl – you deserve to be worshipped!

In many communities, the Goddess as a symbol and a deity still presides over many lives and events throughout the world. As we've discussed, Goddess worship is the worshipping of female deities and female symbols and it takes form in either a personal or communal expression of knowledge and wisdom. In our fast-paced lives the balancing power of female/Goddess energy is needed more than ever, so we believe it's time to put that energy to use. The spiritual energy of the universal female principle provides a much-needed balance and counterpoint to the outer-directed male energy that dictates much of what goes on in the physical world. How one worships or invokes Goddess energy is entirely individual. It can be as simple as making an affirmation or request, then lighting an incense (joss) stick, or it can be a more complicated ritual. We explore the different options below.

Goddess on a pedestal

As we have just explained, invoking the Goddess through ritual or spells is frequently a personal and private experience. This personal experience can give you answers to your innermost questions, and these answers are just waiting for the right time to emerge. All of what you need or want to know about yourself is within you already – you just need to stay aware and allow the truth to surface. Through invoking or worshipping the Goddess you can uncover what lies within your soul, so you can live to your highest potential.

The archetypal Goddess

Accessing the Goddess within must be done with grace, intention, and honour. There are several ways to approach this, but we will do it with simple step-by-step methods. Many of these exercises and rituals are performed when the moment feels right, ensuring the appropriate environment.

A great deal of how this happens is up to you – the essences of these exercises only need love and care. There are instructions to follow until you find your own rhythm or method. This chapter is designed to guide and inspire you as you tap into the archetype of the Goddess energy, held within your DNA. Reading each Goddess profile will enable you to walk in her footsteps. There are charts which are designed so you can access information to create your own rituals.

Now that's powerful!

Goddess psychology 101

Commonality is not a dirty word – as the great psychologist Carl Jung discovered. The human experience is common to us all . . . and it's all about archetypes! In Jungian psychology, an archetype was defined as being an inherited mode of perception or response, which was linked to the human instincts. A pretty cool spiritualist who was way ahead of others in his field, Jung especially believed that our instincts are linked to what he described as "the collective unconscious." Jung believed there were typical patterns of experience common to all humans (much like the physical body is common to all but varies from person to person) and he called these common experiences or themes archetypes. Archetypes give us self-knowledge for they are thumbnail-sketch shortcuts to understanding basic types of human behaviours and as general blueprints they are invaluable – and useful! From such blueprints we each spin off as individuals in our infinite variations. As "models" or the first of a certain form, archetypes allow us to get to the bottom of what makes us all the same in many ways yet at once uniquely beautiful in an infinite number of ways. These archetypes include Birth, Child, Self, Masculine, Feminine, Teacher, Warrior, Ruler, Healer, Artist, God or Goddess, Mystic, Elder, Hero, and Death. He believed archetypes to be patterns of energy that serve a specific purpose. He saw them as being reflective of the many different qualities within ourselves and the experiences that occurred in our lives as a result. The work that Jung did, in establishing the existence of archetypes and the resulting general modes of human behaviours has greatly advanced our understanding of the development of humanity. And knowing a bit about the basic archetypes helps us piece together the jigsaw puzzle that makes us, each of us, aware (and consciously at that) of who we are.

From the above we can now see that the concept of the Goddess and our relationship to the archetypal Goddess is intrinsic to our modern understanding of ourselves. From the initial general archetype of the Goddess, there are several sub-archetypes of the Goddess. Later in the chapter we will explore all of these to enable you to discover which Goddess archetype best fits or describes you, or where you are at this point in your life experience.

Circling the Goddess
GODDESSES AND THEIR MEANING

As we've mentioned earlier each Goddess offers us attributes and qualities that can be applied to your own physical, emotional, and spiritual life. The myths were originally parables for learning particular important lessons about morality and life. This is why they are still relevant for all of us today. Later in this chapter we'll get to the (good) spooky bits! This is where you will learn techniques to invoke the Goddess through ritual and ceremony.

Andromeda: Ethiopian Goddess of dreams Andromeda is the wise Goddess; she knows what is in your heart! Through dreams this woman of knowledge shows how you can gain insights into your life by giving you guidance as to the meaning of your dreams.

Aphrodite: Greek Goddess of love Aphrodite, the Goddess of

WHAT IS RITUAL?

Ritual is the practice of invoking the powers of the sacred, drawing on the energy of the divine, to provide the individual or group with understanding and knowledge. Ritual uses visualization and affirmation. People from all backgrounds and cultures perform rituals and ceremonies to invoke the Goddess, such as chanting words and prayers in order to find favour with their chosen deity.

Rituals are also often related to the cycles and rhythms of life, such as summer and winter solstice celebrations, or whenever someone needs a blessing. Rituals are the oldest form of worship. Rituals invoke powerful symbolism, which resonates and reconnects the individual to their higher power. Rituals reinforce the belief in a true spiritual power or supreme creative force.

It's hard to capture everything the Goddess is, so the attributes we list are by no means definitive nor are they meant to be limiting – they are a working summary if you like, of our own interpretations, with the underlying relevant symbolism and mythology. At the end of our book we list other books that will assist you to find out more about these stories if you wish to delve deeper.

love and beauty, was born from the sea. She represents sex, affection, and the attraction that binds people together. This irresistible Goddess was said to steal the wits of the wise. Aphrodite is also the patroness of arts, letters, craft, and culture.

In Roman mythology she is the Golden One, also known as Venus, the Goddess of Love. Venus has served throughout the ages as the muse or inspiration for many great works of art. In mythology, it is Venus who inspires people to love one another and to celebrate the rites of marriage and partnership. Venus is also associated with the rites of spring and fertility. Though there are many other Goddesses associated with love, Venus reigns supreme.

Artemis: Amazonian divine huntress She is the Goddess of chastity, virginity, the hunt, the moon, and the natural environment. Even though she is a virgin Goddess, she also presides over childbirth and is traditionally the friend and protector of youth, especially young women. Moon Goddess, mother of all animals, it is said that women would sacrifice their hair to Artemis as a token of their devotion before asking her favours.

Athena: Greek Goddess of wisdom Athena is the Goddess of reason in war and peace and she is associated with intelligence, activity, and literature. She is usually shown wearing a helmet and carrying a spear and shield. She is the embodiment of wisdom and purity and represents the intellectual and civilized side of life and war. Athena was not so much a fighter, as a wise and prudent adviser. She is also known as the Holy Virgin or the Celestial Virgin, and she is responsible for dispensing the fates of men.

Baba Yaga: Slavic Goddess of birth and death An Eastern European ancient Goddess who is frequently depicted as a witch-like woman. Baba Yaga is also called the "Old Woman of Autumn" and is associated with the crone energy (wisdom and decision-making). We discuss "crone energy" later in the chapter.

Baubo: Ancient Greek Goddess of laughter Baubo, whose name means "belly," has no limbs or head, and her mouth is her genitals, with breasts that have eyes in the nipples. This was apparently a sight that would make anyone laugh!

Brigid: Celtic Goddess of fire Patroness of poets, healers, and doctors, Brigid is associated with the ritual fires of purification that are able to cleanse even the deepest wound.

Cailleach: Celtic cosmic Goddess The Goddess Cailleach controls the weather, seasons, and the heavens, and is also known for her strength.

Coatlique: Aztec Goddess of female self-sufficiency Coatlique is the protector of all lone women, including those who may be considered to be female outsiders, and those who are filled with powerful thoughts and ideas, helping them to live on the edge. She also helps women find new potential and to bring to fruition their vision.

Demeter: Greek mother Goddess Demeter, also known as the barley-mother, is the Goddess of the earth, of agriculture, and of fertility in general. Sacred to her is anything growing in the earth, as well as all living creatures.

Diana: Roman Goddess of the hunt/Goddess of the chase Patroness of childbirth, nursing, and healing, Diana is the mother of animals, lady of wild creatures, and Goddess of wild woodlands, forests, and hunting. Oak groves were sacred to her and for those who worship her.

Freyja: Scandinavian Goddess of battle The personification of Aphrodite, this Norse Goddess is also connected with acts of war and with the notion of love. Freyja is the ruler of fate, the stars, and magic.

Gaia: The ultimate creation Goddess of Ancient Greece One of the oldest Goddesses, it is said that Gaia has been around since before time. She was worshipped for her prophetic qualities, for being able to foretell fate and what was happening to the earth.

Hecate: Greek Goddess of witches and sorcerers She is the Goddess of darkness, ruler of the dead spirits and, with respect to reincarnation, she is the guardian of any human that has returned to Earth to experience another physical life.

Hera: Queen Goddess Hera is a Greek Goddess, the wife of Zeus, King of the Gods. She is the guardian of wedlock. Her main association is with that of jealousy – and with good reason – for she always had to keep an eye on her husband as he was always taking off with other Goddesses and mortals. Hera also governs all partnerships, be it business or personal relationships.

Inanna: Sumerian queen of heaven A Goddess who was worshipped in the ancient kingdom of Sumeria, Inanna was revered as the Queen of the Heavens and, like the Ancient Greeks' Aphrodite, is the Goddess of love, procreation, and war.

Iris: Greek messenger for the Gods in Olympus The personification of the rainbow, Iris was the Greek Goddess who accompanied the souls of the departed to their eternal resting place.

Ishtar: Babylonian Goddess, lady of victory The Goddess of sexuality, and the ambitious, dynamic Goddess of love and war, Ishtar is a later, more complex form of the Sumerian Goddess Inanna, and their myths are similar.

Isis: Principal Goddess of ancient Egypt Represented by a solar disc between the horns of a cow, Isis is the mother of all creation. She is associated with love, motherhood, marital devotion, healing, eternal life, and the casting of magical spells and charms.

Kali: Hindu Goddess of life/death Goddess Kali, sometimes referred to as "Dark Mother," is the triple Goddess of creation, destruction, and regeneration in the Hindu system of mythology. Kali is the conqueror of time and giver of life to the world. She is all-powerful and is the originator of the creative word.

Lakshmi: Consort of the Hindu God Vishnu The Goddess of Wealth, including a wealth of proper values and spiritual goodness, the Hindu Goddess Lakshmi usually stands or sits on a lotus, which is a symbol of knowledge. To acquire wealth, we must first acquire

SPECIAL GODDESS CULTURAL/ TRAVEL NOTE

On the night of the New Moon in November, women all over India hang brightly coloured lanterns outside their homes and shops. The lanterns glow like stars and this spectacular sight is particularly auspicious as stars are considered to be the jewels of the Goddess Lakshmi. The hope is that the lanterns will attract good fortune and prosperity to their homes during the coming year.

knowledge. Her palms are held down as a gesture of giving. Lakshmi bestows riches on all of her worshippers. In the Hindu mythology, she is said to live in the sky with the stars.

Nut: Egyptian sky Goddess The Goddess Nut was the protector of the dead and her symbols and picture were often found in the tombs and coffins of mummified Pharaohs and their court. It is said she protects the soul on its journey to the underworld.

Persephone: Greek queen of the underworld Daughter of Demeter and Zeus, and wife of Hades, Persephone was known to be a gracious and gentle Queen of the Dead. Persephone also represents the cycle of rebirth. She is all-knowing about the life – death process and will help everyone who needs her guidance on these matters. After she comes out of the underworld, she becomes the Goddess of Springtime. The pomegranate is Persephone's symbol as this fruit contains the seeds of creation, which in turn is a symbol of the cycle of birth–death–rebirth.

Quan Yin/Kwan Yin: Chinese Goddess of compassion Also known as the symbol of purity and wisdom, Quan Yin is the holy mother of compassion and mercy. She is the personification of the principle of boundless compassion and loving kindness. The mere utterance of her name in prayer is said to assure salvation from physical and spiritual harm. According to the principles of Feng Shui (see our Energy Clearing chapter for a full explanation of this ancient

SPECIAL GODDESS
CULTURAL ANECDOTE

Tara is the principal female deity in Buddhism. The name Tara means "She who liberates," she who protects human beings while they are crossing the ocean of existence (samsara). There are two forms of Tara: Green Tara and White Tara. They hold a very prominent position in the cultures of Tibet and Nepal and represent the positive aspects of women. It is said that in the pain of samsara, two tears fell from the eyes of Avaloketishvara, the Bodhisattva of compassion, and were transformed into the two Taras. Green Tara is the manifestation of the wife of King Songsten Gampo of Tibet (5th or 6th century), a princess from Nepal. White Tara is the manifestation of his other wife, a princess of China. These two women are regarded as being the physical manifestation of the two Taras. They are acknowledged for their compassion and for the expansion of Buddhism within Tibet.

Chinese art), the symbol of Quan Yin is used to promote ch'i ener-gy. Ch'i energy is known as positive, auspicious, or lucky energy for a home or business to have.

Shakti: Hindu Goddess The Hindu Goddess Shakti is supreme feminine energy. She is responsible for the creative force that begins at birth. Shakti is the life force by which all the Goddesses were cre-ated, and she is known to bestow her gift of creativity on those who worship her.

Spider Woman: Navajo Goddess of creation The Native American Goddess of the Navajo tribe, Spider Woman gives psy-chic protection to those who seek her. She is in charge of teaching the soul about protection and about the love of beauty.

Tara: The most revered one The Buddhist deity Tara is an extremely ancient Goddess. Tara is worshipped in Buddhist cultures such as India, Tibet, and Nepal. She is the Goddess of self-mastery, mysticism, and spiritual transformation. Tara is the absolute, unquenchable hunger that propels all life; she is also a symbol of a spiritual hunger, and she helps those who invoke her to find release from the purely physical and illusionary world. She is the destroyer of fears and the remover of obstacles. Tara is a Bodhisattva, an enlightened one, who has vowed to incarnate until all beings attain enlightenment. Vowing to incarnate only as a female, she governs the underworld, the earth and the heavens, birth, death and regen-eration, love and war, all the seasons, and the moon cycles.

Themis: Goddess of the oracles Daughter of Gaia, the Goddess Themis rules prophecy, just like her mother. She knows what's in people's hearts and knows what nature and fate has in store for all.

Xochiquetcal: Mayan Goddess of art, dance, love, and music This Goddess from the Mayan culture of South America was said to live on the top of a mountain near the heavens. It was said that those who were faithful to her would spend eternity in her par-adise. Xochiquetcal was honoured by the Mayan people as the "mother of the world."

Invoking the Goddess meditation

Invoking the Goddess is the starting point for the inner journey that we've been talking about. The word invoke means to "call for" with an intensity or with an earnest desire. It also means to make suppli-cation or prayer for, or to appeal for confirmation. This is normally in relation to a "divine being." In invoking the Goddess, we are

WHEN TO INVOKE THE GODDESSES
– THE INVOCATION LIST!

Andromeda: *when you need guidance about your dreams.*

Aphrodite: *when you need help to love and enjoy your body and for finding true love.*

Artemis: *when you need to track down or recover items that you have lost, asking to keep focused on the goal in the distance.*

Athena: *when you need to think clearly in a situation where you have to make a decision.*

Baba Yaga: *When you need to make a decision on matters of grave importance such as life and/or death.*

Baubo: *when you take life too seriously or feel disturbed and need some comic relief.*

Brigid: *when you have been in an accident or wounded emotionally; Brigid aids in rehabilitation and recovery.*

Cailleach: *when you need the energy to continue a project or need physical endurance.*

Coatlique: *when you need strength to go it alone.*

Demeter: *when you need to be patient and generous, especially when you want to jump into something without weighing up the pros and cons.*

Diana: *when you're feeling "hunted" or hounded by others and you need a safety zone in which to feel comfortable.*

Freyja: *when you need help in affairs of the heart.*

Gaia: *when time is against you and you want to be creative or manifest your dreams without time being a concern.*

asking for a response from, or a sign of, or some type of spiritual guidance – help, basically – in the form of intuition. Or maybe we simply want to hand an issue over to a higher being, who we hope and believe can deal with it better than we are able to! We invoke higher beings in many ways ("God help me!" is a common one) but by far the best and most effective way to do it is calmly, consciously, and with a pure intention. You can still be creative though – there are infinite ways to "invoke" – and we would encourage you to devise your own methods too. Use your own judgement and interpretation – as with anything in life, if you don't feel comfortable about something,

Hecate: *when you need protection from earth-bound spirits, including protection from anyone doing you harm.*

Hera: *when you need guidance in relation to a betrayal, or when you need help to make a commitment and to stay faithful.*

Inanna: *when you want to understand the future of a love relationship.*

Iris: *when you need to communicate between aspects of yourself, for example, if you have questions on your direction in life.*

Ishtar: *when you need wisdom, prosperity or wealth.*

Isis: *when you need guidance on how best to use magic or a spell.*

Kali: *when you need to end a situation and start again.*

Lakshmi: *when you need spiritual knowledge or monetary wealth.*

Nut: *when something or someone is dying, ask for guidance on what best suits the situation.*

Persephone: *when you need guidance on ending, letting go, death, and rebirth.*

Quan Yin/Kwan Yin: *when you need protection, especially at night if you are fearful of bad dreams.*

Shakti: *when you want to be creative.*

Spider Woman: *when you want psychic or physical protection.*

Tara: *when you need guidance on spiritual awareness.*

Themis: *when you need guidance about your future plans.*

Xochiquetcal: *when you want to express yourself in a verbal or physical sense.*

then tune in to your intuition to find what will work best for you.

Here are some simple instructions to get you started. (A later chapter, Mind Miracles, provides further meditation instructions, which are also helpful for this process). If you follow these steps carefully and practise your invocations regularly, you will start noticing some subtle (or not so subtle!) and overall positive changes in your life. You will initially feel the Goddess energetically, and then you will know she is definitely with you when you begin to experience the results. The whole point is to get the energy of the Goddess working for you in your life, but first you have to get her here!

Invoking the Goddess – the basics

1 Begin by sitting comfortably, with your back relatively straight but also relaxed. If possible, avoid leaning against anything, including the back of a chair. For meditation, straight-backed chairs are generally better than cushy armchairs.

2 Take three deep breaths, relaxing on each exhalation. Notice how your body feels as you sit. Is it tight around the shoulders, around your back? Sink into your body as you let go of the tension. What would it feel like to be a Goddess?

3 Now turn your awareness to the coming and going of your breath. Notice the rise and fall of your belly or chest as you breathe, or of the sensation of the air entering and leaving your nostrils. Let your attention focus softly but steadily on your breathing. When your mind wanders off (which it will do again and again), gently bring it back to the breath.

4 Continue to enjoy your breathing for five or ten minutes or longer. Focus, breath by breath. Imagine what it would feel like to be a Goddess. What Goddess is guiding you at this moment? Feel the answer intuitively and listen carefully as it may be a very faint voice. The whole purpose of this exercise is to quieten your mind, otherwise you won't hear what your Goddess is saying. When you feel the moment is right, ask yourself: What do I need? Again, note the immediate response. Once again, return your attention to the rise and fall of your breathing. If you do this meditation twice a day – upon awakening and just before going to sleep – you will tune in to the frequency you are meant to and thereby, hopefully, receive the message that will guide you.

It is particularly useful to do this before going to sleep as the subconscious can then get to work in order to help you by revealing the Goddess to you in your dreams.

If you don't know which Goddess you need or which would be best suited for you at this point on your life journey, you may need to ask and wait to see how the information comes to you. And while it may seem to you in your initial meditation sessions that you're not getting anywhere, you really are, and the answers may instead be shown to you in the dream state. Keep a journal and write down the emotions, imagery, and story lines of your dreams. Include as much detail as you can recall, such as key words, colours, and numbers. Match these to the Goddess list to see which Goddess is guiding you. See our chapter on Dreams for further detail.

When you're done, stretch a little, then get up and go about your day feeling energised and supported. Like any art, meditation has a great subtlety and depth to it, and you can, in theory, spend a lifetime cultivating and exploring the practice. But you can also gain enormous benefit just from simply following this simple meditation for five or ten or fifteen minutes, day after day, to invoke your chosen Goddess.

Which Goddess are you
...AND WHAT IS SHE DOING?!

We've given you a fairly long list, however for workability's sake we've whittled this list down to the six major Goddesses that we believe incorporate the most relevant archetypes. This, we trust, will make it easier and simpler to work your own personal Goddess to the max!

Which one sounds most like you? You can be all six Goddesses, but you can only be one at a time. There is no such thing as the "wrong" Goddess for you. It's more a question of efficacy and timing. Choose one that suits you best here and now, for your present purpose. You are not going to relate to all that is said about these Goddesses. There are going to be times when one will appeal or be more relevant to you than others. You can have fun trying others on though – the whole point of the exercise is to open yourself to divine possibility. And one may simply feel more right than the others at certain times, but this sense shouldn't necessarily be one of extremes. As with anything, it's all about balance, and too much of any single thing (or Goddess for that matter!) isn't necessarily the best thing for you.

Accordingly, one word of care is appropriate: It may seem that at certain times one Goddess is in overdrive in your life. You'll feel this in a physical and emotional sense because the influence can be very obvious and usually feels too pervasive or dominating. This is what happens when you are "overdoing" the Goddess. This means the particular "shadow side" or negative aspects of the Goddess in operation are showing up. It is wise to be alert and to try to avoid this occurring, or to at least minimize the effects. And to do this you'll need to watch for signs. For example, if you were "overdoing" the Goddess Artemis, you may be acting too aggressively (as opposed to assertively), feel insecure (as opposed to feeling safe and confident in your abilities), and prefer to be alone to the point of isolating yourself (as opposed to feeling happily independent). These are some of the shadow aspects of Artemis in the context of what the "healthy" or positive aspects of Artemis are. So to compensate for the "extreme" Artemis energy, you could concentrate on healing and overcoming your fears, forgiving others, and practising letting go of the situation. Compassion and love – for both yourself and those around you – would be a great starting point for a longer term remedy in this case.

So, this is why the Goddess archetypes are so helpful. They can be the indicators of where you may gain awareness of your shadow and access to the solutions that are blocking you from whatever is holding you back from reaching your true potential. The shadow elements are considered by the ego to be undesirable or simply not useful, and are therefore relegated to the dark. And (just to be completely confusing!) these same shadow aspects can also be positive in keeping the ego in check, but we must actively and consciously choose to deal with them – we need to truly "engage" and get to the heart of it! Often a woman becomes stronger and wiser by understanding them and working with and through them, rather than pushing them away in denial or projecting their effects on to other people. For the same reasons you may therefore also resist the Goddess you most need, the one who can show you how to heal. You are the one living your life, and if you're ready to face your own shadow and deal with its effects, you will start to really live.

So, young Goddesses, that's the scoop. The ultimate reason for all of this is to gain awareness and understanding of our actions and reactions as this leads us to begin to know ourselves fully.

As you work through the list of the six major Goddesses, see if you can ascertain the most likely shadow aspects. Typically, these are the opposite qualities to those that define the Goddess. An obvious example is Aphrodite (Goddess of love, peace and harmony) whose shadow aspects would therefore include fear, tension, and aggression.

Another method of figuring out where you need to do work or where you may need guidance is to read through the invocation list we have given you for each Goddess and choose the ones that resonate strongly for you. When we say resonate, we mean that either you get a good feeling about the invocation for that particular Goddess or for some reason you don't like it. Both of these reactions can be strong indicators of where you are at!

Bon chance!

Aphrodite

The Aphrodite woman holds sex as a sacred activity. She delights in the gratification of the senses, adornments, and things of beauty of any kind. Touch, smell, and taste are important to her and she operates largely through these for she is a tactile Goddess. She has an inborn aesthetic sense, loving the arts, poetry, and design. In work and career she favours the media, fashion, interior design, or beauty industries.

Keywords: passionate, sensual, a lover of beauty and luxury, creative.

Shadow: possessive, lazy, vain, self-absorbed, a slave to fashion.

Artemis

Artemis is in her element when out of the cities. She enjoys the rugged lifestyle. She plays by her rules and makes her own way in the world without too much male guidance. That's not to say she doesn't want companionship, it just means it's the man who will have to keep up with this woman. She will remain youthful-looking well into her forties. In work and career she is attracted to women's shelters or women's groups, anything that is community based, or a pioneering field, or a solitary profession.

Keywords: freedom, athlete, physical prowess, natural, practical, independent, and individualistic.

Shadow: obsessive, aggressive, feelings of frustration, perfectionist tendencies.

Athena

Athena is out there, the centre of activity, helping and organizing. She is intelligent and self-confident, willing to put herself on the line for her beliefs and opinions. Athena will keep her head in a conflict, and maintains clear vision in emotional situations. If you want something done, Athena makes it happen! Men admire her for her practical way of dealing with pressure, but at the same time they can be intimidated by her, because she can outsmart them with her sharp intellect and her persuasive arguments. In work and career she will be attracted to the corporate world, boardrooms, committees, and academic circles, or anything where she can make herself known and gain recognition for her talents.

Keywords: professional, worldly, transforming, reformer, social organizer, courageous.

Shadow: over-achiever, controller, manipulator, and sceptical.

Demeter

Demeter is the mother of mothers; she has patience and likes to be surrounded by people who need her help or motherly advice. She loves children and wants a family – the whole box and dice.

YOUR PERSONAL GODDESS...
TRY THIS QUICK QUIZ!

The Personal Goddess Quiz is designed to find out which of the six main Goddesses you are relating to today. The Goddess will change, as you change, so it is possible to use the quiz regularly to see which one has you in her sights. And you could use this quiz to ascertain which Goddess you like to be or needs your attention. Grab a piece of paper and get into it. How is she influencing you today?

1. Which is most valuable to you this moment:
    A An audience with a spiritual leader.
    B Fulfilling sexual relationship.
    C A high-flying career.
    D A sports award.
    E An item belonging to a family member.
    F Being the partner of a powerful person.

2. You have some free time. What do you do?
    A Meditate or commune with nature.
    B Call your partner home for an afternoon of pleasure.
    C Go to the gym.
    D Curl up with a good book.
    E Do some cooking or a hobby.
    F Put the finishing touches to a partner's business dinner.

3. What creature do you identify with?
    A Owl.
    B Tiger.
    C Fish.
    D Dog.
    E Cat.
    F Eagle.

4. Which is the single most important quality you need in a partner?
    A Spirituality.
    B Passion.
    C A leader.
    D Intelligence.
    E Loyalty.
    F Powerful.

5. When you entertain, what do you prefer to do?

A   Have a quiet dinner with close friends.

B   Arrange a romantic dinner for your lover.

C   Have a spur of the moment dinner.

D   Like to combine dinner with work.

E   Have dinner with the family.

F   A well planned evening to network yourself or your partner.

6. What is your ideal holiday?

A   A meditation or yoga retreat.

B   A deserted island, with a partner.

C   A wilderness camping trip.

D   You really don't care, anywhere.

E   An organized group trip.

F   Paris or somewhere else in Europe to visit some art galleries.

Check the answers and see which letter(s) you mostly chose. If you checked mostly:

A   you are Persephone.

B   you are Aphrodite.

C   you are Artemis.

D   you are Athena.

E   you are Demeter.

F   you are Hera.

If you got a combination of say mostly Bs and Fs, read the profile for each Goddess, (in this case, Aphrodite and Hera) and see which one most fits where you are today or best suits where you feel you're going. The great thing about this quiz is that you can re-do it at anytime and as often as you like. It may be that you're changing Goddesses daily if you're in a period of massive change in your life. You could also be phasing from one Goddess to another, which possibly means you are in or are about to enter a transitory phase in your life. In addition, you may find that at different times you have a different Goddess in residence! You should also check to see if you are experiencing the shadow aspect of a particular Goddess (be honest with yourself now)...and then get to work!

Unflappable, a whirlwind can be happening and she's dealing with all manner of tasks, calmly and surely. If you have a work or family dinner to organize, just let the Demeter woman take over – she will remember to invite everyone, ensuring that no one is left out. She is also very good with her hands and engages in anything that's craft oriented. In work and career, she is often found in hospitals, schools, church groups, or fundraising.

Keywords: motherly, home-maker, peacemaker, counsellor, nurturing, instinctive.

Shadow: overbearing, fussy, stubborn, and excessively doting.

Hera

Hera is conscious of her position in society. She upholds what she considers important to make a pleasant environment, although she can be a little conservative, and always knows what to say to whom. She is socially adept and always in sync with the correct etiquette for every occasion. Her dignity is the bedrock of her values. Hera is formidable, and will often be at the centre of disputes, debating, and clashing with people. If you are aware, you will appreciate her gifts, respect her... and not tread on her toes!

Keywords: commanding, confident, authoritative, dignified, self-assured.

Shadow: social climber, arrogant, aloof, superior.

Persephone

Persephone is the person who knows how others feel. She senses what you need to feel better, and she's the one that you tell your deepest, darkest secrets to, even if you've just met her. She often needs time alone, to deal with her unseen world. Highly connected to the spirit world, she can appear to be misunderstood and will have an aura around her, protecting her from the outside world. In work and career she is to be found as a counsellor, writer, working with the dying, healer, health practitioner.

Keywords: mystic, sensitive, secretive, spiritual, nonconforming, reclusive.

Shadow: overly sensitive, out of touch, whimsical, unrealistic.

Goddess in the closet!

Each of us is unique in the way our body feels, looks and presents to the world. Some women look like a Goddess in very simple clothes while others need a little more va-va-voom to really make the magic happen. There's no doubt, though, dressing in a way that makes you feel comfortable, is occasion-appropriate, and which expresses your individuality is one of the joys of life.

The following information is to guide you in choosing clothing themes that will enable you to use and to maximize your personal Goddess's energy when you need to tap into her unique qualities. This is not to say that you can't wear what you have in your wardrobe already; it just helps to open you to your Goddess. It's basically an exercise in editing because the chances are, if you are really "doing" or relating more to a certain Goddess, then your recent shopping sprees will show you which one you're into! Did you buy power suits or lingerie? If you have an important meeting or work engagement, wearing Athena's clothes, perfume, and accessories will give you more of her presence, thus enabling you to optimize the opportunity or situation. You might even like to dress like a Goddess that (for whatever reason) you haven't been able to connect with or understand. You never know what might come up for you – maybe you'll find you were born to wear a sarong and lounge about on cushions writing poetry instead of power-lunching with execs and making deals over coffee in the corporate dining room! Try all of the Goddesses on for size and, above all, have some fun with it.

> There is serious evidence that the making of thread and cloth were once religious practices to teach the cycles of life and death and beyond.
> Clarissa Pinkola Estes, *Women Who Run with the Wolves*

Go on, you know you want to . . .

The rules for dressing like a Goddess

Remember: you can only break the rules when you know the rule.

1 The classic "Rule of Seven": This rule is that no more than seven (visible) items of clothing or accessories should be worn at any one time. If in doubt, leave it out! Or at least take it off . . . This is an approach that stylists all over the world often adhere to unknowingly, because less is often more when you want to highlight a person's features. Follow this rule and you'll be a minimalist Goddess with maximum impact!

2 White is one of the most powerful colours to wear, especially if you are going to a business meeting or a place where you need to be powerful. White is also the colour of surrender, but surrender in this case doesn't mean "weak." Power is the knowledge that you can do whatever you need to do. You may or may not exercise your personal power; however, white serves to attract it. Joan of Arc was

one such Goddess who understood the power of this colour – she wore white robes into battle.

3 Put the emphasis on one major item, such as a pair of amazing shoes, or a killer handbag, or perhaps one stunning piece of jewellery. One item is defining and sends a clear message.

4 Polish your toenails with coloured nail polish – it's much sexier to have nude fingernails.

5 Hair should be simple, clean, and well-kept. Only wear hair accessories if you are wearing really simple clothing.

6 Be consistent. Find what works for you and stick to it! Don't become a slave to fashion trends. There's something in Oscar Wilde's saying about fashion . . . " [It is] a form of ugliness so intolerable that we have to alter it every six months."

7 Having a signature fragrance is the mark of a woman who knows herself. Calling all Goddesses: At last you've got the perfect excuse to raid the perfume counter and stock up! You should, however, wear fragrance in subtle quantities. Layer your fragrance instead: The best effect is to use a body wash, body oil, or moisturiser. A spray or a dab of perfume is a final, subtle note. Layering your fragrance means you'll smell beautiful for longer.

The ultimate Goddess Wardrobe Guide

APHRODITE

The Look: Dresses with flair, mixing the unusual with style, and having a few must-haves from top-designer labels. Choosing her lingerie is a sacred act – she cannot have enough corsets, stockings, bras, or anything sensual and sexy. Aphrodite loves to shop and she knows you can get designer labels at half price (although she'll never tell you from where). She can tend to be a slave to fashion – but is never a fashion victim. Being a fashion plate doesn't concern her – she knows what she likes and she just has to look great. Aphrodite wears clothes and uses fragrance in the context of wanting or desiring love. Aphrodite is also usually up on all the latest beauty treatments, and her cupboards are bound to contain a mountain of anti-ageing, anti-wrinkle creams.

Fragrance: Ylang ylang, patchouli, frangipani, jasmine, coconut, vanilla.

Accessories: Everything that's beautiful and has a sensual purpose, or that adds to her alluring energy and beauty.

A strong, positive self-image is the best possible preparation for success.

Dr Joyce Brothers

ARTEMIS

The Look: Dresses casual – jeans and funky, easy clothes best suit Artemis girls. Seriously fashionable clothing is not of great interest to her. If it has anything to do with exercise or sport, she's into it, big time. Ever practical, Artemis will buy two or three of anything at any one time because she doesn't like to shop, or waste time looking. It has to serve a purpose and be functional, above all. Her simple approach makes her stand out in a crowd.

Fragrance: Any clean fragrance based on the simplicity of a woody base – sandalwood, cedar, peppermint.

Accessories: Trainers, key chains, watches, mobile phones. She wears little or no make-up, but she does care for her skin and body, choosing products that are useful but natural.

ATHENA

The Look: Always seen in a power suit, or more formal gear, Athena prefers to be over, rather than under-dressed. Fashionable but non-conformist, her wardrobe will definitely have a little black dress and the right shoes, along with the latest bag, which she'll have had a friend purchase duty-free for her from overseas. She has to be ahead of the "fash-pack." Most of her clothing will be made of natural fibres and she prefers clean-cut designs. She delights in very simple and sexy lingerie – camisoles and cotton underwear are her trademark.

> ALWAYS SEEN IN A POWER SUIT, OR MORE FORMAL GEAR, ATHENA PREFERS TO BE OVER, RATHER THAN UNDER-DRESSED.

Fragrance: A naturally clean, pure, refreshing, and contemporary scent, usually a combination of floral and citrus, more masculine or slightly gender neutral.

Accessories: She loves contemporary jewellery, super chic and smart, as well as clutch bags, hats, and shoes. Her make-up and beauty routine is just that – she'll never go to bed with make-up on. She cleanses, tones, and moisturizes. She always goes for the best brands.

DEMETER

The Look: Very practical in her dress sense, Demeter knows what is appropriate for all occasions. There is no fuss or bother or anything extraneous in her attire. It always looks effortlessly thrown together. She always has the basics. If you are going camping, she'll have the right clothes to wear and people will borrow things from her because she will have what they need. Working clothes are all

GODDESS CHART

At the beginning of this chapter we spoke about ways to invoke and summon the Goddess. Our Goddess chart below is a guide to other elements you can include in your own Goddess rituals which we'll tell you more about later. We just thought we'd give you the cold facts first and you can take it from there.

Goddess	Crystal	Colour	Flower/Plant
Aphrodite	Rose quartz	Pink, white	Linden, rosemary, red rose, myrtle
Artemis	Tiger's eye, moonstone	Green, brown	Willow, pine, mugwort
Athena	Aquamarine	Blue	Thyme, laurel, olive tree
Demeter	Topaz, herkimer, diamond	Yellow, orange, brown	Poppy
Hera	Kunzite	Royal blue	Tiger lily, crocus, hazelnut, orange blossom
Persephone	Bloodstone	Black, white	White rose, lily, white willow bark

organized in order – blue for Monday, yellow shirt with navy skirt – that way she can always be on time. She would rather wear comfortable clothes than an evening dress, but when she needs to impress, watch out – she knows what to wear to have heads turn, and it's always simple but beautiful.

Fragrance: Any refreshing or citrus scents – orange, lime, bergamot, lemongrass.

Accessories: Comfortable shoes are a must. She uses only one handbag till it wears out, but will have a few others just in case the need arises, and she loves hats. She has little time for a beauty routine but has the type of skin that glows without too much fuss, and if she needs skin care, it's usually simple.

Symbols	Essential oils	Planets
Heart, shell, apple, partridge, mirror, honey, flowers	Patchouli, rose, ylang ylang, geranium, jasmine, orange	Venus
Bow and arrow, bee, stag, rabbit	Marjoram, lavender, juniper, rosemary, grapefruit, cedarwood	Moon
Shield, Pegasus, sword, snake, spider, serpent, raven, owl	Bergamot, black pepper, ginger, lime, thyme, sage, peppermint	Mercury
Corn, grains, cornucopia, hare, eggs	Marigold, myrrh, vetiver, neroli, clary sage, marjoram, fennel, lavender	Moon
Crown	Jasmine, thyme, lemongrass, frankincense, sandalwood, peppermint	Sun, Jupiter
Pomegranate, phoenix, cauldron	Myrrh, patchouli, cypress, petitgrain, frankincense	Pluto, Saturn, Neptune

HERA

The Look: Conservative but fashionable, she dresses like a Queen, with style and poise. She can carry off just about any look and this makes her appear larger than life. She feels very comfortable in evening wear, and has an outfit to suit all social occasions, along with hats and handbags to match.

Fragrance: Chanel or any traditional perfumes with light, floral notes, jasmine, rose, lavender, gardenia, freesia.

Accessories: Classic, fashionable. She has every accessory and especially loves earrings – she has a pair for every occasion. She wears make-up – but never too much or too little. She has an eye for what is the best value and gives her the best results. If she sees it advertised, she has to try it.

PERSEPHONE

The Look: Persephone dresses to suit her mood, wearing only colours that mean something to her personally. She looks good in black and can sometimes wear too much of it, if she is in a dark mood. Colour helps to lift her out of her inner world.

So tall she towered before him, so gay her garments gleamed. For hair that rippled round she shone like a fire ablaze, Richly her twisted armlets, her earrings flashed their rays.

Homer, "Hymn to Venus," from *The Odyssey*

Fashion has no place in her life, she would rather wear what other people wouldn't dare to wear, even to the point where she can be out of place in normal social situations. Eccentricity and quirky are her bywords, and she'll check out vintage or recycled clothing shops to find just the thing that works for her. **Fragrance:** Any stronger, more exotic blends, such as those containing spice elements: nutmeg, ginger, musk, myrrh, patchouli. **Accessories:** She loves to improve her clothing with fun and whimsical accessories, adding unusual buttons or working together unusual colour combinations, finishing with scarves and pashminas. With make-up, it's either all or nothing. She can be seen with amazing artwork or have a very clean-cut look. What she puts on depends on her mood.

Create a ritual to honour the Goddess

By now you've should have done the Goddess Quiz, checked out the vibe of your personal Goddess, ruminated on both her positive and shadow aspects, and figured out how to dress. You will now also realize how your credit card on the (rather hard) evidence of recent retail therapy in which you've been indulging (oops) provides an excellent, if scary, record on who you really are based. OK. So you're comfortable with that – well sort of. If not, fear not – we're going to help you to bring it all into some sort of balance so you can call on and work with some serious Goddess energy, and here's the ritual to do just that.

YOUR PERSONAL GODDESS RITUAL

This ritual will assist you to concentrate on and manifest any positive aspects of your personal Goddess that you wish to cultivate. Remember, there is no point focusing on any negative aspects you may have identified with – you just give them more energy if you do! The best way to eliminate something negative is to focus on and affirm the opposite quality. The purpose of ritual is to highlight your intention to the Universe and to the Goddess in question and, also, to help you focus on what you desire.

Step 1: Create the ambience to invoke your Goddess by gathering together the following items to make an altar upon which to conduct the ritual. You will need:

6 candles: choose a colour that represents the Goddess you are invoking (see previous chart). 6 candlesticks or, if you don't have these, use plates or something that will not burn. A table covered with a cloth (see the Magic and Rituals chapter for the ideal colour). The appropriate Goddess oil or Special Goddess blend (see previous chart and chart below). Oil burner.

Symbols of the Goddess (see previous chart). These can be actual objects, talismans or, if they are not at hand (you're not expected

SPECIAL GODDESS OIL BLENDS
– MAKE YOUR OWN

In the chart on page 34–5 we have listed various essential oils that can be used in your personal Goddess ritual. The following special Goddess oil blends are also useful to summon your personal Goddess. The oils will work as individual components to your Goddess ritual, but for maximum effect we recommend you use them in a blend. Start with the recommended base oil, add the essential oils and the recommended crystal to create your blend, and then . . . follow your heart!

Base oil: 100 ml of jojoba
Combine: 50 drops in total of suggested essential oils (see the Goddess chart page 34–5)
Store in: Clean glass bottle
Add: Small piece of crystal for the particular Goddess you're working on – see the Goddess chart page 34–5
Use: On five anointing points – brow, throat, heart, solar plexus, and palms, one on each hand
Timing for creating blend: Full moon where possible, or as follows for specific days for each Goddess.
Goddess Artemis Blend: Full moon or Tuesday
Goddess Athena Blend: Wednesday
Goddess Aphrodite Blend: Friday
Goddess Demeter Blend: Full moon
Goddess Hera Blend: Sunday
Goddess Persephone Blend: Saturday

While you are bathing in water, remember to shower yourself with kindness too! How would you improve your self-worth? We've all got some issues with self-worth on occasions, but instead of focusing on what you don't like, focus on what you do like! Give yourself a kindness break and stop telling yourself what you are doing wrong. No self-criticism, instead, simply appreciate yourself for who you are and how you're becoming a better person all the time.

Make a list of all the positive things about yourself NOW.

Give yourself the gift of appreciation

to find a real phoenix for Persephone or a crown for Hera!), images or drawings are fine to use.

Step 2: Arrange the candles in a circle and place the objects and/or images in an arrangement within a circle that is pleasing to you.

Step 3: Put water in the burner and add 6–8 drops of the oils or of the Special Goddess blend, then light.

Step 4: Light the six candles, affirming the positive aspects of your personal Goddess as you do so. Do this for as long as you feel necessary. We recommend 5–10 minutes before blowing out the candles. Do this every day until the candles have burned down completely.

Step 5: Once the candles are finished, you can "seal" the ritual by burying the candle ends in the garden or in a pot plant. This step is optional and if you choose to, you can also add a few drops of the oil or blend with the candle ends.

Goddess beauty

We each aspire to put our best face (and feet) forward in life, and nothing can make a Goddess feel better than a bit of pampering, especially when there's a higher purpose to it! A beauty routine is pretty much a great excuse to worship the self, anyway, and all aspiring Goddesses should be encouraged to do this as often as possible! Do one or more of these exercises daily to develop a relationship with your personal Goddess. You need to worship if you want to be worshipped...and we say do unto others as you would have them do unto you!

Goddess grooming – the Goddess potion

Goddess, groom thyself! Each day take some time to honour your body. Grooming routines provide an opportunity to meditate and heal our bodies on a daily basis. Our bodies serve us well, and we should be mindful of how much we put them through. That said, a Goddess worth her Epsom salts should never miss the chance to repair, restore, and recover! Although we're all madly rushed for time, using the Goddess potion can become an enjoyable part of your daily routine and the benefits can be truly astounding. A few minutes of concentrated energy can reap spectacular long-term results. It's important to remember to give back to yourself, and sometimes it needs to be just you putting energy back into you!

To make the Goddess potion: Combine 15 drops of rose oil, 20 drops of sandalwood oil, and 15 drops of jasmine oil, with 100 ml of oil of jojoba. Mix well. After you have finished showering, rub the Goddess potion all over your body and, as you do this, imagine you are absorbing the essence of the Goddess. This can also be done in conjunction with an affirmation such as "I am allowing the energy of the Goddess to fill my being, helping me radiate love and joy." Give yourself good vibes to start the day.

Goddess bath

Now here's the hard part for those of you who have to share a bathroom with various flatmates or assorted family members. The first thing you can do is arm yourself with as many candles as you can safely light, fluffy towels, a bathrobe and your CD player, then loudly declare the bathroom to be a de-militarized zone for the next hour or two. Then, quickly shut the door and put on your headphones while you run the bath. Hopefully by the time the rest of your household have woken up to the coup that you've just successfully staged,

GODDESS BATHING SACHET

The Goddess bathing sachet can be hung on the bath tap so that the water flows through it, or it can be fully immersed in the bath. To make the sachet, you will need the following:

* *A handful of rosebuds, lavender flowers, and orange rind*
* *A piece of cotton cloth*
* *3 drops of orange oil*
* *String to tie the satchel together.*

Place the flowers and orange rind on the cloth, then add the oil while reciting, "I am the Goddess." Say this three times and wrap the string around the sachet, keeping your focus on being a Goddess.

Draw the bath, and pop the sachet into the water. While you are relaxing, play some beautiful soothing music, and let the fragrance wash over you, calming your senses and filling you with renewed energy.

GODDESS NATURAL REMEDIES

Sometimes life treats a Goddess a bit roughly – and this means that occasionally you can end up somewhat battle-scarred! Here are our tips for getting you out of the wars and back in top form:

For bruising: A few drops of lavender oil rubbed directly onto the bruise soothe inflammation and skin tenderness.

For shock (post-traumatic stress syndrome): Star Bethlehem flower essence.

For a headache: Breathe some jasmine oil in through the nose. Lavender oil and peppermint oil work well too.

For an upset stomach:
1 drop fennel, 1 drop peppermint oil, 1 drop ginger oil.
Combine these in a small amount (1 tablespoon) of oil of jojoba and rub the combination into your stomach. (Special Goddess tip: This one works wonders for hangovers too – not that you get these though . . .)

For a relationship breakup: 2 drops bergamot oil, 2 drops neroli oil, 2 drops rose oil. Place the oils into an oil burner filled with water. Light the burner and gently breathe in the vapor. You can also use this combination in a facial spray if you're feeling too emotional: Pop it into your handbag for those weepy moments that creep up on you!

you'll be immersed in the bath, safely luxuriating and they'll just have to cope! The beauty of being a Goddess is knowing that the rest of the world can wait! Take as much time as you need to create a sacred space and bring in the Goddess energy through our personal Goddess bathing ritual.

Enjoy . . . moments that creep up on you!

Goddess walking meditation

For those Goddesses who love to sleep in late, this one's a real test! Using our immense powers of persuasion, however, we hope to convince you this test is worthwhile taking. The thing is, to make significant changes in your life, you sometimes have to get out of your comfort zone. In this case it means you have to get out of bed – and early at that! We'd like to show you the benefits of doing a walking meditation but you'll need to set this time aside to do it. The idea is to wake before sunrise and find a place to just walk. It's great if you live on the coast and you can get to a beach, but walking in a park or simply around the streets in your area can be equally beneficial. Even if the environment isn't totally peaceful, don't worry – it will work anyway. Your aim with this walk is to connect with yourself and with natural Goddess energy.

If you have a particular issue or problem on your mind, you may wish to invoke a particular Goddess as you walk.

Before you begin, ask your Goddess to walk with you. Simply say, "Goddess divine, Goddess of grace, walk with me. Connect me with my deepest being." As you walk, be aware of your surroundings; however, try not to allow the details to distract you. Rather, let them flow through you. Continue to do this for as long as you like – 15–30 minutes is enough. When you finish, thank the Goddess; ask for her to be with you during the day or at any time you need support. Just know she is with you!

The Goddess dancing and, um, singing . . .

Admit it: At some stage or another you've secretly longed to be J. Lo, Mariah, or Madonna, or even (bless her) Gwyneth, just so you could grab that mike, jump on stage, and be adored by millions of fans. Well maybe that wasn't your exact fantasy, however, these modern Goddesses can certainly sing up a storm and at least a few of us have been known to hone Karaoke to perfection in syncopated time – in an attempt of sorts to sound even a smidgen like they do (fat chance!). Even if it's in the privacy of your own car, there's nothing quite like cutting loose with a few verses at high speed to make you feel on top of the world while you're revving things up at ground level. Sound waves are known to be healing in certain cases of illness and singing is extremely therapeutic in general – let's face it, it just feels good to do it. Remember those nights "Home Alone" when you put on the newest CD in the stereo system, pulled down the blinds, cranked up the volume, and danced the night away? Well, we recommend that you do this on a regular basis (not necessarily in your underwear "Risky-Business" style, although the Goddess Aphrodite probably would!). However you choose to do it, do so with the clear intention of "singing up" your Goddess.

Sing to heal your body, your heart, and your life. Sing the energy up through your body and out into

When walking observe the trees and all the changes they go through with the seasons. Notice the clouds and the sunset, the sparkling rain, the incredible cycle of nature. Transform your life by living in harmony with the natural energy of the Goddess. This is not a cliché, it's actually the wisest piece of advice:

LIVE IN THE MOMENT!

The place
of the dance
is within
the heart.
Tom Robbins

the atmosphere. Put your favourite music on and repeat the verses following, over and over, to build energy, keeping your focus on whatever your concern is, such as healing your relationship with your body, your lover etc. Follow these instructions for moving your body as you sing (see verse below). Don't worry about what you sound like, only concern yourself with the intention. As you sing each of the lines, make the corresponding physical movement. This enhances the energetic impact of the line you are singing:

Earth my body! (bending to touch the earth, palms facing the earth)
Water my soul! (making a waving motion with hands at womb level)
Air my breath! (hands reaching up to the sky)
Fire my spirit! (hands placed on your solar plexus)

Repeat these lines three times, or for as long as you want or need. The more you repeat them, the more you will go into a trance or meditative space, all of which is very healing.

Another alternative is to repeat either silently or out loud the following verse while you are dancing:

We all come from the Goddess, and to her
we shall return
Like a drop of rain
Flowing to the ocean.
  Repeat
Hoof and horn, hoof and horn, all that dies
shall be reborn,
Hoof and horn, hoof and horn, all that falls
shall rise again!
  Repeat
Richard Gass, *From the Goddess.*

Goddess mandala

A mandala is a road map of the soul, a visual, physical representation of the soul's journey. Mandalas often take the form of very beautiful artwork and they are used in meditation (as an aid to concentration and to take you deeper in your meditations), and they are found in many cultures and religions. They are often in the form of a circle but can also take a square shape. They are symbolic of the infinite nature of the Universe. For more details on the significance of the mandala please refer to our chapter on Chakras and Auras.

Making your own mandala is a simple and effective way of experiencing your own consciousness and your connection to your personal Goddess. Physically drawing what your inner wisdom reveals to you is another way of honouring your inner Goddess.

Gather together some coloured pens, paints, or pencils (whichever you prefer), and some white paper. Sit quietly, centring yourself, pulling in the Goddess energy that you need for the task. Start drawing – don't worry what it looks like, just do what you feel. The symbols that are held within the circle of the mandala are arranged according to what you need to see in order to learn more about yourself. Let the Goddess "draw" through you, for this is another way to access her healing and wisdom. The best results are gained from doing this exercise again and again, until patterns in the drawings consistently appear. These are signs for you from the Goddess. Take notes!

Goddess divination

We'd all like to see the future or if we can't exactly see it, with a bit of a hint, at least we can prepare for what's coming. To find out what the Goddess may have in store for you, wait for a full moon or waxing moon, then gather:

* 1 big glass bowl, about 30 cm (12 inches) in diameter
* Rainwater (enough to fill the bowl)
* Black ink
* An eye-dropper
* Paper and pen.

First, and most importantly, you will need to prepare a special place to weave your spells/rituals. Trust your intuition to select the most powerful place for you to cast your spell. It may be in a cosy corner of your bedroom or outside under the full moon. The most powerful place is always one in nature that is special, or just one that is beautiful. It should also be peaceful – a public park at lunchtime is probably not the optimal choice!

Before you begin, purify your body by bathing in warm-scented water, quietly gathering energy. Take as much time as you need to totally clear your mind, body, and soul.

Prepare a space outside. Imagine you are standing in the middle of a circle. Cast a protective white light around you in a circular motion. This seals the space so that you may begin to work. Sit quietly, let your mind clear, then write a question on the paper, asking the Goddess for guidance. Gently pour the water into the bowl and

In the past few years, a Goddess friend of ours has been drawing and painting mandalas as a hobby. She produced dozens of these artworks and kept them in a small portfolio that over time grew to bulging point. One day, while sorting through the pile, she began to notice there were themes to her artwork. Without even realizing it, over a period of three or four years she had used the same colours and designs in many of the works. In time and through her meditations she began to understand the patterns and the symbolism contained within the mandalas. She says she never consciously set out to do any specific designs and the art she produced was purely spontaneous – she simply believes that her soul knew she needed to say. "I didn't have to try hard to gain awareness and I have learned not to push for answers. They always come at the right time through the artwork, and often months after I've done the painting. For others it may be a different experience but, for me, the mandala-art process certainly helped me on my personal spiritual journey."

let it settle. While you wait, breathe deeply, collecting and building your energy. Then, when you're ready, add eight drops of ink to the water. Trying not to focus, stare at the ink, until your eyes become blurry. As you relax you will start to see images appear. Do this for as long as you can. Draw or write down what you saw. It may take a while to understand what you have seen or intuited. An event in the weeks or months to follow or a conversation you may have with someone shortly afterwards may clue you in to the meaning of the patterns. These are simply signs for you to interpret and they are intended for you to pick up on...but you need to be on the lookout, and soon they'll start to make sense to you. The Goddess reveals all, in good time.

Aphrodite, Goddess of love
FIVE FUNKY RITUALS

Most of us would all like to have more love and passion in our lives. Here's your chance to bring it on! You need to get to the heart of the matter though...Are you in the right state-of-mind for being loved? Are you truly (modestly!) happy with yourself? And if you aren't, how could you expect someone to love you? If you lack self-confidence, your energy will attract exactly what you're putting out. The more we make this energy enthralling, the more likely we are to attract that in our partner. Here are the rituals you've been waiting for – rituals to help draw the right love into your life – the love that is always for your highest good and the highest good of all concerned.

GODDESS ORACLE CARDS

These can be made for your personal use, but they also make a beautiful gift. Create these cards using as much imagination as possible – all-out fantasy works for us! We suggest you use coloured cardboard and paint, and draw or paste images on them that you want and that are meaningful to you. Use the cards when you need a Goddess blessing or a little message from the universe. Close your eyes, breathe deeply, and ask the Goddess for a blessing. Keep these personal oracle cards in a pouch or a special purpose box.

- Trust your feeling
- Celebrate life
- The Goddess protects you
- Initiate new beginnings
- Walk in the moonlight
- Respect your body
- When in doubt, stop
- Abundance is always with you
- The task is yours alone
- Watch for the signs
- Be serene
- Overcome judgement of others
- See only the good in others
- See the beauty around you
- Learn to live in the moment
- Forgive yourself
- Have a massage
- Visit a power place
- Go within, heaven awaits
- Give and receive love without conditions
- Let go, and move through the situation

- Seek wisdom from nature
- Seek your destiny
- Prepare for love
- Whisper a wish at midnight
- Let go of resentment of others
- Nurture your body
- Laugh at yourself
- Surrender to love
- Believe you can do it
- Release your entire struggle
- Comfort and nurture yourself
- Smile at everyone
- Lift your spirit – wear red
- Breathe in life
- Today is for play
- Have faith in yourself
- Tell someone you love them
- Seek a healer
- Tell yourself the truth
- Listen to the silence – that's where the answers are
- Be you – no one is better qualified
- Every problem contains a solution

- Feel your feelings
- Have courage
- Open your heart to love
- Trust in yourself
- Share your smile with a stranger
- Send someone in need an Angel
- Wish upon a star
- Get well acquainted with change
- Be open to change
- Look for the Goddess in others
- Allow others to see the real you
- Cast your worries to the wind
- Wear white to be peaceful
- Live fully today – enjoy!
- Children have a message for you
- Allow pleasure to enter your life
- Dance the anger away
- Connect with friends today
- Speak from your heart
- You need only yourself to be complete
- Watch what you say to yourself

Aphrodite Love Enticer spell

Ah, Mighty Aphrodite! Naturally we're going to appeal to Aphrodite because when it comes to enticing love, she is certainly the Goddess with the "mostest." The time for this spell is any time, any place, because when it comes to attracting love, now is as good a time as any. Now it's time to get to work!

To invoke the affections of Aphrodite gather the following items:

* Piece of white cloth
* Rose petals
* 1 red candle
* Charcoal
* Loose resin of myrrh and frankincense
* Heat-proof dish for incense
* A small piece of rose quartz
* Rose oil
* A symbol that is relevant (see chart on pages 34–5).

To do this spell, it is useful to work at an altar. For this purpose, an altar is any space – a bench, table, book shelf, or otherwise that you deem sacred for the special activities of your choice.

Prepare your altar by covering it with a white cloth. White cloths are neutral and they allow you to focus more readily. In addition, the colour white does not invoke conflicting or over-powering energies.

Sprinkle rose petals around the altar, light the charcoal in the dish, and put the resins on the charcoal.

Hold the dish in front of you and chant your wish: "Aphrodite, I call on you to help bring me my new love, and so it is." Smoke will take your petition for love to the Goddess of Love.

Place the red candle and crystal in the centre of the altar, anoint the candle and crystal with rose oil, and imagine your heart receiving love.

Carve a symbol using the Athame of two hearts joined; focus on your wish as you carve.

Hold the rose-quartz crystal to your heart and recite the following incantation three times: "Guide me and bind me to mother earth, let her show me my truest heart's desire. Hold me in your arms of love, gently rock me, so I can open to my true love, and so it is."

Close the circle and keep the crystal with you to remind you of your wish.

Rejuvenating an existing love relationship

Do this ritual during the week leading up to the full moon. Gather the following:

* 1 red candle
* Jasmine incense
* Yellow cloth.

Before commencing the ritual, prepare your space, clearing away distractions (see Goddess divination section on page 43). Calm your mind by sitting quietly for as long as you feel the need.

Place the yellow cloth on the altar where you have chosen to work. Yellow heightens the energy of the Universe to bring you the desired outcome.

When you are ready, light the red candle while reciting: "Awaken, soul, shed light on my wish of love, blessed be."

Focus upon your specific "Love" wish, with respect to your existing relationship.

Take a stick of incense in your right hand and light it from the candle flame whilst saying aloud your wish in the present tense. (For example: "My true love is with me now.") Imagine what it would "feel" like to have the love relationship you want, at this time.

Let the candle burn for one hour then snuff it out.

Relight the candle daily and let it burn for one hour until it has finished.

Bury the candle in the yellow cloth when it is a full moon.

Aphrodite's love potion
THE ENCHANTRESS BATHING POTION

This ritual will attract love energy to your side with the intensity of a NASA launching pad! The exquisite blend of essential oils is a secret recipe, brought back from the East by Crusaders in the 10th century in honour of Aphrodite. This powerful and potent aphrodisiac will have your potential love eating from your hand – just what every Goddess needs! The timing for this ritual is any time you're in the mood.

Gather together:

* 2 drops each of essential oils of orange, patchouli, jasmine, rose, black pepper, and nutmeg
* Red/pink food colouring
* 1 cup of Epsom salts.

SPECIAL GODDESS ANECDOTE

One of our Goddess friends tells the story of her awakening to the power of the Goddess:

"My earliest awareness of the Goddess came one day when I heard a woman saying she was going to be conducting a workshop on the Goddess. Up until then I had never heard anything about Goddesses, but it was like a light went on in my heart and ever since I have been involved with research on what the power of the Goddess can do and what it means to me. At the time, I could not describe just how hearing these words affected me. Nor could I understand why I even wanted to know about it. I do remember though, that it was a slightly unsettling feeling which left me with a profound sense of urgency – all I could say was there was some energy there and I had to get to the source – and fast! I soon realized that it was no ordinary calling as my research assumed centre stage in my preoccupations. Once I was absorbed, that was that – the Goddess was in my life for good. Embarking on this journey was the keystone to my personal spiritual quest, which continues today. In fact, any time I read about Goddess energy in any space or form, this feeling of being on my own quest returns, almost as if for the first time. I have become more connected with the earth and more powerfully identified with my feminine essence and I know I could never return to my old way of life without pain. What was activated that day is ever present within my heart my soul.

"Whenever I mention the Goddess, people ask me what it means. While the Goddess has many faces and many traditions, I always bring it back to how I see the Goddess in the present moment and that is different every time. To me it's an energy thing and I feel her presence to a greater or lesser degree depending on my own vibrations and moods. Goddess energy is always with me in one form or another – whether I'm happy or otherwise – she's just with me as I'm going along in life."

Create ambience in the space: In honour of Aphrodite, a sensual environment in your bathroom with the use of candles and soft music sets the scene and adds to the effectiveness of the bathing potion. Remember, it's all about enhancing the intention.

Add oils and food colouring to the Epsom salts, mixing in well.

Run the bath, then place the potion in the water.

Soak in the bath. Imagine you are the Goddess Aphrodite with all her powers and her qualities. Breathe in the fragrance, letting it heighten your awareness of love.

If you prefer, you could make up oils into a massage blend, 100 ml of base oil to 50 drops of essential oils in total. Massage the oil into your skin. It works!

Aphrodite's candle rituals

Do this during the week leading up to a full moon. Gather together:

* 1 pink candle
* Piece of pink paper
* Red ink
* Red ribbon
* A handful of rose petals.

Prepare the space in the method outlined above. Cast a circle of white light around your environment and your self. Sit quietly and take three deep breaths, centring yourself.

Hold the unlit candle in both hands, focusing on bringing out the Goddess Aphrodite's loving energy.

Then sit for a moment, collecting your energy, before writing on the paper your wish of love. Ask Aphrodite to assist you in gaining love, understanding love etc.

When you have finished, wrap the paper around the candle and tie it up with the ribbon.

Place the candle in a holder and sprinkle the rose petals in a circle around the base of the candle.

Light the candle and let it burn for one hour before snuffing it out. Relight the candle every day for a week and let it burn for 1 hour.

When the candle has finished, bury it on the full moon.

Aphrodite's lingerie magic!

Do this on the eve of the full moon. The magic begins as you create a box with the aim of transforming a bra-and-pants set or other lingerie item into "Aphrodite's Magic Girdle." Legend says the wearer of the Magic Girdle is made utterly irresistible. Think you can handle that? This is a spell that is conducted in two stages. The first thing to be done is to create a magical box to transform these items.

Gather together:

* 1 pink candle
* A piece of red silk to line box

* A medium-sized box – it can be wooden or paper
  – painted red
* Decorations for box: Hearts, shells and roses.

Prepare the box before doing main ritual. Prepare the space by casting a protective white light around yourself and your environment. This will protect you while you work.

Light the pink candle as you begin to put together the box. Create the box with intention, focusing on your goal as you decorate, affirming your wish for love and passion to come into your life.

When you have finished making the box, put it in a safe place where it is out of your sight for a full week.

The second part of the ritual requires you to gather the following items:
* One handful of rose petals
* 4 drops of pure rose oil (in base, because rose is very expensive), 4 drops of orange oil and 4 drops of patchouli oil
* 4 red candles
* Pink or red sealing wax
* Red cord to tie around the box
* A new set of bra and pants or corset or other preferred lingerie item (choose red or pink to maximize the spell's potency)
* Prepared magical box
* Silk for lining box.

To increase the potency of the ritual, purification of your body is advised. You may want to have a bath before this ritual to enhance your connection with Goddess Aphrodite. Use the enchantress bath potion. Prepare your space and yourself.

Sit quietly and take three deep breaths, close your eyes and imagine a pink light surrounding both you and the space.

Place the rose petals in a glass bowl and add the essential oils. Ask that Aphrodite be present by reciting this incantation: "Goddess of beauty, Goddess of Love, be with me as I ask to be open to love and passion, blessed be."

Light all four candles and, as the flames ignite, know that your wish of love is being spread out near and far to attract the energy of Aphrodite.

Place your underwear set in the box, sprinkle the rose petals over the set, then fold the silk lining over them reciting: "Aphrodite, assist me in transforming these items into your magical girdle, making me irresistible, so mote it be."

Close the box, tie the cord around the box and seal the cord with the sealing wax. Place the candles around the box and leave them burning for a few hours. If you can, leave it for a week and relight the candles each day until they are burned away. Your magical girdle awaits you to be worn. Break the seal when you're ready to wear the lingerie – wear with care...and enjoy!

Astrology

Astrology is as simple and as complicated as life. You can take a bite-sized chunk of it and feel happy, or you can spend your whole life learning. Even professional astrologers are still attending seminars and classes in their old age, so don't think this is something you can knock off in five minutes! Despite that, the interesting thing about astrology in the computer age is this – you can actually get your horoscope wheel, or birth chart, printed out in around 60 seconds. So the basic information that you need can be in your hand very quickly (unlike the old days, when poor astrologers had to calculate everything using logarithms).

The issue is interpretation, though. How do you make sense of that strange wheel when you see it? How do you decode what is, essentially, a map of the moment of your birth, in the place of your birth, at a particular point in time? In this chapter you will find ways to quickly work out what your Moon Sign means (which is by itself just a small part of the information on the wheel), but if you are committed to astrology on a more serious level, you also need to know about the art of prediction.

The theory behind prediction in astrology is this: At the precise second you are born, the planets imprint their energy on your mind, body, and spirit. You pick up the power of Pluto, the spirituality of Neptune, the energy of Mars, and so on – but in a very personal way, which is particular to you. Unless you have a time-twin (another baby born at the same time, and in the same place, as you) your birth horoscope will be as unique as a fingerprint. Like a piece of music in the heavens, the planets "play" a whole mesh of sounds when your umbilical cord is being cut, and you end up as the finished composition.

Prediction works like this – after you are born, the planets keep on moving. They cross the heavens through all the 12 signs of the zodiac, continuing to make patterns and to play different tunes. When you grow up, though, there will be times in your life when the moving planets hit certain chords and notes in your original birth horoscope – which is when things happen!

Media astrologers can use this system to look at your life trends using just your Sun Sign (or star sign) – they use a highly simplified system to do this. For most people, though, prediction means personalized forecasts, based on the time, place, and date of birth. This gives you what is known in the trade as your natal chart, and it's your natal chart that an astrologer considers when looking at the future. Another way of thinking about the natal chart is to see it as a piece of music, or a symphony, on paper, that gives a hint of how a person sounds, and feels, and how they "play" their life.

A smart astrologer can look at a newborn baby's horoscope and see "music" which suggests this person will always be drawn to dangerous, risky, high-energy situations. Why? Because this baby was born when Mars was in the fiery sign of Aries, for example, creating a tense pattern with Uranus, the planet of excitement. At various points in this person's life, whenever Mars and Uranus (which keep on moving) make new patterns in the sky, the "music" of danger and excitement in the personality will be played. And, miraculously, this is when the person in question may find themselves driving a Formula One racing car, and maybe running it off the track. This is where predictions come from. Essentially, astrologers are looking for new notes played in the heavens, which will strike familiar chords in the "music" of someone's personal natal horoscope. Taking our Formula One driver as an example again, it's possible to look as far ahead in his life as the year 2050 if necessary. Incidentally, the information for all these planetary movements comes from something called an Ephemeris, a book the size of a small telephone directory, that lists all the motions of the planets in mathematical order, dating from 1900 to 2050. To a non-astrologer it looks like gibberish, but to an astrologer it contains all the information they need about the future.

People always want to know, "if you see something bad, can you avoid it?" in astrology, the answer is very clearly, "yes." All the warnings and risks are there in anybody's horoscope, right from the day they are born. There are many astrologers who could see danger in Princess Dana's birth chart, for example, at the specific time that she died in a car crash in Paris.

People always want to know, "If you see something bad, can you avoid it?" In astrology, the answer is very clearly, "Yes." All the warnings and risks are there in anybody's horoscope, right from the day they are born. There are many astrologers who could see danger in Princess Diana's birth chart, for example, at the specific time that she died in a car crash in Paris.

Let's get one thing straight. No astrologer can ever "see" death, though. They can pick up danger, and risk, and even crisis, but it's almost impossible to pick the moment of dying. Why? Because death means different things to different people. For someone who has been ill for a long time, and has been in a lot of pain, death can seem like the most peaceful and welcome escape from this life into another one. So it may show up as a Venus – Neptune pattern in the horoscope. For someone who dies suddenly and dramatically in an air crash, though, death could show up as something like Uranus and Pluto meeting up in the house (or horoscope section) dedicated to aeroplanes, which is the 9th House. Because of all the different ways death and dying show up in the birth horoscope, it's just not possible to predict when someone will leave this earth. Everyone's destiny means different things to them, especially when they are departing the planet, so there are a vast number of ways it can be portrayed in the chart.

Happily enough, good news can be predicted in astrology, and there are some simple ways to do it – Adam Smith, our Global Goddess Guru in this chapter, has come up with a quick and easy way of doing it. As a rule of thumb, if you have your personal birth chart horoscope in your hand, you can look at what old-fashioned astrologers used to call "benefic" planets, like Venus and Jupiter, and see what "houses" (or sections of the chart) they are in.

What good luck were you born with? What sort of music was in your chart when you were born? You will need your birth chart to find out. (You can either find the information on the net or order a chart from Equinox, see the Global Goddess Directory.) Once you know, whenever the planets pass over those points in your horoscope years later, the same fortunate chart "music" will be played, and in very specific ways, as you can see below. For example, below we show how Venus can affect you in each of the 12 houses. If your birth horoscope (based on time, date and place of birth) reveals …

Venus in the first house: You were born beautiful and you're destined to draw compliments, win pageants, be photographed, praised, or worshipped for your amazing style, hair, body, or face.

Venus in the second house: You were born to wheedle money out of people in the most charming and diplomatic ways. Your life destiny will always draw bargains, freebies, and fabulous cash prizes to you.

The goddess who is in pole position in life is she who has truly learned to master her mind and who can create apparent miracles at will. This goddess at-the-wheel-of-life has understood the true nature of mind clutter and controls her impulses, swiftly rejecting distractions and bypassing confusion as effortlessly as chiffon glides across skin.

Venus in the third house: Your relationship with a brother, sister, or cousin could be a real high point of your life. You were also born to be a gifted speaker or writer, and destiny will give you chances to do this.

Venus in the fourth house: You were born to love the houses or flats you live in, and fate will also give you chances to be in the most beautiful hotels or home environments. You're a natural home decorator too.

Venus in the fifth house: You have a way with kids and babies and this will mark your destiny and your life. You are also a natural romantic and could easily use this in artistic, literary, theatrical, or other ways.

Venus in the sixth house: Health is happiness to you, and throughout your life you will always be drawn to fabulous therapies and remedies. You could end up being a health professional, or just a fan of massage.

Venus in the seventh house: You are in love with love, and you could have the most romantic partnership or marriage of all your friends. Even as a toddler you will have "special friends" to hold hands with.

Venus in the eight house: Money can cause hassles for other people, but not for you, as you know how to get what you want from other people. You are also drawn to death, sex, and the mysteries of life!

Venus in the ninth house: You could fall in love with someone from another country, or just spend your life travelling. The big wide world makes you happy and you are destined to wander.

Venus in the tenth house: Bosses and other powerful people in your career will love you, and the feeling will be mutual. This placement for Venus makes you enjoy your work and can lead to lots of success too.

Venus in the eleventh house: You adore being part of a group or a good cause, and work very well with a team. Friends are more important than lovers to you, and you will have special female friends all your life.

Venus in the twelfth house: You will learn at a very young age that you want to have special secrets which belong to you, and mysterious interests and private passions are part of your personality and destiny.

Planet watch

IS PLUTO ON YOUR CASE? IS NEPTUNE GNAWING AT YOU?
Without even looking at your horoscope, or paying your friendly neighbourhood astrologer for a consultation, you can guess which planets are affecting you (or playing your music) at any one time. The great thing about astrology is that, after thousands of years of study, astrologers also have a remedy for any problems. Now, check this list:

Moon moodiness: You're feeling emotional, you have stomach problems, you have issues with your mother or stepmother, your periods may be unusual, women in general are more difficult than men!
Remedy: You need to protect yourself and feel safe. Stay at home

and create a base, if you can. Use water as therapy – lots of baths or swims will help. Moon moodiness is complex, though – so see an astrologer.

Uranian craziness: You've had a shock, you feel wired, everything is changing radically and too fast – you feel rebellious, you find it hard to relax, and you may be around mad people, or feel slightly mad yourself. **Remedy:** Freedom is the big thing your soul and spirit is craving, and if you're not building freedom into your life, Uranus can create havoc. How do you feel about change? Or being free? It's something to consider.

Pluto's power punches: Everything, including you, is being transformed at a deep level. People or situations are "dying" or falling apart. Having control (or not) drives you crazy. You're feeling obsessive. **Remedy:** Pluto works so deeply that dreams can be the key. Start keeping a dream diary and it will help you sort out your feelings. Get into nature more too. Watching nature's cycles of endings and beginnings helps.

Neptunian nibbles: This planet can confuse you or take you away from reality! If you have problems with psychic energy, drugs, alcohol (or those who are addicted to any of these), then Neptune is at large. **Remedy:** Ground yourself. Lie on the grass and imagine roots going from your feet down into the earth. Hang around sensible, normal, wonderfully dull people! Kick bad habits. Live in the real world. Build some shelves.

✳ Please note, the above guide is deliberately short and concise, because an in-depth look at all these planetary patterns can take months for you to work through, and sort out. If you think you've found some clues, though, it may be worthwhile ordering a chart, or going to see an astrologer for a consultation. Chances are you have accurately spotted one of these planets having a major effect on your life, so explore it.

Astrology is a mixture of fate and free will. The boundaries of your life – the basic directions and possibilities – are set up by the planets at your moment of birth. After that, it's up to you. There are some things in your life blueprint you can't change – your life lessons, for example, will be set ahead of time, and so will some of the things and people you enjoy, or are drawn to. What you do within those limits however, is purely your free will. Astrology is like a weather forecast. It can tell you when to (symbolically) carry an umbrella to protect yourself, and when to pack a picnic (once again, symbolically) for good times ahead.

Finding an astrologer you like

Playing with some of the concepts behind astrology is entertaining and it can also be a quick fix, but if you're serious about this stuff, go and see a professional. Astrology is now a university-recognized subject, and some astrologers are even studying it for their Master of Arts degree! You need someone who has a diploma or other quali-fication from a school or college which you've already checked out on the internet. The net is definitely your best resource for finding someone. Astrology is so vast now, and there are so many thousands of practitioners, that to list all the varieties here would take too long. Word-of-mouth is also a good recommendation. For a computer chart, though, we recommend you make a one-stop shop at The Astrology Shop online, which has outlets in the UK, USA, and Australia – and carries excellent computer charts from Robert Hand (the future), Liz Greene (the psychology of your relationships), and Robert Currey (an astrologer who can look at everything, if you wish). Visit www.astrology.co.uk for more information.

Serious astrology:

CHECKING OUT THE WHOLE CHART ENCHILADA

If you've never seen one of these scary objects before (see overleaf), welcome to the real world of astrology. There's more to you than just the sign you read about in *Vogue*! This is Goddess Jessica Adams's personal birth horoscope, which has been calculated by a computer, and printed out by a human being, Barry at The Astrology Shop in London. You can get a free chart done for yourself, on the internet, at www.astro.com.

So – the wheel. Where do you start when you're faced with a big circle, a lot of squiggles that look like someone's gone mad with a felt-tip, and little symbols that mean nothing? Well, to begin, at least one of those symbols should mean something to you – the Moon – you can see it at the quarter-past position on the wheel, just on the middle right-hand side of the circle.

The Moon rules what you need. Not what you think you want, but what you actually crave to make you feel secure, comfortable and at home in the world. The slice of the wheel the Moon is placed in tells you the area of your life where these needs will be met. In this horo-scope, Jessica's Moon is in the Sixth House (each slice of the wheel is called a House), which rules work and health. How bizarre! She used to be the health writer for *Vogue* magazine.

You can check your own Moon by looking for the little symbol on your horoscope. What House, or slice, is it placed in? This is where you get what you really, really need. In Princess Diana's horoscope, the Moon was in the third slice, or Third House of the horoscope. This rules our brothers and sisters. Remember her brother's amazing speech at her funeral?

Your Moon is also in a particular sign. At the second you were born, it could have been in Aries, Taurus, Gemini, Cancer, Leo, Virgo, Libra, Scorpio, Sagittarius, Capricorn, Aquarius or Pisces. The chances are high that your Moon sign is different to your regular star sign. The particular sign the Moon happens to be in shows what kinds of needs you have. Once you match the kinds of needs to the area of life where you have your needs, you'll start to build up a picture of yourself, and your life, that is amazingly accurate.

Using Jessica's chart, if you look at the Moon you will see a squiggle and some numbers next to it. The numbers show the degree of the Moon (this is important to an astrologer if he or she is going to read your chart) and the squiggle is the sign of Aquarius. Here's a rundown on all the squiggles so you can interpret yours, when you get your chart done: see the table on page 63.

Matching the information together, this horoscope shows that Jessica Adams has alternative, radical, out-there needs (the Moon is in Aquarius, and it's in the area of work and health). No wonder the crazy woman is one of the authors of this book! Now, work with your own Moon sign and the house (or life department: image, money, brothers etc) it is placed in – chances are you'll find five, six, or seven ways that the theme works in your own life.

Just by looking at your Moon, you can

MOON SIGN?

Moon in Aries: ♈
Urgent, energetic, active needs

Moon in Taurus: ♉
Money-conscious, practical, down-to-earth needs

Moon in Gemini: ♊
Verbal, intelligent, changeable needs

Moon in Cancer: ♋
Emotional, security-conscious, family-conscious needs

Moon in Leo: ♌
Dramatic, creative, proud needs

Moon in Virgo: ♍
Detailed, health-conscious work-conscious needs

Moon in Libra: ♎
Romantic, harmonious, appearance-conscious needs

Moon in Scorpio: ♏
Intense, passionate, obsessive needs

Moon in Sagittarius: ♐
Globally aware, funny, big-picture needs

Moon in Capricorn: ♑
Ambitious, sensible, cautious needs

Moon in Aquarius: ♒
Alternative, radical, out-there needs

Moon in Pisces: ♓
Sensitive, psychic, feeling-conscious needs

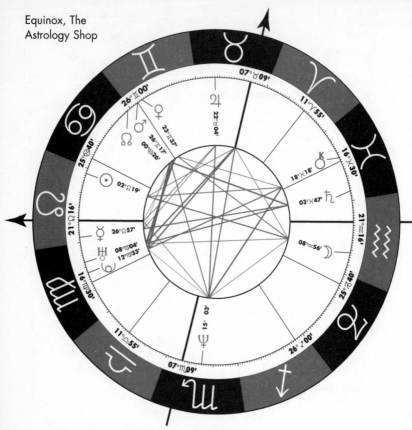

PLANET		KOCH	PLACIDUS	MODE, ELEMENT												
☉	02°♌19'	XII	XII	fixed, fire	☉											
☽	08°≈56'	VI	VI	fixed, air	∂°₇	☽										
☿	26°♌57'	I	I	fixed, fire			☿									
♀	23°♊37'	X	XI	mutable, air		ₑ₁		♀								
♂	26°♊17'	XI	XI	mutable, air			*₁	♂₃	♂							
♃	22°♉04'	X	X	fixed, earth			□₅			♃						
♄	03°♓47'R	VII	VII	mutable, water			∂°₇				♄					
♅	08°♍04'	I	I	mutable, earth		π₁		♀₁		∂°₅	♅					
♆	15°♏03'R	IV	IV	fixed, water		□₇				∂°₈		♆				
♇	12°♍33'	I	II	mutable, earth							♀₅	*₃	♇	♇		
☊	00°♋26'	XI	XI	cardinal, water			♂₇	♂₅		△₄		△₁	♀₁	☊		
⚷	18°♓18'	VIII	VIII	mutable, water	ₑ₁			□₆			△₄		△₁	∂°₆	⚷	
A	21°♌16'			fixed, fire			♂₆	*₃		□₁			7			
Mc	07°♉09'			fixed, earth	□₅	□₂					△₁	∂°₈	△₆			

Jessica Adams
1 hour ahead of GMT
London, England,
51°30'N 00°10'W
Koch House System

	Koch	Placidus
II	16°♍30'	09°♍55'
III	11°≏55'	04°≏26'
XI	26°♊00'	16°♊35'
XII	25°♋40'	22°♋48'

♈ Aries	☉ Sun
♉ Taurus	☽ Moon
♊ Gemini	☿ Mercury
♋ Cancer	♀ Venus
♌ Leo	♂ Mars
♍ Virgo	♃ Jupiter
♎ Libra	♄ Saturn
♏ Scorpio	♅ Uranus
♐ Sagittarius	♆ Neptune
♑ Capricorn	♇ Pluto
♒ Aquarius	☊ Moon's Node
♓ Pisces	⚷ Chiron

| A̗ Ascendant | M̗ Midheaven |

JESSICA'S ASTROLOGY WHEEL/CHART

☉ **Sun:** Who or what is most important to you, your self-esteem, the people or things you identify with. Your ability to communicate by writing, reading, or sign language – plus your travel potential.

♀ **Venus:** The way you give love to others, especially in marriage, but also the way you dress or decorate.

♂ **Mars:** This is how you fight, attack, and defend, and how you take charge and leap into action.

♃ **Jupiter:** Your lucky planet – it shows where life naturally swings your way, without too much effort.

♄ **Saturn:** Your teacher planet – this is what you have to learn, especially at around age 28 to 30.

♅ **Uranus:** The radical planet – this is where you break the rules, change your life, and change the world.

♆ **Neptune:** Neptune shows you how you dream, imagine, and fantasize, and where you are most intuitive.

♇ **Pluto:** This planet describes your power, and where you need total control to change a situation.

⚷ **Chiron:** The wounded healer – it shows who scars you, and what scars you, so you get to help others too.

☊ **North Node:** Hard karma – it's what you need to develop and get better at in this lifetime.

☋ **South Node:** Good karma. This is where life flows easily, because you earned it in a previous lifetime.

Midheaven: Your mission statement – it's what you're here to do in life, and it's often your career too.

Ascendant: Your image or outer packaging – how you come across to others, and how you look.

Immum Coeli: Your family background, home life, and childhood.

Descendant: Your marriage or long-term relationship partner.

start to get a good idea of how a horoscope works. But here's the complicated part. You not only have your Moon sign and House to think about, you also have the Sun, Mercury, Venus, Mars, Jupiter, Saturn, Uranus, Neptune, Pluto, Chiron, North Node, South Node, Midheaven, Ascendant, Immum Coeli, and Descendant. And they all have different signs. And they all have different life areas to work in. And of course, they all mean different things! Some astrologers even use asteroids – help!

You can see why people are prepared to pay money to have an astrologer decode all these squiggles, numbers and symbols. In the meantime, here's the lowdown on what the other planets and points, apart from the Moon, actually mean.

Gifts from the Goddess

Because people are such complicated creatures and have such packed and amazing lives, you can't really expect a magazine or newspaper star guide to tell the entire story. It can do a pretty damn good job, but if you're serious about your life, and you're intrigued by astrology, at some stage you will need this strange wheel object called a personal chart, or horoscope.

If you are in London and want to order an Equinox chart over the counter, drop into The Astrology Shop, 78 Neal Street, Covent Garden, and you can have your personal chart printed out while you wait. For free horoscope birthday cards and screensavers, visit www.jessicaadams.net – who says we don't love you?

The planets not only work in a particular style, in a particular area of your life, they also make patterns with each other (called aspects) which give them their own special flavour. If your Moon is right in the same place as your Mercury, for example, they will be "conjunct," and the effects of one will mix with the effects of the other. Then there's the future to think about. As planets move around the heavens in real time, they will also make passing patterns with your horoscope, maybe setting off the effects of a planet like Jupiter – which is when your luck really starts to roll. Using this method, an astrologer can make predictions to the day, hour, and minute!

It doesn't matter if you are checking out your personality or your future, it's really important that you know the exact time on the clock when you were born, the place (longitude and latitude of the atlas count) and the day, month, and year. Put them all together and a computer, or an astrologer with a book of tables, can create your personal horoscope. It's a life map. It's about you, but it's also about what's going to happen to you. And that's the real-deal astrology and the whole enchilada.

Astrogangs

If you check out your friends' birthdays and star signs, the chances are good that you'll find yourself in one of the following astrogangs. Nobody planned it that way, it's just the law of star sign compatibility. Which signs turn up most frequently in your particular group of friends?

♈	**ARIES**
♉	**TAURUS**
♊	**GEMINI**
♋	**CANCER**
♌	**LEO**
♍	**VIRGO**
♎	**LIBRA**
♏	**SCORPIO**
♐	**SAGITTARIUS**
♑	**CAPRICORN**
♒	**AQUARIUS**
♓	**PISCES**
☉	**SUN**
☿	**MERCURY**
♀	**VENUS**
♂	**MARS**
♃	**JUPITER**
♄	**SATURN**
♅	**URANUS**
♆	**NEPTUNE**
♇	**PLUTO**
⚷	**CHIRON**

Fire Astrogang: Aries, Leo, Sagittarius
Earth Astrogang: Taurus, Virgo, Capricorn
Air Astrogang: Gemini, Libra, Aquarius
Water Astrogang: Cancer, Scorpio, Pisces

THEN THERE ARE BIGGER GROUPS STILL.

Fire–Air Astrogang:
Aries, Gemini, Leo, Libra,
Sagittarius, Aquarius
Earth–Water Astrogang:
Taurus, Cancer, Virgo, Scorpio,
Capricorn, Pisces

Some of these groups will also include boyfriend–girlfriend combinations, for the same reason. People are naturally drawn to each other when their star signs fall in the same group, no matter if it's fire, earth, air, water, fire–air, or earth–water. If you're going to move into the Big Brother house, make sure you're in the right astrogang! Now, here's the lowdown on what it all means.

Fire astrogang

There is a lot of enthusiasm and energy when you get any combination of Leo, Aries, and Sagittarius together. Leo is big on self-expression and creativity. Aries likes to make instant decisions. Sagittarius likes the big picture. Can this combination see sparks fly? Of course. These signs are fiery by nature, and Aries likes an argument just as much as Leo stands on his or her pride. This is the right astrogang to hang around in if you want to go places. If you want a quiet life, though, forget it! These people have no time to waste. A fire group is very creative, and suited to rock bands, dance groups, or arty ventures.

Earth astrogang

Capricorn, Virgo, and Taurus are the most sensible zodiac signs, and this astrogang is full of practical people who have their feet on the ground. This is an excellent combination if you all want to make money. Capricorn will make the contacts, Virgo will check the fine print, and Taurus will do the deals. Did someone accuse you of being a bit boring? You don't really care. You make fewer mistakes, as a group, than the other signs. You are also a lot more natural and normal than some of the flashier star signs around. Earth astrogangs don't have big ideas about themselves. Group holidays are always planned to perfection!

Air astrogang

This is a brainy and brilliant combination of people. When Aquarius, Gemini, and Libra get together people tend to eavesdrop, because the conversation is so good. It's also a bit mad. You can spot an air astrogang a mile off. Look for the people discussing extraterrestrial life forms. One or two of them may also look like extraterrestrials. An air astrogang always has a new age Neville or Nina in its ranks. There may also be a science fiction fan or two. Air astrogangs swap books and ideas, and they basically live on email. The internet was made for air people, who love the endless communication and chat.

Water astrogang

People born under Cancer, Scorpio, and Pisces really understand each other, which is why they tend to hang out together as well. They share each others' passionate loves and hates, as well as the highs and lows of life and love. This can be a very Kleenex-heavy astrogang, because so much late-night sobbing goes on. It's amazing how many heavy issues turn up in the lives of water astrogang people. They have each other to lean on for support, though. Other signs never really get to the bottom of things the way water signs do. Cancer and Pisces sympathize with Scorpio, and in turn they can tell Scorpios their big secrets.

Fire–Air astrogang

If you are part of a larger group of friends who tend to be born under Aries, Gemini, Leo, Libra, Sagittarius, and Aquarius – and very rarely under any other sign – then you are certainly moving in the right circles. These kinds of astrogangs are very common in Hollywood! It can be fun spotting the different personality types in this group. Spot the text message queen, the drama queen, and the crazy chick, for starters. Then go looking for common likes and dislikes. Fire–air astrogangs all love to travel and can't stand being stuck in their own home, or even their own country, for too long. These gangs always have dramas too.

Earth–Water astrogang

This is going to be a very solid group of friends, and it may well last until you are in your sixties or seventies. People may come and go in the meantime, but there will be a core of stayers who are at the heart of this grounded, down-home, caring astrogang. One or two of you will become pretty wealthy, so stay tuned! At least one of your friends, and maybe even you, will make it to the top. As a group you will share your major emotional highs and lows with each other, and there may be some serious relationships coming out of this group later on. One or two of you will swap godparent roles, too, when it's time!

Busted! Star sign dead giveaways

You go to a party and you want to find out somebody's star sign to see if you're compatible with each other. Some Goddesses will ask outright, but what if you're too embarrassed to do the deed? No problem. Just check out our patented, copyrighted Star Sign Bustarama. Photocopy these pages, fold them up really small and keep them in your purse, so you can sneak a look when you're in the bathroom.

ARIES Push in front of someone in a queue. Do they kick you, shove back, or swear at you? This is likely to be an Aries. They can't stand waiting, and they can't let other people push them around – ever. Watch them at the traffic lights. Do they punch the button like a wild thing, even if they know it doesn't make any difference? It's an Aries. The women are ballsy and feisty. They often wear red, or dye their hair red at various times in their lives. The guys are into sport – watching it or playing it. They shout at the tv a lot when their team loses. They stride everywhere. Look for trainers and jeans on the women – they can't deal with fussy frilly stuff.

The person who stands up straightest, and puts on the biggest show, is usually born in late july to late august (Leo). They don't just do things, they perform them.

TAURUS Borrow money from them or lend them money and see how big a deal it is. They either never shut up about how "it doesn't matter, pay me back any time," or they become completely fixated on how much they have to pay you back, and when, and if interest applies. The same rules apply to precious possessions. If you find that borrowing or lending something as small as a cd or a book becomes a major drama, you may be dealing with a Taurus. Shopaholics are often Taureans. The only exception to the rule is the hippy, cash-free Taurus. But they still get thingy if you swap a jar of honey for their lavender plant, and you get a better deal.

GEMINI Blah, blah, blah. The women never shut up. The men talk less, because guys just do, but they are still ace communicators. If you want to know exactly, precisely, how they think and feel about something, just ask. You'll get something from them which could make a letter to the editor of a newspaper, or maybe a novel. They dig mobile phones, answering machines, faxes, and email. They die if they think someone's emailed them and they can't access it. They have nicknames, or go by another name to the one on their birth certificate. A brother or sister is a big deal, for better or worse. They're funny. And they love magazines or radio.

CANCER Their mother is either the greatest goddess of all time, or they're not on speaking terms, or she's passed over and they can't even begin to go near the subject. The mother stuff is crucial with Cancer. They are very, very touchy on the subject, so don't barge in and make any kind of comment without checking if they love her or hate her. They are patriotic, either about the town where they grew up, their country, or the place where they ultimately buy their first flat. Don't knock their special place in the world, ever! As you might have gathered, they are sensitive. They get very emotional, laughing or crying a lot, at full and new moons.

LEO If someone trips over on the street and immediately straightens up and makes a big show that nothing happened, that's a Leo. This sign hates being embarrassed. They are also vain. People who walk past shop windows and sneak a look are always lions. Big occasions, like speeches, weddings, important meetings, immediately prove who the Leo is. The person who stands up straightest, and puts on the biggest show, is usually born in late July to late August. They don't just do things, they perform them. They like perfume, cars, or even clothes that royals, rock stars, or famous people use. Anyone who's had a crazy love life since 1996 is Leo.

The person who has useful friends, or cool friends, is usually a Capricorn. Why? Because they prefer people who can help them look good socially, or get them somewhere in their careers.

VIRGO You can spot a Virgo by upsetting their routine. They won't say anything, but they will have an internal freak-out. Move their toothbrush into the opposite slot on the wall. Screw up their 6 p.m. gym session by insisting you go for dinner at that time. Worst of all, move their cds around. Every Virgo has his or her own system of order, especially for filing and classifying music, books, study or work stuff. The person who looks physically sick when you mess with this system is usually born in late August to late September. Anyone who is experimenting with acupuncture, shiatsu, reiki, or similar out-there body treatments now is a Virgo.

LIBRA Throw some choice discussion topics into the party conversation, like immigration, supermodels, and anorexia, third-world debt, the ethics of banks – and anything on the front page of the paper. The person who agrees with everyone else, on whatever is being said, is Libran. Sometimes they manage to agree with both people who are fighting, at the same time. Anyone who colour codes their outfits is Libran. They like things to match and agree. People who can't survive a year of being single without shredding their underwear are usually Libran. They need to be part of a two-person operation. People who dig art are usually Librans.

Aquarians either look bizarre or, more commonly, they just are bizarre. They don't try to have strange beliefs, habits, jobs, or hobbies, they just have them quite naturally.

SCORPIO Someone who holds your head while you vomit is a Scorpio. Don't be shocked by that! Nothing disgusts them. They are good at getting down, and getting dirty, with you – no matter what is going on. You can also spot

Scorpios by their eyes. They basically stare right through you, or laser through your face. This is especially true when they have sex, or when they kiss you. Scorpios hate with a great passion – it goes deep, it's very quiet, but it's also very scary. Anyone who dumps them in love, or steals their partner, or does the wrong thing to them financially, or at work, will be loathed, secretly, for up to fifty years without knowing it!

SAGITTARIUS They are often funny, or they love funny stuff. They make jokes, they prefer joke or cartoon cards at birthdays, and always get out videos from the ho-ho-ho section of the store. Sagittarians can't resist travelling. They spend money on it and lie about their sick days, just to get away. They get cabin fever easily, which is why they ski, ride, go for long walks, play golf, sail – anything that gets them out of that bedroom. Best way to spot a Sagittarian? Start a conversation about the meaning of life, or god. Say you don't believe in anything. Watch them lecture you within 1.5 seconds. They always have beliefs, and they need meaning.

CAPRICORN The person who has useful friends, or cool friends, is usually a Capricorn. Why? Because they prefer people who can help them look good socially, or get them somewhere in their careers. This isn't a bad thing, it's just a fact of life. The same applies to the person they marry. Why marry someone with your exact salary, background, or success in life if you can be with someone who will take you up, up, up there? The Capricorn's favourite phrases are "now wait a minute," and "hang on," and "Rome wasn't built in a day," and "be patient." They believe that time is the key to everything you want, and impatient people drive them nuts.

AQUARIUS Aquarians either look bizarre or, more commonly, they just are bizarre. They don't try to have strange beliefs, habits, jobs, or hobbies, they just have them quite naturally. You will get the classic Aquarian with a tattoo of a wombat on their head, a pink mohawk, or a safety pin through their knee, but generally they find all that "outrageous" stuff a bit boring, because the common herd is already doing it. Best way to spot an Aquarian? Tell them to do something that everyone else is also doing. Their first question will be "why?" and some of them aren't even that polite about it – they'll just walk out on you. They all have out-there, radical opinions.

PISCES They suffer, with great sensitivity and a few tears (on the inside or outside), when their lives go wrong. They don't tend to bounce back, they bruise like tender peaches. Pisceans also bruise on behalf of other people or animals. They feel every subtle thing, very deeply. They love fantasy. Anyone who thinks the Simpsons is real is Pisces. They dig the ocean and fish tanks, and spas. They love escaping into, or on, the water. their dreams fascinate them. Anyone who tells you their dream, and goes on about it in a rambling way, is Pisces. Anyone who says what you're thinking, before you have to say it, is a Pisces. They are all psychic.

Moon safari
CHART YOUR WAY THROUGH YOUR MATE'S MOOD WILDERNESS

Look up at the sky. Not for Superman (we prefer Lois Lane anyway) but for the Moon, which has a strong and amazing effect on how together, or untogether, the people in your life are feeling. In terms of your love life, you will either get a "Yeah! Let's rock!" feeling at a new moon, or one of those "Sorry I forgot to call you/Um, I'm not sure about our relationship/It's me," not "it's you" moments. The last kind of mood is a full-moon mood, and it's usually temporary, so don't sweat. It's just something that you, or your lover, has to get through. We're just going to give you fair warning about the dates, both good and tricky, so you know when to set up your big beach picnic under the stars, and when to leave the phone or email alone. Allow three days before, and three days after, the dates below, as well as the actual date itself – this is when New and Full Moon energy peaks. This Moon Safari guide applies to the years 2004–2005.

WHY A FULL MOON IS A MAD MOON

A full moon, when you can see the whole white pizza, is packed with emotion and feeling. The sun and moon are exactly opposite in the sky. People do not agree. Inside themselves, people cannot get their emotions to agree either. This is why you will find more tears, tantrums, drinking and emotional craziness when there is a full moon overhead. Be more careful on the roads then. Sometimes people take their conflicts out in their cars by driving dangerously, or in a distracted way. Everything in your life becomes really obvious at a full moon – especially any problems. If something (or someone) isn't quite working, it will be hard to ignore.

2004 Moon safari guide

January 7: Full moon in Cancer.
January 21: New moon in Aquarius.
February 6: Full moon in Leo.
February 20: New moon in Pisces.
March 6: Full moon in Virgo.
March 20: New moon in Aries.
April 5: Full moon in Libra.
April 19: New moon in Aries.
May 4: Full moon in Scorpio.
May 19: New moon in Taurus.
June 3: Full moon in Sagittarius.
June 17: New moon in Gemini.
July 2: Full moon in Capricorn.
July 17: New moon in Cancer.
July 31: Full moon in Aquarius.
August 16: New moon in Leo.
August 30: Full moon in Pisces.
September 14: New moon in Virgo.
September 28: Full moon in Aries.
October 14: New moon in Libra.
October 28: Full moon in Taurus.
November 12: New moon in Scorpio.
November 26: Full moon in Gemini.
December 12: New moon in Sagittarius.
December 26: Full moon in Cancer.

2005 Moon safari guide

January 10: New moon in Capricorn.
January 25: Full moon in Leo.
February 8: New moon in Aquarius.
February 24: Full moon in Virgo.
March 10: New moon in Pisces.
March 25: Full moon in Libra.
April 19: New moon in Aries.
April 24: Full moon in Scorpio.
May 8: New moon in Taurus.
May 23: Full moon in Sagittarius.
June 6: New moon in Gemini.
June 22: Full moon in Capricorn.
July 6: New moon in Cancer.

July 21: Full moon in Capricorn.
August 5: New moon in Leo.
August 19: Full moon in Aquarius.
September 3: New moon in Virgo.
September 18: Full moon in Pisces.
October 3: New moon in Libra.
October 17: Full moon in Aries.
November 2: New moon in Scorpio.
November 16: Full moon in Taurus.
December 1: New moon in Sagittarius.
December 15: Full moon in Gemini.
December 31: New moon in Capricorn.

What It Means For Your Sign

ARIES, LEO AND SAGITTARIUS A new moon in your sign or the other two fire signs is a green light – start something new!

A full moon in Libra, Aquarius and Gemini is uncomfortable – it's time to close chapters and let things go.

TAURUS, VIRGO AND CAPRICORN A new moon in your sign or the other two earth signs is a cosmic thumbs-up for new beginnings.

A full moon in Scorpio, Pisces or Cancer is a signal to wind down and take it easy.

GEMINI, LIBRA AND AQUARIUS A new moon in your sign or the other two air signs will ignite a new beginning in your life.

A full moon in Sagittarius, Aries or Leo is a red light; stop, slow down and review things!

You thought there were just 12 star signs, but think again. There are Taureans who have Aries bits, which make them more dynamic, and there are Geminis with Cancer bits, which make them better cooks.

CANCER, SCORPIO AND PISCES A new moon in your sign or the other two water signs promises a fantastic launch pad for something or someone new.

A full moon represents dilemmas and decisions, so slow down!

The 60 astro types

You thought there were just 12 star signs, but think again. There are Taureans who have Aries bits, which make them more dynamic, and there are Geminis with Cancer bits, which make them better cooks. There are double Leos, who are twice as creative, and then there are Virgos with Scorpio bits, which make them fussy about sex. The keys to the 60 astro types are the Sun, Mercury, and Venus combinations in your chart. You don't need to look anything up, though. Just check out yourself, and your friends, family, or honeys on this no-brainer list. In most cases, the person in question will have two or three things on the list and that's how you spot their classic type. On average, there are five versions of the same star sign. On the day and year you were born, the planets may have been lining up in five different ways to make you an Aries (for example), but either an Aries–Aries, Aries–Taurus, Aries–Gemini, Aries–Pisces, or Aries–Aquarius type. Planets in other signs on your birthday lend their influence. You'll fit one best! You'll notice that some sign types are the same—like the Aries–Taurus type and the Taurus–Aries type. When these two meet, they will click and feel extremely compatible, though only time will tell if this is a friendship or love relationship made in heaven. It's also possible that you recognize yourself, or someone you know, in more than just one of the descriptions for a particular sign type. If so, it's likely that the Sun/Mercury/Venus combination uses up three signs, not two, and so there really will be a mixture of quite a few things! So you can be an Aries–Aquarius type and an Aries–Gemini type at the same time. OK? (See "The 60 astro types" overleaf.)

Are you born to be wild?

There are a certain number of birthdays which contain astro-explosives. They happen once a year, and babies born on those days are literally born to be wild! The most alternative, surprising, unpredictable, stubborn, rebellious, crazy, exciting, electrifying and "definitely different" people you know may be born on one of these days. Maybe you think you, or perhaps your baby, are! Check the list on the next page for the wilder kinds of birthdates.

HOW TO DEAL WITH PEOPLE WHO WERE BORN TO BE WILD!

Anyone born on these special days, and sometimes the day before or day after, is under the influence of the crazy planet Uranus. Give this person a lot of space and freedom. You will notice that their birthday is the time when they seem to behave in the most rebellious, mad, or wild, wild ways. To be on the safe side, never organize a party for these people that is full of risks and no controls. Why? Because crazy Uranian energy is unleashed every time one of these babies (now adults) born on the "wild" days hits their birthday again! If you are in love with someone whose birthday is on the list, make sure that you don't fall into the trap of telling them what to do. These special people are natural rebels and there can be fireworks if they are trapped or forced to fall into line. They have a problem with rules, and often with authority figures – such as parents, teachers or bossy dates!

The special gifts of people who were born to be wild

These Uranus-influenced people are often ahead of their time. What they think or believe today, the rest of the world will tomorrow. They have a natural understanding of the most weird, wacky, and new inventions or forms of technology. They may be a Libra, Scorpio, Sagittarius, Capricorn, or whatever – but often you might mistake them for an Aquarian. They get on with Aquarians, too. Why? Because Aquarians understand them!

At last! The truth about compatibility

You might not have known this, but it's time to spell it out. Just knowing your star sign, and your mate's star sign, is not enough! It can be a guide to friendship, sure, as you can see from the types of astrogangs you fall into. But if you are honestly concerned about living together or getting married, you'll need a lot more than someone else's magazine star sign, and yours.

You need to check out the Moon. This is the key to your emotions, and your partner's. It's also the key to your lifestyle, your comfort zone, your basic needs, and a whole lot of other stuff that is crucial if you are honestly thinking about a serious future together. The Moon is easy to spot, if you haven't done so already. It's crescent-shaped, just like the real moon on a clear night.

Comparing your partner's Moon sign to your Sun sign (your regular star sign) and your own Moon sign can give you a big insight

BORN TO BE WILD BIRTHDATES	
1965	September 8
1966	September 14
1967	September 18
1968	September 22
1969	September 28
1970	October 3
1971	October 7
1972	October 11
1973	October 17
1974	October 22
1975	October 26
1976	October 30
1977	November 5
1978	November 9
1979	November 14
1980	November 17
1981	November 22
1982	November 27
1983	December 2
1984	December 5
1985	December 10
1986	December 14
1987	December 18
1988	December 23
1989	December 27
1990	December 31
1991	N/A
1992	January 6
1993	January 9
1994	January 13
1995	January 17

The 60 astro types

Aries–Aquarius types: Into radical protests, fast computer games, punk beliefs, science-fiction heroes.

Aries–Pisces types: Into water sports, psychic contests, fantasy adventure, Piranha fish, war poetry.

Aries–Aries types: Into aggressive sports, dynamic men as friends or lovers, fast-action jobs or hobbies.

Aries–Taurus types: Into financial competition, business enterprises, expensive sports, fast investments.

Aries–Gemini types: Into speed dialling, speed reading, impulsive short trips away, sports strategies.

Taurus–Pisces types: Into financial fantasies, dream objects and possessions, expensive spas/saunas.

Taurus–Aries types: Into financial competition, business enterprises, expensive sports, fast investments.

Taurus–Taurus types: Into banks with values, investment purchases, designer objects.

Taurus–Gemini types: Into expensive phones, mixing money with siblings, luxury cars, or short trips.

Taurus–Cancer types: Into property investment, mixing money with mothers, and expensive food.

Gemini–Aries types: Into speed-dialling phone buttons, impulsive short trips away, clever "brainy" sports.

Gemini–Taurus types: Into expensive phones, mixing money with siblings, luxury cars or short trips.

Gemini–Gemini types: Into phone calls/emails to brothers or sisters, car nicknames, travel word games.

Gemini–Cancer types: Into phone calls/emails to mum, property strategies, local news or gossip.

Gemini–Leo types: Into ideas and creativity, luxury short trips, royal or Hollywood actor/rock star gossip.

Cancer–Taurus types: Into property investment, mixing money with mothers, and expensive food.

Cancer–Gemini types: Into phone calls/emails to mum, property strategies, local newspapers, or gossip.

Cancer–Cancer types: Into home cooking, mum's family, ancestral real estate, patriotic nostalgia.

Cancer–Leo types: Into luxury residences, royal banquets at home, stars or VIPS in the family tree.

Cancer–Virgo types: Into health food, property details, working from home, family tree research.

Leo–Gemini types: Into ideas and creativity, luxury short trips, royal or Hollywood actor/rock star gossip.

Leo–Cancer types: Into luxury residences, royal banquets at home, stars or VIPS in the family tree.

Leo–Leo types: Into his/her own fame and glory, creative stardom, a leadership role with children/teens.

Leo–Virgo types: Into movie-star health food, analysing celebrities, creative work, jobs with children/teens.

Leo–Libra types: Into royal/celebrity love lives, luxury designer clothes or art, being on the social A list.

Virgo–Cancer types: Into health food, property details, working from home, family tree research.

Virgo–Leo types: Into movie-star health food, analysing celebrities, creative work, jobs with children/teens.

Virgo–Virgo types: Into reading the ingredients on health food, work linked to bodies/fitness/medicine.

Virgo–Libra types: Into perfect relationships, art criticism, body beautiful fitness or health.

Virgo–Scorpio types: Into body/health obsession, perfect sex, reading/writing/talking about taboo stuff.

Libra–Leo types: Into royal/celebrity love lives, luxury designer clothes or art, being on the social A list.

Libra–Virgo types: Into perfect relationships, art criticism, body beautiful fitness or health.

Libra–Libra types: Into romantic relationships, art/photography/music about love, the cause of peace.

Libra–Scorpio types: Into romantic erotica, sexy marriage, "Til death do us part," intense art/music.

Libra–Sagittarius types: Into long distance love, the philosophy of romance, exotic/ethnic art.

Scorpio–Virgo types: Into body/health obsession, perfect sex, reading/ writing/talking about taboo stuff.

Scorpio–Libra types: Into romantic erotica, sexy marriage, "Til death do us part," intense art/music.

Scorpio–Scorpio types: Into sexual obsession, focus on death/the dark side, powerful occult beliefs.

Scorpio–Sagittarius types: Into foreign love affairs, ethnic or exotic belief systems, black humour.

Scorpio–Capricorn types: Into corporate power, sex as a career move, financial structures.

Sagittarius–Libra types: Into long distance love, the philosophy of romance, exotic/ethnic art.

Sagittarius–Scorpio types: Into foreign love affairs, ethnic or exotic beliefs, black humour.

Sagittarius–Sagittarius types: Into overseas adventures, intellectual humour, global philosophies.

Sagittarius–Capricorn types: Into corporate comedy/jokes, global ambitions, overseas careers.

Sagittarius–Aquarius types: Into global politics/causes, new age or scientific philosophies.

Capricorn–Scorpio types: Into corporate power, sex as a career move, financial structures.

Capricorn–Sagittarius types: Into corporate comedy/jokes, global ambitions, overseas careers.

Capricorn–Capricorn types: Into career structure, social climbing (to the top), corporate stability.

Capricorn–Aquarius types: Into corporate revolutions, slow change, older/wiser radicals.

Capricorn–Pisces types: Into fantasy jobs, imaginative ambitions, building fish ponds/ spas/pools.

Aquarius–Sagittarius types: Into global politics/causes, new age or scientific philosophies.

Aquarius–Capricorn types: Into corporate revolutions, slow change, older/wiser radicals.

Aquarius–Aquarius types: Into rebelling against the rebels, changing technology, new radicals.

Aquarius–Pisces types: Into humanitarian poetry/photography, computer fantasy, alternative escapes.

Aquarius–Aries types: Into radical protests, fast computer games, punk beliefs, science fiction heroes.

Pisces–Capricorn types: Into fantasy jobs, imaginative ambitions, building fish ponds/spas/pools.

Pisces–Aquarius types: Into humanitarian poetry/photography, computer fantasy, alternative escapes.

Pisces–Pisces types: Into dreaming about the sea/ water, poems/photography about fantasy/dreams.

Pisces–Aries types: Into water sports, psychic contests, fantasy adventure, Piranha fish, beat poetry.

Pisces–Taurus types: Into financial fantasies, dream objects and possessions, expensive spas/saunas.

Uranus-influenced people
are often ahead of their
time. What they think or
believe today, the rest of
the world will tomorrow.
They have a natural understanding of the most weird,
wacky, and new inventions
or forms of Technology

into compatibility. It's not the whole story, of course. An astrologer will need to check out mysterious stuff, such as your seventh House, your fifth House, your Descendant, and your Venus to really get an insight into what lies ahead. The Moon is a good place to start though. And comparing your partner's Moon sign to your own signs is going to give you stacks more understanding and accuracy than just checking out your normal star signs.

If your Moon sign is . . .

Aries: It helps if your partner's Sun or Moon sign is Leo, Aries, or Sagittarius. You live life in the fast line with a lot of energy and vavavoom, and you don't want a wimpy lover.

Taurus: Try someone whose Sun or Moon sign is Taurus, Virgo, or Capricorn. You are very practical and good with money, or are already eyeing off mortgages – you need someone who gets it.

Gemini: A Libra, Aquarius, or Gemini Sun or Moon will click with you. You never shut up or stop writing emails, and that constant flow of communication is absolutely vital in love.

Cancer: You're emotional and you thrive with a Scorpio, Cancer, or Pisces Sun or Moon. These signs will understand how deep certain family or mother issues go with you, and sympathize.

Leo: Check out life with a Leo, Aries, or Sagittarius Moon or Sun person. You need a fiery person in your love life in order to feel completely satisfied – and proud of who you are.

Virgo: Capricorn, Taurus, or Virgo Sun/Moon sign people will click with you. They understand how important little details are to you, and they have a down-to-earth style you like.

You need to check out the
moon. This is the key to
your emotions, and your
partner's. it's also the key to
your lifestyle, your comfort
zone, your basic needs,
and a whole lot of other
stuff that is crucial if you
are honestly thinking about
a serious future.

Libra: You're in love with love! Try a Libra, Gemini, or Aquarius Sun or Moon sign. These people will be excellent company at parties, and you are an extremely sociable person.

Scorpio: Passionate and secretive by nature, you really belong with a more emotional person, and anyone with Scorpio, Pisces, or Cancer as their Sun or Moon sign could fit the bill.

Sagittarius: Your sense of humour is good, so don't waste your jokes on anyone else except a person born with the Sun or Moon in Leo, Sagittarius, or Aries. They'll click with you quite quickly.

Capricorn: A nice, grounded, sensible Taurus-, Capricorn-, or Virgo-style person could work incredibly well in your love life. Their Sun or Moon will need to be in any of these three signs.

Aquarius: You love freedom and doses of weirdness in your life, so check out someone born with the Sun or Moon in Aquarius, Libra, or Gemini, as they could let you be who you are.

Pisces: You sensitive, psychic creature! Your subtle way of feeling your way through relationships needs the right, understanding partner – try a Cancer, Pisces, or Scorpio Sun or Moon sign.

Global Goddess Guru Adam Smith
HOW TO SCOPE OUT YOUR LUCKY JUPITER RETURN!

At around the age of 12, 24, and 36 you get to experience your Jupiter Return. It's traditionally a time of good fortune and old-fashioned dumb luck! Here's what *Spirit* magazine columnist and Global Goddess Guru Adam Smith predicts for you...

SCOPING OUT YOUR JUPITER RETURN BY ADAM SMITH

Jupiter represents the good news in astrology, standing for optimism, generosity and joie de vivre. The biggest planet in the sky makes us expansive and shows the area where we relax and have confidence that life will bring us what we need. This positive attitude usually brings the best out of any situation, so in effect Jupiter is where we make our own luck.

Jupiter takes twelve years to go round the zodiac, spending roughly a year in every sign. So when we are 12, 24, 36 and so on, Jupiter comes back to its original place in our horoscope to give us double-bubble good fortune. During the Jupiter Return, the area of life governed by our own individual Jupiter sign gets a special lift and we can afford to stretch ourselves, knowing "risks" may work out in our favour. Good fortune at this time may be subtle, but is usually very enjoyable.

Knowing where our Jupiter is means we can prepare for the times when it produces its best effects. The Jupiter Return is usually the best example of this, but we don't always have to wait for twelve years – Jupiter going over the Sun, Moon, or rising sign are also major good times to look forward to.

Ten big astrology secrets
TO KEEP YOU AHEAD OF THE GAME

1 Never sign a contract, buy a telephone, launch a website, start a magazine, or publish a book when Mercury is retrograde, or going backwards. It has a 'shadow' period just before it starts going crazy, too, which you also need to bear in mind. To avoid hassles and rainchecks, don't do anything major involving the written or spoken work/travel during January 1–5 2004, March 24–April 29 2004, July 21–September 1 2004, November 12–December 19 2004. Updates on 2005 and following can be found at our website, 21stcenturygoddess.net.

2 Every twelve years or so, at around the age of 12, 24, 36, 48, 60, 72, 84, 96, 108 (Goddesses live forever) you will have amazing good luck, in exactly the same area or department of your life. What came through for you at age 23–25 will come through again, in a similar way, almost exactly twelve years later. Check it out!

3 If you were born between August 28 1984 and January 16 1995, then anyone born under the sign of Scorpio will bring about deep transformations in your life, or be there when it happens to you.

4 Between the age of 28 and 30 you will experience a major life lesson. It will not be easy. You should not rush your decision. The event or choice will stay with you for a long, long time!

5 Don't do anything major and long-lasting on the day of an eclipse, or three days before and after. The long-term results will not be what you expect.

6   Do expect your birthday, and the days just before and after it,
    to raise issues about your father or stepfather. Pay attention to
    every single detail that comes up – it will affect life for quite
    a while.

7   Ask your family if you were born on a full moon. If you were,
    you're not a werewolf, but you will have two totally different,
    opposing sides to your personality. And guess what? Your parents
    will seem to be opposite personality types too.

8   The dates covered by your star sign (for example, with Leo,
    July 23 to August 22) will always bring a photo opportunity, a
    public speech, your face on TV, your voice on radio, or your
    name in print or on the Web – almost every single year of your
    life! If your birthday is coming up, work on your image, look,
    or style.

9   Always trust a Scorpio with a secret, but know that it will give
    them secret power over you. Never trust a Gemini with a secret,
    especially if it's great information or gossip. It's in their nature
    to pass it on. Don't ever joke about a Cancerian's mother, and
    never start an argument with an Aries if you want an early night.

10 There is no such thing as being born on the cusp. If you were
    born on the date that a sign changes over, you are still one
    sign or the other.

Numerology

As an aspiring Goddess, you can learn truckloads about yourself through understanding the ancient system of numerology, the science of numbers. For those style queens for whom numbers only mean something at the end of a credit-card statement, we're about to blast you into a new trajectory! This is definitely no get-rich-quick-pyramid-selling kind of scheme either (although pyramids do come into it!). And it's not about the winning numbers on the lottery card that you should have bought last week, either. Goddesses, the ultimate winning ticket is the one you were issued at birth – it's the one that contains your numerological destiny. For this is the one lottery card that shows you how rich you truly are. Numerology is a very simple and effective means to knowledge – of life and of self. And as we've mentioned, the more you know about yourself – your real inner self – the better you'll be able to navigate through all of the peaks and troughs of life and come out a winner every time. It's all about the (good) vibrations, and numbers carry these in abundance. And it's all about abundance!

When you start to look at the numbers in your life, you'll soon see that there are patterns within patterns, and a whole universe of meaning to be both discovered and enjoyed. Numerology is a path, a landing strip that guides you in and, when properly considered, another useful tool in your repertoire as a fully-fledged Goddess. If you have always thought about numerology only in terms of your birthday (which is a great and important starting point) then you're in for a real treat, 'cos baby, we've got your number! We'll show you all sorts of ways to look at the numbers around you to really be able to work with the universal energies, to maximize your opportunities, and to better tap into real harmony. After all, energy is a frequency with a particular vibrational quality. And everything has energy. Think about where you live: the number of your house, flat, your telephone numbers, and even your postal code. These can all be very good clues to what the vibes are in your home or area, for better or worse!

The subject of numerology is so massive that what we're offering you here is the snapshot version. To truly understand the finer nuances and subtleties of the science of numbers, you'd need to hole up in your local library for about twenty years, like the experts do. Basically we've tried to make it easy (and fun) for you, and hopefully we've succeeded. Here's our best overview . . . enjoy the trip!

History by numbers ·

Throughout history, cultures around the world have celebrated and revered the power of numerology. Numbers and particular dates and years guided people for many activities, including worship and sacred occasions, but also for seasonal activities such as the harvest and the summer and winter solstices. The mythology from Egypt is full of the significance of certain numbers, however it was the ancient Greeks who were responsible for the system that we rely upon today. Pythagoras, a Greek philosopher and mathematician in the 6th century (BC), played a starring role in linking all things geometric with the spiritual realm. He was absolutely convinced of the inherent mystical and metaphysical essence of numbers, and of their significance to universal law.

The Judeo–Christian calendar has many days that are celebrated as much for when they fall as they are for the intrinsic power of the number or the vibrational qualities they represent. For example, Christmas Day is held on the 25th day (7) of the 12th month (3). These two numbers are powerful spiritual numbers, the positive and negative aspects of which will be discussed below. Even superstitious days (so-called) are pretty much observed in Western culture and those such as Friday the 13th hold special historical significance. Speaking of Western culture, the view of numerology presented here only briefly touches on the significance of numerology in the East. Eastern culture attaches different meanings and symbolic value to numbers, although the overall system is similar in its holistic approach and philosophy.

Living by numbers

There are many ways to look at the significance of numbers in our lives. You may have noticed that a certain number or combination of

---

GODDESS HISTORICAL SOCIETY:
(ANCIENT) SECRET WOMEN'S BUSINESS . . .

Did you know that the superstition about Friday the 13th arose because in centuries past, Friday the 13th was the day that witches gathered for prayer, healing ceremonies, and consciousness-raising? People feared these healers and their powers so much that the leaders of the early church of the day reversed the true meaning of this special day and deemed the gatherings as being representative of bad luck. The poor witches – early Goddesses no less! – were persecuted for a long time because of the fears (that men had) of their powers, which were actually intended for positive use and for general purpose healing. Also, there are thirteen moons in the lunar calendar, and this is why the witches congregated – the thirteenth moon was like the Sabbath to them, and therefore a very powerful time to perform their various rituals and healing ceremonies. The superstition surrounding this date continues today, but aspiring Goddesses can view it as a powerful time to perform healing and energetic rituals such as those described in the chapters Crystals, Oils, and Remedies, and Magic and Rituals.

numbers has a strong resonance for you, or you may be drawn to one number in particular. There is often a correlation between this coincidence and your personal number. In the following text we discuss your soul urge number, which is a number you may be unconsciously drawn to for no apparent reason. We'll look at all aspects, so you get the best view – looking at your full birth date to get your life path number, then your name number and your personal year number. Your personal year number helps you understand what forces may be shaping your present life experience. Now you can't blame it on the weather ...

Your life path number

Your life path number is the key to understanding certain broad characteristics of your personality. Each number from 1–9, 11, 22, and 33 has certain positive and negative aspects that relate to character, relationships, career, your home environment, and even your predisposition physically. Additionally, individual numbers such as your name number, will help you to get more information for you personally.

To calculate your life path number

Step 1: Write down in numbers your full birth date (D / M / Y)*. For example, for a Goddess born on 30 July, 1974: 30/7/1974*.
*Note: For our readers in the United States, having the month first or the day first has no impact on the outcome, which will be the same result numerologically.
Step 2: Add each of the numbers contained in the date 30/7/1974
$3 + 0 + 7 + 1 + 9 + 7 + 4 = 31$
Step 3: Reduce this number (31) to a single digit by adding them together:
$3 + 1 = 4$
The Life Path Number for a Goddess with this birthday is 4.

Note that when you calculate the life number for a person, there are a few exceptions to keep in mind when you reach Step 3. If the numbers in Step 2 come to 11, 22, or 33, then you do not reduce these further to a single digit, as 11, 22 and 33 are what are called "Master Numbers." See the list below for the explanation of each of these.

Life path numbers:
THE GOOD, THE BAD... AND THE GODDESS!

As we mentioned in our introduction, the whole point of life as budding Goddesses is to discover your inner self or true essence. Once this is better known, any goals you might have become easier to attain and your life path/destiny is seen with a higher perspective. Analysing your numerological inheritance is a way to uncover the particular vibrational influences at the time of your birth – which amount to your life path number – and which can give strong indications as to your character and your potential destiny.

The major thing to remember about numerology is that there are positive and negative aspects to all numbers. Yep, you know the drill, there's always a downside to the upside! This is described by various metaphysical gurus (a.k.a. those in the know) as "the duality of life" – or as it is described in Eastern cultures, the yin and yang – and this is the key to understanding why numerology is so fascinating. You can either tend to the negative aspects of your life path number or you can choose to eyeball these potential pitfalls and overcome them, consciously, through application, discipline, and awareness and by doing so tend toward the positive aspects. So, young Goddess – it's all up to you! Viewed this way, it becomes evident that numerology is a practical and, some would say, essential system of knowledge and insight. We have made a character chart (see the next page) to help you get a quick handle on what the numbers make of you. And you should be prepared...'cos it's not all pretty! Later still is a more detailed chart of the various positive and negative aspects of the life path numbers.

Master numbers

A master number within a chart or a life path requires special emphasis and attention, for master numbers possess more potential than other numbers. Due to the double-whammy effect of having the same number twice, they are highly charged, vibrationally-speaking. There are those who believe that we have actually chosen the numbers that will best help us to learn the lessons we need to for this lifetime. The intrinsic connection numbers have with your destiny can make dealing with the vibrational aspects of certain numbers challenging. Due to their intensity master numbers can require time, maturity, and effort to fully understand their impact on you and to get them working properly in your life.

The number 11 – Represents vision: The 11 Goddess is a dreamer, both highly intuitive and a visionary. Most intuitive psychics will have the number 11 somewhere in their groups of numbers, and this is compatible with their ability to "see." Not surprisingly perhaps, some 11 types tend to be neurotic or highly strung!

The 11 Goddess has the intensified aspects of an enhanced 1; she is doubly charged with charisma, leadership, and inspiration. It is a number with inborn duality, which can create inner conflict for her, though. And if she is not careful, she can turn this inner conflict into phobias. The 11 Goddess walks the fine line between illuminated greatness and catastrophic self-destruction.

To reap her full potential and personal power, a Goddess with an 11 in her chart has to utilize her intuitive nature and accept the universal spiritual truths of this number. She's just got to have faith – faith in herself and in a higher power that will show her the way.

The number 22 – combines vision with action: The life of a 22 Goddess is about devoting herself to a higher life, an idealistic (her critics would say unrealistic) vision of what life could be like. Before she can say "tropical paradise + George Clooney," it's time to get back to reality as this grand vision of hers is very unlikely to happen without some obstacles and struggle.

But the clever and canny 22 is often referred to as the Master Builder, turning ideas that to the observer seem overly ambitious into reality. She can practically make wine from water (which could come in very handy on that remote island). This makes her the most likely to succeed out of all of the master numbers. A 22 Goddess has the practicality, methodical and disciplined nature of the 4 as well as the relationship and partnership abilities of the 2. She has big ideas, great plans, and enormous self-confidence. George/Brad/Tom et al may not stand a chance from a 22 Goddess.

If she is not practical in life matters, she can waste her potential and cause herself to experience undue pressures and stress. If she works for the greater good and not just for herself, she will realize all her dreams and grand plans. Teamwork is the key for this Goddess-on-a-mission!

The number 33 – offers guidance to the world: The 33 Goddess is known as The Compassionate, and she is a great influence on the people around her and even beyond. She understands the ripple effect – and synergy – beautifully and always makes her

Which character are you?

LIFE PATH/DESTINY CHARACTER	POSITIVE ASPECTS	NEGATIVE ASPECTS
THE INDEPENDENT (1)	Active Adaptable Loves deeply Monogamous Self-sufficient Ambitious	Lazy Secretive Loner Jealous Self-centred Authoritarian
THE TEAM PLAYER (2)	Cooperative Pro-partnership Peaceful Honest Reserved Analytical	Easily hurt Can be lonely Manipulative Oversensitive Moody Indecisive
THE ARTIST (3)	Sociable Imaginative Expressive Optimistic Artistic Uninhibited	Scattered energy Escapist Extravagant Impatient Irresponsible Vain
THE ROCK (4)	Stable Tolerant Gentle Dignified Loyal Practical	Unexciting Insecure Submissive Obsessive Myopic Antisocial
THE ADVENTURER (5)	Free-spirited Intuitive Dynamic Fun-loving Multi-talented Emotive	Inconsistent Apathetic Self-indulgent Irresponsible Lacking direction Aggressive
THE CARER (6)	Loving Unselfish Dedicated Humane Creative Responsible	Possessive Anxious Apprehensive Critical Fearful Neurotic

LIFE PATH/DESTINY CHARACTER	POSITIVE ASPECTS	NEGATIVE ASPECTS
THE TEACHER (7)	Spiritual **Philosophical** Analytical **Trustworthy** Physical **Stoic**	Pessimistic **Self-obsessed** Inconsiderate **Secretive** Immature **Martyr**
THE ENTREPRENEUR (8)	Dependable **Powerful** Confident **Creative** Driven **Compassionate**	Intolerant **Domineering** Aloof **Difficult** Unemotional **Materialistic**
THE IDEALIST (9)	Ambitious **Humanitarian** Responsible **Kind** Honourable **Artistic**	Cynical **Impractical** Hypocritical **Egocentric** Critical **Abrupt**
THE VISIONARY (11)	Generous **Spiritual** Intuitive **Inspired** Just **Pure potential**	Bitter **Materialistic** Spiteful **Easily influenced** Envious **Indifferent**
THE MASTER (22)	Artistic **Emotionally aware** Powerful **Moral** Worldly **Global**	Lazy **Emotionless** Hypersensitive **Depressive** Misfit **Naive**
THE COMPASSIONATE (33)	Conscious **Highly sensitive** Empathetic **Kind** Loving	Introverted **Anxious** Neurotic **Overemotional** Jealous

presence felt. When expressed in the positive aspect, the 33 Goddess does not focus on her personal ambitions; instead she uses her considerable abilities to uplift people to spiritual awareness. This usually multi-skilled Goddess is also a good communicator. A true 33 has a high level of sincerity and determination and seeks understanding and wisdom before attempting to teach others.

In the negative aspect (sorry girls we do have to go there!), a 33 can often be co-dependent and needy. The 33 that is stuck in the baggage of these downside vibrational aspects may not be able to see the forest for the trees and literally becomes root-bound – for example, by teaching outdated information or refusing to be open to new ideas and resources. She needs to constantly read and update her knowledge. As a 33 it is essential to question everything and not to accept a premise until you have dissected the subject, arriving at a point to see if it's worthwhile passing on. Otherwise a 33 can be seen as egocentric or arrogantly opinionated. Hmmm . . . not particularly attractive qualities for any Goddess!

Note that the number 33 is only regarded as a master number when it is found in the life path as the destiny number. Otherwise 33 should always be reduced to 6.

Numbers and their overall characteristics

1 **The Positive Goddess:** Creative, inspiring, a leader, self-sufficient, and ambitious, this Goddess loves trying new things and developing new ideas. She has a strong drive to accomplish a great deal.
The Negative Goddess: She can be highly self-centred and demand her own way. She can also be extremely bossy, too impulsive, selfish, and egotistical. Oops!

2 **The Positive Goddess:** Loving and thinks the best of people, she is the peace-maker, analytical, sincere in her concern for others. She's a born diplomat, honest and open in word and deed – she'd make a great counsellor.
The Negative Goddess: Can get stuck on the finer details and miss the big picture. Can be apathetic, listless, and pessimistic. Oh, dear!

3 **The Positive Goddess:** She's outgoing, energetic, imaginative, warm, and friendly. She's the one you have the best chats with – this Goddess has exceptional creative skills and is enthusiastic and effervescent.
The Negative Goddess: For no apparent reason she may become moody and tend to retreat. She can be overly critical of

others, impatient, intolerant, or conversely overly optimistic without good reason. Well!

4 **The Positive Goddess:** Hard-working, trustworthy, practical, and down to earth. A doer, this Goddess loves to get things done. An excellent organizer and planner. Great at being an administrator.

The Negative Goddess: To get a job done she may border on obsessive. Has a great need for security, can prove excessively dogmatic, narrow-minded, and repressive. Hmmm . . .

5 **The Positive Goddess:** She's bold, daring, persuasive, versatile, and progressive. Bungee-jumping adventurous, she takes chances and loves her freedom. A trail-blazer, she knows how to motivate people.

The Negative Goddess: She finds it hard to settle into routine, becoming restless and easily sidetracked. May become self-indulgent and unaware of other people's feelings. Tsk-tsk!

6 **The Positive Goddess:** She's warm, nurturing, and happy to be domestic. Reliable, sympathetic and kind, generous with personal and material resources.

The Negative Goddess: She can be over-opinionated. She has a tendency to become overwhelmed by responsibilities and to become a slave to others. She can be too critical and has a tendency to be self-righteous, interfering, or meddling. Uh-oh!

7 **The Positive Goddess:** This Goddess is a deep thinker, and a peaceful and affectionate soul. By nature she's rather reserved and spiritually inclined. She's unique and somewhat eccentric, and she seeks answers to life's heavier questions.

The Negative Goddess: She can be very pessimistic, quarrelsome, and secretive. Stability in her feelings may be elusive. Phew!

8 **The Positive Goddess:** Decisive and forceful, this Goddess handles financial matters and business well. Powerful, confident, accomplished, she has to strive higher and take control. A pretty cool customer, she seeks and likes power and status. She has the courage of her convictions.

The Negative Goddess: Emotional feelings are often suppressed, which may lead to isolation and loneliness. Material gains and rewards often become issues of utmost importance. Warning: Danger ahead!

9 **The Positive Goddess:** She sees the "big picture." Inspired, intuitive, creative. She's a seeker, aiming to improve the world. Compassionate, generous, with a very humanitarian attitude. She's honourable in the old-fashioned sense. She's able to give up material

possessions for the common good. She's both tolerant and broad-minded.

The Negative Goddess: She can develop bad habits, and neglect to attend to life's details. She can get lost in her passions. She quickly finds out what happens from being too materialistic.

The grid of life

Another way to interpret your numerological birth chart in terms of lessons and challenges or your strengths and weaknesses is to map out your whole birth date on a grid. Some numerologists use the Pythagorean triangles, which work in the same way. The grid works on the axis of each of three angles to reveal vertically, thoughts, will, actions. The horizontal axis highlights the aspects of mind, body, spirit that specifically relate to you. The grid reveals where you are "missing" numbers, and this is important as it gives you direct clues as to areas in your life that are in need of attention and/or which are potentially the source of problems. Simply put, a missing number indicates a weakness, however, it can be supported by other numbers in your chart that are stronger, so it's not necessarily a disaster if you don't have certain numbers – and it may even be a boon! The point is, you need to understand the purpose of each axis on the grid and work them both individually and collectively before you will get the full gist. The grid is a kind of blueprint for what your destiny might look like, but by being aware, you can make changes to the outcome, no matter what. In other words, Goddesses, do not fear – anything is possible with mindful awareness and the right approach.

Master grid

The master grid, containing all of the possible numbers, is:				
3	6	9	mind	(horizontal)
2	5	8	soul	(horizontal)
1	4	7	body	(horizontal)
thought	will	action		
(vertical)	(vertical)	(vertical)		

When entering the numbers of your birth date into the grid, note where you have multiple occurrences of a certain number and write them in the same box. Having, for example, three "ones" in your birth chart has significance – it is an indication of a very strong tendency in your character, so you include the number as many times as it occurs. For example, for a Goddess born on August 4, 1988, the grid would look as follows:

$$
\begin{array}{ccc}
- & - & 9 \\
- & - & 888 \\
1 & 4 & -
\end{array}
$$

A person with this many eights would possess great wisdom and be independent. They are also stable and full of joy, which wins them many friends and associates. Turn over to interpret yours.

SEVEN – THE SYSTEMS NUMBER

Seven is the key spiritual number in many religions and cultures. It also has much significance with the power of the 3, since $7 \times 3 = 21$, which, in turn, can be reduced to 3, representing the holy trinity of mind, body, and spirit.

The Seven Deadly sins: Envy, sloth, greed, lust, vanity, anger, pride

The Seven Chakras (energy centres): Base, sex, power, heart, throat, third eye, crown

The Seven Ancient Wonders of the World (seeing as we've been dipping into the past!): The Pyramids of Giza, the Temple of Artemius at Ephesus, the Hanging Gardens of Babylon, the Colossus of Rhodes, the statue of Zeus by Phidias at Olympia, the Pharos (lighthouse) at Alexandria, the Mausoleum erected by Artemais at Halicarnassus

The Seven Days of Creation (hence the seven days of the week!): A self-described "feminist witch" and a true Goddess, Zsuzsanna Budapest knows a thing or two about the power of the days of the week. In her essential hand-book for all (hard) working Goddesses, Goddess in the Office, Zsuzsanna links the seven days of the week with the seven powers Mother Nature has given each of us. According to Zsuzsanna, you can work your week better if you use the energies associated with each day according to what you need to accomplish. Zsuzsanna writes of each day: Monday is for grounding, Tuesday is for using the will, Wednesday for communicating more effectively, Thursday for matters of love and the heart, Friday is for using the emotions and feelings, Saturday is for gaining insights or vision while Sunday – blessed Sunday – is for engaging and accessing the powers of the spirit.

Go with the spirit of each day and have a great week, every week!

Meaning of each axis

Thought line (Vertical): To do with the creative and imaginative process and new ideas or projects. Associated with the innermost thought processes and related to the super-conscious part of the mental plane. Thought creates karma and precedes action. A negative or damaging thought can be as effectively harmful as the actual deed, which may or may not occur. With awareness, you can retract thoughts which do not serve you or the Universe.

Will line (Vertical): Expression of individuality via communication and directness of purpose. The power of choosing actions in fulfilment of one's expressed desires.

Action line (Vertical): Having the ability to plan and execute ideas (seed thoughts that germinate and grow) in a physical form. Having control and awareness of one's physical actions, behaviours, and deeds.

Mind line (Horizontal): The outward mental ability and physical mental attributes such as raw intelligence, ability to rationalize, and to logically structure thoughts. The mind line constitutes the mental processes that are seen and heard by all. Relates to the conscious part of the mental plane.

Soul line (Horizontal): To do with how we assimilate the world. How we record our experiences in this present lifetime at our core level of existence. It represents our ultimate intuitive understanding.

Body Line (Horizontal): To do with the attributes of health, including all physiological aspects, and the ability of the body to maintain itself. It is the physical house that carries thought into existence for our lifetime and, as such, is a record of our genetic blueprint as well as our journey on the earthly plane.

Grids missing an axis

If your grid is missing a complete axis (that is, if you have a row that is completely empty) and if, say, your soul line is completely blank, don't panic! It doesn't mean that you have no soul – on the contrary, what this means is that you may be extremely sensitive to the point of hypersensitivity and you may have an insecurity or inferiority complex. To fill in your missing soul line, the work you may need to do may include taking control of your emotions and recognizing that you have the power not to be a victim of circumstance. It may include being more spiritually tuned in, and exploring more metaphysical and spiritual practices to achieve balance in this area. A missing axis is merely an indicator of an area that will be very significant for you to do work around or to increase your awareness. Call it a message from the Universe if you prefer – instead of worrying about it! It's there to draw your attention to something you really need to notice. So, really, it's all good!

Example of a missing soul line: Here's the grid for Diana, the late Princess of Wales, born on July 1, 1961:

–	6	9
–	–	–
111	–	7

As you can see, Diana's chart was missing her soul line, and as we know from her life, she was an extremely sensitive person and deeply compassionate in her concern for others' welfare.

Your personal name number

OK. So, you always pick a racehorse by the jockey's colours, and you throw pennies in the fountain at the local mall to make a wish, but it's getting late and you're still waiting for your ship to come in! You know you deserve it, so listen up. We've got a better way to increase your personal odds in the race of life and it comes in the form of your personal name number. Your personal name number is different to your life path (destiny) number because your personal name number is calculated by using your full name.

Your personal name number has particularly strong vibrations for you personally. So, in other words, even if you and your best friend were born on the same day, you can still trump her by having your own name number. The alphabet has numerological equivalents, so everything with a name can be analysed on the basis of its numerology – let's start with yours!

Calculating your personal name number based on your full name is done in several steps. The vowels in your name reveal what is called your "Soul Urge," the consonants or remaining letters reveal what is called your "Outer Personality," and the combination of these (adding together the Soul Urge plus the Outer Personality) results in your Destiny number. Each of these is significant and helpful in their own way, and it's useful to understand what the breakdown of each means, notwithstanding the fact that you basically get one number at the end of the whole exercise!

Outer Personality

The Outer Personality is how you present yourself in physical form. It represents the side of yourself that you show to the outside world, or what you've been conditioned and learned to show to others. It is what you naturally do. The names we are given at birth contain numbers which reveal this to us. At a deeper level these tell us our challenges and lessons, both the positive and the negative aspects of how we are seen by the world around us.

Soul Urge

The Soul Urge is what is actually in our conscience or our higher self and is related to the blueprint of our past lives. It is representative of our karmic challenges from previous incarnations and, as such, is about our current mission or life purpose as a result of all that we have incurred as a soul throughout time. Some people are drawn to certain numbers and this is often, coincidentally (or not!), their Soul Urge number.

Destiny

Our Destiny number represents our individual future as designed by our own efforts in combination with our past and present karma. Destiny is changed and created by acting with free will. Destiny is different to fate. Fate represents the set of circumstances bestowed upon you at the time of your birth and relates to such things as your given name, your DNA (your physiological and biological inheritance), and your family circumstances etc. Fate, however, can also be your Destiny, but it is more like the shadow aspect of Destiny if left unexplored. Destiny is active and free-flowing. Fate is passive and counter-intuitive.

Here we show you how to work out your personal name number using your full name. As an example, we've chosen the full name of one of our favourite screen Goddesses, *Titanic* star, Kate Winslet:

Step 1: Write the full name on a piece of paper, leaving plenty of space above and below it. K A T E E L I Z A B E T H W I N S L E T

Step 2: Convert each letter of the alphabet to a number using this chart:

1	2	3	4	5	6	7	8	9
A	B	C	D	E	F	G	H	I
J	K	L	M	N	O	P	Q	R
S	T	U	V	W	X	Y	Z	

Step 3: Assign the numerical values to each letter of the name, placing the values above the vowels (a, e, i, o, u) and, underneath the name, the values of the consonants (all other letters).

```
 1   5  9 1   5         9      5
K A T E   E L I Z A B E T H   W I N S L E T
 2 2       3 8   2 2 8 5   5 1 3   2
```

WOMEN WE LOVE...

Here are the birthdays of some of our favourite celebrity Goddesses. If you want to flex your new found numerological knowledge, try analysing these gorgeous girls...

9 9 1 9 9	(37)	SOUL = 1
CHRISTINA RICCI		DESTINY = 8
3 8 9 1 2 5 9 3 3	(43)	PERSONALITY = 7
BIRTHDAY 12/2/1980	(23)	LIFE PATH = 5

9 5 5 1	(20)	SOUL = 2
BRITNEY SPEARS		DESTINY = 9
2 9 2 5 7 1 7 9 1	(43)	PERSONALITY = 7
BIRTHDAY 2/11/1980	(22)	LIFE PATH = 4

9 5 9 6 3 5	(37)	SOUL = 1
KYLIE MINOGUE		DESTINY = 2
2 7 3 4 5 7	(28)	PERSONALITY = 1
BIRTHDAY 28/5/1968	(12)	LIFE PATH = 3

1 5 5 1	(12)	SOUL = 3
CATHY FREEMAN		DESTINY = 11
3 2 8 7 6 9 4 5	(44)	PERSONALITY = 8
BIRTHDAY 16/2/1973	(29)	LIFE PATH = 11

1 9 6 6 5	(27)	SOUL = 9
MARION JONES	(16)	DESTINY = 7
4 9 5 1 5 1	(25)	PERSONALITY = 7
BIRTHDAY 12/10/1975	(26)	LIFE PATH = 8

Step 4: Add together the vowel values from the line above your name. In this case:

$1 + 5 + 5 + 9 + 1 + 5 + 9 + 5 = 40$

This total (40) should then be reduced to a single digit number: $4 + 0 = 4$. This number (4) determines the Soul Urge.

Step 5: Next, add and reduce the consonant values below your name to determine your Outer Personality. In this case:

$2 + 2 + 3 + 8 + 2 + 2 + 8 + 5 + 5 + 1 + 3 + 2 = 43$

This total (43) should then be reduced to a single digit number: $4 + 3 = 7$. This number (7) determines the Outer Personality.

Step 6: Now, add the Soul Urge (4) to the Outer personality (7) to obtain the Destiny number. In our example it is 11, which, because it is a "Master Number," is not reduced to a single digit. Please refer to our discussion on master numbers and their significance.

Conclusion: Kate Winslet – A master of her own Destiny!

Kate's personal name number is an 11. As discussed earlier, this is a master number, but the other aspects to her numbers give us another interesting perspective on the woman beneath the actor. Kate's Soul Urge is 4, reflecting the need for security, balance and harmony in her personal life. This is in sharp contrast to her public life, the all-consuming and unpredictable film industry, where there is no real security, so she needs balance in other areas to compensate for this.

Kate's Outer Personality is a 7. This number is associated with deep thinking and people associated with this number can tend to appear aloof. A person with a 7 in their Outer Personality is self-sufficient and sometimes insecure, hence their tendency to withdraw. Kate is all of these, plus she has the ability to connect with people in a deep and lasting way.

Kate's Destiny number is the master number 11, which is the big Double F: Fame and Fortune!! As it is well-reported (we know you read *Heat* or *Hello!*) she blasted her way into the stratosphere with her star turn in *Titanic* opposite Leo Di Caprio, and certainly reaped fame and fortune along the way. Even the roles she has chosen throughout her career are in sync with who she is behind the scenes. Being more spiritually inclined, however, life is not about money for Kate. As with the role she played in *Hideous Kinky* (a woman on a spiritual quest) and in *Titanic* itself, where her character (albeit the older version) throws the priceless sapphire and diamond necklace overboard, she does what's best for the greater good – a typical 11.

The numbers and their meaning

The following represents a quick reference guide for each number and the particular vibrational meaning of each.

1	independence	2	relationships
3	creation	4	stability
5	opportunity	6	intuition
7	spirituality	8	infinity
9	completion	11	visionary
22	mastery	33	humanitarian

MISSING NUMBERS AND THEIR MEANING (see page 90)

MISSING 1
Thought level: More likely to be dominated by others and this can result in a certain level of neediness.
Body level: Potential false pride and egotism.

MISSING 2
Thought level: Extremely sensitive to thoughts about others in relation to themselves. Could indicate a lack of self-esteem and inability to respond to criticism.
Soul level: Difficulty making decisions and a tendency to shy away from positions of responsibility and authority.

MISSING 3
Thought level: Tend to be energetically scattered and somewhat lacking in focus in their application of their talents and skill base.
Mind level: Expression is limited by introverted and reclusive behaviour and thought patterns.

MISSING 4
Body level: Low level of energy and difficulty in completing physical tasks.
Will level: Lack of patience and understanding, and the desire or motivation to carry out responsibilities.

MISSING 5
Soul level: Freedom is sought above all else as a primary motivation. The spirit is the focus.
Will level: Being impulsive rather than considered in one's responses to outside communication or situations.

MISSING 6
Mind level: High expectations and perfectionism, intolerant of human foibles and frailty.
Will level: There is a need to respect another's need to follow their individual path and not to control or deny another's point of view.

Missing 7
Body level: They dwell on limitations and this results in physical inaction.
Action level: Emotions are suppressed and this can lead to a paralysis of action in response to the inner critic.

MISSING 8
Soul level: Emphasis should be placed on the non-material or imbalance results.
Action level: Tendency to abuse money and power.

MISSING 9
Mind level: Self-absorption and narcissistic. Thinking only of oneself.
Action level: Acting solely in one's own interest without regard for the greater good.

Goddess special note: Note the significance of the master numbers 11, 22, 33 which are the amplified (extreme) version of the 1, 2 and 3.

Example of doing the numbers on a project name

Goddesses that we are, we couldn't live with ourselves until we had the numerology done for the title *21st Century Goddess*. To make sure the project name had the right feel for what we were planning to produce, we tested it – and so here we are!

The purpose for "doing the numbers" is to discover all of the aspects influencing the project's final outcome. Viewing both the positive and negative aspects of each will then allow an understanding of the opportunities and also of any potential problem areas – before they arise. You may not wish to go with a certain name for your project (or book, film, website, play, shop name etc) if the numerology doesn't seem compatible with your reasons for doing it – in other words, your ultimate goals. Whatever your goals are, of course, can only be known by you. So while this is purely a personal thing, it pays to think clearly what your end game is when beginning anything, and therefore doing the numerology for a project is great for clarity, for making plans, setting goals and realizing visions. For instance, if your business name has a destiny of 4 (which represents stability, security and family), then this may not be compatible with starting a high-risk futures-trading business consultancy as 4 will be too limiting.

What follows is an example of how you can assess the potential of any project that you may be planning, or if you want to register a company name or a business trading name.

Using the same process, for the benefit of all you kick-boxing, garlic-throwing Goddesses, we have calculated each of the three levels for the cult television show: *Buffy the Vampire Slayer*.

Step 1: Write the full name on a piece of paper, leaving plenty of space above and below it.

                 B U F F Y T H E V A M P I R E S L A Y E R

Step 2: Convert each letter of the alphabet to a number using this chart.

1	2	3	4	5	6	7	8	9
A	B	C	D	E	F	G	H	I
J	K	L	M	N	O	P	Q	R
S	T	U	V	W	X	Y	Z	

Step 3: Assign the numerical values to each letter of the name, placing the values of the vowels (a, e, i, o, u) above the name, and the values of the consonants (all other letters) underneath the name.

```
  3           5   1   9 5      1 5
  B U F F Y   T H E   V A M P I R E   S L A Y E R
  2   6 6 7   2 8     4   4 7 9       1 3   7   9
```

Step 4: Add together the vowel values from the line above the name. In this case:

3 + 5 + 1 + 9 + 5 + 1 + 5 = 29

2 + 9 = 11

This total (11) should normally be reduced to a single digit number; however, once again, it is the master number 11, so we do not reduce it. This number (11) determines the Soul Urge.

Step 5: Next, add and reduce the consonant values below the name to determine the Outer Personality. In this case:

2 + 6 + 6 + 7 + 2 + 8 + 4 + 4 + 7 + 9 + 1 + 3 + 7 + 9 = 75

Then reduce to a single digit number:

7 + 5 = 12

1 + 2 = 3. This number (3) determines the Outer Personality.

Step 6: Now, add the Soul Urge (11) to the Outer Personality (3) to obtain the Destiny number:

11 + 3 = 14

1 + 4 = 5. The Destiny number for Buffy the Vampire Slayer is 5.

Conclusion: *Buffy the Vampire Slayer* – A TV show that changes lives!

From the above calculations we can analyse *Buffy the Vampire Slayer* on three levels. The Soul Urge reveals a master number – once again fame and fortune – which indicates key things about the hit show. Firstly, the programmeme is about saving lives. Each show is an archetypal tale of good versus evil with good ultimately triumphing. The show is concerned with the moral high ground and what's best for humanity. This is classic 11 stuff.

The Outer Personality of the show is a 3. The number 3 is about creativity, communication, and personal expression. With highly original storylines and very few stereotypical characters season after season, *Buffy the Vampire Slayer* is unique and unusual by any standards. It's wildly effective in communicating with people

Buffy the Vampire Slayer is a TV show that changes lives!

everywhere and is also groundbreaking entertainment ahead of its time – typical of the number 3.

The Destiny number of the show is a 5. A 5 usually relates to multi-talented people and, in the case of this show, the cast is, especially Buffy. The number 5 is also associated with freedom and adventure – it's all about the love of unpredictability, overcoming obstacles and danger, and, ultimately, it's about the opportunities for change leading to personal choices and freedom. *Buffy the Vampire Slayer* is a television show about exploits and these result in life-changing scenarios for the characters involved. This is why it has been such a cult hit with the youth market, because that's what this age group is usually dealing with in their own lives.

The Triple Goddess: The power of 3

The Triple Goddess is the ultimate symbol of the feminine, representing the three disparate aspects of the female: the virgin, the mother, and the crone. All three aspects are the states that each woman passes through on her journey on the physical plane. All Goddesses should note that these are generic psychological stages and are not necessarily literal. For instance, you may never give birth, but you can successfully pass through the mother stage via creative outlets, nurturing and caring in other ways. In the laws of magic and ritual, all things are done threefold. Affirmations, incantations, and spells are always repeated three times for magical efficacy. There are also three phases of the moon: the waxing moon, the full moon, and the waning moon.

Three is also one of the most important numbers in geometry (the triangle – the three-sided symbol) and has links to the holistic approach of the three aspects of mind, body, spirit, which is the sacred trinity that underlies all aspects of creation, including birth, life, and death. Another representation of this sacred trinity is that of past, present, future. The triangle stands for the ascent to heaven, fire, and the active male principle.

Finally, three heads are better than one. If two of you can't solve a problem, bring in a third party for balance – and a solution. We definitely agree on that one!

Choosing names

Numerology can also be used when picking a name for a child, a property, a business, a pet, or even for your own (new) name. Doing the numbers on all given names can be fun and can add insight about how you might better understand someone else too. It's particularly helpful if someone won't tell you what their birthday is.

Goddesses who wish to change their personal or family names should also be aware that you can never fully eliminate the effects of your true given birth name. Choosing a new name for yourself is pretty major, and it should, ideally, be done with full awareness of the aspects surrounding the name number. Your birth name number has lessons for you to learn and, while you may wish to appear on the world stage with a better sounding moniker or simply be known in a funkier style, you should remember to pay full attention to the numerological aspects. Even if you really dislike your original name (as most people who are motivated to change theirs usually do) it may be a good idea to at least try and understand it. That's not to say choosing a new name for yourself won't have some effect on your destiny – for many people a name change has a major impact on their lives – however, you will still be under the effect of the aspects of the name you were given at birth. Carefully choose your new name with a view to offsetting the positive and negative aspects of both name numbers in a balanced way. Being aware of the influences may really help you to steer a more decisive path in life, if you are operating with full knowledge of what each of your name numbers means for you.

Karmic debt numbers

Numerology can open us to the possible reasons we may experience difficulties in this present lifetime. Our belief is that we all have had many incarnations, accumulating as we've gone along in each lifetime a wealth of information, which may benefit us in our present lifetime – if we can only tap into it. But we may have made mistakes (and we've all bought that cute sweater on sale that shrinks to nothing after the first wash!), or have abused – or worse ignored – the gifts we have been given (and we're not just talking about bad Christmas presents either). With these and other such realizations weighing very heavily on the mind, we can only reassure you that at least, dear Goddess, we are all in the same boat! To balance these errors, in this life we take on difficulties in order to learn a particular lesson. In numerology, these lessons are called our karmic debt.

When looking at a chart many things are taken into account. Take a tip: Please don't beat yourself up if you happen to have these numbers! We advise you to acknowledge them by taking them in your stride and working with them. Nothing numerologically is insurmountable. Carl Jung once said that our greatest gifts come from those things that are from aspects of ourselves we don't like. And there's nothing you can't beat with the right attitude and a bit of knowledge!

The numbers that indicate a karmic debt include, 13, 14, 16, and 19 (prior to the reduction of the totals). These numbers have a greater significance when they are in your life path, Soul Urge and Outer Personality. Different cycles during the course of your lifetime can also draw these numbers to you in different ways, such as house numbers etc. Each of these karmic numbers has their own unique characteristics and their own particular difficulties. Fear not, you can still prevail!

13: Hard work and slow progress

Those who have 13 will have to work hard to overcome obstacles that stand in their way, time and time again. The feeling you may have is one of frustration, with the impression that all your efforts seem futile. And while you may be closer to giving up and chucking it all in, we advise that if you can accept the hard slog and keep doing the task, you'll benefit in a heap of other ways, even if the goal in reality is an impossible one. The point, gorgeous ones, is that the goal itself may not be the point of the exercise! It may be the lessons you were meant to learn simply from having it. If you stick with whatever you're doing and remain undeterred, even if, after all you can possibly do, the goal doesn't manifest, you'll eventually understand the reason why! The trick with this number is to avoid falling into habits of laziness and wallowing in counterproductive negativity. Perseverance and focus are the keys to learning the lessons offered by this number. More often than not, the person with a 13 karmic debt does not direct their energies into one specific activity. They often jump from one thing to the next, scattering whatever energy they need to complete the task. Shortcuts aren't for a 13. Success doesn't come easily and the desire to give up is the greatest temptation. In order to succeed, maintain order and use a schedule. Keep organized, you'll be richly rewarded as your consistent effort is the antidote to any perceived failure. When coping well with the challenges of this number, the person with this karmic debt is

grounded, down to earth, hardworking and reliable. Remember:
The underdog always has its day!

14: Commitment

Usually this karmic debt arises when a person has abused someone else's freedom in a previous life (who's been a naughty Goddess then?). To balance things in this lifetime then, you may experience the feeling of being trapped, overwhelmed, and constantly having to deal with ever-changing circumstances and unexpected problems.

If you can't resign from your job because you have to pay off a maxed-out credit card and you're about to be evicted from your place because your flatmate, who was last seen at the airport, appears to have split with the rent money, or your car is continually in the garage with yet another part needing to be replaced (and what's worse it's out of warranty), you may have a karmic debt number 14 at work. Goddesses with this karmic debt number in their chart will need to be willing to adapt, and quickly, to changes in order to fulfil this debt to the cosmos. In addition, there is the tendency to acting the role of victim, and as if that wasn't enough, the potential is also there to abuse drugs and alcohol, or to be generally self-indulgent. So, lots of pot-holes to avoid here! The lesson here is that with awareness and insight you can avoid the roller-coaster ride of emotions and self-loathing that accompanies all of the above through learning to overcome this particular karmic debt by practising moderation in all things. Mental and emotional stability must be attained in order to avoid being at the whim of the changing fortunes of the external or internal environments. The key to overcoming this karmic debt is commitment: if you follow your heart and maintain beliefs of a higher order (stay on the moral high road girls!), you will succeed in fulfilling all your dreams and desires.

Go get 'em!

16: Thy will be done

The 16 karmic debt holds the meaning of birth, life, and death, the destruction of the old and rebirth of the new. And that's just for starters. The mighty challenge thrown up by the karmic debt

GODDESS CULTURAL NOTE

In Buddhist cultures, such as Tibet and Nepal, traditional prayer beads, known as "mala" beads, are used for repeating and keeping count of one's (meditation) mantra. There are 108 beads on each string and they are often carried in the hand or around the wrist when not in use. A complete meditation session is 108 mantra repetitions and practitioners move through the prayer beads holding each bead to mark the number of mantras they have repeated. Numerologically, this is interesting as 108 can be reduced to 9, which is the number of completion.

GODDESS SPECIAL ANECDOTE

Our very own 21st Century Goddess, Jelena, has changed her name twice, (well anglicized it actually) to Helen and reverted to her original. Interestingly, Jelena's close friends have a special nickname for her: Cherub. Below we will look at the numerology of (a) Jelena vs. (b) Helen vs. (c) Cherub. Her three names reveal her differing challenges and using the same method, we analyse each of them below:

(a) JELENA:

```
  5  5  1      = 11 (Outer Personality)
J E L E N A
1  3  5       = 9 (Soul Urge)
```

To find the Destiny number for Jelena = 11 + 9 = 20, which when reduced = 2.

Conclusion: The Destiny number for Jelena is 2.

(b) HELEN:

```
  5  5        = 10 reduced = 1 (Outer Personality)
H E L E N
8  3  5       = 16 reduced = 7 (Soul Urge)
```

The Destiny number for Helen = 1 + 7, which when reduced = 8.

Conclusion: The Destiny number for Helen is 8.

(c) CHERUB:

```
  5  3        = 8 (Outer Personality)
CHER   UB
3 8 9   2     = 22 (Soul Urge)
```

The Destiny number for Cherub = 8 + 22 which when reduced = 30, which is a 3.

Conclusion: The Destiny number for Cherub is 3.

Jelena/Helen/Cherub have the Destiny numbers of 2/8/3. The number 2 concerns partnership, relationships and commitment, while the 8 is more concerned with material gain. The number 3 is related to creativity, communication, and expression. Jelena related more to the 2 of her birth name and the 3 of her special nickname than the 8, which is the destiny of her anglicized name. She felt the 8 reflected more how she was as a younger Goddess and not where she was going, in a global sense, long-term.

number 16 is to let go of the ego, resulting literally in an instant (karmic!) cleansing of any and all beliefs you may hold about yourself. It's a pretty intense version of a detox, but the good news is (and there's always some good news!) if you can gut out the changes that this number demands, you'll emerge a fully-fledged butterfly, lighter and totally free. Those with this number in their chart have great potential for spiritual growth and self-knowledge. The journey of the 16 is about a reunion with the divine. This karmic debt can be a painful process, as it comes only after much ego control, and the ego (as Gladiator) does not give up its struggle lightly. It will be a to-the-death battle, but there will be a winner. This struggle for control between the ego and the divine will is a huge undertaking. It may have those Goddesses with a karmic debt number 16 in their charts running for the hills! It can be pretty full-on stuff to deal with but the trick here is to meet it head on if necessary, do your best and then release it to the Universe and surrender to the divine. Spiritual rebirth can take place only after one has been thoroughly tested on the nature of life itself. Feeling humbled in the face of disappointments or even tragedy, while still showing humility and compassion, is the key for a 16's success. Because a Goddess with this number is often highly intuitive and often does have a lot of knowledge, she needs to be careful not to view the rest of the world as inferior, thus isolating herself from others who may be key helpers for her on her rocky path. Let's face it, no matter what, an alienated or lonely Goddess is definitely not a happy camper in the cosmic scheme of things! If, however, she can develop faith by placing her destiny in the divine hands of the Universe, a Goddess under the influence of the 16 can still make supreme headway.

GODDESS SPECIAL NOTE

In Marianne Williamson's beautiful and impassioned book, A Woman's Worth, she notes on page 8 that in olden times, 4.15 a.m. used to be considered the witching hour. Perhaps you've had a spell of insomnia where you wake regularly at this time . . . so if this happens, relax, it's just your inner (witch) Goddess trying to wake you up! So, when you do, use the time to pray, meditate, positively affirm, and forgive. You may also have very strong intuitions and creative ideas at this time. Use it wisely and scribble down any ideas you may have (even if you're still half asleep); they may look very interesting in the morning after you've had a cup of tea! **Remember, Goddess, your thoughts are powerful.**

19: Interdependence

The karmic lesson of the Goddess with the karmic debt number 19 in her chart is that of learning to understand the notion of interdependence and of the proper use of power. As Marianne Williamson says, "The purpose of life as a woman is to ascend to the throne and rule with heart." It is every Goddess's duty to understand power and to wield it fairly – with both love and compassion. In doing so, she will learn her most valuable lessons yet: To contribute to the world or humanity at large and be able to be counted upon as an upstanding member of the human race. The Goddess with the 19 in her chart may sometimes come across as needy, however, with much personal struggle she can overcome the need to control even though she is not always used to listening to others or accepting their advice. She's a stubborn Goddess, the 19, and she tends to resist help, often to her ultimate detriment.

Her obsessive desire for independence tends to dominate every time, which can turn potentially positive outcomes against her. The key is to be deeply connected to the wider community, helping, supporting and assisting others and learning to graciously accept the same in return. So, the lesson here is not to worry, help is at hand!

Moving house by numbers!

Moving house is always a pretty significant event and the numerology of your new abode can give you plenty of clues as to the sort of experience you can expect living there. It's always a "feeling" thing anyway – you know when you walk into a place whether it suits your energy or not – however, by being aware of the numerological implications of the flat number and/or street number, you can work with the corresponding energies. If you want to increase your social life and be more active, then moving into a home with a seven vibration will not work very well, as this is more for a spiritual retreat, or for spending more time alone, in a calm and peaceful manner. For those who want a busy and action-packed schedule, find a house with the numerology of a five! If you are looking at a flat, then the flat number, not the street number, will be the most significant aspect of the numerology for

1
2
3
4
5
6
7
8
9

Home numbers hot list

Below is a shortlist of the positive and negative aspects of numbers for the home.

POSITIVE VIBRATION	NEGATIVE VIBRATION
Great for creative projects	Too much isolation
Fresh start/Individual expression	Tendency to selfishness possible
Originality is enhanced	Chaotic internal environment
Good for self-development	
Equality and partnership	Heightened hypersensitivity
Harmonious living/Great for happy marriage	Outside world is shut out
Nature is key	Tendency to give too much to others
Artistic pursuits successful	
Holistic: mind, body, spirit	Too many energies: chaotic
Positivity will be the mood	Financial problems if not watched
Personal development focus	Pressures to expand or change
A real energy centre for you/Great for socializing	
Balanced, calm atmosphere	Not social enough
Earth energies: Grounded	Over-organized or regimented and "safe"
Good to build a business/Space shared with others	Not relaxed: Work orientation
Opportunities are rife!	Too much activity
Lots of change/Social aspects positive	Hard to unwind
Use intuition wisely	Things can seem overwhelming
Work and play merge/Good for relationships	
Family orientation/Loving energy for kids	Too much introspection
Sense of duty enhanced/Compassion, love the focus	Energy drain due to neediness
Beauty and décor important	Fantasy shuts out reality
Spiritual pursuits fruitful	Energy can be too "quiet"
Solitary meditative energy	Money can be hard to obtain
Peaceful atmosphere/Deep thought and reflection	Tendency to alienate others
Financial abundance/Emphasis on material gain	Too "out there" in the world
Fame and respect flourish	Material goods may be scarce
Domestic order, structure	Money seems to come and go
World energies influential	Too much energy on others
Loyalty from friends, family	Not enough childlike fun
Wisdom, compassion flow	Not thinking of yourself enough
Great for "moving on" mentally	

Note: Generally speaking the master numbers 11, 22, 33, do not apply to house numbers which should be always reduced to a single digit.

you. The street number should be calculated individually as this will give you other influences to take into consideration while you are living there. The same method can be applied to your postal code to get an idea what the vibe is like in your area.

To calculate your home numerology

Take the numbers of the address where you live and add them together. For example:

411 Itchy Palm Road, Coconut Beach = 4 + 1 + 1 = 6.

This home has a 6 vibration so it is an excellent family home as it is all about love, caring, community, and children.

Flat 2, 25 Leaf Road, Flowerville = 2 and 2 + 5 = 7.

This flat has the vibration of the 2 – great for relationships and partnership. The other significant influence is the actual street number, which has a 7 vibration, the number representing the spiritual or inner life. This street number suggests a total retreat for a relationship to develop with the individuals each growing spiritually.

3A Petal Road, Lotustown = 3 + 1 = 4.

Using the alphabet grid from before, convert any letters after the house number to a number. Hence A = 1, B = 2, etc. This home has a 4 vibration.

SPECIAL GODDESS ANECDOTE

One of our Goddess friends lived in the house number of 36 as a child, which carries the vibration of a 9 house. The energy of a 9 house is that of community (lots and lots of neighbours and local friends dropping in all the time), a global outlook (her family travelled a lot) and she spent her entire childhood there until she went away to boarding school. As a student, our Goddess friend lived in a 14, which is a 5, meaning lots of social activities and opportunity as well as risk, change, and adventure. As a graduate in her first job she lived in a house with the number 1 (individual evolution), and then met and moved into a flat with the number 2 with a boyfriend (relationships and partnership). Interestingly enough, she moved with the same boyfriend into a number 1, where under the pressure of conflicting careers in conjunction with individual pursuits and priorities the relationship ended. Happily single and running her own business, she presently resides in a shared-living arrangement. The number of her current house carries the 5 energy. Needless to say, she is a very busy (and socially in demand) Goddess!

Goddess in the home

If you think back over all of the different houses you have lived in, it is possible to track your personal evolution. It can be a very useful exercise to look back – right to your childhood homes if possible – and see how things have developed for you, quite literally from birth!

This can then give you the perspective to see where you may find yourself now and how things can potentially progress. You can then consciously steer your direction – if you want a family energy, then you may try to find a 6 house that suits as opposed to a 1 home number, which is more slanted towards individual energy. If you want to get your material house in order, then choose an 8 and so on. The right place will come to you at the right time, as with everything in life, so if you can't move for whatever reason, then think a bit beyond the obvious and feel what lessons you may still have to learn by staying where you are.

The personal year cycle

What is the personal year cycle? Goddess, it's where you're at . . . in life! Personal year cycles are a twelve-month period revealing your personal, inner process for twelve months in terms of the vibrational aspects of your numerology. These numbers are influenced by all your other numbers, which make up your chart, including your birth date as we've discussed above.

Each of the numbers carries a different energy and focus, and each will suggest major changes or events that are more likely to happen within each of these cycles. Your Personal Year number is not necessarily the same as the World Year number. For example, we are presently in 2004, which is a 6 year, however, you may be in a 9 year, which is the end of a cycle for you personally. Anyway, we're going to show you how to calculate your Personal Year number, because that will give you the best clues as to what's going on for you right now and also what's likely to come!

The World Year number affects everyone, more in the sense of its overriding influences. It's not necessary to be in the same cycle as the World Year number. You can be "out of cycle" but this is not necessarily a bad thing at all. For example, you may be getting married when your Personal Year number is a 1. This number carries with it the energy of individuality and of new ventures and independence. The vibrational aspect of the World Year number (in the case of the year 2004, the number is 6), will still kick in regardless, reflecting the energy of hard work, security, and balance. The energy of the World Year number will make itself felt regardless of whether you are aware of its effects or not.

Personal Year cycles reflect a lot of what is below the surface of your outward life and, when investigated in conjunction with the plans you may have, they provide the ability to bring to your awareness things that need your attention for your current purpose. The Universe knows how! Your instincts may be telling you it's time to do certain things, and the vibrational aspects can, therefore, be useful as a backup tool to actions and decisions you may make. It pays to honour those instincts because you can miss out on capitalizing on certain energies and then you may have to wait until they come around again in the next nine-year cycle. The knowledge that there's always next time is good news for those of us who like to procrastinate, however, we're all for doing it now rather than risk missing out! Sometimes it can be brutal, but it is always amazing! It's all the more reason to take a deep breath, drag out that much-scribbled-on notepad again, and find out where you're up to in life!

How to calculate your personal year

Add your month of birth, your day of birth and the current year together, then reduce to a single digit.

Example for a Goddess born on 7 August, 1979, for the year 2004 is 7/8/2004 (D/M/Y)

7 + 8+ 2 +4 = 39 = 12 = 3

The personal year number for this Goddess is 3. She is at the most creative time of her 9-year cycle.

Personal Year 1 – New beginnings

A Personal Year 1 is the beginning of a new nine-year cycle for you. Exciting new adventures and new challenges await you this year, as well as the initial clues of the journey or path you may take over the next nine-year cycle. It's a time to clarify your goals and dreams, and to take action.

Make sure you are healthy because you are going to need your strength and extra energy to move these new projects. Hard work may be necessary, so set your house in order. If you are unwilling to answer to change and make the move, your prospects may be delayed until the next cycle begins in nine years' time.

You may have felt for a while now that it's time for adventure or a major change like a new job, new friends, or a new relationship. If trekking the Himalayas or that holiday in Morocco has been calling you, this is the time to do it! This is the 1's energy getting you into the groove. Clearly set out what you need to do and work toward these goals. Fear may prove a problem. If so, stop – but not for long – ask yourself what the fear is and then, as the saying goes, do it anyway! The past will tend to disappear, leaving the way open for these new challenges. This is a great time if used to its full advantage. Enjoy this "sowing" time . . . because the seeds of the future are held within a Personal Year 1. Get into it.

Personal Year 2 – Partnerships and cooperation
A Personal Year 2 is a wait and see time; a year when you may find yourself in the background and very much in a new stage of personal development. You will truly feel you are a work-in-progress at this time. This is not a time to force any issues or push forward too hard. It is a time for cooperation and building relationships that will benefit you in the future; a year for accumulating, collecting, and waiting. Be prepared for delays and detours. Your key is patience. Positive accomplishments are unlikely. All plans are on hold and trying to push will only result in frustration and anger. And we don't think that will solve your problems! The reward of patience is patience.

This year is about you helping others and it revolves around two very important words: "team work." It's about learning to use your abilities to work more productively. This can be difficult for you if you have chiefly worked alone in the past. Partnerships of all kinds are up for review, including marriage, family, and friendships. They may bring with them a tendency for emotional extremes such as depression, but before you reach for another tub of ice cream the news isn't all bad – a deepening of feelings and commitment in these relationships also happens within a 2 year. So you do have something to look forward to after all!

Personal Year 3 – Creativity and communication
The Personal Year 3 is very social, with creativity being an important part as well. It is a year when you will want to spend time with old friends, form new friendships, or broaden your social circle. Romance and love affairs may bloom. Hurrah! You are inclined to live life to its fullest now, but resist the temptation to completely give in to having a good time. You will need to pay the piper sometime, and probably sooner than you think! Be careful not to scatter your energies and undertake too many things at the same time.

A Personal Year 3 is a good time to open yourself to creative talents, particularly those related to the arts, and verbal or written skills. It may not be a gold-star year for business or career, but take heart – if you don't have too frivolous an attitude or make any rash decisions, it won't be that bad. And it may be the start of something else altogether!

Personal Year 4 – Hard work, but steady progress!

The Personal Year 4 can come as a shock to some. It's the horror flick you've been dreading and now you've got the starring role! There's no way around it, this is a time of really knuckling down and doing the hard stuff. The task at hand is the re-establishment of self-control and self-discipline. You knew you'd have to pull your weight eventually and you probably had just a bit too much fun last year, but your responsibilities and commitments will increase and with that so will the workload. Just remember to keep breathing – Om your way through it – and just do the best you can. This year sounds awful, but keep in mind that in reality you're building an entirely new way of being and operating. The true nature of what you achieve in this year can only be revealed over the full duration of the nine-year cycle.

It can be a very frustrating year, when it seems as though all your greatest efforts fail to produce the results you desired or planned. It may even feel like you are forever taking one step forward and several more back, however, it is time to get organized and plant yourself well down on mother earth! You'll have extra pressure on you due to the extra responsibilities, so it is wise to watch your health and diet in a personal year with 4 energy, as you may become more susceptible to burnout or illness. Get your rest and recovery strategy in place early – this year it's a bit of a marathon! Interestingly, the positive aspect of this is that if you embark upon a new health and fitness routine in a 4 year, you will have a much greater chance of it being a successful long-term programme due to your overall levels of diligence and discipline.

This year, you'll need to dig in and dig deep.

Personal Year 5 – Change and freedom!

The Personal Year 5 is a year of major changes (again!). Horizons are expanded, inspiring you to make new friends, connections, and contacts. You will truly be the networking queen this year and along with a bursting Palm Pilot, your mobile phone and e-mail will run hot. A Personal Year 5 brings excitement and adventure and a good deal more freedom. It's time to kick off those mules and be footloose and fancy-free. Yeeha! Newly barefoot and feeling fabulous, old routines will suddenly bore you. *Quelle surprise!* Seeking new directions in a constructive way will pave the way to glory!

The main issue you face is scattering your newfound energies in every which way. Your ability to channel these energies and to be effective with them will be essential. This new energy gives you the get up and go to change anything including your career, place, country of residence, or relationship(s). The only word of caution – try not to do it all at once!

Personal Year 6 – Harmony in love and family

A Personal Year 6 tends to bring with it further responsibility and concerns for family, loved ones, and close friends. Sacrificing time and money for friends or family is more often the case in a Personal Year 6.

Projects and other endeavours will seem to be moving very slowly. This year is not really a year for major accomplishments, it's more for the internal structural and emotional changes. Chill out with family and friends. Be a couch potato more often. It's time to let up a bit on the pace. Any emotional interaction with those who are close to you is going to be fantastic during a 6 year, so this is the year to tell someone you love them, or ask someone to marry you. And, girls, it doesn't need to be a leap year either! What are you waiting for – another 6 year?

Personal Year 7 – Learning and reflection

A Personal Year 7 has the potential to be a very introspective one and you will have time for plenty of reflection. What have you been doing for the last few years? Now is the time to (hopefully) get your head around it. This year provides you with some relief and enough time to get to grips with and acknowledge the various hidden aspects of yourself. It's a spiritual period for most, and one in which spending a good bit of time in contemplation is healthy – and wise. Spending time alone is not unusual during a 7 year. Free yourself up from unnecessary outside responsibilities in order to capitalize on the energies and maximize your prospects for personal growth. Shut your bedroom door and think about things – deeply. Cocooning brings splendid rewards for Goddesses with an introspective bent this year. Your efforts will pay dividends.

Reflect on the past and plan your future projects. In this headspace you will have the resolve to handle any situation, and long-term solutions for problems will become apparent (finally!).

One of the most rewarding activities you can do during this period is study, write and research. A Personal Year 7 increases your ability to analyse, think, and articulate your philosophies and your deepest needs. People may view you as being somewhat reclusive or detached. This year is not necessarily the time for making new friends or relationships or focusing attention on anything (or anyone) preventing your time alone. Many people will find themselves single in a 7 year and it can be very hard for people in relationships or who have a family. Often it's actually what creates the tension in those relationships that needs your attention, and it's the reason you want to be alone. Meditation is the key to your sanity. Make the time to cool out and you'll feel better for it.

Personal Year 8 – Attainment of goals with the winning post is in sight!

A Personal Year 8 is a full-on power year! This is a time when all your efforts over the last few years are paying off and you can truly see all the reasons why you've been slaving away. A Personal Year 8 brings you to a period when big decisions are finally sorted, or you are able to get closure on things that have been outstanding for a long period of time. Major achievements are brought to completion or to fruition. Take advantage of this expansion of energy for you will exude self-confidence and authority this year and others will be receptive to your ideas at this time. You are at your peak of power and status potential, strike while the iron is still hot; activity is your key to success. It's time to strut your stuff.

Personal Year 9 – Completion and closure

A Personal Year 9 is a year of completions, a time of endings, and of saying goodbye to outmoded behaviours or belief systems that no longer serve you. It's all about taking inventory and doing an emotional spring-cleaning. Scrutinize old values and ideals and check their use-by date! It's the year for a cleansing of the mind, body, and soul.

Clean and clear out cupboards, and drawers, write letters or send emails to people you haven't seen or spoken to in a while and clear up any broken agreements or communication. It's time to get your emotional and physical house in order (we recommend you do both: please see the Energy Clearing chapter for more details). Rearrange furniture, renovate, and/or clean your home. Use this time to get rid of old unwanted clothes, furniture, or possessions. Give anything that you no longer like or use away to charities. All of these activities are vital for a 9 year to be successful. Don't succumb to any escapist tendencies. If you need to get away, commune with nature or take long walks. While walking, reflect on how you treat people and how you look after yourself and others around you. Don't waste a single moment – instead, walk for atonement! Clear the deck for the beginning of a new nine-year cycle and . . . congratulations new Goddess – you made it!

Tarot for absolute beginners

You've seen the cards, you've heard the rumours about their powers and you may even have a pack yourself. This ancient future-seeing system can also reveal secrets about the past and present, if you know where (and how) to look. But first, what should you expect when you leave yourself in the hands of a professional?

Seeing a tarot reader

Don't be afraid to ask the price when you call up to book a tarot reading, or when you approach someone at the local market. There's no law against knowing how much it's going to cost you, or how long it's going to take. Ask if there is a tape to take home afterwards. If not, make sure you have something to take notes with. Choosing a tarot reader is best done by word of mouth. Advertising is fine, but personal recommendations are best, and if they come to you about a tarot reader who never advertises at all, that's even better. A psychic who doesn't have to pay to let people know about his or her work is usually one of the most accurate and thoughtful in town!

There are no rules with tarot readers – you can get spiritual types who talk to you about karma and guides, and scary people who really aren't that skilled, but make a lot of dramatic declarations about your future! Feel free to spend a couple of minutes quizzing your tarot reader before you make the appointment and pay the money. What sort of things will she or he go into? Are you allowed to ask specific questions? You can work out a lot about your reader just from this short, polite series of questions. Anyone who doesn't have time to reassure you, won't have time for the other stuff either. And a couple of minutes can help you sort out if you are dealing with a freaked-out Glastonbury hippie, a wannabe reader from Brighton with no experience and no idea, or, if you're lucky, a kind-hearted natural psychic who is also a true professional – that means accurate, sensitive, trained, experienced, and with plenty of time for your questions.

Here are some simple do's and don'ts for a tarot reading

Do:

* Tell the reader if they are on the right track. Don't just sit there with your arms crossed, your mouth zipped, and a "Hey, impress me" look on your face.
* Point out if something doesn't make sense, or you don't understand it.
* Remember that all the reader is doing is picking out your likeliest

possible future – it's not the future because there is no such thing. There are many destiny roads for you. All a tarot reading does is turn a spotlight on the most obvious and likely one, at the very minute you are asking about it.

* Sort out payment method before you begin – if your reader doesn't take credit cards, come prepared with cash.
* Enter into the spirit of the reading. Before the first card is turned over, silently ask your guides and angels to help the reader help you.
* Listen to advice and return to your notes, or the tape. This is especially important if you think the rest of the reading – the non-advice part – is really accurate. It proves your reader is worth listening to. You're paying for the guidance you hear in a tarot reading, so you may as well take it seriously.
* Allow time for glitches. Tarot readers are frequently right about the event, or the person, but wrong about the time frame. Don't just assume everything they say will happen next week, or even next month. The results of a reading can take up to two or three years to come to fruition.
* Get a second opinion, in another reading, if you have any doubts. Chances are, you'll be amazed as the same cards come up, or the same interpretations are given. If both readers are good reliable psychics, then the chances are high you'll have confirmation both ways.

Don't:
* Don't get addicted to your tarot reader. You only need a reading twice a year, for guidance, and only more frequently than that if you are in real trouble about something. Any more than that and you are becoming dependent.
* Don't lose your common sense. If your reader says something that is absolute gobbledegook, don't assume it's divine guidance just because he/she has a deck of cards in front of them. A good reading will usually back up and support what you already believe, or know, for at least part of the session.
* Don't put up with interruptions from the phone or the answering machine. You can politely request that a reader devote all his/her time to you. Professional tarot readers don't let other bookings come in while they are supposed to be attending to you, or deal with their kids running in and out.
* Don't be afraid to go over anything at the end if you're not sure what the reader meant. This is doubly important if anything bothered you as the cards came up!
* Don't stretch your tarot reader's time. Most people are only human

and will try to be polite and give as much as they can to you, but by trying for more, more, more, you will actually drain your reader's energy. Be thoughtful, and when they wind things down, take the hint and get your purse!

Choosing a deck of tarot cards

If you'd like to try reading the cards for yourself or your friends (and we hope you do!), then you'll need to buy a pack of tarot cards. They resemble normal playing cards, except for one thing – the pictures of animals, people, mysterious objects, and ancient symbols in the illustrations contain a secret code of meaning. And that meaning is your key to the future.

There are plenty of different tarot decks to choose from now, and you can see a selection of these at websites like www.tarot.com and www.2.dgsys.com/~bunning/top. Most major bookshops or new age shops will have at least four or five decks on display, but do ask at the counter for an opened pack that you can handle and "feel" as your intuition will be the best guide in selecting the right pack for you. The obvious way to choose your personal tarot cards is on appearance – if something looks right, or you love the pictures and colours, then take it seriously. Do check that you are buying traditional tarot cards, though. There are plenty of variations on the tarot theme. For example, you can buy animal cards, angel cards, and Egyptian cards. You want tarot, which means Major Arcana and Minor Arcana. The Major Arcana is easy to spot, as you'll find symbols like the Sun, the Moon, the Empress, the Emperor, and the Star. The Minor Arcana is just four suits – Cups, Staves (also called Wands or Rods), Swords, and Coins.

As a general rule, you should feel excited or inspired when you look at your cards. If you feel uneasy or a bit weirded out, they are not right for you. These cards are going to be with you for life. They're also going to change your life! So take your time, and check with your gut feelings (also known as your solar plexus chakra). Can you imagine being able to meditate on one of these cards for ten minutes? Do you like, or love, the look of the Kings and Queens? Do you feel truly motivated or intrigued by the Magician? Tarot is an emotional business so it may sound weird, but you need to feel something quite deep about these coloured pieces of cardboard in your hand! Some readers say you need to fall in love with the cards. Basically, the bigger the emotional attachment, the more vivid and powerful your readings will be. Goddesses who are feminists may prefer to use the Motherpeace deck. If you'd like to use something that's been around forever, use the Rider-Waite deck. The Morgan-Greer deck is a popular choice for beginners too.

Setting the scene for a tarot reading

Whenever you do a reading for yourself or other people, it's a good idea to make it private. Why? Because if there are other people watching, it may result in people feeling shy or embarrassed, which will make it hard to really open up and be honest about what the cards reveal. This is why gypsies used to work in tents. Shut the door, take the phone off the hook, switch your mobile off, and let people know you are not to be disturbed. Burning good quality incense or a candle is also a good idea, because it heightens the vibrations. It also makes the reading feel special, or sacred, and it is – after all, you don't look into the range of future paths every day! You can also heighten the psychic vibration by playing classical or ambient music at a low volume. Music without words is best, because if you hear song lyrics being sung you might find yourself being influenced by them. Nobody wants to sit down for a tarot reading and be told, "It's raining men!" just because Geri Halliwell's playing in the background.

Finally, it's always a good idea to say one of these things to the Universe before you read: "Please help me to help myself" if it's for you, or "Please help me to help them" if it's for someone else. Your sincerity is the magic ingredient that makes for a good reading. By the way, if you are sensitive to the spirit world, you may feel a spirit standing next to you as you read. This is perfectly normal. They will be there to impress upon you which card to pick, but also to give you extra information relating to the card. This doesn't happen to every-one, though. But if you do get extra help, remember to thank your guide from the spirit world later.

How to make your tarot reading truly psychic!

How can you read for yourself? The answer is, by making your tarot reading truly psychic. You're the best person to experiment on, by the way. You can read for yourself weekly, or even daily to begin with, just to feel confident with the cards. Write down the results, noting what you got wrong as well as what you got right, in terms of your predictions coming true, and that way you'll learn the basics. Only when you have the simple meaning of the cards established in your mind can you proceed to a truly psychic reading, and that takes a little work. Here's how to start.

First of all you will need to lie down, or sit down, in a comfortable position (face it, do any psychic exercises ever ask you to get uncomfortable? – but, hey . . .). Essentially, to be psychic you need to get into the psychic state, which means leaving the real world state behind. The real world is all about noticing if your hand is itching, or feeling like you want to munch on a chocolate bar, or worrying about what your friend meant when she emailed you to say you resembled an elephant. The real world is everyday, trivial, and full of noise – from the TV, from stereos, from cars outside, to barking dogs. None of this has anything to do with waking up your sixth sense, which is what you need to do in order to read tarot psychically. So please, prepare to leave the real world for half an hour!

Now you're comfortable, you need to get into that sixth-sense state. Do this by closing your eyes and breathing through the top of your head. No, we are not insane. You literally breathe as if you were pulling the air in through your hair parting. Quickly pull this breath down through the top of your head, through the bridge of your nose, your throat, your chest, your stomach, your womanly bits (to be polite), your thighs, your legs, and finally let it out through the soles of your feet. The reason you have to breathe like this, reasonably quickly, is sheer oxygen supply. If you spend all day dragging that one breath through all these body centres, you could start turning blue – and nobody likes a blue Goddess unless she's Tibetan.

Take ten of these breaths. You can "see" the breath, too – it's a beautiful, sparkling, golden-white cloud of pure light and air. Each time you breathe out, give yourself a mini break before returning to the task of pulling that magical breath in through the top of your head again. After a while you'll feel the coloured air sparkling through your body – even though you can't imagine why!

After ten rounds you need to rub your hands together. You're preparing your tarot hands. These are not the hands you wash up with, or apply exfoliant with, or type with. They are full of psychic energy, and they are about to become your main sixth-sense tools as you literally "feel" the cards in your hand. Now practise narrowing your eyes, opening them wide, and narrowing them again. These are your tarot eyes. You're going to see stuff with them that you don't normally see! So, with tarot hands, and with tarot eyes, prepare yourself for a psychic reading like no other!

First, pull out a card by swishing the cards around, in a very sensitive way, until you can almost feel a card saying, "Pick me" with your fingers. When you look at it, try to see more than just the picture. What does the picture remind you of? What emotions can you see on the face of the person pictured on the card? Are there

THE 21ST CENTURY GODDESS CODE OF ETHICS FOR TAROT CARD READERS

Say it loud and say it proud. If you're going to read the tarot for other people, you have to have a code of ethics, or you're going to run into trouble – or, create it for people you read for! It might help to run through this every time you do a reading.

CODE 1 I will never tell anybody anything that I personally would not want to hear.

CODE 2 I will always ask the universe to "help me to help them" before a reading.

CODE 3 I will always respect the power and wisdom of the tarot when I read.

CODE 4 I will read the tarot knowing that the future is flexible and can be changed.

CODE 5 I will keep the tarot reading private and confidential for my subject.

any hints or clues in the card? Let yourself tell a kind of story with it. If you see words, or other pictures, hidden in the folds of the fabric depicted in the card, or the shape of the clouds in the background, don't be afraid to let yourself take them seriously.

Jot everything down fast. Don't be afraid – nobody else is going to see this except you, so who cares if you're wrong! Let yourself say, "This reminds me of..." and finish the sentence. Here's a real-life example, using the Queen of Wands.

The card shows a woman in a gold robe, with two lions at each knee, holding a wand, or branch of wood, with a black cat in front of her. A sunflower is in her other hand. Imagine you have just drawn this card. What else do these things remind you of? Let's say this is your card for the next week. What would you expect to experience, or find? Don't say cats and sunflowers! But if you say, "Someone born under the sign of Leo the lion," or "A piano teacher, because my piano teacher used to be called Mrs Gold," then you're getting somewhere.

If you have a pack of tarot cards nearby, you can try this method right now. Find the Queen of Wands (or Queen of Staves as she is sometimes known) and focus on the card. If this is your card predicting the next seven days, what might you forecast for yourself? Don't worry too much about the actual meaning of the card in the No-brainer Tarot Dictionary. Just go with what your stomach is telling you. Wave your hands around if you like – that can help the flow!

Always close down after doing a powerful psychic reading. Here's a quick exercise designed for that purpose.

Close-down exercise

Lie down on the floor. Curl yourself up into a tight ball, the way you used to when you were small. Hear your breathing slowing down and relaxing, in this tight ball. Imagine that you, as a little ball, are about to be covered by a much bigger ball – in fact, it's a huge sphere of white light. This light covers you and protects you. Say out loud, "My tarot reading is over and my sixth sense has gone to bed." Get up and shake out your arms and legs. Don't worry that your psychic ability has closed down entirely – it will still be there for emergencies, if you need it. It's just that your supersensitivity has now been switched off! (You need to do this, otherwise you will be having some very bizarre conversations with your family or house-mates for the next few hours.)

The No-brainer Tarot Dictionary

We have compiled this dictionary based on our personal experience, knowledge and tarot training – some interpretations may differ slightly.

The Minor Arcana

The Minor Arcana (see pages 124–5) is the section of cards in the tarot deck which relates to ordinary, everyday events. If these cards turn up next to Major Arcana cards, you may be up for a life-changing experience, but most of the time if you turn up Minor Arcana cards, you are looking at the temporary and less important aspects of life. The Kings, Queens, Knights and Pages attached to the Minor Arcana suits (cups, staves or rods, swords, coins) refer to real people, whose jobs or personalities tie in with the meanings of each suit. The King of Coins, for example, is a money-minded man. The Knight of Swords is a tough, active younger male.

The Major Arcana

The Major Arcana (see page 126) is the smallest section of cards in the tarot but it is also the most important. If you turn up Death,

The Minor Arcana

Ace of Cups: A new friendship or love relationship. A birth. True emotional happiness and satisfaction.

Two of Cups: A partnership between two people – for any kind of reason – and it's a good one too.

Three of Cups: A party or other celebration – anything from a house-warming to a wedding to a big eighteenth…

Four of Cups: Being blind to what you've got. Being blessed, or lucky, but also feeling short-changed.

Five of Cups: Healing from sadness and loss. Getting over it, so that a truly fresh start can be made.

Six of Cups: People or places from the past that play an important part in helping future decisions.

Seven of Cups: Confusion, due to too many choices. If this turns up as a "future" card, the advice is wait!

Eight of Cups: Using inner strength to deal with a hard situation – but it has a definite solution or ending.

Nine of Cups: The feel-good factor is high. There is satisfaction and happiness, and often a happy heart.

Ten of Cups: When ten cups appear on a card, wishes and desires come true, and a longing is satisfied.

Page of Cups: A young person with fair colouring, or a period of learning and study, and deep thought.

Knight of Cups: A young man with fair colouring, or travel for a man who is either coming, or going!

Queen of Cups: A woman who loves her home, her dog or cat, and her shopping. She's good news.

King of Cups: A man who has a big heart, a caring nature, and a natural talent for making love work.

Ace of Staves: The birth of a bright idea, or the birth of a child. The start of a new job or great project.

Two of Staves: A partnership or shared agreement which is based on money, a lease or a mortgage.

Three of Staves: A new career, a new deal, a new position or a letter, email, or phone call with good news.

Four of Staves: A lease or mortgage, a move of house, or sometimes a holiday which feels just like home.

Five of Staves: Lots of talking, faxing, emailing, or phone calls to get a solution to a difficult situation.

Six of Staves: Two or more people in perfect agreement about a situation that needs lots of talking.

Seven of Staves: More than one problem area that needs to be handled carefully in order to succeed.

Eight of Staves: Travel bringing friendship, or even love. Or staying put but meeting wonderful foreigners.

Nine of Staves: Making the most of what is there, when there is no other option. Keeping things intact.

Ten of Staves: Taking more on, for work or other reasons. Being responsible for taking a heavy load.

Page of Staves: A talkative young person, or a trip away. This shows a busy time with lots of calls or plans.

Knight of Staves: A young man who has a good phone manner. Or, a trip or house move. Sometimes a visitor.

Queen of Staves: A woman who is educated or intelligent. She is really good company and is independent.

King of Staves: A man who knows how to talk. He is likeable but he is about words, not mega-deep feelings.

COINS

Ace of Coins: A cheque, cash sum, or direct deposit, following a rise, bonus, win, deal, or promotion.

Two of Coins: Money, a home, or possessions. Managing a situation where two sides both want a fair go.

Three of Coins: Renovations, decorations, a mortgage, or a lease. Good profits from a job or project.

Four of Coins: Money is the number one preoccupation and nothing else matters.

Five of Coins: Financial loss. This card can also show someone dealing with emotional or romantic loss.

Six of Coins: Organizing money. Sometimes, sorting out a mortgage, lease, or possessions. Accounting.

Seven of Coins: Slogging away to make money in the long term. Doing the right thing to see final rewards.

Eight of Coins: Excellent career results. Professional training, promotion, a raise, bonus, or special praise.

Nine of Coins: A fantastic work or money result. Buying domestic appliances or home decorator items.

Ten of Coins: Lots of money. This is the result of a big work achievement or a business-minded marriage.

Page of Coins: A dark child. Or, news and special plans about money, work, business, or travel.

Knight of Coins: A young man who is steady and sensible. Or, news about money, business, work or travel.

Queen of Coins: A woman who is good with money or business and really cares about her lifestyle too.

King of Coins: A man who actually understands the stockmarket! This guy is fair, honest and practical too.

SWORDS

Ace of Swords: Wham, bang, crash, wallop! This is the start of a job or relationship which takes you over.

Two of Swords: Everything is stuck, nothing is moving. For one reason or another, things are in limbo.

Three of Swords: A loss which has a strong effect on the emotions. A challenge which needs inner strength.

Four of Swords: The body recovers or heals. This healing may be needed because of stress or due to an illness.

Five of Swords: The unpredictable or difficult side of human nature is on display. People are not easy.

Six of Swords: Travel or a visitor from far away. If it's travel, big life improvements are the result.

Seven of Swords: Coping with problems linked to possessions or money. Being aware of the risk of loss.

Eight of Swords: Being locked in by a situation. Feeling trapped. There is a solution but it's down to timing.

Nine of Swords: Being aware of the body, and the care or attention it needs. Looking after health issues.

Ten of Swords: People are not perfect, and this card shows why. Big life changes call for staying power.

Page of Swords: An energetic young person. Or, a business, work, or financial offer which requires care.

Knight of Swords: A sporty or high-energy young man. Or, instant decisions and sudden changes or u-turns.

Queen of Swords: A tough woman who can really help with a problem but probably won't want cuddles.

King of Swords: A man who does not give in easily. He is strong and serious and good at finding solutions.

The Major Arcana

The Fool: Starting all over again with a big-life step that involves challenges, but also a lot of fun.

The Magician: Using special skills, talents, or even qualifications to make money and find real success.

The High Priestess: A person who teaches wisdom, understanding, and sometimes special, hidden knowledge.

The Empress: A child or baby, or a happy marriage. Alternatively, a lifestyle which offers contentment.

The Emperor: A boss or employer. Alternatively, a man who is extremely strong and supportive.

The Hierophant: Doing things the traditional or conservative way. Following religious or spiritual advice.

The Lovers: This is true passion and partnership, with Cupid hovering overhead. Beautiful romance.

The Chariot: Travel, or vehicles. Alternatively, a time of great energy and effort for a worthwhile goal.

Justice: A fair result. Sometimes, a balanced partnership with both sides equal. Justice is done.

The Hermit: Spending time alone in order to understand yourself, or the Universe, a lot better.

Wheel of Fortune: Life is full of ups and downs, just like a TV game show, and this card shows highs and lows.

Strength: Finding inner courage and amazing coping skills to deal with life's challenges or problems.

The Hanged Man: Dangling between the old life and the new life. Being temporarily stuck while life changes.

Death: The death of the old, and the birth of the new. But first, something must be let go of.

Temperance: Peace and quiet, health and harmony. Relaxing, renewing, reviving, and finding real balance.

The Devil: The temptation to do the wrong thing, or to accept situations which do nobody any good.

The Tower: Radical change, and the need to start all over again. A wake-up call that has to happen.

The Star: Success. Hopes and wishes coming true. The Universe is definitely helping out right now.

The Moon: Lots of emotion, but not much common sense. Imagination, psychic powers, and intuition.

The Sun: Children or babies may arrive. Wonderful warmth and happiness in friendship or marriage.

Judgement: A happy ending to a situation which had to finish eventually. The chance for a new start.

The World: Travel or moving home. Or, the end of a job or project which brings success or praise.

Temperance, the Lovers, the Hierophant or any of the other colourful cards from this section of the deck, you may be about to experience a relationship or event which could change your whole existence! The most famous card in the Major Arcana is Death, which describes a situation "dying away" leaving room for a new beginning. All the images on the Major Arcana cards are dramatic, highly symbolic and sometimes tied into ancient myths and occult meanings.

Get to know the guy cards
THE FOUR KINGS

Tarot books should give you a much more complex and lengthy interpretation of the cards than our No-brainer Dictionary. You'll find the books we like and use in the Global Goddess Directory at the back of the book. We are prepared to go into more detail, though, on the age-old subject of guys!

There are four cards in the tarot which specifically refer to guys, and particularly guys you might end up having relationships with. Here's your in-depth report on the guy cards – the King of Cups, the King of Swords, the King of Coins, and the King of Staves (or Rods).

The King of Cups – Mr weddings, parties, anything

This man loves to party. He's an ideal wedding guest, or a good date. He's sociable and he likes being in a relationship. That cup you see him holding is actually a champagne glass, or at least a can of beer. The cup also represents his emotions and feelings. He's got a lot to give, to the right woman. Let's hope it's you, baby! He's generous. Expect good presents.

The King of Swords – Mr action man

He's ambitious. He sets himself goals and achieves them, through sheer tenacity. He's got a hard edge. Don't mess with him. That sword in his hand isn't real, of course, but he could be a mean hand at fencing competitions, or even playing a game such as Dungeons and Dragons. He's a bit of a tough guy, so don't say we didn't warn you. But that's sexy, too!

The King of Coins – Mr moneybags

He's either richer than most, or he's just hung up on money. Do not borrow £10 from him and think you can forget about it. You can't. This guy is very organized and practical. He's got his life sussed, or at least he'd like to – and he keeps on going on about it! He's slower-moving than the King of Swords. He still has goals, mostly financial, but they take time.

The King of Staves – Mr mobile phone

This guy lives for text. He's also good with email. He has a lot of ideas, and some of them might even work. He usually has one or two books on the go, and he knows what's going on in the news. Feelings and emotions aren't his strong point. He lives in his head, and this can be frustrating sometimes for the women in his life. He's smart, and he can be funny too.

The past, present, future spread

There are many different tarot card "spreads" or patterns you can choose from. The Celtic Cross is the best-known spread. This involves laying out ten cards, in a cross shape, with another line of cards going up the right-hand side. It's quite complicated, however, and if you are starting out with tarot cards, you might prefer the Past, Present, Future spread. It only takes five minutes – and it's not hard to decode.

1 Set the scene for your reading (see the "Setting the scene" section earlier in this chapter).

2 Shuffle the cards face-down without looking at them. Shuffling doesn't have to mean anything more than mixing them up. You're not appearing in "Casino!" Spend as short or as long a time as you like, mixing up the cards. What is your gut feeling? When your instinct, or stomach, tells you that the cards are ready, stop.

3 Separate the cards into three piles, all face down. All three should be roughly the same size.

4 Pick one card off the top of the first pile to show the past, one card off the top of the second to show the present, and one card off the top of the third to show the future. Turn them over and look at them, using the No-brainer Tarot Dictionary to decode them.

5 Spend a few minutes writing down anything else that occurs to you as you look at the cards. OK, you might be looking at a picture of two dogs howling at the moon, but what else comes to mind? This is especially useful when you are reading your future card. Your psychic ability and intuition can come into play if you let your mind roam and wander as you gaze at the picture. Write down what you see, and come back to it later. You may be surprisingly accurate about your own future!

6 People always want to know when their future card will come true. With Past, Present and Future readings, it can often be judged by working out how long ago your past card was true. In other words, you know the event that the card is referring to, but how many weeks, months, or years ago did it happen? That's your clue. For future timing, just count forward the same number of weeks, months, or years.

Example reading:

EMILY'S PAST, PRESENT, AND FUTURE

The guinea pig for this reading is Emily, a 21-year-old student who is currently at fashion college in London.

Past: The Magician – Using special skills, talents or even qualifications to make money and find real success.

Present: The Star – Success. Hopes and wishes coming true. The Universe is definitely helping out right now.

Future: The World – Travel bringing friendship, or even love. Or staying put but meeting wonderful foreigners.

Emily thought the Magician card for her past was spot-on. She says that she started a market stall three months ago which made her a lot of money. She was selling homemade candles on the stall, and it was so successful that she became a regular seller at the markets. Emily said the picture of the Magician, with objects on a table, even reminded her of the stall with all the goodies laid out on a tablecloth!

Emily said that all her wishes and hopes really were coming true in the present, so the Star card was also correct. She had enough money to buy herself the things she'd always wanted. She had a fantastic bunch of friends. She was in a happy relationship with a guy who cared about her. And her studies were also going really well. "The card shows quite a lot going on, and that's how I feel," she says. "It's like there are lots of departments of my life all taking off."

For the future, we counted forward three months, because the past card pointed to a time frame that was three months earlier. "That's too weird," Emily says. "I already know this card is true, because I booked a flight to Thailand for three months' time." The landscape shown on the card even looks a bit like a tropical setting. "I am meeting up with my friends there as well," she says, "so it looks like friendship not love, but that's fine by me, I've already got a gorgeous man."

Example reading:

JESSICA'S PAST, PRESENT, AND FUTURE

Now that you're getting the hang of it, here's another example reading, but this time with a lot more psychic energy being used. In this example, the cards are being read not just for their basic meanings, but also for what the reader can "see" in the cards. In this example, Goddess Jessica is reading for herself – just to prove it's OK to do it! After giving the cards a good shuffle, this is what came up.

Past: Two of Swords – Everything is stuck, nothing is moving. For one reason or another, things are in limbo.

"This sounds like where I was a year ago," Jessica says. "The woman in the card looks like me as well. She's got short dark hair. Even the Moon looks droopy in the sky, which is how I felt for a while. Everything was stuck and I couldn't see a way to get out of it. In the end, I moved, which was the perfect solution. But I do remember not being able to see a way forward a year ago. That's why the woman in the card, who looks like me, has a blindfold over her eyes. Her socks are bright yellow though, which I take to mean I was optimistic about the future. The lines on the sea also remind me of lines of words on a piece of paper. A year ago I was writing so many chapters of my novel it was all I could see!"

Present: King of Cups – A man who has a big heart, a caring nature, and a natural talent for making love work.

"Well, this could be a bit embarrassing," Jessica comments. "I know exactly who this man is. He's a friend of mine, and yet it could easily turn into a romance. He does have a big heart, it's quite true." Looking at the King of Cups card more deeply, Jessica can also see more clues hidden in the illustration. "The thing around his neck looks like a gherkin. I always think of gherkins as spicy, so I think this could be quite a spicy romance. And I think the fish might be his ex-girlfriend, because I know she was a Pisces, which is the sign of the fishes. I'm glad the fish is swimming in the opposite direction, though!"

Future: Knight of Cups – A young man with fair colouring, or travel for a man who is either arriving, or going!

"Well, I hope this means he's arriving," Jessica comments. Using her psychic side, Jessica feels good about the results. "The guy in this card looks like he's a man on a mission, and I think he might be bringing me a present when he lands . . . let's hope it's from Tiffany's!"

Creating a personal tarot workbook

People often ask, "What if I don't like the cards I get?" The answer is, learn to work with a personal tarot workbook. This is like a diary, with all kinds of scribbles and sometimes sketches in it, which allows you to work with the cards, and work with your future – even heading yourself away from problems, if necessary. Just find a book you really love the look of, in your local store or market, and set it aside as your own personal workbook.

To start using the workbook, remember to do this – any time you get a card which isn't what you hoped for, draw two more cards and put them next to the one you don't like. Let's say you get the Tower, which is usually about change – and not always change you are comfortable with. What can you do, if this is a verdict on your future?

Pick another card immediately, and put it next to the card you just pulled. This new card shows the contributing cause – something, or someone, which is influencing your life, so that you're heading in that "blah" card direction. Now, pull out one more card and once again put it next to those other two cards. This new card shows you another choice, hopefully a more positive outcome, now that you are aware of the cause or source of the "blah" outcome!

Example reading: MADELEINE'S CAUSE AND CHOICE

Here's a real-life example. We actually tried it on a New York Goddess called Madeleine, a medical student who was doing Past, Present, and Future for herself.

Past card: The Chariot – "This is so true," Madeleine enthused. "Last year I got my L plates and a new car."

Present card: The King of Cups – "That's my boyfriend, Peter," Madeleine said. "He's a total party animal and I love him."

Future card: Wheel of Fortune – "I don't like this at all," Madeleine said. "It's too up in the air. The people on the wheel in my card look as if they're terrified. Does this mean I'm doomed to have an up-and-down year?"

We got Madeleine to put two more cards down, one for the source or cause of Wheel of Fortune, and another card for a more positive choice she could be making – once she was aware of the cause of the future problem.

Cause card: The King of Coins – It turned out that Madeleine actually had another guy interested in her – Matt – and, you guessed it, his father worked for a big finance company and he had his own investments and gold credit card at the ripe old age of eighteen. "It looks like Matt could turn my life upside down, if I let him," Madeleine said. "He's the cause of my Wheel of Fortune, so that's right." She sneakily admitted that part of her wished he would turn her life upside down too! All of which leads us to the next card.

Choice card: The Lovers – "What I think this means," she said, "is that if I am aware of Matt maybe turning my life upside down, and avoid him, I could actually achieve true love with Peter after all. Is that right?"

The answer to this is, you'll never know until you start your workbook. In this case, Madeleine's gut feelings are guiding her. A workbook will allow you to explore the cards, track your progress, check out what is happening (as it happens) and be ready to follow the full wisdom of the cards, once everything is revealed.

Madeleine started by making a rough sketch of the five cards and putting it in the front of the book. She wrote out the meanings, from our No-brainer Dictionary, and then wrote out fuller meanings from other tarot books. She dated each entry she made in her workbook, to see how things were shaping up. As she suspected, Matt, the King of Coins, did eventually make a move on her. She was ready, though. After weeks of meditating on the beautiful and romantic image in the Lovers, she decided she would much rather have that than the hectic, crazy Wheel of Fortune. "Sure, I know the Wheel of Fortune shows ups, but I don't like the look of the downs," she told us.

Madeleine told Matt she already had Peter in her life, and carried on her relationship with him. And then, "You'll never believe it, but Peter went back to his ex-girlfriend, Clingy Cathy, a few weeks later," Madeline told us. "Turns out she was a total party animal too, and he thought they were made for each other." Just when she was beginning to despair of the cards, though, the Lovers did turn up trumps after all. "Within a few weeks I met a new guy called Alex, who took me on the ferris wheel at an amusement park, and then a few days after that, we had the big, major pash," Madeleine says. "I think this is the beginning of real love, which is what the tarot predicted would happen. The funny thing is, if I hadn't told Matt to go away, I might be with him now – and I would never have met Alex. Can you believe it?" We can – if you sincerely and seriously use your tarot workbook and journal.

Making predictions for friends and lovers

To read for anyone who is close to you, it's important to be objective. Remove yourself from the reading as if you were a Romany gypsy in a caravan, passing through. It's hard though! What if you see yourself showing up in the cards you are drawing for friends, or a lover/partner? Time to remember the golden rule: Before you start say (out loud or in your mind), "Help me to help them," and you will then get out of your own way!

Step back from the cards as if you were telling a story, and even if you do think you see yourself in one of the messages, just describe this person by gender, appearance, attitude, and so on – don't say, "Ooh that's me!" and lose the plot, or give biased advice. Leave it to your friends or your favourite babe to figure it out.

Some spreads are better suited than others to people who are close. Try one of these for each of the special people in your life. We've chosen them because they're not too heavy or serious, and you won't get funny looks from either your friends or your main squeeze by doing them!

For a friend: The magic two-card reading

Shuffle the cards and then get your friend to shuffle them. Ask him/her to spread out all the cards face-down on the table, and just pick two. The first card shows what your friend already knows about his/her life. It's the, "Wow this is obvious!" card. The second card is what your friend doesn't know yet – what is just around the corner, over the next few weeks.

For a lover: The good news week reading

Get the one you love to shuffle the cards, after you have finished shuffling. The cards are all spread out face-down on the table. Ask the person to pick just one card, which will describe a special week in the very near future – within a few months, in fact. This is their lucky turning point, and it will show the person, event, or change which truly brings about a Good News Week for them!

The lovers card ritual to encourage romance

You can use tarot cards to help create the life results you want – they're not just for peering into the future. This ritual will help deliver exactly the right level of romance you need, at the time. (Hint: what you think you need may not always be the case!) At the very least we've found this special ritual tends to encourage interested emails or calls, a tiny bit of flirting at a party, or the arrival of a very eligible single person who is dropping big hints. At the most, this ritual can be extraordinary and help draw a fantastic and permanent love relationship into your life – even your future husband. It all depends on what your guides think is appropriate for you right now, and what your higher self knows that you need. So if you're ready, willing and equipped with a tarot deck, let's go!

Step 1: Choose ten of the qualities you'd like in a lover from the following list. Take your time and choose carefully. Then write down those ten words on a nice piece of paper (that means not your regular mouldy old lined schoolbook paper, please!)

The list: Compassionate, educated, funny, intelligent, caring, sensitive, kind, loving, sexy, attractive, healthy, organized, articulate, adventurous, family-oriented, secure, stable, unusual, energetic, comforting, relaxing, clever, emotionally intelligent, creative, talented, special, hard-working, romantic, passionate, ambitious, successful, unique, offbeat, mysterious.

Step 2: Above the ten words on your piece of paper, write this sentence, next to the date. "I now draw someone with these qualities into my love life, for the highest good of all concerned."

Step 3: Lay the Lovers tarot card on top of the piece of paper, and sprinkle salt over it.

Step 4: Shake off the salt into a glass, and add some of your favourite perfume or essential oil.

Step 5: Wrap the Lovers card in the piece of paper you wrote on, and put it under your pillow.

Step 6: Take a bath or shower using the salt from the glass, singing or humming your favourite happy or romantic love song as you do so!

Step 7: Spend one night with the card and paper under your pillow, asking your guides and angels to help you on your search for romance, then return the card to the pack, and keep the piece of paper folded somewhere special and private. Check back in a day, a week, a month, or even six months: chances are, someone with all or most of your top-ten qualities should have crossed your path and given you some very interested looks – or maybe an offer you can't refuse!

Step 8: We want to hear your results, Goddess, so email them to Lovers Card Ritual Stories at our website, 21stcenturygoddess.net

Gotta go! The "moving on" spread
FOR BIG LIFE CHANGES

Tarot is actually designed for people making changes. That's why so many tarot readers get to see people who are switching jobs, moving house, splitting up relationships, or doing other drastic things. People want to know if they are making the right decision, and they also want to know what their next move should be. This spread is designed for you, if you're moving on from a situation. Perhaps you plan to lose weight, if you've always been overweight. Maybe you plan to stop being poor and start being rich. Maybe you want to leave a painful family relationship behind you. Perhaps it's time to say "Gotta go!" for love-life reasons, or work reasons, or basically... any kind of reason.

To begin, look at the cards spread face-down. Choose at random, following gut feelings, and lay them up, in a row of five, so you can see exactly what you've chosen.

1st card: What you think you're leaving behind.
2nd card: What you're really leaving behind!
3rd, 4th, and 5th cards: The three choices ahead of you.

The choice element in the last part of this reading is important. It reminds you that the future is made up of different pathways – if you really like the look of one of these cards, pull it out of the pack and look at it often. Meditating on the picture can help you "pull" this destiny choice towards you, every day – but remember, only when you've left the situation you were asking about. The second card in this sequence, the one which shows you what you are really leaving behind, is often the most interesting one. It will certainly help you go deeper into your situation.

Going deeper

The tarot was designed to cover all bases – the simple, small-scale side of life, as well as the big stuff. To go deeper, you will need to work with each card, one at a time, to really uncover its true meaning for you. Start with the No-brainer Tarot Dictionary as a general guide, but then really look at the pictures, and start to brainstorm. Tarot was designed to pull out all the psychic insights of the person facing the card. It also reflects what we call archetypes – universal symbols which every human being knows and understands, no matter if they are living in a hut in Africa, or a ritzy flat in New York

TELEPHONE TAROT – DOES IT WORK?

Quite a few magazines, websites, and newspapers offer an instant tarot line these days, where you do the work by calling up, then waiting for the computer to choose you one or more cards. These services are a lot cheaper than paying for a full personal consultation with a reader, but they can also be useful – in a limited way. The best way to describe telephone tarot compared to personal tarot is like this: fast-food hamburgers versus a three-course meal. Sometimes all you want is a burger, which is fine. The extra depth, sensitivity, and accurate touches you get from a real live tarot reader are what you pay for, though – plus their ability to see some things clairvoyantly about your life, through the cards. (Clairvoyance is the psychic talent which enables you to "see" pictures of the future in your mind's eye). Some people complain that a telephone, or at least a telephone company's computer, couldn't possibly have any psychic energy. That's missing the point. Like every oracle, telephone tarot works "in the moment." Basically, it's your intention and sincerity, and your desire to seek an answer, that counts, not the actual method! With oracles you can pull a card from a deck, flip an I Ching coin, swirl tea leaves around in the bottom of a cup, interpret the shape of a passing cloud, or swing a pendulum. These are all future-seeing devices which work, simply or in complex ways, depending on the intention of the questioner. If you mean it when you call, you'll get the answer you need to hear, and there's nothing random about it. Scientists influence the results of experiments by deciding to peer at what is going on. You influence the results of your own life by deciding to peer at it, too!

City. You will know you've "got" the tarot when you gaze at a card such as the Empress, with all her blooming flowers and her feminine, fertile body, and find it seems familiar to you – or at least it rings some bells. If you start dreaming about tarot images, then you'll really know it's in your system. But how can you go deeper if you're an absolute beginner? The workbook that you use for your personal readings is a good place to start . . .

Tarot card triggers

Use any of the cards that appeal to you in the Major Arcana to start your discovery of the deeper side of tarot. Do you like the look of the

Fool dancing off the cliff, or are you drawn to the Magician, with his strange selection of tools and magical instruments? The Emperor on his throne can be an amazing symbol to uncover, or perhaps you prefer to work with the High Priestess. Just the fact that you are choosing one Major Arcana card over another to work with can tell you a lot about your personality, and particularly your current situation in life. So don't treat your choice of card as an accident! Perhaps the card has chosen you . . .

Your tarot notes

Begin by noting down what the card means to you, without thinking too much about it. Of course you know the No-brainer meaning, or you may have some good tarot books by your side to give you the full lowdown. To really know tarot, though, you almost have to step into the card and imagine meeting the character who is in that scene. What would he or she say to you? And what questions would you ask them? What replies can you imagine receiving? Look at the background, the landscape, any animals in the picture, any natural elements such as lightning bolts, or even the small chains which link the man and woman in the Devil card. It's all there for a reason . . . it's just up to you to decode and discover it all. And that's the way to a deeper and much more meaningful tarot reading, both for you or your friends.

How to do a horoscope spread

You don't have to know anything about astrology to do a horoscope spread. This card layout just borrows the idea of the twelve houses (or life departments) from astrology, and follows a wheel pattern, just the same as the one you see in a natal horoscope.

This is a big spread, which involves a lot of time and energy, so it's best to do it once a year. If you're feeling OK the day after New Year's Eve (you saint!) then it's brilliant to do this on January 1st, right at the start of the year ahead. Otherwise, just treat it as a twelve-month prediction for your life. Remember, if there's anything you're not crazy about in the reading, you can use your workbook, and the two-card "cause and choice" method to come up with creative and smart ways to work with the future, rather than have the future work against you!

Basically, after you set the scene for your reading and shuffle, you need to choose twelve cards. Lay them out in a wheel, placing them anti-clockwise, with the first card at the quarter-to position, the second card below that, the third card below that, the fourth card at the half-past position, and so on – your last card will be at the ten-to position.

A special hint: Wherever you draw Major Arcana cards, expect that life theme or area to be hugely important in your next twelve months. The Major Arcana are all listed in the No-brainer Dictionary – they're the big life subjects, such as Strength, and The Devil, and so on.

The table below describes the areas affected by each card.

1st card: Your image this year. How you look. Your reputation, and how others will see you.

2nd card: Your money this year. Your possessions. What you buy and sell. What you own or earn.

3rd card: Brothers and sisters over a twelve-month period. Short trips. Your car or other transport.

4th card: Your house or flat. Your family or housemates, other than brothers and sisters. Your living conditions and your relatives.

5th card: Your love life as opposed to serious, permanent relationships. Kids or babies. Creativity.

6th card: Your job or part-time job. Your health and wellbeing. Work experience or housework.

7th card: Your main lover or partner. Alternatively, the person you used to go out with or live with.

8th card: Other people's money and its effect on you. Taxation. Wills. Investments. Loans. Banks.

9th card: Travel to other regions, states or countries. Education. Publishing. Self-education.

10th card: Your career. Alternatively, your exam results or qualifications. Your success or ambitions.

11th card: Your friends. Any groups you belong to, such as charities, clubs or teams. Your social life.

12th card: Your inner self. Your soul. Your spirit. Your private world. All your secrets – sshh!

EXAMPLE:
THE HIGH PRIESTESS

To some writers, like Juliet Sharman-Burke, the author of the wonderful guide *The Mythic Tarot Workbook*, the cards have links with well-known myths. For The High Priestess, Juliet writes that this may be, "Persephone leaving behind the daylight world of her mother, Demeter." What films, books, myths, songs, or stories does this card remind you of? But first of all, do you like the High Priestess or not? Some people find her wise and inspiring. Others find her scary and too powerful. Is she a witch to you, or a magical force for good? When they look at this card, some people are reminded of Morgana le Fay, the famous sorceress in the King Arthur legends. Others sometimes see someone they actually know – like the local naturopath – while others might be reminded of media "priestess" figures, like the astrologer Mystic Meg. It's worth your time to explore not only the High Priestess, but also every other Major Arcana card, as not only will you never forget the meaning of the card, but each time you see it, you will go deeper in your readings!

Crystals, Oils

Crystals, essential oils and flower remedies have been recognized for a long time as having enormous potential for healing our bodies and emotions, and for helping us tap into the earth's psychic energies. These psychic energies can give us some more oomph in our magical workings and can help empower our Goddess rituals (see the chapter on Magic and Rituals). In this chapter we will give you the basics of crystal magic and the ways you can use crystals for healing and for magic. We have also included information on using aromatherapy oils and those fabulously subtle, but effective, Bach Flower remedies. Check out how to use and blend these remedies to help heal many forms of emotional distress and discomfort.

d Remedies

Crystals

Have you ever had the experience, when passing a jewellery store, of stopping to gaze more intently at a beautiful piece of jewellery? Was it the silver or gold that caught your eye or was it the precious or semiprecious crystal that was set in the middle? Attraction to a particular stone can tell you a lot about your keen fashion sense and about what you may need psychically and emotionally at the moment – whether you need to feel balanced, protected against negativity, or whether you need to boost your self-esteem.

If you actually get hold of that crystal, you can tap into its physical and psychic energy and use it to feel the balance or protection you need. For example, if you are attracted to hematite – a heavy, black stone – you may unconsciously want to get some relief from an overwhelming feeling of anxiety. Get a small sample of it to help you feel grounded. As hematite is an excellent crystal for releasing worries, carry it with you or hold it in your hand to help you feel free to think clearly about how to alleviate your feelings of worry or anxiety.

Many of us are aware that we have become estranged from the earth. But now the "old ways," those ways that understand the powers of nature and natural substances, are once again becoming accessible to those of us who desire to use them. When a stone calls to you to pick it up, whether lying in a riverbed or on a velvet pillow, you have just come in contact with your inner self, a part of you that is essential for making your dreams come true.

A great deal of stuff has been written about crystals, as more and more information has come to light about how and why crystals are formed. When reading about the formation of crystals you really get a sense of how powerfully linked they are to the energy of the land from which they came. These crystals, having absorbed and retained the energies and subtle vibrations of the earth around them, are a concentration of the earth's physical and psychic energy.

Different crystals have different psychic characteristics. After centuries of experimentation and work, magical practitioners and healers have worked out how to use them for various purposes, such as deflecting negativity and attracting the appropriate energies or powers to create positive outcomes – wealth and love, as well as balance and health. Crystals work on a cellular level, shifting and aligning the energy around them to match their own energy. They can even subtly move the energy within your body. The body is known to store all our hurts, traumas, and negative thoughts in particular areas of the body. We can sometimes feel quite strong pain in those areas. By placing the right crystal over a sore area, the crystal can help shift the pain, as well as release any emotional issues related to the soreness.

We have put together for you a quick guide of some of the most popular crystals with enough information about their particular powers and energies so that you can work out how you want to use them for your own magical workings or healings. With experience comes knowledge, and with knowledge comes the quest for more knowledge. If you know nothing about crystals, we hope we can share with you our surprise and delight about how effective crystal magic and healing can be. If you already know something about crystals, you will appreciate how powerful this stuff can be and how you just keep on learning new ways of using them.

As the descriptions that follow are only guides, you are free to add your own experiences and beliefs. You may even wish to question what is written, as there are considerable variations in a number of books as to the particular energy of a certain crystal. Questioning the information in various books and weighing up their content and your experiences is very important for your own self-discovery. It will help strengthen your psychic abilities. However, don't let any negative beliefs hold you back.

Choosing your crystal

There are many ways in which you can choose your crystal. If a particular crystal "calls" to your intuition, find out what it is and read its description in the list provided. A crystal "calls" to you if you feel drawn to its colour, texture, or general appearance. It "calls" to you if you just simply want to touch or stroke it. You may feel a desire to hold the crystal close to you or to keep it in your bag or pocket. Go with it – you are already doing some serious crystal magic!

Another way of choosing a crystal is to simply read the information about each major crystal, stone, or resin described in this chapter and to choose one or more of them based on their descriptions, which may include their associations to a certain power, magic, and lore.

A crystal's energy may be described as projective – this means that it has the ability to project a certain form of energy, such as protection. Alternatively, the crystal can have a receptive energy, which means that they are able to store a particular form of energy, such as love or support for a particular activity.

The crystals, stones, or resins we have selected for you below are all pretty easy to find and are not particularly expensive. While you are reading the descriptions, keep in mind the following questions to help you work out what type of crystal you need:

* Do you need help with a physical problem?
* Do you need help with an emotional problem?
* Do you need a stone to help empower a spell or Goddess ritual?
* Is the stone for you or for someone else?
* Do you need to give or receive energy?

Aventurine: This green stone increases perception and creative insight, enhancing your creative talents and motivation and stimulating the existence of opportunities. Aventurine is used to strengthen mental powers and eyesight. It soothes emotions and is used for healing the heart and for alleviating heartache. It is also used for the acceptance of self and others, and for inner peace. Wear it over your heart to soothe a broken heart and also to ward off anxiety and fear.

Agate: This stone aids strength and courage, and compels truth. Agates come in various colours, each one having a different energy, which resides within the stone. The blood-red agate gives strength, courage, longevity, love, healing, and protection. In ancient times it was used to ensure that the earth would produce a plentiful harvest and that the soil would continue being fertile. Use it in love spells for purity. There are five main types of agate:

* Banded agate, which increases energy and eases stress.
* Black agate, which offers courage and success in competitions.
* Black and white agate, which can help protect a person against physical dangers.
* Blue lace agate, which can help relieve stress and reduce family quarrels.
* Green agate, which can help improve the wearer's health.

Amber: This golden yellow resin, derived from the fossilized resin of coniferous trees, is worn to protect against psychic attacks, and is an aid to furthering ambitions and lifting the spirits. In ancient times, amber was ground into a powder and mixed with honey or oil of roses for various physical ailments. Amber is perhaps the oldest substance used for human adornment. Its energy brings luck, healing, strength, beauty, and love. As amber was once a living substance – sap – it was believed to contain the very essence of life itself. Amber has been used for nearly every purpose in magic and is highly prized for its talismanic powers of protection.

Amethyst: Sometimes known as the "Stone of Venus," amethyst has a calming and soothing influence. It also has the ability to transmute negative energy into positive. It's very effective as a healing stone because it helps protect the wearer by soaking up the negative feelings projected towards him or her by others. It also aids in the prophetic arts, increases spiritual awareness and guidance, and helps purify and regenerate all levels of consciousness. Wear an amethyst to help reduce the incidence of nightmares or to reduce feelings of anger and impatience.

Amethyst ranges in colour from light to dark purple and, when placed on your third eye during meditation, has the ability to enhance energy patterns beneficial to the body and to help release negative energies from the body.

Try this great way of helping to release an emotional pain or to alleviate the intensity of a physical soreness. Sit quietly while holding a small piece of amethyst in one hand. Take three deep breaths. Concentrate on your pain and imagine that you can move the pain out of your body and into the piece of amethyst in your hand. Send all the pain you feel into the stone. Throw the stone into the ocean or bury it into the ground, visualizing that the pain is now detached from your body and is being absorbed by the ocean or earth.

Aquamarine: A light blue, clear stone, the aquamarine has a receptive energy that can assist in attracting inspiration and enhancing creativity. It is used to help reduce fears and phobias, release emotional trauma, and calm nervous tension. It has been known to be favourable for travellers, helping to protect them against accidents. Aquamarine can be worn as a protective amulet to ensure good health. To enhance a feeling of calm during a particularly stressful time, hold or place an aquamarine at your throat and imagine that you are breathing the calming blue light of the stone into your body. With every breath you take, feel a sense of calm wash over you.

Azurite: This beautiful deep blue stone has a receptive energy and has long been used to increase psychic powers and abilities, and to invoke spiritual guidance. It's also good for remembering dreams and for giving you a sense of clarity about your future path. Hold one in your hand when trying to decide something about your future and you will find that you may be given new insights about the best path to follow.

Bloodstone: A favourite stone for healing and improving the circulation of both blood and energy, bloodstone helps renew and balance your energy when you are feeling stressed out, and is very effective at removing emotional blockages and clearing blocked energy from both the physical and non-physical body. If you are going through a stressful time, such as at exam time, wear bloodstone as a talisman to protect you from the accumulation of stress. Young girls were given a piece of bloodstone, which is green with red flecks, at menarche (when they first began menstruating) to remind them of the power of their blood. As bloodstone helps with the circulation of blood, place the stone on your lower abdomen if you are suffering from menstrual cramps. Because it is green, bloodstone is sometimes used in wealth, money, and business spells.

Carnelian: This orange-red stone brings its owner joy and dispels apathy. It gives protection and energy, aids in concentration, and helps stimulate the mind, improving memory retention. In Ancient Egypt, it was believed carnelian could promote peace and harmony, and it was worn to prevent skin diseases and for general good health. Sometimes known as the wish stone, wear a piece of carnelian near your heart so that your dearest wish will be fulfilled.

Citrine: This pale yellow, clear crystal stimulates openness and awakens the mind. It encourages tremendous healing on both emotional and mental levels, helps unblock subconscious fears, and serves as a natural relaxant. It also develops self-discipline, enhances self-esteem, manifests creativity, and enhances your self-will. Put a small piece of citrine in your purse, wallet, or anywhere you put money to promote the accumulation of money and a sense of abundance. As the crystal has a projective energy, also carry it to invoke a sense of protection.

Fluorite: This stone, which comes in various shades of purple, green, and blue, accesses the visionary mind, bringing spiritual ideas into an earthly existence. It's a powerful stone that can be used to connect with your own spirit guides. It also protects from interference from other energy forces, enhances concentration and meditation, as well as balances the mind and increases its mental powers. It's also considered to bring good luck. Holding it while meditating is believed to help manifest your innermost wish.

Garnet: This crystal enhances self-esteem, alleviates bad dreams, encourages success in business, and is thought to assist in seeing into past incarnations. It also stimulates happiness, peace, balance, patience, inspiration, and persistence. The garnet, which is usually a deep fiery red, ranges from orange-red to pink-red, has a projective energy and is used for healing. It promotes a healthy, cheery disposition and is good for mental depression. The garnet is worn or used in magic to enhance the body's power by strengthening the aura and creating a shield of protection for its wearer. Garnets were once exchanged by parting friends to ensure that they would meet again. Exchange a piece of garnet among your friends to ensure consistency and loyalty in your friendships.

Hematite: This powerful, heavy, black metallic stone absorbs negativity, and is capable of drawing illness away from the body. Also known as the worry stone, hematite is calming to the emotions, and is considered an excellent grounding stone that helps maintain a balance between body, mind, and spirit. It alleviates worry and anxiety, allowing for mental clarity. If you hold a piece of hematite tightly in your hand and ask a question, you will find that the stone will help the answer to come to you. Wear hematite as an amulet for strength and courage if you are involved in a battle of wills or words, such as in a courtroom situation. Keep a piece of hematite with you to help you succeed in legal battles.

Herkimer Diamond: This special variety of quartz crystal, also known as the dream crystal, is excellent for helping you feel balanced and alert. This clear-coloured crystal works with the complementary energies of yin (female, passive energy) and yang (male, active energy) to help you attune spiritually, and it aids in bringing teachings from the dream state. It enhances visualization, astral travel, and dream recall, as well as helps amplify and store thoughts. If you are feeling overwrought about a particular problem, place the crystal under your pillow so that the energy of the stone will encourage you to remember those dreams and therefore help provide some insight about how you can resolve your particular problem.

Jade: This sacred, creamy green stone is believed to bring good fortune, prosperity, and longevity to its owner. It is also a symbol of divine revelation. It stimulates practicality and wisdom, and is thought to provide a link between the spiritual and the mundane. For many centuries jade has been revered as a sacred stone in China and is still revered by the Chinese today. As the stone can be used to access your higher guidance through dreams, place it under your pillow to encourage a sense of emotional balance.

Jasper: Used to safeguard personal independence, jasper is said to bring inspirational warnings when there is a danger of unfair domination from others. It aids and comforts during distress, and helps balance emotions. There are three basic types of jasper:

* Red jasper has a projective energy and is worn for protection, able to send negativity back to its source.
* Green jasper has a receptive, healing energy and can be worn to promote sympathy for others with emotional or mental problems.
* Brown jasper has a receptive energy and can be used for grounding and centring yourself. If you live with your head in the clouds, wear brown jasper to ward off danger.

Kyanite: This transparent or translucent stone never needs cleaning or clearing as it doesn't accumulate or retain negative energy vibrations. This mineral's energy is unlimited in its applications, which makes it one of the best stones for aligning your emotional, intellectual, physical, ethereal, and astral bodies. It brings tranquillity and a calming effect to the whole being, stimulates communication and psychic awareness on all levels, and dispels anger and frustration. Kyanite helps facilitate meditation as its energy is accessible, gentle, and balancing. Place it under your pillow if you wish to recall your dreams to help you solve a difficult problem in life or if you wish to connect with your spirit guide.

Lapis Lazuli: Deep blue in colour with flecks of real gold, this is the stone of Isis, an ancient Egyptian Goddess. Prized for its prophetic capabilities, it is an uplifting stone and will boost your psychic awareness and promote a sense of gentleness in the wearer. It stimulates and strengthens the mind and body and helps attune you to a sense of spiritual awareness. It also aids with success, helping you utilize your talents, expand the awareness of your intellect, and enhance your spoken communication skills. When worn next to the skin, it shelters the wearer like a shield, giving a sense of healing and strength.

Malachite: Called a magic stone, malachite is a favourite stone for travellers and other adventurers. It stimulates clear vision and insight, represents hope and inner peace, and is believed to protect wearers from danger. It can be used as a child's talisman to help them sleep soundly and to protect them from bad dreams. It increases a sense of abundance in all areas of life. This stone, which is banded in brilliant, varying shades of green, supposedly has equal amounts of negative and positive energy, giving the stone its ability to enhance the balance between physical and spiritual life.

It is used to release repressed emotions and is believed to aid physical detoxification. Place a piece of malachite in front of your computer or television so that it can absorb undesirable energies, including radiation emanating from these pieces of equipment. Also place a piece of the stone in each corner of a room to cleanse it of toxins. Because of their ability to absorb negativity so readily, it is a high maintenance stone, needing cleaning virtually on a daily basis.

Moonstone: Moonstone is a powerful stone representing the energy of the Goddess. Translucently milky with tints ranging from white-yellow to blue-grey, in blue, white, or pink opalescent shades, moonstone aids in bringing forth memories of past lives. Carry a piece of moonstone with you for protection if you are travelling over water. The stone can also be carried for good luck. It is also believed to promote unselfishness, and opens the heart to humanitarian love and hope. It's good for alleviating premenstrual symptoms, and it regulates moods and enhances feminine energies.

Moss agate: This translucent stone with flecks of green is believed to bring the wearer happiness and wealth and also assists in making and keeping friends. It aids in the restoration of energy, increases the ability to ward off self-induced anger and inner bitterness, and is used in healing. There are three varieties:

* Green moss agate balances emotional energy.
* Red moss agate balances physical energy.
* Blue lace moss agate gives a sense of tranquillity.

Obsidian: Obsidian is a naturally occurring glass; it is simply lava that cooled so fast that the minerals contained within didn't have time to form. The ancient Aztecs fashioned it into mirrors, and in Mexico obsidian is still fashioned for use in scrying – a magical technique where you can see images form within a crystal or other natural substance, providing an answer to a question or concerns a future event (see later in this chapter). For some, the blackness of the stone allows easier contact with the subconscious mind, promoting a sense of spiritual awareness. It has a projective energy and is used for grounding – absorbing dark energy and converting it to white light.

Peridot: This light green, clear stone has receptive and protective energies that promote health, wealth, and sleep. It is used to counteract negative emotions and is calming to the spirit, helping to dispel fears. It is also used in wealth-attracting spells, and is worn or carried for general healing purposes. It was once worn as a means of gaining foresight and divine inspiration.

Quartz: Considered the stone of power, quartz is used for harmony and healing, helping to amplify the energy in both the body and the mind, and stimulating positive thought processes. It can be used to help you receive information from the spiritual world. There are four main types of quartz:

Clear quartz is a clear type of quartz that amplifies energy and is able to deeply cleanse the aura. It has a healing quality, which can be used to draw out pain. It is also believed to promote clarity and wisdom, and is a good stone for meditation. It is a very potent stone, which can be worn to protect you from negative forces or vibration. As it has such a powerful effect amplifying energies, cleanse the crystal regularly to keep it free from negative influence.

Rutilated quartz is a clear, powerful electrical conductor, with golden, copper or blue-grey fibres or rutiles. It amplifies energy, thoughts, and can be programmed for healing (see below on how to programme your crystal for a particular purpose). The crystal intensifies and deepens altered states, making it an excellent stone to have with you if you feel a bit restless when you are in the middle of your meditation, or if you want to enhance your clairvoyant or tele-pathic abilities.

Smoky quartz is a smoky brown-black stone that helps you over-come depression, nightmares, and stress. The stone can range from having quite a strong haze (or inclusions) to a virtually clear brown-black colour (free of inclusions). If the stone is a clear brown-black, it will be more powerful in inducing deep meditation. It can be used for channelling energy from the Universe and for tapping into a source of higher guidance.

Rose quartz is the ultimate love stone. This light to medium milky-pink crystal aids in the enhancement of self-love and compassion, intuition, and emotional balance. It reduces stress and tension, and cools hot tempers. It has vibrations of universal love and inner serenity and helps the heart recover from all wounds. Rose quartz is invaluable for helping heal emotional pain, and enhancing a positive outlook. Wear or carry in your pocket or bag a piece of rose quartz to attract a flow of love, fidelity, and a sense of a happy relationship. If things go wrong in your love life, place the crystal on your heart to soothe its energy. You will soon feel more settled and open to understanding where your relationship went wrong.

Rhodonite: A pink stone with black highlights, rhodonite is used to activate love, making the wearer able to attract or keep a loving partner. It balances yin/yang energies, and helps achieve your highest potential within a relationship. Considered the other heart stone, it helps build self-esteem and confidence in love. It strengthens the power of your mantras, affirmations, chanting, singing, and toning. Place a piece of rhodonite over your third eye (the point in the middle of your forehead) to help activate your intuition and inspire you when you feel down and stressed.

Topaz: A crystal that enhances the prospects of success in all endeavors, topaz also aids in restoring physical energy and emotional calm, and helps protect the wearer from external stresses. Topaz is a mood elevator and has been used to help people who suffer from insomnia and depression. It also stimulates creative-thinking processes and is instrumental in allowing the visualization of the success of a new project to manifest in the physical world. Wear a topaz ring on your left hand or carry a piece of topaz in your left hand pocket if you are feeling melancholy – you will soon feel much better.

Wear blue topaz to help you align your thoughts and actions with your higher self, which will allow you to write freely and express yourself creatively. A clear gold topaz will attract abundance, while a light blue topaz will aid your ability to communicate.

Tourmaline: Supercharged with magnetic and electric energy, tourmaline promotes astral projection and also works as a protective shield. It consumes negative energy without releasing it into the atmosphere. Use a piece of tourmaline for meditation, or if you are trying to solve a problem, as the crystal enhances visions and allows a person to see with compassion, teaching us to expand our limited concepts of thinking and to become more flexible and understanding. The crystal comes in a number of colours, each of which has its own specific uses:

* Pink tourmaline has a receptive energy, attracting love and friendship and promoting sympathy for others.
* Red tourmaline has a projective energy and is worn to promote courage.
* Green tourmaline has a receptive energy and is used to attract money and success in business. It will also stimulate creativity.
* Blue tourmaline also has a receptive energy and will help alleviate stress, as well as promote a sense of peace and a restful sleep.

Turquoise: Turquoise, which comes in shades of blue ranging from deep sky blue to a beautifully soft greenish hue, has a receptive energy that promotes courage, friendship, healing, and luck. It is a sacred stone to many Native American tribes – a piece of turquoise is a required tool in the Apache shaman's medicine or power bag. This protective stone helps ward off danger and clears one's path of pitfalls. It is excellent for both spiritual and physical alignment – wearing turquoise can help speed the healing process. It is also valuable for grounding as well as for vision quests and astral travel. Place a small piece of turquoise on your third eye (in the middle of your forehead) to help you psychically connect with a higher power. Do this when you feel the need for guidance if a problem seems too difficult for you to resolve. It purifies all levels of being, physical and non-physical, and is capable of handling strong negativity, which it absorbs, helping to protect the wearer from the evil eye.

Cleaning your crystals

When you bring home a crystal, stone, or resin, which you feel that you would like to work with, the first thing you must do is to cleanse or clear the crystal of any negative energy it may have retained when it was sitting in a store, or when it was on transit to you. Many new age stores will automatically cleanse a stone for you, but you may like to still do a further cleansing ritual to welcome your new stone to your home as well as remove any unwanted, negative vibrations. Follow this simple yet effective ritual, which is spread over three or four days, to thoroughly cleanse your crystal. The ritual is also a wonderful way to rejuvenate the power of crystals that you have already been using. Before starting the ritual, gather the following tools and ingredients:

* A container large enough to hold your crystal
* A trowel to bury your crystal in the earth

* A glass bowl full of seawater or salty water
* A white cloth large enough to cover the glass bowl
* Some incense or a smudge stick made from a tied bundle of dried sage, sweet grass, or cedar; or a crystal cluster large enough to hold the crystal being cleansed; or a bowl with some rose petals, honeysuckle flowers, or orange blossoms.

On day one: Place your crystal in the container and put it outside for 24 hours so that it captures both daylight and the light of the moon (preferably the full moon). Do this for all stones except amethyst, fluorite, and turquoise, which may fade in sunlight. Instead, bury these stones in the earth for 24 hours or visualize them being surrounded by a white light that cleanses them of all the negative energy they contain.

On day two: Bury the crystal in the earth for another 24 hours. (Skip this step if you are cleansing amethyst, fluorite, or turquoise as you already buried them on day one.)

On day three: Place the crystal in the glass bowl filled with seawater or a mixture of salt and water. Make sure the crystal is covered with the water. Cover the bowl with the white cloth. Let the crystal soak for another 24 hours. Do not do this step for carnelian or turquoise as both these stones should not be cleansed in saltwater – instead, place them in a bowl of fresh spring water for 24 hours.

On day four: At this stage you may do one of the following to finish cleansing your crystal – let your intuition guide you to choose one:

* Pass the crystal several times through the wafting smoke of the lit stick of incense or smudge stick (a smudge stick is a bundle of herbs – sage, cedar or sweet grass – that have been bound up for easier use);
  or
* Place the crystal on a large crystal cluster of either amethyst or clear quartz for another 24 hours (a crystal cluster is usually a small slab of naturally formed crystals);
  or
* Soak your crystal in a bowl of water containing rose petals, honey suckle flowers, or orange blossoms for 24 hours.

Please note that any time you use your crystals, and before cleansing it, thank your crystal for allowing you to tap into its energy. If you've been doing a lot of emotional healing and releasing your negative emotions into your crystals, you'll also want to cleanse them. Make a habit of periodically clearing or cleansing your crystals even if you haven't been using them for meditation or healing work, if only because they do get dusty – a cleansing will help rejuvenate their energies.

Charging your crystal:
CHOICES, CHOICES, CHOICES

Charging your crystals is in some ways the opposite of cleansing them, as you are activating or amplifying their energy. There are quite a number of ways a crystal can be charged. You may place your crystals on a quartz cluster (a small slab of naturally formed clear crystal), as quartz is well known for its ability to amplify the energy of any crystal with which it is in contact.

Crystal can also be activated with sound. Hold a single-note chime near the crystal and strike the chime gently several times. This will have a harmonizing effect on the crystal. Alternatively, if you like to chant and have made it a regular practice, place your crystal near you while you practise, especially if you want to use it as part of your meditation practice.

During your meditation you could simply hold the stone in your hand or set it in front of you as a focus. If you are part of a meditation group, you can charge the crystal with the group's healing energy, directing it for a particular purpose, such visualizing that the energy is directly helping heal a sick or emotionally unhappy friend. Remember, if doing any powerful work like this for another person who is absent from the group, always ask their permission first.

Your thoughts and intentions can have an activating or deactivating effect on crystals. If your thoughts have been gloomy, make sure to cleanse or reprogramme your crystals as soon as possible.

You can also charge your stones with the energy of the seasons, as well as the psychic energy of a particular day of the week or of a certain phase of the moon. You can tap into these energies to help amplify the crystal's vibrations by simply burying the crystal in the ground during a specific day to charge your crystal with the particular energy that the earth is manifesting at that time (see further on for a breakdown of what each time means).

You can also bury the crystal in the ground to give the land around you a particular gift, such as protection or purification, to help reclaim the area, create a beautiful garden, or to help return energy to the ground.

Yes, to tap into the moon's energy, just leave the stone overnight in a place outside where it will not be disturbed.

Seasonal: Link your crystal with the energy of the seasons by burying it in the earth on the following day of the solstice or equinox. The solstices and equinoxes vary a day or so each year, and they also occur at different times of the year depending on whether you are in the northern or southern hemispheres. The chart below will give you a good guide to their timing.

Moon phases: The energy of the moon changes according to its phases and other significant times, such as full moon. Put your crystal out overnight to link into the following energies:

* New or waxing moon: Empowering new beginnings.
* Full moon: Promoting a sense of abundance.
* Waning moon: Banishing old habits or ways.
* Dark of the moon: Promoting contemplation about the future.

Days of the week: The concept that each day of the week corresponds with a planet goes way back a long way, and it is an important basis for magical workings (see the chapter on Magic and Rituals) as it is believed that each day relates to a particular type of energy. Use the opposite chart to decide when to charge a particular crystal so that it links into the energy of that day.

Equinox/Solstice	Type of energy	Northern Hemisphere (Exact date varies)	Southern Hemisphere (Exact date varies)
Spring equinox	Helping the growth of new projects	21–23 March	21–23 September
Summer solstice	Counting your blessings; thanking someone	21–23 June	21–23 December
Autumn equinox	Harvesting your dreams	21–23 September	21–23 March
Winter solstice	Renewing your life by letting go of the old and asking for the new	21–23 December	21–23 June

Programming your crystals

Once you have chosen your crystal(s), you can dedicate or programme it for personal use, either for healing or for attracting or deflecting energy. To do this, gather your crystal and the following tools:

* A coloured candle (choose a colour that is appropriate – see the ritual chart on page 188 – for instance a red candle for love, a white candle for protection or a green one for abundance), also don't forget the matches and a candleholder.
* A stick of your favourite incense, such as sandalwood, and an incense holder.

Before starting your programming ritual, sit quietly and contemplate to what use you want to dedicate your crystal. Breathe deeply and evenly, focusing just on the purpose of your dedication, creating an atmosphere of meditation. When ready, visualize a circle of shining, pulsing blue light swirling around you and your immediate area, giving you a sense of protection.

Day of the week	Energy of the day	Which stone to charge
Monday (Ruled by the moon)	Heightening intuition and inner feminine power	Moonstone, bloodstone
Tuesday (Ruled by Mars)	Strengthening goal setting and motivation	Garnet
Wednesday (Ruled by Mercury)	Aiding communication and increasing study skills	Any blue stone, such as aquamarine, lapis lazuli
Thursday (Ruled by Jupiter)	Focusing on wealth, success and luck	Jade, citrine
Friday (Ruled by Venus)	Focusing on romance and love	Rose quartz
Saturday (Ruled by Saturn)	Invoking balance and patience through inner wisdom	Clear quartz
Sunday (Ruled by the Sun)	Helping radiate joy and peace	Tiger's eye

Position the candle and incense in their respective holders and light them. Hold the crystal above your head and visualize its colour radiating light down through the top of your head, washing over you and moving down to the earth. Recite the following dedication (or make one up along similar lines): May the power that is held within this crystal, guide and help manifest [insert your purpose here] in my life. And so it is.

Finish by snuffing out the candle and incense, and then sleep that night with the crystal under your pillow. Keep it in a special bag, either silk, cotton or any other natural fabric, when it is not being used.

Using crystals for guidance

The crystal repair kit
(DON'T LEAVE HOME WITHOUT IT!)

Here is our special mix of 13 lucky crystals, which you should always keep with you, just in case. Over time gather the following 13 crystals and keep them properly cleansed and charged as described above. Keep them in a silk pouch with a list of their meanings or in a small silk-lined box. Anytime you need guidance or help, sit quietly with your eyes closed and think of a question you would like to have answered by the stones. Take a deep breath, clear your head and your heart, and reach your hand into the bag or box to choose one of the stones. Read below what the stone means.

If you would like to further invoke the stone's special energy into your life, simply carry your chosen stone with you, either in a little pouch around your neck or in your pocket.

* Amethyst: Protecting against drink driving and invoking a sense of calm.
* Aquamarine: Helping to protect against accidents and grief.
* Carnelian: Balancing creativity and mental processes.
* Citrine: Enhancing personal power and bringing abundance.
* Clear quartz: Enhancing clear thinking and amplifying energy.
* Fluorite: Protecting against interferences from negative energy forces.
* Jade: Inducing relaxation and invoking luck.
* Jasper: Enabling the acquisition of a positive outlook.
* Lapis lazuli: Releasing stress quickly and aiding relaxation.
* Malachite: Bringing harmony into your life.
* Obsidian: Protecting and grounding your energy.
* Rose quartz: Helping you feel compassionate about yourself and others.
* Turquoise: Purifying and dispelling negative energy.

Using crystals for protection

Crystals offer a safe way of protecting yourself against negative forces. Their strong vibrational energy can absorb, reflect, or deflect negative energy, or even replace it with a more positive and harmonious energy pattern.

The strength and sweetness of friendship depend on sincerity tempered by sympathy.

Anonymous

For personal protection, if you always seem to feel drained after being with a particular friend, instead of limiting the times you see that person or dropping them entirely from your life – particularly if they are going through a very emotional time and need your help – wear a crystal that will help you stay grounded, such as hematite, or that will protect you from being completely drained of energy, such as obsidian or turquoise.

To protect your home, place a protection stone, such as turquoise or smoky quartz, outside your home by the front or back door or below a vulnerable window to keep it safe from burglars.

To protect your office, find a place where people spend a lot of time – for example, the lunch room or reception area – and choose a stone that brings harmony or balance, such as kyanite or rose quartz, or that cleanses the space of negativity, such as clear quartz.

To protect your car, keep a stone in it, such as red jasper or aquamarine, to secure it and to help keep you safe from accidents.

Late night crystal cleanse spray: You can make the following spray to use on a daily basis to wash off the day's bad vibes, cleansing away all the negative energies that have been directed at you and have been floating around you during the day. This is also a great spray to use after being at a late-night party when you feel a little drained from meeting a lot of people. It is made on the night of a full moon. You will need the following seven crystals (you may have already got these for your crystal repair kit – see earlier in this chapter), ingredients and tools:

* A piece of clear quartz, amethyst, lapis, malachite, tiger's eye, jasper and garnet
* A cup of seawater or saltwater
* A glass bowl, large enough to hold a litre of liquid
* A litre of purified water, enough to cover the crystals
* A spray bottle.

During the evening of a full moon, cleanse the crystals by washing them in the seawater or saltwater before placing them in the glass bowl with the purified water. Leave the bowl outside or near a window overnight to catch the light of the full moon.

On the following day, remove the crystals from the water and tip the charged liquid into the spray bottle. Dry the crystals and either put them back in with the rest of the crystal repair kit or keep them in a clean bag made from natural fibres for future use.

To use the spray effectively, start with your head and spray the crystal cleanse all over your body, finishing at your feet.

Using crystals for divination and insight

Crystals have long been used to divine the future or to gain insights into a problem that you wish to see resolved. Various techniques can be used with crystals – one of the most powerful includes the time-honoured practice of scrying with a crystal ball. Scrying is the practice of strongly focusing on an object or a natural substance, such as water or fire, until you begin to see words, symbols, or images appear within or on the surface of the object or substance. This is quite hard going but, as the results are often very powerful, it is certainly worth persevering with.

How to scry using a crystal ball: Choose either a clear quartz ball (the clearer the better) or any other type of crystal ball that takes your fancy. Sit quietly with the ball in your hands on your lap and focus your energies on the question you have in your mind or the fact that you wish to see the future. Close your eyes, taking three deep breaths. Slowly open your eyes, place the ball on a piece of black cloth and stare into it. Continue breathing deeply, evenly and slowly, and wait for an image or relevant thought to come to you. Don't push this – take your time.

After a while you may start to see fuzzy or fleeting images on the surface or within the crystal. Do not focus on the images yet, but continue to think on your purpose. Depending on the strength of your concentration, you may find that images click into focus and you will see an answer to your issue. Sometimes, the image may appear in your mind or a thought will occur that answers your question or fulfills your need. Keep a journal of what you see or feel while scrying.

This is not an easy process and it may require a bit of practice. Start scrying for about 15 to 20 minutes at first. If it doesn't work, it may be that you aren't to know the answer to your question yet. Try another day. Practice is very important. Perhaps do it a few times a week to start with – this is an art, and it will take time before you become proficient.

GEM ELIXIRS

Gem elixirs are made by soaking a particular gem or crystal in purified water. The water is taken internally, and it works on the physical, emotional, mental, and spiritual level. Gem elixirs release dissonant energies, allowing subtle energy to flow more easily and integrating the energy to heal unbalanced states. To create your own gem elixir, gather the following:

❋ A crystal of your choice
❋ A clean bottle (choose any size but make sure that the neck is wide enough so that the crystal or gem can be dropped into the bottle)
❋ Enough distilled or spring water to fill the bottle

Place the stone in the bottle and fill the bottle with the water. Charge the water by placing it in a spot outside where it can be exposed to both daylight and the light of the moon undisturbed for 24–48 hours.

Drink one full glass of "energetically charged" water until you feel a shift has occurred in your health, or simply pour some of it into your bath. Leave the crystal in the bottle so you can use again.

Using crystals for healing

Crystals have an inherent power to balance, rejuvenate, and re-energize the body's energy. Using crystals for healing can be one of the best ways of helping your body heal itself – they can have quite a life-changing effect!

A very simple technique for healing and unblocking energy flows in your body involves placing a particular crystal on the area that feels pain or discomfort and visualizing that the crystal's energies are drawing out the negative energy into itself. Throw this crystal into the sea or bury it into the ground to let the earth re-absorb the pain from your body.

Alternatively, if you have chosen a crystal that is specifically targeted for healing a particular area or is charged to help with your health, hold the stone in your receptive hand (your right hand if you are right handed or your left hand if you are left handed) to absorb the crystal's healing energies.

Crystals can also be used to finely tune the chakra system, a series of seven energy centres running along the centre of your body (see the chapter on Chakras and Auras for a full rundown of this system). If one of these energy centres is blocked, perhaps because you have experienced some trauma or unpleasant experience or your physical system is under stress for some reason, such as indigestion, the area surrounding the chakra may feel clogged and the energy will become stagnant. This can lead to certain related organs experiencing difficulties because they are not getting the energy they need to operate to their best potential. For instance, you may get problems in your reproductive organs if the energy of the second chakra is blocked, or in your liver if the energy of the third chakra is stagnant.

Each chakra resonates with a particular colour, following the sequence of colours in a rainbow. Like attracts like – crystals of a colour that corresponds with a particular chakra can be used to help unblock the energy flow in the relevant area. (See the chart below for a short list of crystals that resonate with a certain chakra.) The crystal's energy vibrates with the same frequency as the colour of the chakra, releasing the stored energy of the blockage. Once the energy is activated, it flows along the energy lines into the relevant organ and reactivates the organ's energy.

Crystals also have the ability to facilitate emotional equilibrium.

CHART OF THE CHAKRAS
AND THEIR CORRESPONDING COLOURS, CRYSTALS AND PARTS OF THE BODY

Chakra	Colour	Crystals	Parts of the body
First chakra Base (root)	Red	Garnet, hematite, obsidian, smoky quartz	Feet, legs, rectum
Second chakra Lower abdomen (sex)	Orange	Carnelian, citrine, jasper	Sexual organs, large intestine, bladder
Third chakra Solar plexus	Yellow	Amber, citrine, tiger's eye, topaz	Stomach, liver, kidneys
Fourth chakra Heart	Green	Aventurine, malachite, rose quartz	Heart, lungs, breasts
Fifth chakra Throat	Blue	Aquamarine, lapis lazuli, turquoise	Throat, thyroid, mouth, brain, nervous system
Sixth chakra Third eye (middle of forehead)	Purple/indigo purple fluorite	Amethyst, kyanite, Eyes, ears, nose	
Seventh chakra Crown	Magenta	Clear quartz, Herkimer diamond, moonstone	Skin, whole muscular and skeletal system

When our emotions are out of balance, there is a subtle energy repression that can close down one or more chakras. If an event is particularly traumatic, the whole chakra system can shut down. Certain emotions or traumas trigger the chakra to close, however, crystals can be used to help dissolve these blockages and heal the memory of those feelings.

Crystals can be used in a variety of ways, but we have found that placing the crystal on the body at the point of the relevant chakra is the most effective. Use the crystals either one at a time, or in combination with each other, so that you can connect one chakra with another and support the emotions. For example, you can unite the head chakra with the chakra at the heart by placing a heart crystal on the crown chakra and a crown crystal on the heart. The combinations are endless – ask for guidance from a health practitioner versed in chakra healing if in doubt.

> Those are our best friends in whose presence we are able to be our best selves.
> Charles W Kohler

Using crystals to tune up and balance the chakra system – a special ritual: Choose a crystal to match the colour of each of the seven chakras, remembering to cleanse and/or programme these crystals using one of the methods given earlier in this chapter.

Create a space that is quiet and peaceful. Lie on the floor or the bed, and place the appropriate crystal on the corresponding chakra, letting the crystals realign or reactivate the chakra energies in your body. You could also place the crystals in the same position but underneath you or even slightly away from you.

Spend 15–20 minutes meditating or just relaxing with the crystals in place. Once you have finished, remove the crystals and place them in a glass bowl filled with distilled water to cleanse, leaving them for 24 hours.

You can do this simple ritual as often as you need. If you are working on a particular issue, do this short ritual daily so that you will have the maximum amount of energy available to resolve the issue or until you gain an important insight, which is instrumental in helping you finally tackle the problem.

Magical Aromatherapy

The oils of scented plants and flowers have been used for centuries because of their powerful effects on the mind, body, and emotions. Recently there has been a tremendous resurgence of interest in these oils and their abilities – used for both healing and magical workings.

Our aim in this section is to introduce you to the amazing qualities of essential oils for both their therapeutic and magical purposes. You can use these oils individually, or in appropriate combinations to refresh a room, to relieve minor ailments, relax the mind and body in the bath or with a massage, and to use their scent to power a particular type of magic. They are especially effective when used on a day that governs the ruling planets whose energies correspond with that of the particular plant or herb.

How to mix special oil blends

Before you start gathering your ingredients, make sure you use only pure essential oils. There are many fragrant oils on the market, but they don't have any magical effects. You may have to pay a little more for the real essential oils, but it's worth it! Really expensive oils, such as pure rose oil, can sometimes be purchased by the drop – just ask you local supplier. If you are using pure rose oil in a love potion, you will be assured that you are truly attracting real love to you.

IMPORTANT
Never use essential oils undiluted on the skin as they can cause irritation, and you should never take oils internally.

Blending essential oils is very simple and can be done with only a few tools. There are various blends of oils that you can try out, which by their inherent qualities will be tailored for helping you achieve a particular purpose, such as attracting love, studying more effectively, or gaining abundance and wealth. However, you can amplify the power of your oil blend and dedicate the blend to your specific purpose by doing the following small ritual.

First decide what you would like to achieve and check the chart on page 165 to put together a blend of essential oils that will support your intention or purpose. Have a look at the blend suggestions in the special oil blends table and gather the essential oils that you would like to blend. To blend these essential oils, you will also need:

* A 250 ml bottle with a secure lid
* 200 ml of a base oil of apricot or sweet almond
* A black cloth large enough to wrap up the 200 ml bottle.

Think of the purpose of the blend you are going to make. Pour your energy into the purpose while you measure out approximately 100 drops in total of essential oil per 200 ml of base oil. If your blend is made up of two oils, measure out 50 drops of each essential oil into the 200 ml bottle of base oil. If the blend is made up of three oils, measure out 33 drops of each, and if the blend has four oils, measure out 25 drops of each.

You are an alchemist with the power to charge the oil blend not only with your intention, but with your own energy. With each drop you measure out, focus on what you want the blend to help you achieve. With each drop, hold the bottle and swirl it in a clockwise direction three times, recite the following words:

The power of the oil, The power of my thought, The power of my wish, Come now. Blessed be.

Tightly close the bottle with its lid and wrap the bottle up in the black cloth. Put it in a safe place in your bedroom or on your Goddess altar if you have one – see the chapter on Magic and Rituals. Every day, perhaps when you first get home from work or when you are about to go to sleep, take out the bottle, swirl it in a clockwise direction and say the following words:

May the spirits of this oil, Help bring my highest good. So mote it be.

Fourteen special oil blends

Here are 14 special oil blends that will help you get through some of the more important aspects of life, smelling quite sweetly!

1 Specific purpose To enhance Goddess power
Special oil blend Frankincense, lime, myrrh, patchouli, rose, sandalwood, vetiver (Blend all of these, or choose three oils that you prefer.)

2 Specific purpose To enhance success
Special oil blend Basil, cinnamon, patchouli

3 Specific purpose To perform well in an interview
Special oil blend Lavender, orange, rose

4 Specific purpose To ease the pain of breaking up
Special oil blend Bergamot, neroli, rose

5 Specific purpose To perform well in a new job
Special oil blend Basil, ginger, orange, grapefruit (Use all four, or choose three oils that you prefer.)

6 Specific purpose To attract money
Special oil blend Basil, cinnamon, ginger, peppermint, vetiver (Blend all of these, or use three oils that you prefer.)

7 Specific purpose To attract luck
Special oil blend Cinnamon, clove, cypress, peppermint, thyme (Blend all of these, or use three oils that you prefer.)

8 Specific purpose To enhance study
Special oil blend Basil, lemon, ginger

9 Specific purpose To protect from gossip
Special oil blend Black pepper, clove, geranium, marjoram, petitgrain, pine, sandalwood, thyme (Blend all of these, or use three oils that you prefer.)

10 Specific purpose To protect from jealousy
Special oil blend Juniper, lavender, sandalwood

11 Specific purpose To enhance friendship
Special oil blend Bergamot, grapefruit, lime

12 Specific purpose To enhance psychic powers
Special oil blend Lemongrass, nutmeg, sandalwood

13 Specific purpose To attract love
Special oil blend Coriander, lavender, orange, rose, ylang ylang (Blend all of these, or use three oils that you prefer.)

14 Specific purpose To increase prosperity
Special oil blend Cinnamon, chamomile, ginger, orange (Blend all of these, or use three oils that you prefer.)

When you blend the essential oils to perform well in an interview, sprinkle a few drops on your CV to attract success in your job application. To perform well in exams, before going into the exam room sprinkle the study enhancement blend on the pen you will be using for writing your exam paper to improve your memory recall and do your best in the exam. To increase prosperity, rub your prosperity blend on your wallet or purse or on anything that represents a bit of a gamble, such as a lottery ticket. Sprinkle your friendship or love blends on the letters you send to your friends or lover to subliminally forge stronger bonds in your relationships.

TO MAKE A BLEND OF ESSENCES

Place four drops of each of the remedies you have chosen in a 25 ml bottle (available from your local chemist), then add one teaspoon of brandy and top up the remainder of the bottle with purified water. Shake the mixture well so that the remedies are completely dispersed into the water. Such mixtures do not keep forever. They usually keep for a few months, but you can keep them in the refrigerator to extend their shelf life for six months.

CHART OF ESSENTIAL OILS, THEIR USES & CORRESPONDENCES

The following chart lists some of the most common essential oils and includes useful tips on what the oil can be used for both therapeutically and magically. We have also included the best day of the week to use the oil. The chart below is compiled from information gathered through extensive research and from our own experience.

Essential Oil	Aromatherapy and emotional uses	Magical uses	Ruling planet Day of the week
Basil	Stimulating, clarifying, focusing, good for mental fatigue	Purification, protection attracts money	Mars Tuesday
Bergamot	Uplifting, enhances creativity, antidepressant	Protection, attracts prosperity	Sun/Sunday
Black pepper	Warming, helps the circulation	Lust, courage	Mars/Tuesday
Cardamom	Refreshing, invigorating, aids digestion	Love, aphrodisiac	Mercury/Wednesday
Cedarwood	Helps focus, acts as a sedative, antiseptic	Protection, enhances spiritual awareness	Uranus/Wednesday
Chamomile	Relieves tension and anxiety	Prosperity, meditation calming, antidepressant	Moon Monday
Cinnamon	Aids poor circulation and lethargy, warming, anti-fungal	Passion, strengthens psychic awareness	Mars Tuesday
Clary sage	Relieves muscle tension, abdominal pain, alleviates premenstrual symptoms	Protection, grounding	Mercury Wednesday
Clove	Antiseptic, analgesic	Divination, lust	Mars/Tuesday
Comfrey	Soothing to the stomach, helps clear the lungs, alleviates bruising	Safe travel	Saturn Saturday
Coriander	Stimulant, antispasmodic	Lust, love	Mars/Tuesday
Cumin	Tonic, antispasmodic, carminative	Aphrodisiac	Mars/Tuesday

Essential Oil	Aromatherapy and emotional uses	Magical uses	Ruling planet Day of the week
Cypress	Antiseptic, sedative, astringent	Purification, healing, calms jealousy eases the pain of loss	Saturn Saturday
Dill	Aromatic, aids digestion	Protection, clarity	Mercury/Wednesday
Eucalyptus	Antiseptic, antiviral, antibacterial	Purification, healing	Saturn/Saturday
Fennel	Cleansing, warming, anti-inflammatory	Purification, protection	Mercury Wednesday
Frankincense	Antiseptic, astringent, anti-inflammatory	Courage, spirituality, nightmares	Sun/Sunday
Geranium	Antidepressant, mild analgesic, calming	Courage, protection, happiness	Venus/Friday
Ginger	Strengthening, warming, stimulating	Prosperity, attracts money	Mars/Tuesday
Grapefruit	Antidepressant, antiseptic, diuretic	Purification	Mars/Tuesday
Jasmine	Uplifting, antidepressant	Love, luck, aphrodisiac	Jupiter/Thursday
Juniper	Antiseptic, diuretic, detoxifying	Protection, prevents theft	Jupiter/Thursday
Lavender	Calming, comforting, antiseptic, balancing	Love, protection	Mercury/Wednesday
Lemon	Antibacterial, sedative, digestive	Healing	Neptune/Friday
Lemongrass	Strong antiseptic, bactericide, refreshing	Psychic awareness	Venus/Friday
Lime	Antibacterial, diuretic, stimulating, refreshing	Healing, protection	Venus/Friday
Mandarin	Antispasmodic, Revitalizing, aids digestion	Cleansing	Moon/Monday
Marjoram	Sedative, Soothing, analgesic	Protective	Mercury/Wednesday
Myrrh	Stimulating, anti-inflammatory, empowering	Spirituality, healing	Jupiter/Thursday

Essential Oil	Aromatherapy and emotional uses	Magical uses	Ruling planet Day of the week
Neroli	Antidepressant, sedative, antispasmodic	Happiness and health, attracts love	Sun/Sunday
Nutmeg	Stimulating, aids digestion, warming	Psychic powers	Moon/Monday
Orange	Antidepressant, antispasmodic, uplifting	Luck, love	Sun/Sunday
Palmarosa	Stimulant, antiseptic, anti-rheumatic	Healing	Venus/Friday
Patchouli	Sedative, anti-inflammatory, calming	Love, passion, attracts money	Pluto/Saturday
Peppermint	Analgesic, expectorant, energizing	Healing	Mercury/Wednesday
Petitgrain	Sedative, digestive, nurturing	Protective, empowering	Sun/Sunday
Pine	Antiseptic, stimulant, inspiring	Spirituality, cleansing	Jupiter/Thursday
Rose	Soothing, antidepressant, inflammatory, indulgent	Love, clairvoyance	Venus/Friday
Rosemary	Stimulant, antispasmodic, astringent, awakening	Purification, love, mental power	Jupiter/Thursday
Rosewood	Stimulant, antiseptic, sedative	Physic awareness	Venus/Friday
Sage	Antispasmodic, antiseptic, astringent, balancing	Riches, cleansing, promotes wisdom	Mars/Tuesday
Sandalwood	Sedative, anti-inflammatory, stabilizing	Spirituality, manifests wishes, protection	Moon/Monday
Tea tree	Antiseptic, anti-fungal, antibacterial, purifying	Cleansing, purification	Saturn/Saturday
Thyme	Digestive, antiseptic, diuretic, energizing	Healing, prosperity	Jupiter/Thursday
Vetiver	Sedative, relaxing, grounding	Luck, prosperity	Moon/Monday
Ylang ylang	Aphrodisiac, soothing, sedative	Love, passion, peace	Venus/Friday

Bach flower remedies

Bach Flower Remedies are essences made from plants. An essence is the preserved vibrational substance – or vital life force – of the flower or plant that is used for healing and to prompt deeper levels of health and wellbeing. The essence can include a part of the plant, such as stems, leaves, roots, buds, or it can be a distillation of the whole plant. The flower or plant essences act upon the non-physical body rather than the physical body, influencing our feelings, thoughts, beliefs, and unresolved emotional traumas. Users of vibrational essences may find that, as their thoughts and emotions change, their physical symptoms will also shift.

Essences are made by first placing the appropriate part of the flower or plant in pure water. It is then left in sunlight for a period of time. This creates the "mother essence." This essence is then diluted, combined with a preservative (alcohol or glycerin), bottled and then sold for use. The clear, meditative intentions of the people making essences amplify the transfer of the plant's energies into the water.

You can purchase mother essences from health practitioners, health food shops or you could search the Internet under "Flower Essences."

How to use flower remedies

Flower essences are generally taken internally by placing two to four drops under your tongue, or by taking the same number of drops diluted in water. Taking these by mouth is the most popular method, but the essences can also be applied topically in a bath or compress. Take a remedy or a blend of remedies several times a day until you feel better.

Bach flower remedies chart
SELECTING THE RIGHT ESSENCE

There are no wrong choices. Selecting a remedy is up to you, your health adviser or practitioner. It depends on what is happening with your life or emotions. The chart on pages 170–1 lists the key qualities of each essence. In making your choice, follow your intuition or "gut feelings."

Check out the negative emotion column and see which descriptions match to how you are feeling now. The positive emotion column indicates what type of energy you can invoke by using the corresponding remedy.

Take your time going through the chart and use the far right column to tick the remedies you feel would suit you at the moment. Perhaps use a pencil so that you can reuse this table or photocopy it and have a permanent record of the different types of remedies you felt you needed at a particular time.

Most sources suggest using no more than 3–4 different essences at any one time. So, choose a maximum of four essences and keep a diary to record their effects.

Flower essence blends

When you or someone else is in distress or is experiencing an emotional spiral, whether it is because of the loss of a loved one, the experience of a life threatening accident, or the worry of facing a challenging situation, the following flower essence blends will help to soothe and balance your emotions.

* Physical and emotional shock: Bach Rescue Remedy (You can purchase this already made up, or you can blend your own remedy using Star of Bethlehem [trauma], rock rose [terror and panic], cherry plum [fear of losing control], and clematis [helps one to stay conscious].) Use this blend if you are going to the dentist, facing a job interview, going through a driving test or any other form of examination, or if you are undergoing an operation.
* Sleeping problems: Rock rose (nightmares), white chestnut (worrying thoughts), and agrimony (restlessness from repressed worries).
* Worrying about others: red chestnut (irrational anxieties), chicory (concern for others, neediness), and holly (jealousy and suspicion).

DO ESSENCES DIFFER FROM ESSENTIAL OILS?

Yes! Essences are not the same as the essential oils used in aromatherapy. Unlike essential oils, they are unscented and unflavoured. Through special preparation, an essence contains only the energetic properties of its mother essence.

Remedy	Keywords	Negative emotion before the remedy
Agrimony	Mental torment	Dislikes being alone, feeling stressed, restless at night
Aspen	Unknown fears	Unconscious anxieties and vague fears, nightmares
Beech	Intolerance	Narrow-minded, critical, judging, must have total control over a situation
Century	Weak-willed	Timid, easily imposed upon and finds it difficult to stand up for themselv
Cerato	Seeks advice	Talkative, constantly asks for advice, distrusts own judgement
Cherry plum	Breakdown	On the verge of a nervous breakdown, suicidal feelings, violent impulses
Chestnut bulb	Repeats past mistakes	Very slow to learn from life, attempts to forget unpleasant experiences
Chicory	Possessive	Over-possessive, demands respect, wants attention, uses emotional black
Clematis	Dreamer	Absent minded, preoccupied, lives in the clouds
Crab apple	Self-hatred	Feelings of despair, disgust, feels unclean
Elm	Responsibility	Overwhelmed by responsibility, temporarily doubts capabilities
Gentian	Despondency	Negative outlook, melancholy, pessimistic
Gorse	Despair	Hopelessness, depressed, no energy
Heather	Self-centredness	Self-concern, self-absorbed, poor listener
Holly	Jealousy	Hatred, envy, suspicion, greedy
Honeysuckle	Living in the past	Nostalgic, regretful, frequently feels hurt or injured
Hornbeam	Weariness	Can't cope, exhausted, feels deprived of vigour
Impatiens	Impatience	Irritable, frustrated, tells others to hurry up
Larch	Lack of confidence	Feels inferior, feels a failure
Mimulus	Fear of known things	Frightened of life, shy, very sensitive physically
Mustard	Deep gloom	Black depression, gloomy feelings, at the mercy of one's own feelings
Oak	Worn out	Despondent, hopeless, feeling overworked
Olive	Exhaustion	Deep inner tiredness, feeling washed out
Pine	Guilt	Blames self for others' mistakes, introverted, feels unworthy
Red chestnut	Overprotective	Self-sacrificing, worries about other people and their problems
Rock rose	Terror	Sudden physical or mental emergencies, naked fear or panic
Rock water	Repression	Self-denying, perfectionist, dominating
Scleranthus	Uncertainty	Indecision, extremes of emotions
Star of Bethlehem	Anguish	Mental despair, no hope or sense of peace
Vervain	Impulsive	Highly-strung, fanatical
Vine	Domineering	No respect for others, greedy, demanding
Walnut	Transitions	Unclear about life's direction, in mental torment, argumentative
Water violet	Pride	Aloof, superior, feeling withdrawn
White chestnut	Mental chatter	Keeps going over and over the problem mentally, suffers unwanted tho
Wild oak	Uncertainty	Vague notions, uncertain what to do
Wild rose	Apathy	Underlying hopelessness and sadness, chronically bored
Willow	Resentment	Blames everyone else, irritable and spreads gloom and doom

Positive emotion invoked after the remedy	Tick applicable
Cheerful, laughs at worries	
Fearlessness	
Tolerance, kind to self and others	
Self-determination, believes in themselves	
Intuitive, trusts self, acts wisely	
Calm, courageous, retains sanity	
Learns from the past and puts into action those lessons	
Concern for others, secure self, gives without expecting anything	
Grounded, realistic	
Sees things in the right perspective, harmonizing	
Capable, efficient, confident	
Unshakably confident	
Faith, hope of recovery	
Sympathetic to others, good listener	
Understanding, tolerant	
Has learned from the past, and doesn't cling to it	
Strength and courage to face the present and the future	
More relaxed and diplomatic, less hasty	
Determined, perseveres	
Under control, no irrational fears, calm	
Serenity, cheerfulness, feeling stable	
Endurance with stops along the way, strong	
Great inner strength, vitality	
Takes responsibility, shares burdens of others without taking them on	
Able to cope mentally and physically for self and then others, keeps a cool head in emergencies	
Courage	
Flexible, brings ideas to fruition	
Determination, calmness	
Strong, inner calm	
Enthuses and inspires others, calm	
Loving, wise, understanding	
Quiet, inner peace, knows direction in life	
Acts in humility, creates atmosphere of calm	
Balanced state of mind, clear headed	
Assists in making a decision	
Interested in life, inner freedom to explore life	
Optimistic, takes responsibility for actions	

Magic and Ri

What has magic and ritual got to do with the 21st century?
Well, quite a lot really, as many of us are beginning to use
magic and ritual to find a balance to all the challenges
and the hectic pace of 21st century life. We seem to be
more keen than ever to look to the past – through its folklore, mythology and magic – in search of inspiration and
meaning as we realize a lot of the "noise" and pressures
around us now are not really what life should be all about.
Magic has certainly captured our imaginations and
hearts, inspiring the creation of a dazzling array of modern charms, spells, and potions that are based mostly on
old magical traditions. This stuff really works – a new car
when the old one breaks down, an expensive holiday
after you have worked long and hard finishing a tough
project, more money in the bank account so you can finish your education...no problem! To power your magic,
however, you need some help from the Goddess, and
that's where ritual comes onto the scene as a respectful
way of seeking Her wisdom and support.

ls

The material contained in this chapter features very simple, spiritually based, earth magic. We will show you how to use magical energy to cast spells, make amulets, potions, and charms, set up ritual space, and connect your own Goddess energy with some other powerful mythological Goddesses who have been around a long while and know a thing or two!

But that's not all! You'll see that most of the stuff you will need to do magic or to set up a special Goddess ritual space will generally be ordinary objects and ingredients – stuff you usually already have around the house! This is an important point because we believe that magic is around in all things and in everything we do.

We also believe that seemingly ordinary activities, when done with love, purpose, and a sense of ritual, can create a life that becomes quite magical without trying. We would like to show you how you can bring ritual into your every day life, providing a doorway to spiritual growth and development.

So, just put the key in the door and step through into this powerful realm of magic.

Blessed be!

As is often the case when doing anything new or when going down a new path, we need a bit of guidance from others who have gone down that path before us, and magic is no exception. So, please, follow our guidelines as there are some rules and codes that all practitioners of magic need to follow.

However, feel free to change, rearrange, or substitute items and spell ingredients, such as herbs or oils, to suit you and your purpose. Don't be afraid to experiment and, above all else, keep an open mind.

Sometimes, along the way, you will meet with seemingly contradictory information. Don't panic! Examine the evidence and make a decision according to what feel is right for you. Develop and learn to trust your intuition or inner guide.

Our wish for you is to be able to receive as much from magic as we have. Just give it some time and attention, although the more you commit to magic the more you will get out of it. If you follow the guidelines of magic with wisdom and respect, magic will happen for you.

Hanging out with a Goddess:

The power of ritual

A superstitious awe has too often veiled the importance of ritual in helping us connect with our spirituality. Unfortunately, it can be seen as something far removed from the daily life of an average person, and as something that only strange people would think to engage in. But think about it! All of us perform rituals every day. Do you shower daily? Do you brush your teeth every morning? Do you make up your bed before having breakfast (now let's not go too far!)? Do you find that you do certain things to bring you luck? For instance, do you wear a favourite outfit for important meetings or dates?

Rituals to connect with our own spirituality and with the energy of a bigger source, such as the Goddess, work on similar lines. Goddess rituals, in fact, virtually all spiritual rituals, are a series of simple steps that help us move out of the tensions of everyday life and into another realm where we can hear ourselves think properly. It is also a place where we can feel at peace, balanced, and able to ask for help, advice, or simply energy to power a spell or other magical working, such as making an amulet, charm, or magical potion.

These rituals are intended to respectfully tap into the energy of the Goddess. Within a specially created and protected ritual space, you can call to the Goddess and she will appear. You may see, hear, or feel her presence, and when you do, you will be in a fabulous position to ask her questions and to allow her to help you improve problem areas in your life – for example, your health or love life.

Just ask the Goddess!

If you are interested in ritual, have we got some great Goddesses for you to meet within your special ritual space! In magic, the moon represents feminine, psychic powers. One of the most important Goddess rituals you can do to link into your own psychic power and spiritual wisdom is one that honours the Triple Goddess, each aspect honouring the passage of a woman's life, from maiden, through mother to crone.

Calling for help

How do you ask a Goddess for help with a troublesome issue? The first step is to know your Goddesses. See the Goddess chapter and do some extra reading about the Goddesses, so you can invite the right ones into your ritual space to help you with the issue you need advice about. For example, if you wish to spice up your love life, the Roman Goddess of love, Venus, or Her Greek equivalent, Aphrodite, may be your best bet. Above all else, the Goddess should be invoked with the power of positive thought, trusting that she will appear when you ask politely and respectfully for her to be present.

In the following ritual, we are going to ask the Goddess Athena to help us in resolving an argument with a friend. Athena is the messenger of the Gods, and she has the ear of all the powers that be. Asking for her help will let you connect with her wisdom, giving you an insight as to how to resolve your dispute.

Athena will ask something of you though, before she will help. This is a usual practice. In any request for the Goddesses, you will usually first need to perform a task, sometimes to show your sincerity or worthiness. In mythology, it was often a journey in search of a magical item that led to an initiation.

By going through the following initiation, you will come away with a new awareness of your situation, which will help connect you with your deeper knowledge. This initiation marks the entrance into a secret Goddess cave; it opens the door to higher learning or self-development, while marking your spiritual transformation.

First, ask yourself whether you really want to resolve your current situation. Next, write a request to the Goddess Athena asking for guidance about your dispute or about any related concerns. The request may be in the form of a prayer or a song.

Upon waking the next day, read out your request or prayer with feelings of compassion and sincerity.

Do this every morning for the next six days. That's it!

Although this is a very simple ritual, doing this on a daily basis will put you in the right frame of mind to help you listen to your inner guide, your inner Goddess. On the seventh day, take particular note of your thoughts after saying the words one final time. The Goddess Athena will help guide you along your week's journey, your initiation, teaching you to listen to a deeper wisdom about how to resolve your dispute. Follow your new thought processes to effectively resolve your issues with your friend.

What you can do with magic

Ritual is a very effective way of putting you in the right frame of mind for making magic happen in your life! So, let's have a peek at what magic is.

What is magic?

Dictionary definitions talk about magic being a "deliberated process" where you are able to make something happen without anyone seeing exactly how you were able to do it. Magic is simply a way of causing change to happen by consciously wishing for those changes to occur. Simple?

Of course, it's not quite so simple! For one thing, our thoughts can get in the way, especially those pesky negative ones. You know the ones – "Oh, I don't deserve a good relationship." "Why should I be so lucky and happy?" "I'm not worth the trouble." First off, get rid of those real quick. The only trouble is that we did take quite a long time to acquire and fine tune these negative thoughts so they tend to stick around like a bad smell.

It's important to remember that you are definitely not the only one who's got them hanging around. For centuries, people have been developing ways of crossing from the world where these negative thoughts live – known as the real world – to another space – known as the sacred ritual space – where they can get on with changing their life for the better.

THE INITIATION

An initiation is one of the most ancient of rites. It marks the psychological crossing of a threshold into new territories, knowledge and abilities. The major themes of the initiation are suffering, death and rebirth. The initiate undergoes an ordeal that is symbolic of physically dying, and is symbolically reborn as a new person possessing new knowledge.

Positive thinking
THE KEY TO POWERFUL MAGIC

Thoughts have their own form of energy. For example, if you have a lot of negative thoughts, you will attract negative energy to you. Similarly, believe it or not, if you have a lot of positive thoughts, you will attract positive energy to you.

Once you have begun to think positively, you will find that your outer life will "magically" change to reflect your inner thoughts. If you are a habitual "negative thinker," retraining yourself to think in a more positive way will take some time. Be patient, it will be worth it. Take the time to sweep that closet full of negative thoughts clean so that you can see the world with new awareness.

The first task of performing effective magic is to start reprogramming the subconscious mind to eliminate negative thoughts. This can be an ongoing task that lasts a lifetime. You must sincerely believe you can consciously cause things to happen. If you don't, you will find that it takes a whole lot longer for your magic to manifest.

Brain power
Magic is the art of blending your "thought energy," your psychic energy, and the energy of something larger than you, such as the

TAKING CARE OF THE DETAILS
Watch your thoughts; they become words.
Watch your words; they become actions.
Watch your actions; they become habits.
Watch your habits; they become characters.
Watch your character; it becomes your destiny.
Unknown

earth or the Goddess, to transform your life. Techniques, such as visualizations, affirmations, and meditations, will help you be clear and steady in your thought processes so you can effectively direct energy for the outcomes you desire. This is really what magic is all about.

Use your imagination creatively to see your goal clearly. Consciously choose to use your words in a positive manner. Create images in your mind to bring about a positive outcome, and use those images to help manifest your wishes. The more you can imagine your magical goal, the sooner it will become reality.

You will need to develop your powers of concentration for magic because part of the ritual or magical working will usually require you to retain an image or thought for some time without becoming distracted. It is important to control your thoughts and be as focused as possible when you are working magic.

Another way of making your ritual or magical working more effective is to use or channel your feelings into what you are doing. Direct these feelings into all the actions you need to perform during a ritual or magical working, such as setting up the ritual space or when speaking certain words.

Speaking from the heart

The more power and feeling you can muster when speaking during a ritual or a magical working, the stronger will be the effect. Of course, the intention of the spoken word is a vital factor in the success of magic. Incantations are words spoken, chanted, or sung within a ritual. Prayers, which are like spoken incantations, are a powerful way of attuning and communicating with the Goddess as a heartfelt expression of a request for guidance and aid.

EARTH MAGIC CAN HELP SOLVE MANY OF THE MINOR CRISES AND PROBLEMS FACING US AS INDIVIDUALS TODAY.
Scott Cunningham, *Earth Power: Techniques of Natural Magic*

Does magic really work?

A question we get asked often is, "Does magic work?" Well, what we can say? For us it has, and for many others we have worked with it has. We have had lots of letters telling us it worked for them. If in doubt, try it for yourself.

What have you got to lose?

What you can't do with magic

Magic uses very subtle energy, and without the knowledge of how it works, we could harm or upset the natural balance of the energy flow around us. Energy used for good can also be used for bad. When performing your spells, always remember the adage, "As you sow, so shall you reap." It is believed that you will be repaid three-fold for the kind of energy you send out into the world. This means that you will receive three times the good – or three times the damage – you have caused. Here are a few more universal laws that you must observe if you want to practice magic.

Harm none

It is exceptionally important that you honour all living things – including animals and birds – and harm none of them. This is the most basic rule of magic: Harm none – not you, nor your enemy. Magic is an act of love and involves bringing more love and joy into the world; there's enough hatred out there without creating more.

If you do send out hatred or curses into the world, you shall certainly attract the same energy back on yourself, and sometimes your repayment will not come in the form that you expect!

You have been warned!

This rule is very important to abide by. If you hear of people practising negative magic, such as black magic, don't be tempted. Remember that when you misuse energy, sooner or later it will come back, in multiples!

Even just threatening to hex or put a curse on someone is violating the "Harm none" rule, so be careful to not even say any words that can be seen as a curse.

Do not dominate or manipulate others

It's very important, too, that magic spells performed to attract a lover are not used to manipulate them against their wishes. We would suggest you only do love spells to ask for your highest good as well as the other person's highest good.

And if you want to use magic to help a friend or family member, ask their permission before you do, and abide by their wishes.

Setting up a special ritual space and getting your goddess altar happening

Creating an altar will keep a focal energy point for working with magic, as well as providing a special space for working magic. You can have a permanent altar, but it's best to create one as and when you need it, unless the spell or ritual requires you to leave items on the altar for a period of time.

If you don't wish to have a permanent altar on which to keep your chosen ritual tools, keep your magical goodies instead in a box so that they can retain their energy. Wrap herbs or mixtures in a cloth to protect the energy from being exposed to light or other items in box.

Before you start any ritual or magical working, it is important that you prepare and charge your tools and ingredients. There are a number of ways you can charge your magical equipment, such as bathing them in the light of the full moon or cleansing them in running water.

What's on the altar: The basic altar kit

All traditions have their own tools of the trade. The following are tools used by Wiccan practitioners. We personally use only one or two, or a combination of these, depending on the ritual. You can take out or add what you like, but it is important to have some of these items if you intend working with magic, as they help focus and build energy – two vital factors in working magic. Most tools correspond to certain elements of nature, such as earth, air, fire, and water.

Images of the Goddesses: You can place these on your altar to petition for guidance and support, or to honour them.

PROTECTIVE CHANT

Visualize a triple circle of purple-coloured light around your body while chanting the following words to invoke a sense of safety around you.

I am protected by your light O gracious Goddess, day and night.

....

Another version to chant is: Thrice around the circle's bound Evil sink into the ground.

A coloured cloth: Used to both cover the altar and to add power to the magic that is being performed, each colour has a specific magical purpose (see the chart later in this chapter).

A grimoire: A book that can be used to record rules, spells, magical techniques, and the meaning of different herbs and crystals.

An athame: A magical knife that has a black or dark-coloured handle to absorb power and a dull and double-edged blade (this tool corresponds with the element of air).

A wand: Used to direct energy to a particular spot (this tool corresponds with the element of fire).

Sticks of incense and an incense holder or a small bowl to contain herbs and resins for burning.

A cup: To contain water used for purification within your ritual space, or wine, depending on the ritual (this tool corresponds with the element of water).

A measure of salt: Used to purify a space for ritual and to protect the space from negative psychic energy.

Candles of different colours, stable candleholders, as well as a candle snuff to extinguish the flame after you have finished your ritual or magical working.

A pentacle: A five-pointed star used mainly by Wiccans for protection. The five points on the pentacle represent the spirit and each of the four elements: earth, air, fire, and water (in a ritual situation, this tool corresponds with the element of earth).

A bell: Used within a specific part of a ritual to call for support or in recognition of the words being spoken or after the recitation of a particular incantation.

A broom: Often used to purify the space before a circle is cast. To make a witches broom, it is suggested that you use an ash staff, birch twigs, and willow binding – ash is protective, birch is cleansing, and willow is sacred to the Goddess.

Optional extras for special magical workings

Here is a list of objects you can get for special magical workings when you're preparing to cast a spell or making some magical objects or potions. Feel free to add to the following rudimentary list as the need arises.

* Bowls: Used to hold herbs or other magical items.
* A selection of appropriate crystals: Used to ground, protect or energize a ritual.
* A selection of appropriate herbs and essential oils: Used to attract or

protect certain energies during a ritual or spell.
* Mortar and pestle: Used to grind herbs.
* A cauldron (black lead pot that can withstand heat), which can be used for burning objects or substances.
* A selection of jars and bottles: To store herbs and oils once they are charged with positive energy during a ritual or a magical working.
* A selection of differently coloured pouches: Small bags that can be used for spells and charms.

Taking care of your magical tools

Don't forget to put your tools of magic away in a special box each time you finish your ritual or magical working, taking special care to keep them clean and pure. As you do more and more ritual or magical work, you will find that your tools will become an extension or expression of your magic.

Easy set up rules for a goddess ritual

When deciding to do a ritual, think about where you would like to do it. This can be your bedroom, a park, or a nature retreat. This ritual space need not be permanent – it only needs to last as long as the ritual itself.

As you need to concentrate on what you are doing, it is important that you should choose a place where you will not be disturbed. Once you have chosen that ideal spot, remove anything from that space that may distract you. Let anyone who may interrupt you during your ritual know that you do not wish to be disturbed for a while. If you are interrupted once you have begun a ritual, the psychic power you have built up will be dissipated quite drastically and you may end up feeling ungrounded and jittery.

It is essential that you choose a spot where you feel safe and that it is a space with, preferably, some contact with the natural world. As often as possible, perform your rituals out of doors, such as by the sea or in the mountains.

Once you have found just the right place, set up your altar and gather the ingredients and tools you will need for the work.

WOMEN CONNECT WITH THE GODDESS THROUGH RITUALS, CELEBRATING THE GODDESS AND THEMSELVES.

Next, you will need to prepare yourself, both mentally and physically. Whatever you do, don't perform rituals or spells when you are feeling unwell, angry or emotionally upset. Also, don't do it if you are under the influence of any form of drugs, including alcohol.

Getting ready for the ritual

There are several things you need to do to properly prepare yourself before doing a ritual or magical working. So that you can really concentrate your energy and heighten your psychic awareness for the ritual, consider fasting for a few hours before the ritual as a form of body purification.

Just before the ritual, cleanse your body by taking a bath or shower. You can use herbs or soaps with essential oils that correspond with the purpose of your ritual. If you are doing a Moon Goddess ritual, use white soap, or if you are doing a ritual with a love Goddess, like Venus, use a cake of soap or shower gel that is rose scented. You could even sprinkle the floor of your shower or the water of your bath with the appropriate herbs or with the petals of a rose!

When you get out of the bath or shower, wear clothing made only from natural fibres. If you prefer, you can skip getting dressed and go skyclad (nude) into your ritual space. Whether you are clothed or not, it is advisable not to put back on any jewellery or your watch.

When you feel ready, walk into your ritual space or sit in another area where you feel safe and take some time out to meditate. Concentrate on your breathing, making sure that it is rhythmic and deep, and aim for feeling calm, balanced, and totally present within your body. You will find that you get the most out of your ritual or magical working if you are in this state of mind.

The power of the circle

Remember to use protection

Once you have gathered your tools and ingredients, prepared your space, cleansed your body, and calmed your mind, stand in the middle of your ritual space and cast a circle that encompasses your altar and is large enough so that you can move freely around in it.

To cast a circle, hold up your hands to raise energy from your body, close your eyes, and call out in a loud voice:

I cast this magical circle for creating my wishes.
I invite the Goddess to be here.

Draw to me only those energies that work with love and light!
Let all other energies be gone.
So mote it be.

While you say these words, imagine a white light wrapping itself around your body and the altar, moving in a circular motion.

Energy kicked up in a magical circle is very powerful and, as you want this energy to be concentrated, this circle will help contain the energy. This circle will also protect you from any negativity while you are doing the ritual. If done right, a cast circle can block any unwanted influences and keep you safe from being disturbed.

Always cast a circle before each ritual and close the circle when you are finished. To close a circle, say the following words:

Thank you Goddess for being present.
Hail you and farewell.
Blessed be.

Imagine that the white light is closing in into the centre of the circle and that it is flowing out of sight down into the earth.

The basic ritual

Designing your very own rituals

It can be very empowering to design a ritual for yourself. There may be a number of valid reasons for you to get on and do a ritual. You may have a goal, such as improving your relationships or doing a spell to attract a new lover. A ritual can also be tailored for a particular purpose, like celebrating an event or achievement. A ritual can also be extremely helpful in giving you a chance to remove yourself temporarily from the hustle and bustle of everyday life – very important stuff to keep us sane!

You will need to choose which Goddess you would like to invoke during your ritual. What is the first name that pops into your head? What do you know about her? Read up about your chosen Goddess. Goddesses usually have symbols, semiprecious stones, coloured candles, bells, or other special magical objects attributed to them with which you can decorate your ritual space to make her feel welcome.

Use your intuition as to what you want to use as a magical tool or object for your ritual. If you feel wrong about a certain stone or other object in your ritual space, even if a hundred books say it is fine and right, get rid of it. You are Goddess of your own ritual space!

Next you need to choose what words or invocations you are going to say during the ritual. Words are a very powerful way of invoking your chosen Goddess and will work by themselves – for example, you could recite poetry that fits with your chosen Goddess – as long as you speak the words with sincerity and with a strong belief in what you are saying.

Ritual is not a matter of simply following instructions such as, "light three sticks of sandalwood incense and one blue candle." The real power of ritual comes from what you bring to it in terms of your feelings and the objects that you have gathered in your ritual space or altar.

If you notice a particular stone when you are in the process of designing your ritual, and it seems to "speak" to you in some way or is a reminder or symbol of the Goddess or the purpose of your magical working, pick it up and incorporate it into your ritual. Alternatively, you may just simply hold it in your hand as you are doing your pre-ritual meditation.

If you are doing a ritual for a specific purpose, include everyday objects on the altar as a symbol of success or encouragement. For example, if you are looking for strength and courage in a new business venture, try placing a business card on the altar as you do the ritual.

For a ritual designed to remove an emotion, influence, or person from your life, try writing the name or an appropriate word on a slip of paper, then concentrate all your feelings, worries, and temptations onto it. Incorporate the action of burning this piece of paper into your ritual and watch the connection between you float away with the smoke.

Take some time to design and carry out a ritual, no matter how short or "trivial" it may seem to you. In fact, just have some fun with it, as long as your actions and words are meaningful to you. Doing a ritual does not need to be serious to be effective. Sometimes, the more you laugh and feel relaxed in your ritual space, the more powerful is the energy you are channeling into the ritual.

After a couple of rituals, you may find that you are doing some of the same things to set up your ritual space and to get mentally or physically ready for your ritual or magical working. Perhaps you always wear a specific piece of clothing, always begin with a certain short prayer or invocation, or always include a special coloured candle. Take notice of these constants as they may be helping you to enter into the right "ritual mind frame."

Special moon Goddess rituals

The moon and Goddess energy have been inextricably linked for centuries. The important phases of womanhood – maid, mother and crone – are even believed to correspond with the three main phases of the moon – new or waxing, full and waning, or dark – respectively.

Rituals can be designed to honour the Goddess as a young maiden, mother, or crone during the appropriate phase of the moon. These rituals are powerful ways of tapping into the energy of the Goddess at a particular transition through the night sky. So, what rituals should you do at a particular time of the month? Let's take a look!

Maiden Goddess energy at new or waxing moon: The new or waxing moon corresponds with energy of the Goddess as a young maiden.

Maiden Goddesses include Athena and Persephone.

The Goddess in this phase holds the promise of new beginnings, of regaining or understanding the urges of youth, of excitement, and carefree erotic freedom, being willing and able to explore new ideas and concepts. She is innocent in some ways, but she is also a seductress who recognizes the power of her sexuality.

Do a ritual during this phase of the moon if you feel that life has lost some of its magic or if you want to expand your awareness.

Mother Goddess energy at full moon: The full moon is when the moon's psychic energy is at the height of its strength and power, radiating the Goddess's mature, creative power. Mother Goddesses include Demeter, Ishtar, Isis, and Lakshmi. The mother Goddess radiates your creativity, power, and a sense of empowerment from within, at full strength during the phase of the full moon. The full moon symbolizes a period when a woman reaches the peak of her creativity and fertility.

There is a ritual called "Drawing down the moon" (see below), which helps to capture these energies for projects, love, or success, and when you need that extra boost of energy to get what you want. In this ritual, you feel as if you are connecting with the light of the full moon and anchoring the energy that the light brings within your soul. A woman who does this kind of ritual empowers herself like with no other ritual.

Full moon rituals are as powerful done alone as they are in a group. However, you need to feel safe and comfortable if you are doing these rituals in a group.

Crone Goddess energy at waning or dark moon: The waning or dark moon phase corresponds with the energy of the Goddess in the guise of the crone, an archetypal wise old woman who has experience and compassion, as well as the profound understanding to enjoy her accumulated wisdom about life and death. She is the gateway to rebirth. Crone Goddesses include Hera and Hecate. Waning or dark moon rituals are best conducted to help you make an end to an unwanted relationship or to get rid of any emotional hurts.

Tapping into the power of the Triple Moon Goddess: In many magical traditions, there is a belief in the Great Goddess, the most powerful form of female psychic energy. This form of energy is often also referred to as the Triple Goddess, who is the total sum of the psychic energies of the maiden, the mother, and the crone, and is usually invoked during the full moon. Working with these three aspects of the Goddess, you can connect with the phase you are in. You may be young but have the crone energy; you may feel old and need the energy of the maiden. We live in a world that has taken away some part of our birthright to be in the right phase for our soul. Use moon rituals to help reconnect you with the right female psychic energy for you.

The Triple Goddess is a loving presence that waits and watches while you feel her energy – it's like knowing when you are going to bleed. Sometimes when you have had some troubling experiences and the pressure of your outside world is getting to you, you may sense the pull of the light of the full moon. This sensation is the Triple Goddess tapping on your shoulder, asking for you to reconnect with her. Try out the following ritual, called "Drawing down the moon," by invoking the Triple Goddess to help you reconnect with a strong female psychic energy.

You can do this ritual either by yourself or gather together a group of close friends. If you are going to do this ritual with some friends, you will all need to feel a sense of alignment with each other before starting. Take some time out to feel centred around each other and to talk about what's been happening in your lives, perhaps sharing the reasons that have led you, will help you feel the need to reconnect with your psychic energies. This will help you collectively join your energies in preparation for the ritual.

When doing this ritual in a group, you must also keep a balance between giving all your energy as a group towards the purpose of the ritual and getting the energy back from the Triple Goddess as an individual. When you do receive this energy, let it permeate through your body and soul. Do not be tempted to expend the energy quickly – relish it and let it nurture you.

Drawing down the Moon: On the evening of the full moon, follow the instructions in this chapter to set up your ritual space and prepare your mind and body for the ritual. Do not have any alcohol before the ritual and do not eat anything until the ritual is finished. Gather together three bells and place them on an altar. If doing this ritual in a group, preferably with three or more friends, work on consciously feeling that your energies are connecting together. Also keep focused on the fact that you want to call in the Triple Goddess in her three guises as maid, mother, and crone. Choose among yourselves who would like to work with what aspect of the Triple Goddess. Read what each aspect represents and make your choice. Also choose who should lead the ritual and which three people should ring the bells.

When you feel ready to start, stand or sit in a circle holding hands. Cast a protective light around you and the space and feel the noises and worries of the outside world melt away.

Focus all of your energy into your intention of calling in the Triple Goddess. The person who is leading the ritual will call the Goddess by chanting the following words or invocation three times (repeated by the others in the ritual):

O Glorious Goddess, maiden, mother, crone,
You that has created all that is,
The silver one that restores our lives,
Help us to pull your energy into the circle,
So we can be guided by your wisdom,
Blessed be.

At the end of each recitation, three people should chime their bell.

By chanting these words you are raising power to connect with the Triple Goddess. Keep holding hands (except when you need to ring a bell!) and walk around inside the circle in a clockwise direction. Keep holding hands until it feels right to stop. This may indicate that the energy you are generating through movement, chanting, and intention is reaching its height.

Feel this energy within your protected circle and pull it into your bodies. Experience the energy and sense whether it is bringing you any messages or insights from the Goddess, which you can later use to create changes in your life. Let this wonderful feeling soak in.

When you are ready, close the circle by thanking the Goddess and all should give their thanks, saying:

*Thank you for touching my life and allowing me to live
   my full potential.
And so it is.*

After you have finished the ritual, remain silent for about five minutes before you all share what your experience was like. This will give you some time to process your thoughts and feelings. These experiences will be different for each person – some may not get much at all and some may feel that they have received an invaluable insight that will help them feel more attuned with themselves. It's OK no matter what happens – everything is perfect.

When to do what type of ritual or magical work

There are many types of rituals for you to try, depending on what you want to achieve. Here is a great rituals' chart to help you work out what day of the week and during what moon phase you should consider doing a particular ritual. The table also lists the colour of fabric you should use as either an altar cloth or as a garment specially worn for the ritual. Colour is a particularly potent way of attracting or repelling certain forms of energy, and it helps heighten the energies you're working with.

Colour Material	Meaning	Days to charge	Moon Phases
Orange	Legal matters, success, attraction	Tuesday, Wednesday	Waning
Blue	Protection, healing, compassion	Monday, Sunday	Any time
Pink	Emotional love, overcoming anger	Friday, Saturday	Eve of full moon
Green	Luck, fertility, healing	Tuesday	Waning
White	Truth, halting gossip, breaking a curse	Any day	Waxing
Yellow	Friendship, wisdom, happiness	Any day	Any time
Purple	Wealth, power, strengthens willpower	Tuesday, Thursday	Full moon
Red	Passion, sensual love, courage	Friday, Saturday	Eve of full moon or full moon
Black	Absorption, destruction of negativity	Friday	Full moon and waning

Moon Goddess amulets

This moon Goddess ritual involves making and charging an amulet to heal a broken heart. Do it during the phase of the waning moon. Gather together the following items:

* White (or silver-coloured?) craft clay
* 2 drops of peppermint oil
* A silver-coloured altar cloth
* Three white candles and holders
* A handful of angelica and basil
* A small bottle or container of bergamot oil
* 2 drops of clove oil
* A sharp pin
* A small bowl of spring water.

You may want to celebrate the Triple Goddess energy through dance – as she has often been worshipped in dance since ancient times. Incorporate some dancing during your full moon ritual to help generate energy or during rituals celebrating the eight seasonal festivals of the year, such as the winter and summer solstices and the spring and autumn equinoxes.

Fashion the craft clay into the shape of the full moon. Sprinkle it with the peppermint oil and let this amulet dry overnight, bathed in the light of the moon.

Prepare an altar by placing the silver cloth over a stable surface. Arrange the candles in a triangle on top. Sprinkle the herbs on the altar, and position the oils, pin, bowl of water, and moon amulet on the altar so that they are easy to reach.

Hold each candle and anoint it with bergamot oil, focusing on your intention to release the pain of your broken heart. Allowing forgiveness to fill you, carve the symbol of a fish into each candle with your sharp pin.

Once you have completed anointing the candles, place them into the holders and light each one as you recite the following words.

Allow my heart forgiveness, releasing all pain,
Cast out fear and grant me peace.
So mote it be.

Now take the moon amulet and pass it through the flame of all three candles, remembering to keep focus on your intention to release your pain. Sprinkle it with water, while reciting:

I wash away and purify my soul.

Hold the amulet against your heart and sit quietly for a short time. Carry the amulet with you until your heart feels whole again. When you need to top up the energy of the amulet and its healing powers, sprinkle it with two drops of bergamot oil and two drops of clove oil.

Goddess charms

Pouches, caches, and charms have been used in most magical work for centuries and are possibly the most popular form of folk magic. Known as wanga, gris-gris, mojo bags, or putsi-pockets, these bags are found in all cultures around the world. They are stuffed with various empowering ingredients – herbs, feathers, spices, barks, and crystals – that bring health, luck, protection, or any other desire.

These charms were either worn by the maker or given as gifts to others. They were also positioned in a prominent place in a room or home so that they could be seen on a regular basis.

You can make your own personal lucky charm by first getting a square of silk, leather, or fabric woven from natural fibres, measuring about 15 cm x 15 cm (6 inches x 6 inches). The bag must be large enough to hold a few items. Also choose the colour of the fabric so that it will heighten the energies you want to harness (see the rituals chart earlier in this chapter).

Use the symbols chart below to select the most appropriate items for your purpose. Combine the various ingredients together and, as you do, stay focused on your purpose – for example, love, luck, health. Fasten the bag very tightly with string or ribbon in order to keep the contents from falling out. Make sure, however, you can easily untie the bag so that, if you wish, you may refresh the charm by sprinkling a few drops of essential oil onto the contents.

To make the pouch yours, sit quietly and focus your mind on your wish or intention, making it as real as possible. Hold the pouch in your hands and bring it up to your nose to smell it. Do this daily, or as many times as you need, or until your wish is fulfilled.

Type of Charm	Luck	Success	Money
Colour	Green, purple	Orange, yellow	Green, purple
Crystal	Jade	Citrine	Aventurine
Symbol	Four leaf clover, dice, butterfly	Star, bee, dragonfly, ladder	Gold coins, star, keys, wheat
Herbs	Basil, mustard seeds, anise, holly, corn, nutmeg	Cinnamon, Irish moss, vervain leaves, poppy seeds	Echinacea, coltsfoot, allspice, bergamot, jasmine cinnamon, dill, mint
Essential Oils	Ginger, rosemary, lemon, orange	Cinnamon, rosemary, bergamot, chamomile, clove, ginger, orange, patchouli, jasmine	Clove, nutmeg, thyme, vetiver, bay, pine, sage, peppermint

Symbols

Symbols add a new energy to your charm. The symbols opposite are the most common, but they are only a very small representation of what can be used. Symbols can be drawn on paper, be the real item, or be made out of clay – use your imagination. Another way to bring a symbol into your life would be to look through old magazines and find pictures symbolizing your wishes.

Artemis protection charm

Prepare your altar, ritual space, as well as your mind and body, and when ready gather the following ingredients in a cane basket or a cloth bag. (If using a cloth, place ingredients in the centre of the cloth, lift its corners to make a ball shape and tie the cord around the ball as tightly as you can.)

* A small packet of powdered ginger
* A handful of rose petals
* 3 drops of sandalwood oil
* 3 drops of geranium oil
* A pinch of orange peel
* A piece of purple cloth, 20 cm (8 inches) square
* A length of blue cord, about 15 cm (6 inches) long.

In order to activate the magic of this charm, wait until the moon is full and bright. Take the ingredients in the cane basket or a cloth bag with you as you go for a walk in nature. Find a safe "power place," such as under a friendly tree, and cast a protective circle of energy around you. Sit within this circle with your basket or bag for a while, meditating on the moon.

REMEMBER, THE MOST POWERFUL CHARMS ARE THE ONES WE CREATE OURSELVES.

Gather your power and, when you feel ready, spread out the cloth and create the charm by adding the ingredients to the cloth one by one. Focus on charging your charm by channelling your energy and intention into each ingredient. Draw up the corners of the cloth to make a ball in the centre, and then wrap the cord tightly to securely enclose the charm ingredients.

Take the charm in both hands and feel it emanating a magical, shimmering energy. Visualize a mist surrounding you, moving in and out of the charm. Focus all your energy on the protection you need. Hold the charm to your solar plexus and sit for a while taking in the energy of the charm. As you do this, clearly ask Artemis for her strength and protection.

Finish with closing in the mist around you and the charm. Keep the charm with you or place it in your home, car, or bedroom.

Ishtar prosperity charm

During the phase of the waxing or full moon, prepare your altar, ritual space, as well as your mind and body, and when ready gather the following ingredients:

* A pinch of mustard seed, dill, clove, fennel, sage
* Two small bowls
* A couple of drops of cinnamon, orange, and patchouli oil
* A green candle and a holder (and some matches)
* A green cloth as big as your hand
* A piece of parchment
* A coin (preferably one that is gold coloured)
* A small piece of citrine
* A piece of gold-coloured string.

Mix all the herbs in one bowl and all the oils in another bowl. Place the bowls and other ingredients around you or on your altar, so that they are close at hand. Sit quietly nearby and focus on raising your energy to empower your charm. Call in Ishtar, reciting loud and strong:

Ishtar, Goddess of wealth and prosperity,
I call you here to witness my wish.
Blessed be.

Then upon the candle carve a pound symbol, your initials, and your astrological symbol. Next, anoint the candle with the oil mix. Spread out the cloth and sprinkle the herb mix onto it. Take the anointed candle and gently roll the candle in the herbs, keeping your focus on your wish for wealth and prosperity. Place the candle in the holder and light it, reciting:

May the spirit of Ishtar burn bright,
May my wish always have firm foundation,
Goddess Ishtar, I need no jewels, nor bags of gold,
But may my purse or bank account have enough to behold.
Blessed be.

Gaze into the candle flame, breathe deeply and evenly, and write your wish on the parchment. Fold the paper into three, place it on the cloth and add the coin and crystal. Bind it all together with the gold cord, wrapping the cord around the bundle three times while focusing on your wish. Keep the charm with you until your wish is fulfilled.

Remember to hold, squeeze, and smell your charm periodically to remind you of your wish and it will soon be granted.

May the Goddess Ishtar smile upon you!

Quick money charm

During the phase of the waxing or full moon, prepare your altar, ritual space, as well as your mind and body. While focusing your intention on getting money fast, place a piece of green cloth, approximately 20 cm (8 inches) square on your altar. In the middle of the cloth position a small picture of a star and then sprinkle the following ingredients onto the picture.

* A couple of bay leaves
* A pinch of powdered cinnamon and nutmeg

Next, slowly add nine drops of patchouli oil, seven drops of vetiver oil and three drops of clove oil drop by drop. With each drop say the following chant:

Money green, money mine,
Send to me quick fast money.
And so it is.

Collect the corners of the bag together and wrap a length of green ribbon, about 10 cm (4 inches) long around it three times to make a pouch while repeating the above chant. Hold the charm to your heart and take a deep breath, squeezing, and smelling the bag.

JELENA ONCE USED THIS QUICK MONEY CHARM AND IT WORKED WONDERS. WITHIN A WEEK, SHE HAD THE MONEY SHE NEEDED!

Special Goddess spells

Athena "Protection" spell

This powerful spell can be performed during the phase of the waning moon. Find a place that you can leave untouched, not disturbed for three days. Set up this space for ritual as usual, focusing on the purpose of your spell. Continue focusing on the purpose of your spell as you prepare yourself for ritual, and as you gather the following ingredients:

* A stick of sandalwood incense
* 8 black candles and holders (and matches)
* ½ cup of sea salt
* A pinch of powdered thyme.

Cast a protective circle of energy around you and light the incense. Arrange the eight candleholders in a circle. Hold the candles between the palms of your hands, directing all of your intention into the candles. When you feel that the candles are charged, place them in their holders, and sprinkle salt around the holders. Light the candles, reciting out loud the following words:

Athena, I call you to witness this flame, the flame of protection,
Let your protective light shine on me at all times, banishing all
    negative energy.
Blessed be.

Sit quietly watching the flame of the candles for a few moments, then visualize blue light surrounding you. As the candles burn, know or feel that they are burning away any negative energy floating around you.

When the candles have burned one-third of the way down, snuff them out while reciting the following words:

Extinguished – all evil, negativity, and harm.

Repeat this ritual for two more nights. On the last night, after the candles have burned away to almost nothing, bury their remains with the sprinkling of thyme somewhere where they will not be disturbed.

Demeter "New Project" spell

Begin this spell during the phase of the waxing moon. Prepare yourself and your chosen space as usual for a ritual and get a sprouted grain, such as wheat, to cast this special spell to encourage the success of a new project. Hold the shoot of grain in your hand above your head and recite the following poem:

Life continues to be fruitful in a world that is ever being
    penetrated by all forms of death.
Goddess Demeter, who bears such great gifts,
Who brings the seasons,

Sovereign, Doe,
You and your beautiful daughter, Persephone,
Be kind, and, in exchange for my poem,
Give me the courage to bring new energy into my life that my soul
  wants and needs.

Place the wheat on your altar until the next full moon. Then bury or burn the grain to allow the energy to return to the ground.

Kali "Letting Go" spell

Use this spell to ward off the evil eye, to dissipate any negative energy directed at you, or to cut the ties that bind you to a particular person or emotion. Do this spell during the phase of the waning moon, finding a ritual space outside preferably and near a body of water. Prepare yourself and your space as usual for the ritual and gather the following ingredients, placing them on the altar:

* A piece of paper and a pen
* 3 drops of sage oil
* A small piece of obsidian.

Draw a pentagram on the paper and stand on it with your hands above your head, calling Goddess Kali in a loud strong voice, saying or singing the following words:

Goddess Kali, I petition you,
The Goddess of destruction and regeneration,
Please help cut these ties that bind me to —
  [say the name of the person or object you want to let go of].
May this be done with love and compassion.
So it is.

Sprinkle the oil on the earth around you and hold the crystal in your left hand. Visualize that you are draining the energy you hold about this person or issue into the stone.

When you feel ready, close down the circle, carry the stone to the edge of the river, lake, or sea and throw it in as far away from you as possible. The water will cleanse the emotions from the stone so that it will sink harmlessly to the bottom.

Thank the Goddess for her help and leave an offering to the earth for absorbing your negative energy – a piece of hair or a crystal of your choice are good examples of an offering.

Perfect potions and scented oils

Make your own "luck oil"

Measure out three drops of the following essential oils for every 15 ml of base oil, such as olive oil, and store in a clean, decorative bottle.

* Ginger
* Basil
* Thyme
* Anise
* Mint

Sprinkle a few drops of this mixture on your pen before an exam, add a few drops to a CV, a tax return, or a loan application, and good luck should come your way.

Comfort potion

To make a potion that brings a sense of comfort and peace, gather together the following ingredients and add them in a bowl:

* ½ cup of rock salt
* 1 cup of Epsom salts
* A few pieces of lemon peel
* A couple of lavender spikes
* 2 drops of lemon oil
* 2 drops of lavender oil
* Red and blue food dyes

Mix these ingredients in the bowl and put the mixture into your bath or into small sachets that can be hung over your bed or placed on your desk, if you study or work at one.

Spice up your love life potion

In a bowl, measure out the following ingredients:

* 1 cup of Epsom salts
* 3 drops of tangerine oil
* 3 drops of grapefruit oil
* 3 drops of lime oil.

Mix the ingredients together and use the mixture to add a fragrant touch to a bath, which you may take before going out on that special date.

Table of scented oils

Potions and scented oils have been used since antiquity, and have a very powerful way of attracting certain energies to the wearer. Some of these blends may not be pleasant-smelling, but they are still able to attract a particular type of energy that you may desire to have around you.

LOVE POTION	HAPPINESS POTION	FRIENDSHIP POTION	BROKEN HEART POTION
Rose oil, ylang ylang, black pepper, orange, jasmine, patchouli, ginger	Lime, grapefruit, bergamot, lavender, neroli, geranium, rosemary, basil	Lavender, orange, lemon, cedarwood, sandalwood, frankincense, peppermint	Neroli, bergamot, grapefruit, Roman chamomile, marjoram, sandalwood, rose, cypress, myrrh

Chakras and /

The pure light in a moment
of awareness in your mind is
the Buddha's essence within you.

ZEN MASTER LINJI

ras

The conscious (cosmic) Goddess

We talk a lot about energy throughout this book and the various ways that you can hook into and transmute it to effect change in yourself and in your life. This chapter is for the Goddess who wishes to understand the energy connection between her material (physical) self and her spiritual self. You are, quite simply, a body at work – and on all levels at that. And you're going to have to get into your body to really get into this chapter! We believe that as humans we exist materially and spiritually simultaneously. The chakra and the aura energy systems, and our own physical bodies are the key to this coexistence on the material and spiritual planes. They are there-fore the key to healing any dis-ease or lack of ease which exists between our mind, body, and spirit.

These energy "systems" are the critical links or portals, between your physical body and "consciousness." Now, consciousness may sound a bit "out there" as a concept but it is an important idea to consider. Consciousness has been described as the ultimate aware-ness or enlightenment and it's what advanced practitioners of medi-tation (such as Buddhist monks, Sufis, and other spiritual "seekers") are pursuing when they spend hours, days, or even decades in con-templation and in just "being." Consciousness as such is that which is beyond thought or logical comprehension and this is why the aim of any meditation practice is to transcend or rise above thoughts you are aware of. Consciousness is the great leveller of all that is human and it serves to remind each of us that we are all a part of some-thing infinite and far greater than our individual selves.

Being in line with consciousness or universal energy is what we believe we have been sent here to do and the first place to start is with our own energy fields. We need to get those nicely balanced – in alignment – and get on track and on purpose to be able to devel-op our full potential and express our true essence.

Above all, remember: You are a potent energy centre on each level – mind, body, and soul – and once you come to grips with this, both in a theoretical and practical sense, you will understand what it truly means to be a Goddess.

Goddess – heal thyself

Hinduism is an ancient religion and philosophy which has given many gifts to humanity, both spiritual and material in nature. The Hindu chakra system is one such gift and can be described as the energy system at work in and around the body. "Chakra" is a Sanskrit word (from the old Indian language which is preserved in literature, but is extinct) meaning "wheel of light." We all originally came from light, and these wheels are our own personal connection to the ultimate light source, the Divine Source. Philosopher and psychologist, Carl Jung, referred to the chakras as "gateways to consciousness," and he believed that through them a person could communicate with the Universe and receive cosmic energies in return. This is consistent with the Hindu belief.

Chakras are the energy centres in the "auric" or "etheric" body that are linked to the physical body of each person. You can think of it as you having a cosmic form of your own physical body that is purely energy and, invisible though it may be, it emanates and resonates with every thought, action, and reaction. The simplest way to view it is perhaps, ironically, scientifically: we are matter and all matter is energy (according to Newton's theory), and accordingly we are energy. And, as individual energy sources, we therefore each "vibrate" at different levels.

The chakras are the focal energy points which vibrate at a particular frequency. Each chakra emanates a corresponding colour and each is connected to corresponding organs in the body. In turn these are connected to a correlating energy band on the aura. If this concept is kind of hard to get your head around, think of it as the energy that's given off by the organs as they function, the way food gives off an aroma whilst it's being cooked. Like wheels, the chakras "spin" in a constant rotation, reflecting an energy that is constantly, in effect, from the body.

The chakras form one line from the crown chakra to the base chakra in line with your spine (see illustration on page 204). They can literally "spin out" too, and this is when some fine-tuning or rebalancing is necessary to bring them back into alignment. We list below the directions for massage for both males and females so you'll be able to rebalance yourself – or your best friend! Goddess energy that is balanced has all of the chakras, vital body organs and aura bands in perfect harmony and alignment.

One technique to begin tuning into your own energy field is to really become aware how you feel energetically when you are with another person or how you feel when you go to a particular place.

It's especially handy if you're going for a job interview or some situation where you're either meeting people for the first time or you enter a new environment for the first time. The contrast with this and how you usually feel, say, when you're just at home, or visiting a friend's home, or a place you feel familiar, will heighten your conscious understanding of your own subtle energy field.

Sometimes you meet someone and their energy positively goes "zing!" or the complete opposite happens – you feel uncomfortable or you instantly feel the need to withdraw. This is when you (and your energy field) have crashed up against someone else's energy field, which is either drawing you in, or repelling you. This also explains why you just "click" with someone the instant you meet them or, conversely, you may experience an instant dislike of someone without even knowing them. You have a karmic energy connection with them and this probably means there are lessons for each of you. Now you can understand why that guy in IT just doesn't mesh with your vibe – it's an energy thing! And, sometimes, someone whose energy previously used to be very "in sync" with yours, is suddenly putting out a different vibration or frequency. This can be particularly uncomfortable, especially if it's your boss, best friend or boyfriend! You can't help it. You'll just have to accept that, for better or worse, the vibe has simply changed and the whole energy of the situation or relationship is no longer the same – and adapt accordingly. The question to ask here – and you will need to be brutally honest with yourself in order to feel the true answer – is it my stuff or theirs?

Don't be confused – these are great signs to pay attention to, for you are instinctively picking up on the energy field, which may or may not mesh with yours. You may not be meant to "go there!" Your energy field is therefore a frontline tool in your daily life as it can direct you to where you need to go to fulfil your own destiny.

In other words: Don't repress it – address it!

Auras – light up your life!

Auras are the bands of light surrounding all living things. The aura in humans is an electromagnetic field, which is seen by certain people who have a developed psychic or clairvoyant ability. This field is seen in the form of coloured rays radiating from the spine. The word "aura" has its origins in Latin and means "breath of air." The dictionary definition is "a subtle emanation proceeding from a body and surrounding it as an atmosphere." Sometimes your aura may only be sensed by you or felt by others, but on occasion (and some say with practice) it can be seen.

The auric field consists of coloured bands matching those of the chakra system. As each chakra has a related colour, so too does the auric band. Colour can also be used as a healing tool and as part of chakra therapy. Later in the chapter we will discuss the way colour can alert you to potential or actual imbalances in your chakra system and how you can then use certain colours to restore harmony and wellbeing. Properly understood and then tuned into, chakras and their related auras can be extremely potent healing devices, for they are the energy centres that relate directly to our physical, mental, and emotional states. They are the key to our "wellness" and its counterpart – illness. They can be used for the diagnosis and recovery of all sorts of emotional and physical blockages.

You need to tune into your own auric field to protect yourself from being too "open" and, therefore, vulnerable to energy "attacks" by people who don't have any sense of boundaries. You will intuitively sense when you've been too expansive or, conversely, too restricted with your aura. And learning to adjust your aura is part of the process of tuning in energetically to your own levels – you need to acknowledge when you're depleted, when you've got energy to spare and so on. The lessons are sometimes hard won and it can be a painful learning process if you're not conscious of what's happening or what's going on around you energy-wise. Being either unaware of your own energy field, or just plain being in denial of what it is and the effects it has on you physically, can lead to imbalance in the short term and even illness if the imbalance continues long term.

One of the differences between Eastern and Western medicine is that the West has traditionally focused only on the (largely observable) physical symptoms of the physical body in the context of "illness" or "dis-ease." Holistic medicine is that which looks at the whole person and everything that is going on for them which may have caused the illness or dis-ease in the first place. Dis-ease is, literally, a lack of ease or harmony, and energy flow has been affected in some way. The East – and indeed many indigenous cultures throughout the world (such as Native American, indigenous Australian, African, and Mayan cultures among others) – have traditionally treated the person holistically. This can mean their lifestyle, family, and even their entire village can be involved in an individual's healing therapy. It's not just about a specific body part of an individual, it more interestingly becomes what this individual's illness or dis-ease really represents as a symptom of the greater, wider picture. This is the mind, body, spirit approach to individual and collective healing which we believe is the future.

It's an intuitive thing too. Often we instinctively know what's causing our physical problems but we lack the necessary knowledge or the courage to work on the source directly. The trick is to work with the chakras, which basically allow you to plumb your own subconscious and get to the root of the issue or whatever it is that's blocking you and preventing you from reaching your full glory. So it's not just physical: true healing has to be mental and spiritual as well ...

The wonderful thing about this is that after reading this chapter you will know that you have the power to heal yourself – you just have to do the work. You'll probably also be able to see how others around you may be blocked. That can be a real eye-opener and sometimes very painful too, especially where others are involved. So before you go rushing off to tell Aunt Mabel that her recurring heart problem is because she has a blocked heart chakra from never getting over her first boyfriend thirty years ago, take it easy! Look at – and to – yourself first. This work can be pretty full-on. Just like energy clearing, emotional clearing can be very tough. To first get to and then understand the source of your pain, whether it is emotional, physical or mental – or, as in most cases, a combination of either of these – you must be prepared to ask the really hard questions about each, and then learn from whatever you discover. You must also be prepared to learn about yourself, both the good and the bad (and sometimes the very ugly!), and face all of the aspects of your being that you have repressed through fear or conditioning. Healing the gaps or removing the blockages is then viewed as your personal mission towards wholeness. In other words, you will be moving towards the "completion" of yourself, which is in line with your destiny. Our lives are spent most rewardingly when they are directed towards wholeness and wellness of self. Then we can show up each day and contribute to others in the best way possible. Quite obviously this is a journey, and most likely it won't happen overnight, however, do try to keep in mind that what is whole is accordingly

THE SEVEN CHAKRAS & ASSOCIATED BODY AREA

Seventh chakra — crown chakra

Sixth chakra — third eye chakra

Fifth chakra — throat chakra

Fourth chakra — heart chakra

Third chakra — solar plexus chakra

Second chakra — sex chakra

First chakra — base chakra

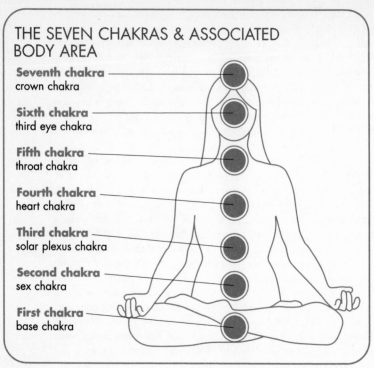

FOOT AND HAND ASSOCIATED CHAKRA MASSAGE PRESSURE POINTS

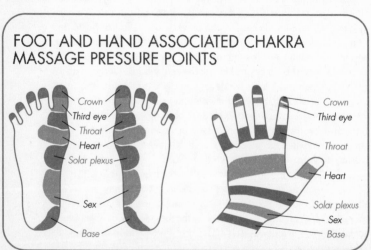

Crown
Third eye
Throat
Heart
Solar plexus
Sex
Base

Crown
Third eye
Throat
Heart
Solar plexus
Sex
Base

complete – and you may as well at least try to get there in this life-time . . . and save yourself another trip!

The basic chakra system

OK. Now we're getting down to the technical bit. For some Goddesses this stuff may be a bit dry to read, but as a necessary stepping stone to your ultimate personal glory, we can only advise you to try and hang in there! So, here goes . . .

Traditionally, there are seven chakras: crown (top of the head); third eye (between the eyebrows); throat, heart, solar plexus or power chakra; the lower abdomen or sex charka; and the base chakra. Each chakra is associated with a particular region of the body and each has its own purpose and is a source for healing therapy. When any of the chakras are out of balance, healing is required. Rebalancing the chakras restores vitality as well as unity to their combined functioning. Mantras and tones as well as massage can be applied to each chakra for healing. Ultimately, having and maintaining one's chakras in balance is essential for one's individual soul to be united with the collective or universal soul.

There are other theories supporting the existence of up to 32 chakras. These include the "back side" of the original seven and around eighteen or so further smaller energy centres in and around the body. For our purposes – and this is more than enough to get you started – we will focus on the seven major chakras. For Goddesses who wish to further explore this topic, please flip to our Goddess Library for additional references.

The following is a breakdown of the main individual chakras, beginning with the highest to the lowest. They have been numbered accordingly.

Seventh chakra: crown chakra

Location in the body: The top of the head in the centre.
Qualities: This chakra is where the unification between the individual and the Universe occurs. The crown chakra represents the culmination of the other six chakras, for here the complete physical, mental, and spiritual human is connected with its higher self and the source: pure consciousness.
Ultimate expression: The self is seen as a pure being with no limitations.
Lotus flower symbol: The lotus with 1000 petals.
Glands/organs: Central nervous system, pineal gland, right eye,

brain, cerebellum, skull.

Associated colours: Magenta, white, gold.

Key crystals/minerals: Amethyst, diamond, alexandrite.

Astrological relationships: Saturn, Neptune, Capricorn, Pisces.

Mantra and tone (related sound): The related mantra is "Om," which resonates to the musical note B.

Massage/essential oils: Frankincense, Lotus.

Balanced: Complete understanding of the self as being essentially connected to the Divine Source and as an individual who is part of the whole. Focus is on the greater good and "consciousness," not just on the personal.

Unbalanced: Egocentricity, recurring fears and/or worries, confusion, depression, general sense of dissatisfaction with life.

Sixth chakra: third-eye chakra

Location in the body: Centre of the forehead between the eyes/brows.

Qualities: Perception of the individual as actually "being." Psychic qualities are activated and the sense of the cosmic is the reward of awareness. Concentration and focus leads to an intuitive knowing and understanding the spiritual connection that is one's essence. This chakra is described as being the gateway for spiritual understanding.

Ultimate expression: The self is a "knowing" being for whom awareness is all.

Lotus flower symbol: The lotus with 96 petals.

Glands/organs: Pituitary gland, left eye, sinus, nose, ears.

Associated colours: Indigo/violet.

Key crystals/minerals: Lapis lazuli, purple fluorite, clear quartz.

Astrological relationships: Venus, Mercury, Uranus, Sagittarius, Aquarius, Pisces.

Mantra and tone (related sound): The related mantra is "KHAM" which resonates to the musical note A.

Massage/essential oils: Rosemary, Jasmine, Patchouli.

Balanced: The psychic, clairvoyant and intuitive qualities of the individual are very active and vivid dreams are common when the third-eye chakra is in balance. Great wisdom and creative solutions are easy to attain. The signs on the spiritual path are also easy to read as the individual's awareness level increases.

Unbalanced: The individual is concerned solely with material pursuits and neglects spiritual matters at personal cost. The intellect dominates and yet concentration is difficult. The conscious mind is often overwhelmed with too many fearful and conflicting thoughts.

Fifth chakra: throat chakra

Location in the body: The throat area, underneath the chin and above the inner collarbone.

Qualities: Relates to the communication of emotions and regulates the transition of the self towards inward reflection. Is the base for all aspects of sound on the physical and metaphysical (vibrational) planes (voice, laughter, crying etc). Represents the true expression of the individual self.

Ultimate expression: The self is a being who is freely able to communicate this essence to the Universe.

Lotus flower symbol: The lotus with 16 petals.

Glands/organs: Throat, thyroid, vocal cords, lungs, neck.

Associated colours: Cyan, turquoise, light blue.

Key crystals/minerals: Turquoise, aquamarine, lapis lazuli.

Astrological relationships: Venus, Mars, Uranus, Taurus, Gemini, Aquarius.

Mantra and tone (related sound): The related mantra is "HAM" which resonates to the musical note G.

Massage/essential oils: Lavender, sandalwood.

Balanced: Harmonious, powerful and clear communication of the

GODDESS POP/CULTURAL TIP

It started with Gwen Stefani of the rock group No Doubt and found its peak in Madonna's Ray of Light phase at the end of the '90s. The phenomenon that saw aspiring Goddesses the world over sticking beautiful jewels and decorative spots known as "bindis" between their eyebrows – the position of the third-eye chakra – is rooted in the ancient. The word bindi is derived from the Indian word "bindu" meaning "source" or starting point. In India, the women have been wearing bindis for centuries and a spot is placed on the third eye to symbolize the "piercing of the veil." The piercing of the veil refers to the process of attaining enlightenment – or ultimate awareness – where the spiritual pilgrim or seeker transcends the level of reality and perceives "pure consciousness." There is also a connection to the "OM" symbol. The visual representation of the "OM" symbol is that the three shapes underneath the dot represent the path of the pilgrim. The "dot" at the top of the symbol represents the soul that has "pierced the veil" and through attaining enlightenment, transcended. This is also linked, symbolically, to the reason married women in India have a painted red dot between their eyebrows signifying their status. This also refers to the loss of the hymen (the veil has literally been pierced), and to the loss of their virgin status in the act of consummating the marriage.

truth. Reality is expressed easily and readily without fear or favour. All communication is creatively based in the divine, so silence is used as effectively as sound and intuition is trusted above all.

Unbalanced: Knowledge is not communicated well or wisely. Things are misinterpreted or misunderstood and explanations become clouded or distorted perceptions of the truth. Ignorance or lack of discernment can be a symptom of imbalance as well as depression. Fear of speaking your truth.

Fourth chakra: heart chakra

Location in the body: Centre of chest, heart region.

Qualities: Literally at the heart of the chakra system. It is the mediator between the top three and the lower three chakras. It is the great processor through which all emotion, compassion, and intuition is channelled. Healing and emotions are generated and balanced by free-flowing love.

Ultimate expression: The self is loved, and this love is then expressed to the whole, which is equally loved.

Lotus flower symbol: The lotus with 12 petals.

Glands/organs: Heart, circulatory, or arterial system, rib cage, upper back, arms, lungs, hands.

Associated colours: Green.

Key crystals/minerals: Emerald, tourmaline, jade, rose quartz.

Astrological relationships: Saturn, Venus, the Sun.

Mantra and tone (related sound): The related mantra is "Yam" and the tone resonates to the musical note F.

Massage/essential oils: Rose, geranium.

Balanced: Unconditional love is freely offered and one's connection to the spiritual and the physical world (the natural environment) reflects the individual's state of passion, bliss, and ecstasy with life. Seeing and accepting the positive aspects in all events is the tendency rather than the exception.

Unbalanced: Problems with the heart recur. Anger and fear rule impulses and freedom from worry is impossible. The ability to be compassionate is severely reduced and selfishness becomes habitual. Love given is conditional and transactional in nature.

Third chakra: solar plexus (power) chakra

Location in the body: The solar plexus, including the region above the navel.

Qualities: Rules the impulses and is the centre of desire. The personality is integrated with the alignment of impulses, free will, wishes, and expression of personal power.

Ultimate expression: The formation of the self as a being, as expressed by the personality through free will and tempered with desire.

Lotus flower symbol: The lotus with 10 petals.

Glands/organs: Adrenal glands, pancreas, nervous system, abdomen, lower back, stomach, liver, spleen, digestive system, gall bladder.

Associated colours: Yellow.

Key crystals/minerals: Yellow topaz, citrine, amber, tiger's eye.

Astrological relationships: Mars, Mercury, Jupiter, the Sun, Leo, Virgo, Sagittarius.

Mantra and tone (related sound): The related mantra is "Ram" and the tone resonates to the musical note E.

Massage/essential oils: Ylang ylang, lemon, lime.

Balanced: Emotions are vital and free-flowing, the individual has an overriding sense of tranquillity and exists in a state of calmness. Free will and personal power are each exercised intuitively and spontaneously without fear.

Unbalanced: Emotional blockages are common and panic is the overwhelming feeling. The individual is incapable of trusting in the process or "going with the flow," and places too much emphasis on getting their own way and disregards the better solution for the greater good. Anger, fear, and hatred are the common responses.

Second chakra: lower abdomen (sex) chakra

Location in the body: Lower abdomen to the navel area.

Qualities: The centre of sexuality, relationships and creativity. The male and female energies are harmoniously blended and balanced to create relationships, which serve the intentions of the Divine Source.

Ultimate expression: The giving birth to Self as a being as expressed through the sex drive and the creative impulses of free will and personal desires.

Lotus flower symbol: The lotus with 6 petals.

Glands/organs: Genitals, reproductive organs, spleen, bladder, kidneys.

Associated colours: Orange.

Key crystals/minerals: Coral, moonstone, fire opal.

Astrological relationships: Venus, Mars, Mercury, Moon, Cancer, Libra, Scorpio.

Mantra and tone (related sound): The related mantra is

"Vam" and the tone resonates to the musical note D.

Massage/essential oils: Petitgrain, ylang ylang, sandalwood.

Balanced: The individual gives and receives in equal measure without difficulty. Surrender to the process of sharing is possible and relationships are harmonious and deeply connected. Openness of heart, body, and mind ensure that joy is the life experience. Sexual expression is one of unity and spiritual transcending.

Unbalanced: Sexual problems and an inability to give or receive in surrender to universal energies. Staying locked into the purely physical or functional expression of sexuality. Trying to control situations and emotions in relationships lead to needs and expression being repressed. Jealousy and mistrust are symptoms of the closed heart, mind, and body.

First chakra: base (root) chakra

Location in the body: Base of the spine.

Qualities: The centre for the individual being linked with the world in physical form; the basis for self-expression and ambition, tempered by the desire to evolve, protect self, and survive. The base chakra is the foundation of existence upon which the personality is built in connection to the Divine Source.

Ultimate expression: The self is understood and expressed as a physical being expressing its existence through its evolution.

Lotus flower symbol: The lotus with 4 petals.

Glands/organs: Adrenal glands, lymph system, colon and intestines, bones, teeth, nails, legs, arms.

Associated colours: Red.

Key crystals/minerals: Ruby, garnet, pyrite, hematite.

Astrological relationships: Saturn, Mars, Aries, Taurus, Capricorn.

Mantra and tone (related sound): The related mantra is "Lam" and the tone resonates to the musical note C.

Massage/essential oils: Marjoram, cedar.

Balanced: The material world is recognized as the ground level of existence but with a clear view to the spiritual. The individual is deeply connected to nature and trusts in the universal laws. Stability is sought and self-reliance and independence are the goal. Personal boundaries are in place and those of others are respected.

Unbalanced: The material world is overwhelmingly the focus and matters of spiritual concern are disregarded and ignored. The pursuit of personal material gain is the sole purpose and the ego rules the basic survival instinct, preventing the heart from alerting the individual to universal energies. Insecurity, greed, and stress are the primary

GODDESS FLIGHT DECK

In one of the many jewels contained in her remarkable book, The Energy Body Connection, Pamela Welch notes that the pituitary gland (which is one of the parts of the body associated with the third eye chakra) is found in "a groove of the sphenoid bone." This, she writes, "is composed of two wing-like structures. This is symbolic of the ultimate expansive flight that our consciousness will take as it is illuminated with the spiritual wisdom of the sixth chakra. Here, as we expand in consciousness and increase in the light of spiritual wisdom, we prepare to experience union with the Divine Source of all things."

So, now that you know you have a little angel in mind, the question is: how many frequent flyer points do you have?

life experience. An inability to let go and to "flow and let flow." Personal boundaries are weak and the individual crashes in on the boundaries of others without consideration.

Goddess at the wheel of life!

The chakra information above bears close inspection in order to discover where you may need to do your clearing and rebalancing work. Goddess, there are no limits to what you can achieve once you've plugged in! In physical human form we are imperfect, however, we have the spark of the divine within and this is the perfection within each of us. So if you work from the outside in – as it is said in Zen Buddhism "the way in is the way out" – and start to examine where your natural vitality and energy is being blocked, you'll be amazed at what can happen. Now you can rewrite the script which has thus far prevented you from experiencing your full potential.

The patterns of addiction and old habitual behaviours are long past their use-by date, but you have to recognize this and tune in to what will replace them and serve you best on your present path. Simply put: If you have or have had health problems in any of the chakras, these are an indication of mental or emotional blocks. When the chakras are in balance, you feel a positive connection to all that is joyous – it's hard to rock your Goddess chariot under these circumstances – and everything really is possible! This is why clearing and rebalancing the chakras is so critical. The more energy that flows freely through your chakras, the easier it will be to be yourself.

THE TANTRIC GODDESS

Now, we won't include a sealed section here, but some of you may have already guessed the link between the kundalini and the lower chakras. And what a link it is, possibly the ultimate – according to India's *Kama Sutra*. Well-known throughout the world by (acrobatic) lovers because of its creative approach to the sexual act and to sensuality in general, the *Kama Sutra* literally means love lessons ("kama" meaning love and "sutra" meaning lessons). For those Goddesses who are still furrowing their brows, the *Kama Sutra* is the ultimate guide to love and sexuality as practised between consenting adults, of course.

The source of the *Kama Sutra* is in the ancient Indian religion of Hinduism. According to Hinduism, the sexual act between two people can be the same in nature and purpose as a meditation. As such it is capable of raising the kundalini energy. This in turn awakens all the chakras and through their mutually experienced bliss the individuals are able to attain enlightenment. For Hinduism, sex is a sacred act, which can free the two individuals from their earth-bound karma. (Note: Karma is different to kama although some would say they are intrinsically connected. Karma means "action" or "deed" and the reaction or event that occurs as a result of one's own actions is said to be one's destiny.)

It's all about sacred sex . . . so do try this at home!

Raising the kundalini

It's not a shipwreck that's being brought up to the ocean's surface – in the yogic tradition it's the creative life force that lies at the base of your spine (in the base chakra) and it's how you can link and acti-vate the seven chakras. The kundalini is described variously as being "a coiled serpent" and "the essence of mother earth" or "the supreme life force," but for our purposes we'll call it "the creative life force." It is "earth energy."

The universal energies or "heaven energy" enter through the top of the head – the crown chakra – and "meet" the kundalini or "earth energy" as it rises through the individual chakras. The meeting or virtual collision between the two energy flows, top and bottom, heaven and earth, are what is said to cause the spinning of the charkas – hence the reference to them as wheels.

The creative life force or earth energy is in operation in varying degrees through the chakras in all individuals, however, intense meditation can raise more of this life force to spread through and "activate" the chakras. The idea is that in the process of spiritual awakening the kundalini energy raises through each of the chakras until it hits and fully activates the seventh – the crown chakra. In many people the serpent energy lies unawakened – asleep at the base of their spine. When it does rise from sleep, it only really gets as far as the first three chakras as it's not being "fully engaged" as such. For them, the main issues are survival, sexuality, and power. Others who wish to be fully realized understand the need to activate the higher chakras. Once again, however, it's all about balance – you should not stimulate some chakras or a single chakra over others. The higher and lower must be in balance: as on earth, so in heaven! There are those who devote their lives to achieving this cosmic balance in their attempt to realize the ultimate union with the Universe.

Yoga – the path to unity

And speaking of kundalini energy, one of the most popular methods of uniting the chakras is the practice of yoga. One branch of yoga called kundalini yoga incorporates specific exercises and "asanas" or body positions to raise the kundalini energy as we've been discussing.

There are other branches of yoga, however, and yoga in many of its forms (ashtanga, karma, and hatha yoga amongst others) has been in the headlines and the popular media. It has reached its peak asana, if you like, ever since music industry stalwarts Sting and Madonna, actor Gwyneth Paltrow, and supermodel-turned-yoga-guru Christy Turlington have made it the activity of the millennium. Bikram yoga is another very popular branch of yoga, and is a type that sees devotees sweat it out in a room that is pre-heated to 40 plus degrees in temperature (to aid in the elongation of the muscles, silly!). Ballet dancers have known this technique for years. Phew! It's enough to drive a Goddess to the nearest bar(re)! Like dance, yoga is a far from trivial pursuit and serious practitioners work on it for an entire lifetime. Goddesses take note: It is definitely not step aerobics or boxercise! Yoga is an ancient system of physical culture that is incapable of being a fad. To obtain real results in yoga requires a dedication and a strong personal discipline, but the results are more than worth the input. Want to be calm, centred, serene, and glowing with energy and vitality? Yoga is the ticket.

The word yoga is a Sanskrit word and it has its roots in the English word "yoke," meaning to link, unite, and to place under discipline or training. Defined in a more general sense, yoga is a method of training designed to lead to integration or union. Seen in the light of our current discussion of the chakras and their ultimate union, it is then possible to understand how yoga can assist in their combined functioning. Yoga is a primary method of keeping the chakras aligned to allow more of the kundalini energy to flow upwards to meet the in-pouring cosmic energy – union and integration.

The Salute to the Sun is the classic and most popular yoga sequence, and it is easy to teach yourself from one of the many books or videos available. You could also attend yoga classes to get personal instruction. If The Salute to the Sun sequence is done in the morning on a regular basis, you will reap your rewards in improved posture, increased mental clarity, and balance. And don't we each want all of the above!

Spa chakra – energy therapies

Massage, aura-soma colour therapy, and yoga are three of the most effective and immediate direct methods we know for getting your chakras in shape. Check yourself into your own home spa to begin your treatment!

GLOBAL GODDESS GURU TIP

Leslie Kenton's essential handbook for rejuvenation and de-ageing, *Rejuvenate Now*, has a tip for those Goddesses who wish to get going on their new energy programme. Leslie – who is without doubt one of the legendary contemporary Goddesses writing in the area of health and beauty internationally – has a very cool detox routine for the psyche. This can be done using various techniques: affirmations, meditation, autogenics (mental exercises and affirmations designed to turn off the body's fight or flight response mechanisms and replace them with calm and relaxed responses), yoga, and martial arts. She calls it a "Psychic Scrub." Leslie believes that beneath our old habits and patterns is ultimate freedom of self. She calls it encoded or old "stress" and writes: "The false ideas, notions, and habit patterns that suppress and squander our life energy make us highly susceptible to early ageing. They represent psychic and spiritual rubbish which is not only a big energy drainer but can cause as much free radical damage as living on junk food or taking drugs."

Leslie believes you can detox the psyche just as you can detox the physical body to release new and life-giving and affirming psychic and spiritual energies. She recommends doing a physical and psychic detox at the same time for maximum results.

Massage

Apart from the physical areas on the body that directly relate to the chakras as outlined on pages 205–10, you can also massage both hands and feet to assist and enhance healing and unblocking. The areas should each be massaged in a consistent direction. It should be done in the correct direction for each chakra, irrespective of whether you are stimulating the chakra through the hands, feet, or the major corresponding body parts. This is because the spin direction of each chakra alternates and is different and opposite for males and females. Therefore consistency is the key! See the illustration on page 204 for the corresponding positions to massage on the hands and feet. And you shouldn't wait for there to be a willing massage partner around either – self-massage is equally effective. Just grab a few of the appropriate oils listed and let your fingers do the walking . . .

Again, we urge all Goddesses to try this at home!

Chakra	Massage/female	Massage/male
Crown	Anticlockwise	Clockwise
Third Eye	Clockwise	Anticlockwise
Throat	Anticlockwise	Clockwise
Heart	Clockwise	Anticlockwise
Solar Plexus	Anticlockwise	Clockwise
Lower Abdomen	Clockwise	Anticlockwise
Base	Anticlockwise	Clockwise

[see the illustration of hands and feet, and massage points on page 204]

Full-body massage also works wonders and a sensitive and experienced massage therapist will be able to gently pinpoint the areas that are not free in your body. Having a massage on the chakras that need to be stimulated is a worthwhile exercise to shake things up physically. This is why some people feel the need to cry or release emotion during a massage session. Massage is an excellent tool for wellbeing and for long-term health. In India, babies are given massage regularly by all members of the family, to strengthen and stimulate their growing energy fields and relieve stress.

Aura-soma colour therapy

Aura-soma colour therapy is a fascinating therapy system for rebalancing your chakras and the aura. As we've noted before, "aura" means "breath of air," and the word "soma" is the old-Greek word for "body." The word "soma" also has its origins in Sanskrit, where there are references to it being some sort of "divine drink" which is capable of transporting the soul into spiritual bliss or ecstasy. Why colour therapy at all? Well for one thing, we believe that understanding colour helps you to understand life! We are picking and choosing colour all the time, both consciously and subconsciously, according to what's going on in our emotional, psychological, and spiritual lives. "When there's 'no colour' in your life" is an old saying with a basis in fact, for when there is no light, you tend to feel a bit drab or down. How many times have you reached for that bright dress or shirt on one of those gut-wrenching PMT-type days? That's why it's really no coincidence when you find yourself in an "orange" phase, or when you can't seem to find anything in your wardrobe but pink or blue.

There are certain needs that your auric system has and your choices are in one sense feeding it what it requires in order to be better balanced. Using colour also promotes insight, and in the context of aura-soma therapy, it is an aid to self-knowledge. The colours help people to break down any resistance to change and to address areas of their lives where they have perhaps been in denial. Colour works on illness and wellness at the same time and is thus a holistic system of healing. The healing colour vibrations in conjunction with the ability for physical application on the body make aura-soma a unique colour-therapy system.

The aura-soma colour-therapy system is the lifework of Vicky Wall, a British pharmacist, and consists of choosing from a collection of 102 bottled colour combinations of essential oils and water from the Glastonbury Well in England. Wall was an elderly blind woman whose highly developed sense of intuition and clairvoyance led her to discover and develop the "balance" system, as she called it. Vicky Wall believed in colour as a means of communication and healing for the spirit. Practitioners of aura-soma colour therapy can be found in locations around the world. For those Goddesses who wish to have a one-on-one session, please refer to our Global Goddess Directory for details of how to contact a practitioner near you.

The aura-soma system itself is described as "non-intrusive and self-selective soul therapy" that helps to increase self-awareness and ultimately one's full potential. The bottles contain mesmerising combinations of colours, which in some instances resemble precious gemstones. Indeed Vicky Wall called them "jewels." We call them energy in a bottle! Some contain a single colour, others two colours. They are displayed so that the light shines through the bottle, intensifying the colour clarity, enabling the process of selection. This selection process is individual and normally consists of picking four bottles, which are then analysed in a specific order:

Bottle 1: Represents your true purpose: Soul Purpose
Bottle 2: Represents issues from the past: Gifts and Challenges
Bottle 3: Represents the here and now: Present Tense
Bottle 4: Represents your future potential: Future Perfect

Each colour combination selected is analysed in detail. Then, one bottle of the four (usually the second one chosen) is retained to be applied directly to the relevant chakra(s) of the body after shaking the oil and water (with the left hand only) to mix them fully. You can also use the oils just by meditating on the bottle itself – merely looking at and concentrating on the colours is healing in itself.

Each bottle contains universal energies which reflect both positive and negative aspects. It should be noted that the colours you choose are capable of stimulating your awareness and can also be comforting or relieving, however, the actions and changes that they may bring up for you are completely in your court. For example, they may illuminate or bring up for you certain fears you may be having around your relationship, however, you are the only one who can take the measures required. So, like anything, the theory and the practical application are two very different things. These are simply tools to show you the direction you may need to take.

Example of bottle selection: One of our Goddess friends is a designer in the cut-throat fashion industry and had just given birth to her second child when she came upon the aura-soma colour-therapy system. She picked the following bottles (in order):

Bottle 1: Number 54 – name: Serapis Bey
– clear top and clear bottom
Bottle 2: Number 1 – name: Physical Rescue
– royal blue over deep magenta
Bottle 3: Number 99 – name: Feminine Leadership
– olive green over pale pink
Bottle 4: Number 11 – name: A Chain of Flowers
– clear over pale pink

Bottle 1: Number 54 – The therapist was fascinated by our Goddess friend's selection as she had never seen anyone pick the clear bottle first. The clear oil works on all the chakras and is related to the tarot card the Page of Swords and the main theme of this bottle is cleansing and detoxification on all levels. The positive personality aspects of the clear bottle are that of having strong personal ideals – they have clarity around them as indicated by the clear oil. Vicky Wall used to call people who chose this bottle "the rainbow warrior," meaning that they had the potential and were strong enough in character to awaken the rainbow within them – in other words, to awaken and balance the chakras and to have them at one's full disposal. They tend to hold on to the past, feel largely unprepared for things that life throws up, and suffer enormously when this occurs.

Bottle 2: Number 1 – This bottle relates to the tarot card the Magician and the purpose of this bottle is to help one understand and accept that everyday life is spiritual. This is also called "the healer's bottle." The person knows their ideals and has strong leadership qualities. This bottle is calming in emotional crises and assists in connecting the person with their life purpose.

THE SPOOKY GODDESS: ESP ALERT

We've all heard about "the sixth sense," and most have probably seen the film by M. Night Shyamalan starring Bruce Willis and Hayley Joel Osment, but did you know the sixth sense has its basis in the sixth chakra – the third eye or brow chakra? In Pamela Welch's wide-ranging and informative text *The Energy Body Connection* she writes: "We all have the ability to open up our eyes to the non-physical world. In fact, children do it quite naturally before they are taught otherwise." Pamela believes that because the third eye is the opening to spiritual wisdom and intuition, extrasensory perception (ESP) is also located there and this is the sixth sense. She also tells the story of her three-year-old daughter who one day pointed up into the air in front of her and said, "Teacher, Mommy, teacher!" while apparently gazing at a spot for some time. Pamela concluded she was acknowledging and interacting with someone she couldn't see, and while she could feel some sort of presence, her daughter's ability to actually see it left her in awe.

It is interesting to note that in the film it was the young boy (played by Hayley Joel Osment) who could "see dead people," and this serves to remind us all that in the non-material world, at certain levels of experience, we are still children. And to many, this is the real world of the sixth sense.

Bottle 3: Number 99 – "I love helping women" our Goddess friend declared when she pulled this bottle. "I definitely feel as though it's my life mission at this point." Well put. This bottle is all about using one's feminine intuition and leadership skills to show direction and to do so with confidence and flair. Certainly it accurately reflected her present life and life's work as the Head Designer for a busy fashion label.

Bottle 4: Number 11 – The fourth bottle selected refers to the future – and in the case of our fashionable Goddess friend, it is all about her having the clarity of mind to love her own soul. Perhaps it was a sign that she will be moving into a new phase of being more inner-directed than outer-directed. The basis of the fashion industry is that it is more concerned with externals than intrinsic soul issues. The selection of this bottle by our Goddess friend, who is in a challenging phase of her life, is quite telling of her current transition and her likely new direction as mother and business woman.

Om ... What's my mantra?

Other methods of rebalancing the chakras include repeating a particular mantra (a tone or sound vibration such as the musical note of a phrase like "Om") or by focusing on a visual representation of a mantra, namely a yantra. There are many ways of repeating a mantra: it can be verbal, whispered, written, thought, or chanted. To develop the psyche, the mantras are verbal, and to develop the emotional personality, the mantras should be chanted. So now you know why the teachers made you write lines like, "I will not be late for class" one hundred times or more! That was their visual and mental mantra for you!

In the table of chakras and their properties that we listed earlier, we also listed the musical notes that go along with each of the chakras. Most of us do not have the musical reach of Mariah Carey, but don't be deterred – you only have to reach a very low octave of the note to get results!

Mantras can also take the form of a saying, for example, "Om namah shivaya." This means "I bow down to Shiva" – Shiva is a major deity in the Hindu belief system. The word "OM" is the universal sound and is linked with the crown chakra (see page 204).

Other mantras are designed to be chanted in a group setting. The effects of group chanting can be more powerfully transmuted, especially if it is for peace, health and general wellbeing of a community or society as a whole.

To develop the intellectual personality, mantras can be visualized in the form of a yantra. Yantras are physical and visual symbols of the mind, and concentrating on these symbols assists in harmonizing your energies. Yantras are said to improve the faculties of concentration and memory retention. They are vehicles for liberating consciousness, and we may change them or bring in new symbols regularly to keep our own evolution progressing.

Certain yantras are coloured in according to certain traditions. The yantra for the Goddess Durga (another of the powerful Hindu deities) is traditionally yellow. The Goddess Durga is the creative and dynamic energy behind everything in existence. She is represented by the colour yellow because yellow is an intermediary colour in the dispersal of light. At one end of the colour spectrum is violet and at the other end is red. Red is said to be symbolic of creation, of the rising sun; violet is the end of creation – destruction – and yellow is positioned between the two extremes: preservation.

Chakra alert!

So you've had a big night out on the town, clubbing, drinking, and generally partying, and now you're sure you've unbalanced a few chakras (and a few other things to boot!) but you don't know where to begin to re-balance or how and if you will ever feel normal again! Here's our brief guide to show you what common addictions or activities, when conducted in excess, affect the chakras.

Firstly, excessive toxins affect not only particular energy centres directly, they have an effect on your body's entire system. Smoking and excessive drinking are known to be common addictions for those with heart chakra imbalances (inability to love freely or unconditionally), so these exacerbate the problem when done on a long-term basis. So too, excess caffeine consumption is a common problem for those with an imbalance in the solar plexus chakra (emotionally instability) and excessive meat and dairy consumption is typically associated with an imbalance in the base chakra (survival and fear-based issues). Sex addictions are obviously associated with imbalances in the sex chakra (inability to transcend fear of emotions). So, we'll presume that if you're not actually addicted to any of these, you may be a tad prone to over-indulging! Certain foods can help bring you back to the land of the living. So while you're sipping on that water, get your best friend, your mother, or your flatmate to make you some nutritious recovery food! The rule of thumb here is to go with fresh foods in the colour band of the affected chakra. Check the chakra chart and information on pages 204–10 again if you're not sure which one's which.

Generally speaking, the heart chakra responds well to green, leafy vegetables such as spinach, broccoli, lettuce, beans etc. Similarly, the solar plexus responds to the yellow group of foods, for example, squash, sweet corn, even carrots. Eat red apples and tomatoes instead of red meat for the base chakra and replace dairy products with foods such as (non-genetically modified) soy, which is an excellent source of protein. In the future, if it happens that you've hit the circuit in excess, you'll be able to put into place at least some sort of recovery programme that involves your chakras' health! Obviously cutting down on and even eliminating the toxic substances mentioned reaps a zillion other benefits for your health. We recommend all Goddesses have a health routine, which incorporates a sensible food plan and a sustainable exercise programme. You will be on fire if you do – you'll be an unstoppable energy ball. And that's what we want you to be!

Angels and Sp

Unless you've seen a fairy, an angel or a spirit guide, or heard their voice – or watched them produce amazing results in your life – it can be hard to believe in them, we know. But try to see it like this: If you can believe in the world of molecules and other tiny particles (you can't see the quantum world, but scientists know it's there), and if you can also believe in the bottom of the ocean (another mysterious, unseen world), then maybe you can make the leap and also trust there is another world still, full of miraculous beings.

t Guides

Most cultures believe in angels or similar spiritual forces, designed to do good. In the Christian Bible, angels act as messengers (an angel appeared to Mary, telling her that she would give birth to a son) and "angels of mercy" get humans out of danger. In Native American culture, people believe that hawks are spirit messengers, and their feathers are used in healing ceremonies. So even birds can have angel-like qualities. Some angel experts, like the American writer and lecturer Doreen Virtue, believe that angels can even incarnate in human form, so when you meet these special angel – humans – it's literally a case of "entertaining angels unawares"!

The only way you're going to find out any of this is by being open to the possibility that angels, or angelic forces, are truly out there. That's the first big step. The second step is actually seeing, hearing or sensing them or some evidence of them.

If you take this chapter to bed with you, don't be surprised if you wake up and see morning light, or even the light still on in the hall, showing big, rainbow-coloured rings around it. This beautiful shimmering light is something that lets you know an angel or spirit guide is around and very pleased that you're starting to read up on their influence at last.

In ancient times, people drew angels with huge, white, feathery wings. We now believe that painting wings was one way of illustrating the massive white, shimmering light that seems to gather around angel bodies. Angels work for the light (literally the light as opposed to the dark) and they often come to us as colours or sparkles, or just masses of bright light, which you can actually see going straight through solid objects. Some truly psychic and gifted Goddesses even see angels appearing just as they do in books and paintings – with robes, and haloes, and wings. Circles or bands of light, white or rainbow coloured, are a sure sign that you have an angel around you, though. Watch out for it.

Spirit guides

Everyone has at least one spirit guide, and sometimes more, to help them in their lives. They are often from Chinese and Native

American cultures, because these cultures have strong belief systems that encourage them to volunteer for the role of "helper" on the other side, once they die and leave this earth. You may not know it, or you may be happily aware of it, but there is someone in spirit who is always there to show you the best choices to make, or to move in mysterious ways that result in your hopes, dreams, or prayers being answered. Don't necessarily expect your spirit guide to look like you, or even speak your language, although they will find a "mind language" to communicate with you telepathically, so you can understand them!

Some psychic artists can see your spirit guide. If you go to any of the Mind Body Spirit festivals in your area (they take place all over the world, usually twice a year) you may be lucky enough to find one of these psychic artists, who can sketch your spirit guide, for a fee.

Your guide is likely to be from a culture where belief in the afterlife was strong, and he or she may have passed over recently, or even hundreds of years ago. You might find that you have a Tibetan guide, an Indian guide, or a Native American guide, for example. Don't worry if you don't have access to a drawing at a festival, though. It's possible to see and meet your guides in other ways, which you'll read about in this chapter. For the moment, you only need to understand the special purpose of your spirit guide.

Basically, the fact that they last lived on Earth many hundreds of years ago has helped give them the big picture on your life. They can see past, present, and future possibilities of your life. So when you're stuck, or lost, or dealing with a problem, they have a real advantage in being able to point the way forward. They also have centuries of experience! Your guide typically has more information than you about a situation – they have total vision.

Even though we sometimes think we know what we're doing, we're really only living our lives with limited vision. We can only see today, or tomorrow, and we certainly can't see the big picture. It's like knowing you live at the end of your street, but not being able to see the rest of the map. Spirit guides have the map, and in their world it is their job – and their joy – to steer us through life, whenever we ask for assistance. Sometimes, of course, they intervene on our behalf, especially if we're going badly wrong. Have you ever been about to get into a car with someone who's been drinking, and felt an urge to get out, or almost heard a voice saying "Don't go!"? Well, that was probably your spirit guide. There are lots of people with similar stories. But for true spirit guide "flow" in your life, you need to learn how to open the door to their world.

Who is your spirit guide?

Meditation helps get you out of this world and into the other world. It builds the telephone line, or television cable, which connects you to the spirit people and your spirit guides. Remember, the spirit world has a different energy system. It's lighter and faster than our world. Unless you meditate, you will find it hard to make contact with them, and try as they might, your guides will find it really hard to contact you.

Practise the meditation that follows until you really feel you've clicked with your guide. You might see a face. You might get a sense of a very loving, amazing presence around you – some people cry when this happens, because it can be so emotional. If you are clairaudient (you have a natural ability to hear the spirit world) you may hear your name being called, or even hear their name. All sorts of things can happen in this meditation, but remember: Practice makes perfect. You have to be willing to give this a go several times, but once you have made contact with your guide you will never forget it. Here's a tip – don't have any fixed expectations about what your guide might look like, how old they may seem to be, what gender they might be, or what country they might come from. This makes it easier for them to come through. If you resist them with your mind, for example, if you tell yourself "There's no way I could have a 100-year-old Chinese healer on my side!" then it's harder for them to get through. Just trust, and let go.

Your spirit guide meditation

Sit cross-legged on the floor, at a time when you won't be disturbed. Don't cross your legs too tightly, just feel relaxed – lean up against the wall or bed, if you like. Ask the Universe, or any spiritual force you believe in, to help and protect you as you seek your spirit guide. This begins your meditation!

Now, imagine you are in the shower. Instead of water, you are being showered with gold drops of sparkling light. Stay in this "shower" for as long as you like. How will you know when it's time to stop? Simple. You'll feel blissed out. You may even catch yourself smiling. Something is already beginning to work now – your guide is in touch and helping to "tune up" your aura so that the vibration not only feels good to you, it also helps match their vibration, so it will be easier to make contact.

The shower of golden light rain has now stopped, and you are drying off – basking in a bubble of white light. Feel it all around you, under your legs and bottom, around your shoulders, over your knees, and under your feet as well – really cover yourself. Feel it going over the top of your head, covering the sides of your body, and even covering your fingertips.

Now that you are in this white space, imagine a white door. It can be any kind of door you like, but it must be bright, sparkling white. Now open the door. You will see, sense, feel or hear your guide, who is waiting behind this door. Don't force anything! Just let it happen. It's very common for people to break the connection at this point by saying, "Oh it's my imagination" or "I'm scared," or (worst of all) "This isn't working." Don't be too bothered by this kind of reaction if it happens. Just let it drift over you and keep on focusing on the white space you are in. If you really aren't getting it after a few minutes, then let it go and try again another day.

A good result will involve some, or all, of these effects:

* A familiarity – a sense that there is nothing new in what you are experiencing, that it's exactly what you would expect to find!
* A true sense of something, or someone, who has endless wisdom, kindness and love.
* An answer to a problem flashes into your mind.
* You see, in your mind's eye, a face, or the outline of a person, or a symbol (for example, with a Chinese guide, a Chinese dragon) which gives you a clue as to the identity of your guide.
* Scents or special smells can sometimes drift into the air – of course, they're not really there at all, but your sixth sense can detect them. For a Native American guide, you might "smell" burning sage, which is a typical herb used by that culture.

Don't jump if you hear a voice, just as if there was a voice in the room. You are privileged to hear it and you may also have the special psychic gift of clairaudience.

Finally, remember your spirit guide will always be a wise, philosophical, kind, and loving presence in your life. This is the biggest giveaway of all – if you sense or know this, then you really are in the presence of your guide. Don't accept any substitutes!

Making friends with your spirit guide

Like any friendship or teacher–student relationship, there needs to be patience, respect, a sense of humour, time, and mutual appreciation with your guide. Once you have met your guide in this way, he or she may pop up again, perhaps when you least expect it. Pay attention when this happens – your guide is around for a reason, so check what is going on, who the people around you are, and the situation you are in. Guides work with telepathy, so they will beam the information through – go inside yourself and chill out for a minute, and you'll get what they are trying to convey.

You may also want to ask your guide for . . . well, guidance! . . . on a regular basis. This is fine – you can never ask too often, but they may not always respond. Some things in life are there for you to go through by yourself, or you would never learn anything and your soul would not progress. All our souls are unfinished objects, like pine furniture which needs to be treated and polished. Our job here on planet Earth is to work on our souls, and this sometimes means we have to go through stuff in order to learn – and it's not always easy. At this stage your spirit guide will be watching and waiting, never interfering – but always on your side too. They'll be right back with you when your solo lesson is over.

Your spirit guide also loves it when things go right, or when there is something to celebrate. At moments of great happiness or excitement, you may feel a shiver going down your spine, or you may feel someone standing behind your shoulder. Don't worry – your guide is there to share in your happiness. When you get a great exam result, land a wonderful job, meet someone special, have a baby, or achieve any of life's high points, your spirit guide will often be there, applauding and thoroughly enjoying what's going on! It sounds odd to say it, but spirit guides are only human – well, they were, once upon a time – so they love to know that your life is working out, with a little assistance from them.

Cosmic good manners

Spirit guides have to obey spirit world laws, which means they cannot help you unless you ask first. A silent and sincere appeal to them, or even an out-loud request, will work wonders. It doesn't matter what words you use, but your attitude does count. A request to your guide has to come from the heart. Don't be surprised if the most miraculous or amazing things happen, very quickly. Spirit guides, in the right situation and circumstances, can organize things rapidly and sometimes in ways you could not have imagined. Do leave it up to them, though. They have to suss out the most effective, fair, and achievable way of fixing things for you, and it's not always the way you thought! They also have to consult the spirit guides of the other people who may be involved in the equation. The solution has to suit everyone perfectly, and it has to be for the highest good of all, otherwise it's just not possible!

When a spirit guide provides an answer or solution in your life, or even a miracle, you typically won't even be able to begin tracing how it happened – it all seems so incredible. But you must make a point of saying thank you. If someone did you a massive favour here on Earth, you'd certainly send a heartfelt card, email, or even flowers or chocolates. Tune into your spirit guide in the golden rain/white light meditation, if you like, to really build the connection, and make sure you are suitably appreciative. Like anyone else, your guide loves to see thanks from the heart. It's good for their evolution too, as one of the ways their soul progresses in the spirit world is to successfully help us humans. You'll find more on the art of thanking late in this chapter.

ARE YOU READY TO PHOTOGRAPH A FAIRY?

It's very easy to believe in angels, as the Earth is currently experiencing a huge wave of interest in them, and it's almost hip to say you've had contact with an angel. But what about fairies? What's more, do you think you could photograph one? Maybe it's because they turn up in so many kids' books, but a lot of people feel they left the world of fairies behind when they turned nine years old. All we can say is, think again. Tiny nature spirits, with wings, are also a reality and they exist in the same mysterious, invisible world as angels do – but on a different sphere.

William Bloom, a real Global Goddess Guru, writes about his first encounter with fairies (also called nature spirits, or devas) when he was going for a walk with his small son and dog one day. He found a circle of fungi in the countryside: a fairy ring. Bloom felt an impulse to help clean up the fairy ring and get rid of all the old stones, branches, and rubbish. He says, the fairies then gave him an elf suit for his trouble! "Of course there are people – especially sceptics, cynics and scientists – who would like me actually to prove everything," William writes in his amazing book, Working with Angels, Fairies and Nature Spirits. "Unfortunately, they cannot see my lovely elfin outfit. They could, however, see the certificate for my PhD in political psychology. I value my doctorate and my elf suit equally."

We have our own fairy story to tell too. Two years ago, Jessica decided to create a special corner of the garden near her home, on the east coast of Australia, just for fun. She put out some small, wooden Buddhas on top of the shorn-off tree trunk outside her shed, and cleared away all the old bark and weeds from the area. She found a huge, beautiful, purple amethyst crystal which had been stuck in a desk drawer, and put it next to the Buddhas. Next, she hung a small mobile from the tree overhead. The tree had been bound up with rope, which was cutting into the bark – it almost looked like the tree was hurting, so she cut the rope away as well. After that, Jessica just forgot about it.

She went away for a while, and left her neighbours to feed the cat while she was gone. Upon her return, something amazing had happened. The neighbours told her that a special kind of fungus had grown on the tree trunk where she had put the crystal. It was a rare fungus, normally seen in wild places – and it glowed bright white-green in the dark! Apparently while she had been away, people in her street had actually been walking up to the garden to see it for themselves. True evidence, perhaps, of fairies at work. But that's not the end of this story, though. Some time after this, Jessica got back some photographs of her garden. To her amazement, she saw what looked like a tiny fairy queen, and also a tiny Aboriginal figure, hidden in the picture – right where the glowing fungus had been. To see this strange photograph for yourself, visit the website for this book, 21stcenturygoddess.net and use your magnifiying glass.

The five-star fairy voucher system

To attract fairies into your life, try something they love – giving great gifts. They also have a huge sense of fun, which is why the five-star fairy voucher system seems to work so well. You couldn't be doing anything sillier or more ridiculous with your time, on one level, but on another level, it's the kind of dumb, funny, generous, and bizarre thing that fairies truly love. Who wouldn't appreciate a five-star favour, anyway? Fairies are drawn to children and childish things, and no matter how old you are, this five-star favour voucher system can really work – if you are prepared to pretend you're a kid all over again.

Basically, five-star fairy vouchers are a few steps on from the tooth fairy, who used to leave a pound (or more if you had a multi-

FIVE–STAR ✳ FAIRY VOUCHERS IN ACTION

* **Gourmet magic:** The next thing they cook will be TV chef standard with a voucher that reads, "This voucher entitles you to some gourmet magic. Keep it by your side the next time you cook. The results could be Jamie Oliver!"

* **Big night beauty:** At their next big party or event, this person will be extra beautiful.

* **Pennies from heaven:** Expect a fairy bonus when you least expect it!

* **Word magic:** When you need it most, at a speech or a meeting, the words will come. This voucher can read, "This voucher has been sent to you by the fairies. Use it when you have to make a speech or write something important, and the words will flow."

* **House power:** This voucher guarantees fairy help with your next lot of housework.

* **Kissy Kissy:** The fairies will deliver you the best kiss you've had in ages – wait and see.

* **Creativity boosters:** Fairy inspiration guarantees a painting, poem, song or story you love.

* **Interview magic:** This voucher is to be used at your next major job interview.

* **No smoke:** Fairy power will help you in your quest to give up cigarettes – valid for a year.

* **Discount dazzlers:** The next fabulous thing you want to buy will be – magically – reduced.

These are all small things, but they are exactly the kinds of treats, freebies, gifts and magical experiences that fairies can help with. Now, make up a few of your own. But remember, the best fairy vouchers are made by hand, come from the heart, and are small enough for a mouse to carry in a Prada handbag by moonlight. A fairy told us that.

millionaire fairy) under your pillow for every tooth you lost. The five-star fairy voucher system involves you creating a tiny "gift" voucher, using the smallest piece of paper you can draw on, then giving it to someone who you believe needs one. Just make sure it's really a five-star favour! There are no such things as ordinary old favours in the fairy world – that's left up to the humans. Keep it anonymous, for even more fun – imagine the look on someone's face if they receive a fairy voucher and have absolutely no idea who sent it! Just put one in the mail and let it go!

You can use glitter or bits of feather stuck to the paper that you make the voucher with. You can also draw fairies on the voucher, for extra impact, or just cut out pictures of fairies from magazines. If you're really gung-ho about this, you can make your voucher the size of a postage stamp, or smaller, which the fairies like even more – they think tiny things are hilarious, as it's such an effort for us to get down to their size! As soon as you mail or give your voucher to someone, the fairies will automatically be drawn to that person, and that situation – and even though you are giving something small, and the results will be small too, they will still have the extra magical five-star element when they do happen! Try it and see.

Rubber bands and feathers
ANGELS IN OUR MIDST

It was Goddess Anthea who first told us about rubber bands. "They're angels' halos which have slipped off," she said, picking one up off the ground. "I always pick them up because they're lucky." After that, everyone was picking up rubber bands. In fact, walking back from Goddess HQ in Avalon, Australia, the three of us – Anthea, Jelena and Jessica – all found matching red rubber bands within a few minutes of talking about this angel phenomenon. We interpreted this as a big "Go, Goddess, go" sign from the angels, especially as they knew we would be giving them a starring role in this book.

Another key angel signal is little sparkles of light. These are like tiny pinpricks that appear in the corner of your eye. When you feel dizzy, you may have "seen stars" sometimes (not like the Tom and Jerry cartoons – it's a medically recognized reaction that involves lots of winking and flashing light sprinkles in your field of vision, often after you've got out of bed too quickly). Angel signals are similar, but different. An angel "flash" with a tiny silver-white light sparkle (the size of a pinhead) is actually a double message. The first message is, "pay attention to this moment," and the other half of the message is "Yes! Yes!" So if you happen to be reading a significant line in a book, or having an important breakthrough thought, or even meeting someone you know is going to be vital to you, that sparkle is an angelic way of saying, "Yup, we agree, this is important." Watch out for it. These light sprinkles are unusual, but when they take place, there is definitely something in the air...

Apart from slipping rubber bands on your wrist, you can also look out for feathers, especially white feathers. This is another angel symbol that lets you know they're around and they're looking out for you. We know someone in New York who gets these feathers – at the rate of three or four a day sometimes – when she's facing something important in her life. How do they get there? Well, you could say that pigeons and sparrows donate a few, but how to explain the perfect white feather that appeared on Goddess Jessica's coat when she was having a spiritual healing session in London? The healer couldn't believe it, and neither could Jessica – but it was there.

Angels sometimes create coins in your path for the same reason. There is an old saying that goes, "See a penny, pick it up, and all the day you'll have good luck." See what happens! Some people get rubber bands constantly, others get feathers, and there are those who find coins. Sometimes these coins are foreign, which makes it even more interesting. Sometimes they date from decades ago – as long ago as the 1950s in one case we heard about – all of which convinces us that this is more than just someone dropping his or her small change on the ground. Try it yourself. Next time you're walking down the street, hoping or wishing for something, or worrying about something (both of these attract angels who want to help) check out what you see in front of you. Is it a rubber band, a feather, or a coin? If this keeps on happening to you, there are angels around.

Heaven help me!
DIAL 333 FOR ANGEL RESCUE

This is a special meditation which will help you contact your angels. The angelic helpline number, 333, is special, too. Three is a powerful number in many cultures and belief systems. And three threes are amazingly powerful! In her wonderful book, Healing with the Angels the angel expert, Doreen Virtue, says that this number means, "The ascended masters are near you, desiring you to know that you have their help, love, and companionship." Normally people tell you to find somewhere quiet and private to meditate, but as you may be urgently dialling 333 in crazy situations sometimes (noisy parties, crowded streets) it will help you to learn how to do this any time, any place, anywhere. So let's try it now, no matter if the TV is on in the background, your mobile is ringing, or the dog is freaking out the cat next door.

Step 1: See in your mind's eye a gold telephone. It's beautiful and shiny, just like a gold necklace, a gold sequined halterneck, or gold Christmas tree tinsel. It glitters. It may be an old-fashioned telephone

---

ANGEL HINTS AND TIPS

Because the angel world is well aware that you could be easily scared or freaked out by their sudden appearance in your room, the angels find other tricky, clever ways to let you know they are around. There's the appearance of rubber bands, feathers, or coins. Or you might be gazing at a wall and notice that the lamp in the corner is making a definite wing shape, in the shadows on the curtains – just as you happen to be reading the angel chapter! There are many other ways angels can find you without scaring you. You might get an angel birthday card. You might even meet a real person who helps you out, when you are truly feeling lost or alone, only to find that this person has vanished, or nobody else saw them. Sometimes angels stretch the joke and turn up in human form with the surname Angel, or the name Michael or Gabriel – two well-known angels.

---

with a wheel on the front, with ten dialling holes, or a new telephone with a touchpad. It could be a Mickey Mouse phone. It's up to you. It's your personal direct 333 angel line, so create it the way you want it. And yes, it can be a mobile if you wish.

Step 2: This phone is unusual. There are only three numbers on the dialling pad or wheel. And you guessed it – they are 3, 3 and 3. See the numbers clearly. What colour are they? You can choose the colour of the digits. Some people choose black numbers on a gold phone, others have bright blue, white, or rainbow colours. Don't change your design around by the way – try to stick to the same phone each time you dial.

Step 3: With your pressing problem or urgent question in mind, take the receiver off the hook and hold it to your ear. Remember, you are still doing this in your mind's eye. You may actually see everything very clearly, even with your eyes open – or more likely, you will get a sense of what you see. It's like you can visualize it, imagine it, even if there are no pictures in front of your eyes. It may help to switch your gaze to the right of you, staring off into the distance. This position is easier for your eyes, so you will see the receiver more clearly.

Step 4: See yourself holding the receiver up to your ear, and dialling 333. What is the dial tone like? It's probably your regular dial tone, but maybe not. Some people have gold angel phones which have an echo on the ring. Some people hear an almost musical ring instead of the usual "brr brr." Let it ring for as long or as short as seems right. Then, leave your mind blank and open. Leave a space!

Step 5: Still in your meditation, let your angel know the problem, or the situation. Silently explain that you have dialled 333 on the "Heaven help me" line for a special reason, and be as honest as you can about what is going on. Don't try to cover anything up – your angel knows what's really going on anyway! Your issue may be related to your appearance, your money, your car, your parents, your sexuality, your health, your previous boyfriend, your exams, your holiday, your home, your career, your friends, or just yourself. Spell out your question or request, though. You can say it out loud if you want, but your 333 angel will hear just as effectively if you "think" your sentences into the phone. Take as long as you like. It's very important to go through everything until you've said all there is to say. Remember to leave a gap after each sentence, too. You may find, to your total surprise and delight, that your angel answers you by popping a thought into your head. Inspiration, in a lot of cases, is just another word for angel telepathy.

Here's an example of a real-life 333 "Heaven help me" phone call, and how it worked out for the person who called.

Amy had lost her dog, Butch, a young and crazy Labrador, after she had let him off the lead in the park. After five days, one advertisement on the radio, and lots of door-knocking around the neighbours, she was panicking. Her parents thought that finding Butch was Amy's responsibility and her sister was too busy to help. Consequently it was all down to her. The weather got bad – rain started pouring down every day – and Amy couldn't sleep at night because she was worrying about Butch shivering in a bush somewhere, starving. Finally, she rang her gold phone (just created) and dialled the magic 333.

"It was a really weird experience because it was the first time I'd tried it," Amy says. "Anyway, I saw myself pushing the buttons, 333. Because I was desperate, it only took one ring and my angel picked up the call. I just explained everything – how worried I was about Butch, how he was a young and crazy dog but he didn't deserve this punishment, how I didn't know if someone else had him now ... just the whole story!"

While Amy was pouring her heart out on the "Heaven help me" line, she found something interesting happening. "I was doing this quite late at night, and I hadn't been able to sleep, and I had a headache, and felt really tired, but also really hot and bothered," she says. "Well, in about five minutes I started to feel really relaxed and sleepy. It's almost as if my helpline angel was trying to fix that as well!"

Amy left gaps after each "thought sentence" she was sending and got nothing back, until she told her helpline angel this: "I just said, 'I'll work in the local chocolate shop all my school holidays if it means I get the money to find him'," she explained. (Amy has a regular holiday job in a confectionery shop.) The next thing Amy knew, she thought of several things all at once. "It wasn't like me coming up with them either, they just sort of popped into my head," she says. "I didn't hear my angel speaking, but I am sure this was my angel's suggestion!" The magic things were:

1. The chocolates in the shop are everyone's favourite in town, because they look so good tied up with their trademark pink ribbon.
2. Chocolate would make a great reward for anyone who could find Butch.
3. Butch likes chocolate too.

Amy says she had a "zinging" sensation after this that left her feeling really hopeful, excited and inspired. She knew the solution. She would go back to the park and leave a trail of chocolates for Butch to follow home – crazy though it sounded, she was convinced it was worth trying. And she would also buy the biggest box of chocolates from the store, complete with pink ribbon, take a photo of it, and make photocopied posters to stick up on all the local lamp-posts and walls.

The happy ending to this story was that: four days after Amy put her box of chocolate reward posters up, she got two calls about her dog. Butch had been staying with a family on the other side of town, after he had followed their dog (a girl dog, of course) home! But wait, there's more. What about the chocolate trail in the park? Well, Butch never found it – he was too far away. But the boss of the confectionery shop where Amy had her holiday job happened to see some of his marzipan truffles on the grass. He was so entertained by what she had done, he offered her the prized weekend slot she had always wanted – at double pay. This goes to prove something else about angel power, and the magic of the golden 333 "Heaven help me" phone. Angels love to do something more than you ask for. Once you call, they have permission to scan your whole life and situation, so not only the problem you have will be solved or soothed, you'll frequently get an added bonus. It seems that Amy's 333 angel knew a way to find Butch, but also a way to get her the extra holiday cash she required!

Your shopping angel

You might think that shopping is too trivial and shallow to attract an angel, but there are several zillion angels, built for all sorts of reasons. If you knew a fellow Goddess on a shopping trip, desperately trying to find the right dress for an important party, at the right price, but with only two hours to find it . . . well, would you want to be an angel for her, if you could be? This is the way the angels feel. They're only too happy to help, but you must ask – and so many people don't. Angels who live for kindness and beauty naturally want to be kind enough to help you find the beautiful frock of your dreams. But first of all, a few basic rules for your shopping angel.

You have to really mean your request. Could you do this by yourself, without help, or is it really important to you to find this item?

Be specific. Ask your shopping angel to guide you towards a certain colour, shape, price range, or whatever else it is you are specifically looking for. If it's more an abstract idea, like, "I want my legs to look longer in jeans," then put that in too. The more detail you can give your shopping angel, the easier it is to either guide you towards what you desire, or even (this happens too!) come up with a better alternative.

Put your logical brain to bed. Your head may "think" your chosen item is going to lie in the biggest department store in town – the one you always go to – but if ten minutes after your angel request you just happen to walk past a garage sale advertisement pinned to the local noticeboard, take it seriously. Your shopping angel may be urging you to check out the secondhand stall instead. To let your angel work, you need to switch off that part of your head that follows common sense or logical rules, because often the answer lies outside those rules. You might think your perfect pair of winter boots is awaiting you at a shopping centre, but what if your angel knew there was a secondhand pair of Gucci platforms in just your size, at a tiny price, at a funny little vintage store up a hidden alleyway? Be open to what your shopping angel suggests.

If you have a time limit – for example, if you have a whole two weeks to find a coat, or even just one shopping Saturday to find your father's birthday present – be specific. Angels work on different time to ours. You need to be absolutely clear about just how much time you have to find your perfect shopping item so they can work in with your schedule. This is sometimes the reason why people call in their shopping angels and get disappointed because, after one whole day shopping around town, they have no results. Essentially, they forgot to let their angel know their time limit. If you just wish for "the best secondhand car in town" but forget to specify your time frame, your angel might deliver it to your door five months later!

As always with angels, be polite, sincere, humble, hopeful, genuine, and respectful. And with your very first result, thank your shopping angel (out loud, if possible.) That way you build a friendship. Show your joy and happiness whenever you wear that item/drive that car/see your father enjoying his birthday present. This is the shopping angel's payback – they get to share in your joy.

Angels work in mysterious ways, and you will never know exactly what goes on behind the scenes when your shopping angel has pulled yet another miracle out of the bag. Sometimes it's just a "feeling" you get to go to a certain store. That feeling is a psychic hint, transmitted over the airwaves by your shopping angel. Your shopping angel can arrange for you to bump into people who have just seen the exact thing you're looking for, or even whisper to bookstore assistants to put certain books (the one you're looking for, natch) to the front of the store. And by the way – if a book flies off the shelf at you, pick it up and take a look. Most times, this is a book you are meant to read or buy!

To put in your request to a shopping angel is simple. Just count your money, work out your budget, figure out your absolute deadline for finding this miraculous object, and then say (out loud or in your head), in your own sincere words, a short request. And by the way, if you keep on getting lucky with your shopping angel, each time you try it again, remember to thank your winged wonder for the last amazing result you had. Angels are just like us, they love to be thanked.

Be an angel!

Angels can't do all the work, so you may as well help out while you are here on planet Earth. There's a car sticker around you might have seen that says "Practise random acts of kindness and senseless acts of beauty." This is exactly what you should be doing if you are trying to be a human angel. Here are some ways you can achieve this.

Feed other people's parking meters if you can see that their time is about to run out – and especially if you can see a parking meter attendant marching up the street. It only takes a few coins and you will truly be performing an angelic act.

If you like the way someone is dressed, or has their hair, tell them. Compliments about physical appearance may seem corny or obvious, but they really work. Always pass on compliments from one friend to another. If someone in your circle of friends has something nice to say about a person behind his or her back, be sure to let them know. Half the time people don't!

Always remember birthdays with a snail-mail or email card. Always remember Christmas cards. Once again, it might seem old-hat and obvious, but a lot of people don't bother. And an angel always will!

Do the washing up. You will be amazed at how this can change someone's day, or night. Water someone else's thirsty plants if you can see they are wilting.

Send anonymous Valentine's Day cards to males and females. Choose people you know who never get anything, or don't expect to. This is a cool thing to do around February 14th every year. It's got to be anonymous, though. This adds fun and mystery.

If you see a tourist with a map on a street corner looking lost, stop and help them so they don't have to ask first. Always give up your train or bus seat to anyone who looks like they need it. It doesn't matter if they're old, young, pregnant, or not pregnant! This is truly the act of an angel.

Whenever you hear about a job vacancy in your world, tell as many people as you can. You could be giving someone the break they need, but without that information, they will never know.

This is pretty basic, but if you see someone crying – anywhere, any time, even if everyone stares – make sure you are the person who walks right in to see what's going on. You may be able to help, you may not, but the fact that you bothered counts. That person won't forget it.

Always buy a spare raffle ticket for someone you know – or even someone you hardly know. The spare ticket could be a winner and it only costs a few coins. Always buy a copy of *The Big Issue* or other publications that benefit the homeless – homeless people need angels more than anyone else. Remember, in all these examples above, an angel will automatically be drawn to the situation when you help out. So you will also be attracting angel power to that person as an added bonus!

Why it's vital to count your blessings

Angels love people who say "thanks" as much as anyone else. Think about it for a second. If your primary job is to help out humans, how would you feel if all people ever do is ask – and ask, and ask. Try to make it a rule that before you make an angel request, no matter if you're dialling 333 or calling in a shopping angel, you first make a note of all the good or lucky things about yourself and your life, and say, "Thank you," either out loud or to yourself. Counting your blessings is an old-fashioned thing to do, but like most ideas which are handed down over the generations, this notion has survived because it works, and because it's important.

You might think you don't have any blessings, especially on days when your PMT is all you can feel, but most people should be able to find ten blessings to count, and you can too. Angels love gratitude. And of course, when they do you a favour, or deliver a miracle, that's also worth a big vote of thanks. One of the best ways you can express your gratitude is to be an angel for someone else. This is also known as sharing the good fortune, or spreading the joy. If you count your blessings and share your good fortune then an angel will always find it easier to work with you, as you will be lifting your human vibration closer to the angel vibration that they work on. Here are a few things you could run through, when you're thinking of the parts of your life that you should honestly be thankful for. And, yup, the angels will be listening.

Your looks – what were you born with that you really appreciate? It might be your hair, your legs, your teeth – whatever. Everyone has a beautiful feature that they should be thankful for.

Just being born in places where you have money, freedom and education is like winning the world lottery. Why? Because there are so many millions of people in this world who are poor, or who have to live without true freedom. So – it's a no-brainer. You can begin by being grateful for winning the lottery of life, just by coming into the world in your own particular country. Think of all the refugees who would give anything to be in your place!

Think about your clothes, CDs, books, or other possessions. Think about your money situation. Even at your most broke, you still have more than the average person in Rwanda or Kosovo. Even when your wardrobe seems sadly depleted, we bet you've still got more T-shirts and pairs of shoes than you know. Give thanks for what you've got. Really savour and appreciate what you own, or what you've received as birthday or Christmas presents.

Everyone is born with someone special either in their immediate family or circle of relatives or friends – an important, influential parent, step-parent, sibling, aunt, uncle, cousin, grandparent, niece, nephew, housemate, neighbour, or whatever. You know this is a special connection and you were born with it, so be grateful!

What do you love, or like, most about your house or flat? Say thank you to the Universe.

What's lucky about your work, school or college situation? Apart from anything else, you can be grateful that jobs or study courses are on tap for you. There are many places in the world where (believe it or not) teenage girls fantasize about having the chance to go to school.

Are you in a happy relationship right now? Have you ever been blessed with a wonderful love relationship, even if it didn't last? Do you know for a fact that someone special is interested in you right now? It's all thanks-worthy!

If you've ever had an amazing holiday or you have one coming up, you know what to say. Friends are always worth being grateful for. A good friendship is hard to find.

Anything else that you know in your heart is a total luck-draw in the game of life should be a reason for you to thank your angels. Maybe you got a car for your eighteenth birthday. Maybe you were born with an amazing swimming talent. Perhaps you're one of the top-five science students in your class, or you've just landed the work experience ticket from heaven, or the dream compliment from an oh-so-powerful boss. You know what to say...

Three miracles from the angels

Angels were made for miracles, and they have three to deliver to your door right now. As you can see, the next page is full of stars with numbers – fifty, to be exact. Take a moment to look at these. You have no idea where this exercise is taking you, or what those numbers mean, but you have to trust that you will find miracles that seem absolutely right. Why? Because you need them so much – and the angels know that. You will need three dressmaker's pins. To begin, read this sentence and "think it" at the same time:

"I would love to see three miracles in my life, from this second. I trust the angels to help me achieve them. I'm open to heavenly help and angelic assistance. Please show me what's out there for me, starting now!"

Close your eyes, and gently move the book around. Just shuffle this page from left to right, side to side, until you really can't remember what was where. Now, take a pin and make your first choice by sticking it onto the page, still with your eyes closed. (We don't mind if you leave pinpricks in our book, honestly – we think it's worth it!) Write that number down. Repeat this exercise twice more, until you have three numbers. Now match the numbers you picked and discover your miracles!

Tip: You can't do this exercise too often, or it won't work. Once a year is enough. You also have to be in the right frame of mind – in other words, this isn't a way to kill time on a rainy Sunday afternoon. You really have to need and want those angelic miracles, and be prepared for a true sense of wonder and appreciation as the angels unfold them in your life.

THE MIRACLES!

1 **The miracle of beauty:** The angels promise that beauty will be brought into your life, either through your own appearance, or through beauty in other people, animals, places, objects or environments. Beauty is entering your life.

2 **The miracle of respect:** The angels believe it's time for you to be respected and honoured by other people. They know your reputation matters to you, and they say it's now possible for you to be admired and appreciated in the right way.

3 **The miracle of personal change:** The angels can see that you are ready to change, either in terms of the way you look, or the way you present your personality. They know a transformation can happen more easily than you might think.

4 **The miracle of confidence:** The angels believe the time has come for you to truly feel confident and shine brightly, in front of an audience, or just in front of family, friends, people you love or like, strangers, and anyone you need to impress.

5 **The miracle of abundance:** How would it feel to have exactly what you need and want in your life? To never feel broke, or to always have just what you require in terms of objects and possessions? This miracle is now possible, from today forward.

6 **The miracle of money discovery:** Discovering that you don't need money as much as you think is a true miracle. The angels are ready to show you that there is more to life than cash, or being rich. They are ready to show you other riches right now.

7 **The miracle of returned objects:** You seem to have lost something, or those close to you have had something stolen, or mislaid. Whatever has gone from your life, or gone from the lives of those you care about, will be returned or replaced in kind.

8 **The miracle of rewards:** Everyone deserves to be rewarded for the work they put into life, and the angels are telling you that it's now possible for the universe to give back to you, for all the energy, time, and effort you put into your work or life.

9 **The miracle of words:** You can create magic with what you say, or write, and the angels are now hinting that it's time to start

speaking up, or using your computer more, or even trying to become a writer. Words are your miracles.

10 **The miracle of mobility:** You are about to find that getting from A to B, or even discovering your local area, is miraculously easy and enjoyable. Perhaps you are on your way to getting a driving licence, a mountain bike, or just a great short holiday.

11 **The miracle of family ties:** Step-parents, godparents, grandparent, cousins, brothers, sisters, aunts, and uncles are on a special and miraculous list in your life right now. Expect something special and wonderful, either through one of these people, or just for them.

12 **The miracle of learning:** The angels are happy to tell you that, before too long, you will be gaining a qualification, enrolling in a course, or just reading and listening wisely, as a special subject becomes totally within your grasp at last.

13 **The miracle of family:** Thirteen is lucky in this instance so don't be too worried if you've stuck a pin in this number! The angels are telling you that whatever you currently think would be "a total miracle" in your family might just happen.

14 **The miracle of ancestors:** Ancestors, ranging from your grandparents all the way back down the family line, can now be the source of something special and wonderful. Don't be surprised if these unknown relatives start to play a part now.

15 **The miracle of home:** Home is where the heart is, and the angels know it. This could bring about the ideal home base for you, or enable you to make changes to your place that truly make it feel like a home. Open up to the miracles.

16 **The miracle of belonging:** The angels say it's time you realized that you can belong to a place as much as you can belong to a person. What is your homeland, or what do you consider to be your homeland? Is it this country, or would you be more at home in another one? This miracle could lead you there.

17 **The miracle of romance:** Romance is different to love. It's not about that serious, heavy, life-time commitment. It's about sweet nothings, and flowers, and chocolates, and magical nights, and anything else you dream up. It's a miracle!

18 **The miracle of children:** Children and babies are the keys to a miracle in your life, from this moment forward. The angels will find the best way to bring this about, but one way or another you will find kids now add something to your life.

19 **The miracle of creativity:** It takes inspiration, and something else – a mysterious X factor maybe – to turn a creative effort into something that is really special. This miracle can now occur for you, you only have to make the first move.

20 **The miracle of self-expression:** Madonna sang, "Express yourself," and look what it did for her! The angels believe it's time for you to let your heart, soul, personality, and character pour into something creative or artistic. It's time to be yourself.

21 **The miracle of good health:** This is a really amazing miracle promise to see, and the angels believe that your good health is now very close – it's just going to take one key person, event, situation, or set-up to bring it to your door.

22 **The miracle of balance:** You need balance in your life, and the angels can see it. They now want you to know that the perfect balance between mind, body, and spirit harmony is achievable. Who or what will bring it to you now?

23 **The miracle of work:** You might not think work is a miracle at all, but if you are working in a job you dislike or feel unrewarded by, or if you are without work, this is a wonderful miracle to pick. The right job for you is now possible.

24 **The miracle of efficiency:** Wow! You might not have believed this, but you are very close to becoming the most efficient you've ever been. The miracle of organization and order in your life is not to be sneezed at, and it's within reach.

25 **The miracle of the ex factor:** The angels say something wonderful and miraculous is now possible for your ex partner, or through your ex partner. What that will be, only time can reveal. But hope and wish for the best for both of you, and wait!

26 **The miracle of true love:** This is the miracle every Goddess secretly wants the most. If you are willing to meet the angels halfway, to respond when the right person appears, and to believe and trust – then a true loving partnership can happen.

27 **The miracle of love healing:** This choice of miracle reveals that you need to repair some of the damage in your current relationship, or make things better between you. Perhaps your partner will do it for you, or another person can help out?

28 **The miracle of equality:** Every love relationship or partnership needs balance and this choice promises that you will meet someone who can create this with you, or find ways to make your current relationship a lot more equal.

29 **The miracle of security:** Security sometimes has to come from knowing that there is a pile of money, or a home, or some other important resource, that you can call your own. This choice says that other people will help you find it.

30 **The miracle of financial savvy:** Every Goddess would probably like to be totally organized financially, or a genius with pounds and pence, but this can be hard to achieve. The angels now believe it's possible for you, if you meet them halfway.

31 **The miracle of miracles!:** This is a very unusual choice, but the angels insist that it's one of the most important miracles you can expect. Basically, the other world out there – the spiritual, hidden, mysterious world – is coming closer!

32 **The miracle of life cycles:** Every ending in life and nature is followed by a beginning. Every death is also followed by new life, or rebirth. This very natural, organic, environmental lesson will be spelled out in your own life, by the miracle of new life.

33 **The miracle of global adventures:** Global adventures can come to you because you travel or move to a new place, or because you make friends with someone from another country. The angels say this miracle is now open to you, so enjoy the experience.

34 **The miracle of education:** Education might sound like a boring miracle, but the angels are shaking their heads, and saying that the gift of learning and acquiring knowledge is something that will change your life in powerful and fantastic ways.

35 **The miracle of journeys:** A journey is anything you can take by plane, by boat, on foot, by car, or on a bicycle or motorbike. Did you know that one special journey was in your destiny? This miracle will broaden your horizons in every way.

36 **The miracle of understanding:** Understanding people whose backgrounds, countries, cultures or customs are different to your own is certainly a miracle for those who are narrow-minded! You're about to learn from those who are different ...

37 **The miracle of success:** Lots of Goddesses love seeing this one because it promises so much. But first, the angels want you to define your notion of success. Is it the best mark in your course, the hottest job in town, or something else?

38 **The miracle of achievement:** You are on course to a truly major achievement, one which you will never forget, and one which will always make you feel good about yourself. It may seem impossible at times, but the angels say this miracle is close.

39 **The miracle of recognition:** Everyone gets to be a star, or a legend in their own lunchtime, with this miraculous promise. The angels believe it's time that other people recognized your talent, achievements or accomplishments. Go for it!

40 **The miracle of ambition:** You may have chosen this because you're not all that ambitious. Maybe it would seem miraculous to yourself and others if you got motivated? Maybe you need more time or energy to feel this way. It's here!

41 **The miracle of friends:** True friends who like you for yourself are the miraculous promise of this number. The angels say you will either rediscover just how fantastic one of your friends is, or you will make a new friend who is solid-gold.

42 **The miracle of groups:** Belonging to a group of people can be a special and life-changing experience, and even if you don't think your membership of a netball team or a quiz team (or any other group) is that big a deal, the angels see miracles.

43 **The miracle of healing friendships:** You seem to have chosen this number because there is a problem with a friend of yours, or maybe you have broken a friendship, or lost a friend. Healing the rift or damage is now possible thanks to this angel choice.

44 **The miracle of ideals:** An ideal is a noble vision, or a truly wonderful idea of what the world could be like. This choice says you are about to discover just how big an idealist you are. The angels say every ideal can also become a miracle.

45 **The miracle of solitude:** So many people freak out when they see the word solitude, but it can be a wonderful thing. It doesn't mean being lonely, it means being alone – and that's quite different. The angels say private time can be a miracle.

46 **The miracle of secrets:** Perhaps the miracle here is that you can actually keep a secret, or rely on someone else to keep them for you! The angels believe that one particular secret, in the not too distant future, has a miraculous purpose.

47 **The miracle of peace:** Peace of mind and inner peace could be the biggest miracle of all, especially if you are stressed out, or have a whole bunch of people or demands intruding on your life. With angelic help, inner peace is now achievable.

48 **The miracle of self-knowledge:** Do you really think you know yourself? This number says that you could actually know the real you a lot better – and maybe get over some hang-ups or phobias. Angelic help will assist you to discover yourself.

49 **The miracle of trust:** Perhaps you have had your trust in other human beings destroyed, or shaken a little. Either way, it might seem like it would take a miracle for you to trust again. The angels love this choice and will help you one hundred per cent.

50 **The miracle of faith:** It's time for you to discover who and what you have faith in. It may be God. It may be one of the Goddesses. It may be something you can't even name. Belief in a higher power, or creative cosmic intelligence, is close!

BE AN ANGEL

There's a car sticker around you might have seen that says "Practise random acts of kindness and senseless acts of beauty." This is exactly what you should be doing if you are trying to be a human angel.

Psychic Power

Everyone is psychic

You just need to find out if you are better at smelling, hearing, feeling, seeing, or sensing information. To be psychic basically means you have super knowledge. You might go on a date with a guy and sense things about his personality, or even his family, that turn out to be correct later. If you are moving into a flat and you "see" pictures in your mind's eye of ginger cats, you may discover that the person who lived there before you was feline crazy. Psychic ability is something everyone has, in stronger or weaker degrees. It helps us communicate with each other without having to use the phone. It could even mean we can move objects just by thinking about it (although this is rare).

Your own accuracy as a psychic depends on a few factors. First, do you believe that you can do it? Second, do you feel good about it? (Fear will put you off.) Third, was anyone else in your family well-known for his/her way with tarot cards, tea leaves, or seeing ghosts? (Strong psychic ability can run in families and is often passed down from grandmother to granddaughter). In the same way that everyone can cook, or at least learn to boil an egg, it's true that we all have the potential to be psychic. This ability can range from diluted – the ability to know who is about to text-message you before it happens – to very strong – you might be able to see people who have died, and even hear voices.

Your psychic wavelength quiz

When you think of lavender do you imagine

a) Holding a velvety lavender stalk?
b) Seeing miles of purple lavender fields?
c) Smelling fresh lavender oil?
d) Hearing the wind rustle through fields of lavender stalks?
e) Instructions for making lavender bags?

If we say the word "chocolate" to you, do you

a) Taste the velvety texture in your mouth?
b) See the foil wrapper and the writing on the label?
c) Smell the cocoa and cream scent?
d) Hear yourself munching it?
e) Think about the pros and cons of eating it?

Finally, if we ask you to imagine Brad Pitt is standing next to you right now, what do you find easiest to dream up?

a) The feeling of his stubble, or the softness of his skin.
b) The colour of his eyes.
c) The smell of his aftershave.
d) The sound of his voice.
e) The kinds of things you might talk about.

Find your psychic wavelength

Take this quick test to discover which psychic wavelength you operate on. Your first thought will be your best though, so stick with that.

Depending on your answers, you operate on touch, sight, smell, hearing or sensing (also called "knowing"). You may operate on two levels at once, so if you have a close call between, say, the B or D choice, perhaps you are capable of hearing information tele-pathically and seeing pictures too. But in any case, checking your answers overleaf will help you find your strongest kind of sixth sense ability.

Mostly As: You should be able to feel a drop in temperature if someone in the spirit world is around you. You might get excited shivers down your spine if your spirit guide wants to communicate good news to you. If you try to predict the future for yourself or other people, you might talk about the way things feel to you (rough or smooth) or you might describe things as hard or soft. You're very sensitive!

Mostly Bs: You are clairvoyant! You "see" pictures in your mind's eye. If you practise this ability you could eventually become accurate with tiny details. Instead of just seeing a plumber's truck around a guy, for example (you may be psychically detecting that he's a plumber), you may see the number plate, or the writing on the side of the truck, or even how clean the back window is. Pay attention to images or symbols in your dreams. They could be accurate pointers to the future.

Mostly Cs: You operate on smell, and tune in psychically to people and events by "sniffing" them out. You may even have noticed unusual scents or fragrances around you, even when there is nothing in the room to cause them. If your great-grandmother used to love peppermints, for example, when she is visiting you from the spirit world you could get a strong minty smell. If you're looking for a new housemate, you may go on smell, not because he/she actually comes wafting in on a cloud of Chanel – or garbage – but because your nose twitches and you "sniff" their personality.

Mostly Ds: You are clairaudient. You can actually hear words, or music, psychically. This is a very unusual version of psychic ability. People who have it sometimes become professional mediums – in other words, they can actually hear people from the spirit world speaking to them. If you ask your spirit guide a question out loud and then remain quiet for a few minutes, with a clear mind, you might even hear the answer coming back. Sometimes you may hear your name called – especially as you fall asleep! This is a definite giveaway to clairaudient ability. Information relayed this way often comes in brief snatches. It's unusual to get long sentences. You might just get one word rushing past your ears. Why? Because the spirit world operates on a much faster vibration than the earthly one.

Mostly Es: You are probably clairsentient. You just "know" things and yet you haven't felt a drop in temperature, seen someone in spirit, smelled a fragrance, or experienced any other clue. This is quite a common ability. Typically you may feel as if you have always known something about a person or situation, and yet if you question yourself, you'll realize the information is new, and there's no way you could have picked it up from another source. You get lots of hunches if you're clairsentient. Classically you'll pick numbers in raffles (or not) because you just "know" they are, or aren't, going to win.

Why we're all psychic

Centuries before the internet, and text messages, and telephones, most ancient cultures used to rely on sending information, and receiving it, over long distances – using only our imagination and concentration. This ability is still with us, though people hardly use it any more. However, in times of crisis or emergency, when people desperately want to reach each other (but there's no phone), psychic ability often comes back. That's when you'll have a funny dream about your friend, only to realize that at the moment you had the dream, she was in a skiing accident. Alternatively, you might suddenly think of your Great Aunt Muriel for no reason, only to discover that she's just won the lottery. Extreme emotion, especially excitement or fear, seems to transmit across invisible airwaves. If you get used to sending and receiving information in this way when you're a kid (and adults around you encourage it too) then by the time you are in your twenties, you might have developed telepathy quite strongly. Telepathy is simply the art of sending and receiving information without the annoying jingle on your mobile!

Simple telepathy for absolute beginners

Have a friend in one room, and put yourself in another room. Each of you should have ten ordinary household objects to "send" to the other one at a time. It might seem clunkier than email, but then again, hey, it might just work! Basically, you need to find out if you're a receiver or a sender. Some people are very good at both, other people may be gifted only at one method of telepathy. Here are some objects your friend might be concentrating on trying to deposit in your mental in-tray.

* A vacuum cleaner
* A coat hanger
* An orange
* A book

You can do complicated stuff too. Maybe you've got a fluffy bunny pyjama case – well, consider "sending" that object too. However, the quality of your message depends on using all your sense channels to transmit it to your friend. In other words, even though you've worked out that you are clairaudient (you hear) or clairvoyant (you see), you will need to pull together the entire package – sight, smell, feel, sound, and so on – to really push your message through. If you really want your friend to get that fluffy bunny case, you may picture the rabbit, "smell" rabbit food, hear a rabbit munching on grass, or silently say the word "rabbit" to get through. If you really try all the options, the message for your friend will be that much stronger…

TELEPATHY IS THE ART OF SENDING AND RECEIVING INFORMATION WITHOUT THE ANNOYING JINGLE ON YOUR MOBILE!

Spend about five minutes on each object. If you both close your eyes and concentrate on this exercise, and gently encourage each other (criticism at wrong guesses tends to turn down psychic ability) then you should find your ability to send or receive increases with each attempt.

If you do this with your boyfriend, you may develop a closer relationship, but it will also mean that, ultimately (especially if you stay together for a long time), you will be able to know what is on the other person's mind from time to time. This can happen naturally between couples too. Have you ever been lying on the couch with your boyfriend, not speaking for an hour or so, then started a conversation, only to find that you both come in at the same place, and start talking about the same thing? That's natural telepathy. If this happens to you and your main squeeze all the time, then "sending" things like fluffy bunny pyjama cases should be simple.

The psychic secrets of flowers

Do you want to read psychically for a friend, in a charming and old-fashioned way? We have a method that does not involve tarot cards, or throwing runes over your left shoulder. Instead, you just ask your friend to go out into the garden and pick one flower that she/he really identifies with. You want your friend to pick out a flower that "speaks" to him or her. It's worth spending a long time making the choice. The kind of fragrance, colour, petals, and texture that your friend selects will give you important clues about personality, future, and destiny.

When your friend has found the right flower, hold it gently in your hand and start to think about three things – past, present, and future. Take them in turn, and try not to let the fact that you already know certain things about your friend get in the way of your reading.

Let's just say your friend has chosen a huge red rose which you meditate on, waiting for pictures to come into your mind. For the past, you might get an impression that someone in her life was keeping secrets from her (because the petals are so tightly closed), or you might even see an initial in the petals – perhaps an A, which refers to her old friend Angus or Alistair! For the present, perhaps you feel the rose wants to open up more, but it can't. Is that how your friend might be feeling? With a bit of practice, you can personalize your flower reading and work in a deeply intuitive and sensitive way to give your friend quite accurate information. The golden rule, though: Do unto others...Always give the kind of psychic reading you would be happy with, and be gentle with people, even if you think that red rose has a whole lot of thorns!

Protect yourself
WITH A PSYCHIC SLEEPING BAG

Your aura is an energy field that goes right around your body. Think of it as your personal force field. Sometimes, when you are feeling more sensitive than usual, or just more tired, other people, or even other people in the spirit world, can affect your aura and influence the way you think or feel. Having an operation can also affect your aura! The most common aura problems come from other people invading your mental, psychic, and spiritual space, though. Without being too paranoid about it, there may be times when you wonder why on earth you are thinking constantly about a particular girl or guy that you don't even really care about that much. It's possible that this person is concentrating very hard on you, and because they are pouring out psychic energy, they have managed to get through your protective barrier, to influence you in a subtle way. Whether they meant to do this or not, it's not that great for you – or for them – and this is why a psychic sleeping bag can be a very good protective measure.

There are other reasons to get into your psychic sleeping bag, too. The more psychic work you do, the more open you are to any kind of person at all in the spirit world – even people who are troubled, or who want to make trouble. Don't be scared about this, just think of it in a commonsense way. When you work with ESP, you are open. It's just like opening a door in your kitchen. Pretty much anyone can come in when you are open, unless you protect yourself. Having a psychic sleeping bag is a protective measure, like having a latch on the door.

Ask your angels and guides to help you put on your sleeping bag.

WHAT THE 20 DESTINY TIME STONES MEAN

1   means, wait one day
2 means, you'll know the answer in two minutes
3   means, ask three people over three months
4 means, wait four days
5   means, the answer will be clear in five weeks
6 means, give this situation six months
7   means, think about it for a week
8 means, eight hours are all you need to work it out
9   means, nine months gives birth to the solution
10 means, wait ten days
11 means, wait eleven days
12 means, this answer requires a year
13 means, expect the unexpected
14 means, the answer comes slowly over a fortnight
15 means, you'll know after two weeks
16 means, four months should answer your query
17 means, the answer is clear in seventeen days
18 means, a long answer develops over 18 months
19 means, the solution you need has its own natural rhythm and trying
    to get results on a deadline won't work. Your life has its own
    music now
20 means, at twenty past the hour, you'll understand

It needs to be spun out of white light instead of white nylon. The cover is white, shiny, and reflective. Anything or anybody which isn't there for your highest good will simply bounce off that amazingly brilliant white cover. Physically get into your bag, standing up. Shuffle into it with your feet first, pull it up around your waist, up over your shoulders, and pull the hood over. Tie the drawstrings under your chin. Imagine the white light from the hood spilling over your face as well, like a beautiful, brilliant spotlight. Now say this: "I am protected." Do this whenever you feel the need. You should certainly try doing it any time you engage in a lot of psychic work.

Make your own Destiny Time Stones

You will need 20 stones or pebbles for this, and do pick stones which are big enough to write on. Don't just grab any old bits of gravel, either! These are your personal stones, to be kept in a silk scarf, or a drawstring bag, and they will help you make some important decisions if you really make them your own.

Wash the stones in warm water with a little essential oil, if you have any. Lemon or sage are both very good, and the stones will always carry a little of those scents. Get any dirt off, pat them dry, and then sit down with a gold or silver metallic pen – you can find them at most stationery stores. Number each stone from 1 to 20 following the meanings provided in the box below. If you don't have a drawstring bag for your stones, keep them in a handkerchief you really like or, better still, a gorgeous silk or cotton scarf, tied in a knot at the top. This is your own personal oracle for those times when you feel hopelessly stuck, lost, dazed, or confused! All you need to do is ask, sincerely and simply, for the correct qualities to bring to the situation which baffles you. You need time to sort things out, and your Destiny Time Stones will give you the cue.

We asked Jamie, a tall, dark, and handsome dude who works in an advertising agency, to throw his stones. Jamie's question was, "How do I get a better job?" He went to quite a lot of trouble drawing on all the numbers and words so we figured he might take a while to find the stone, but he jiggled the bag around for a second and immediately pulled out 13 – "Expect the unexpected."

In a few weeks, Jamie had his answer. He was offered a chance to leave the advertising agency and work part-time as a stand-up comedian.

The stones speak to you only if you take them seriously. Make sure you mix them around properly in your bag or scarf. Remember, a complex question can have a speedy answer – or something which seems really simple, like wondering how long you should wait before you get your hair cut, will make you wait for months!

Ghosts and other mysteries

People have different theories about ghosts. Some say they are imprints on the atmosphere. If someone was very upset and emotional (for example, someone who had just lost her head to Henry VIII), then somehow all those icky feelings will stick in the atmosphere, just like grooves on a record. Whenever a clairvoyant person is around (someone who can see psychically), the "record" of that time will play, revealing the rather distressing picture of a headless spook in a big medieval ballgown, wringing her hands and walking up and down corridors.

In actual fact, ghosts are very rare. And there is nothing to suggest that what you see, or hear, or experience in a haunted place is an imprint. A ghost is actually a person who has died, and either refuses to go towards the light (the light is variously known as heaven, nirvana, or the summerland) or, more strangely, doesn't actually realize that she/he is dead.

Ghosts are rare because both these circumstances are also extremely rare. What is out there beyond the light (the light you see when you leave your body) is so fabulous (the best gardens you ever saw, for a start) that nine out of ten human beings can't say no. Besides, at the point of death, there is always a friendly spirit guide or family member waiting to take you over. It's also highly unusual to find a dead person who hasn't actually realized that he or she has gone. It happens sometimes if the dying person was using drugs or alcohol quite heavily. It can happen, on extremely rare occasions, when there is nobody from the spirit world to collect the person who has just left their body.

And what does it feel like for the poor, unknowing ghost? Mediums who have been in contact with spirit people say that they explain it this way: A huge fog! The lost person can see and hear real, living people around them, but they can't make themselves known or heard. (This is why objects get moved sometimes, or electronic equipment gets fiddled with – it's a way of getting attention.) Time and space mean nothing to such lost spirit people. Instead, it's like one great big mist, and one enormous ball of confusion for them. They can be stuck there for years, in a big time–space fog – and not know it.

TRUE PSYCHICS HAVE A GIFT. . . AND THEY WANT TO USE IT FOR HUMANITY.

If you suspect you have a ghost in your house, call the experts. There may be a local spiritualist church in your area, or just a particular priest in your local regular church who has a reputation for helping these poor spirit people move on. And what about the ghosts who simply stubbornly refuse to go to the light? They just need a little gentle persuasion – but once again, by an expert. Don't try to set up as a ghostbuster without help. People who have died and got stuck, or lost, can't hurt you – the most they can do is scare you a little, as occasionally they have a way with television sets, or radios, or microwave ovens (spirit world energy connects well with electricity). Nevertheless, these are complex people, caught in complicated situations, and you need a highly spiritual, caring and experienced expert to deal with it.

Spook alert

Psychic no-go zones you need to avoid!

Over the years we've encountered some really weird experiences and people in our psychic travels, and now is the time to talk about them – especially if you want to know what NOT to do on your psychic explorations.

Never use a ouija board

When people die, they really don't change that much. If they were a nuisance when they were alive, always making prank phone calls, sending stupid junk email, or even trying to freak young Goddesses out, they will also be a nuisance when they are dead. Unless they develop spiritually, they can hang around with the same bad energy and bad habits that were there during their time on earth. What do you think a spirit world creep, vandal, or loser really wants to do? Right, move a glass and scare the false eyelashes off you! We have heard some really nutty stories about teenage guys, in particular, using ouija boards over the years. One terrified bloke we knew used it to get his exam results – and ended up ringing the Salvation Army as his house got turned into a real-life X-Files location.

What you need to know is this. When a bunch of you deliberately try to communicate with spirit people but you don't know who they are, and you don't really care (except you want to have some fun, or scare yourselves stupid), then you are basically issuing one giant invitation to any dead creep around to get involved with you. Would you throw a party for people you had never met, or let everybody in your town in? Of course not. You'd get people who'd wreck your kitchen, pour your bubble bath down the loo, and rip your fishnets to shreds. A ouija board is the same. You have to be really, really lucky to find a high-level, spiritually aware, cosmically cool spirit person to communicate with. Most of the time, you're opening yourself up to any old dead person who happens to be floating by. And with your shared group psychic energy, you are creating something like a huge force field for that spirit-world person to use. That's why the glass goes zooming across the board. And it's sometimes why doors can fly open, and you may even experience genuine disruptive poltergeist activity. Don't risk it!

Beware the psychic power tripper

Anyone working psychically who doesn't come from compassion and humour, caring and common sense, is a little bit dangerous.

Why? Because although their information may be accurate (especially about certain chunks of your future), it actually does you no good. Avoid people who charge you a lot of money. Are they charging more than a doctor or a good masseur? If so, ask yourself what their motives are. A true psychic has a gift he or she wants to use for humanity, and although they have to earn a living from it, they will never price their gift beyond a certain level – after all, why should poor people be shut out of spiritual advice? If you sense a rip-off, run a mile.

Watch out for psychics (amateurs or professionals) who say you MUST do this, or you SHOULD do that, or you WILL experience such and such. The future is a delicate business. There are a few aspects of it which certainly are fixed in time. They were set up and organized a long time ago before you were born, and you were part of the team who chose it all to happen to you! A great deal of the future is free will and full of choices, though. It weaves around the predestined stuff like a huge web or (if you live in London) the London Underground. Depending on where you just came from and where you stand now, a psychic can probably talk about your choices, and maybe even spot a couple of predestined things (the number or gender of kids you'll have, for example – this is frequently chosen before you are born). Nevertheless, anyone who waves his or her arms around and gives you the impression that you HAVE to follow a certain aspect of advice (or doom will prevail), or that absolutely everything is written, fixed, and chosen – well, you know where the door is.

Handing over your power

You are here to live your life, with a few psychic tools, but not to flip around like a goldfish in a pond, letting every decision come back to a rune, or a psychic vision, or a dream. You made the choice to be human with good reason – you wanted to come down here to this planet and learn lessons – and also enjoy yourself. If you hand over your power to a system, or a psychic, or a tarot reader, or anything else, then you are missing the point. A little intuition and spirit-guide help is a great thing, but even the wisest and kindest angel in the world is not going to run your life for you. The biggest miracles and the most magic we have seen come from this combination – independent action plus spooky help. In other words, if you want to go to Bali to learn how to surf, then for heaven's sake, book the ticket, buy the board, and do the trip – only then will your psychic ability allow you to find the right beach, or the right price for the board. Try to blend your personal power with your amazing intuitive power, and you'll have the kind of life you've always wanted!

Don't give in to doom merchants

Never accept anything from a psychic that rattles you or freaks you out. He or she may be the greatest thing since sliced tarot cards, according to your mates, or they may be incredibly famous (or expensive). Nevertheless, if you hear stuff that you don't like about your past, present, or future, and it's delivered to you in a way that you find insensitive, or even just plain dumb, well then – you are entitled to stop the reading right there and leave! A lot of gloom and doom with anyone – be they astrologer, guru, or crystal ball expert – is never a good thing. It's not accurate either. Do you really think your future is so black? You are free to question and challenge anyone who tells you about accidents, in particular. If they can get this bare "fact" about your life, why can't they also give you the date, place, and circumstances? We rest our case. A psychic will occasionally get accurate information about a potential accident, and you are certainly meant to hear it – but only in order to avoid it! Vague mutterings about seeing danger are useless. All they do is scare you. And a good professional psychic or medium won't even pass it on, unless they can also give you specific helpful information which will assist you to avoid any potential accidents.

FANATICAL FRIENDS

Watch out for friends who get all excited and freaked out by psychic stuff, but don't have a clue what they're doing, or why they're doing it. Of course the world of tarot, I Ching, ESP, or whatever is fascinating, otherwise we wouldn't be writing this book. But it is not a cheap thrill. You always need to know where your fanatical friends are coming from, especially if they offer to throw your tarot cards. A little maturity and wisdom can definitely be a good thing in this regard. The occasional look at the future, in order to make smart decisions that benefit everybody, is a natural part of life – future-seekers and mystics have been part of every major civilized human society and culture. There is a massive difference, though, between, on the one hand, musing on life choices in the tarot and learning about yourself and, on the other, pulling out a tarot card like a madwoman every five minutes, to make it give you the "right" answer about a boy you like. Encourage your fanatical friends to take up roller-skating instead.

Wondering about doom and gloom predictions is very common, but all you need to know is this – while it is sometimes possible that a psychic can see an accident coming, or at least the risk of one, a good reader won't just terrify you, he or she will instead pass on handy information about your car that needs fixing, or a tendency that you have to speed, or even give you information about a particular stretch of road, and the conditions there. This is all practical stuff, and you are meant to hear it. Remember, without a psychic you could probably get the same information from your local friendly policeman, a wise friend, or a garage mechanic. As it is, you are being given a special, privileged, cosmic shortcut to this information. If it sounds like common sense, and you figure it's probably timely advice – and if the rest of the reading adds up too – then you should probably heed it. What you DON'T need in your life, though, is a self-proclaimed expert who drones on, "I see divorce, I see floods, I see the dog biting you in the bum, I see bankruptcy..." Get out of their negative energy field, Goddess, and don't look back!

Test your psychic IQ

You will need pens and paper, a pile of magazines you haven't read before, and peace and quiet for half an hour. You are going to pick up information psychically about people by concentrating on their picture in a magazine feature story, and writing down facts about their lives only by looking at their faces. Give yourself plenty of time to do it, and don't edit yourself, or think too hard about what you are writing. Just try to see pictures, feel things, "smell" situations around people, or use your other main psychic sense that you discovered in the first test in this chapter.

Try not to go on what makes sense or what you think you know. You may be staring at a picture of a rich woman in an evening dress, but does that necessarily mean the lady in the photograph is wealthy at the moment? By the way, you can do this exercise with photographs of celebrities like Jennifer Aniston, as long as you haven't read the interview or the story, and as long as you aren't the Numero Uno Aniston Expert on the planet.

When you are finished, go through your list and give yourself ticks and crosses, or marks out of ten. Practise until you find your average going up. This way, you will also get to know your own psychic rhythm. The facts you pick up could astound you, and you may be surprised to find out it's the information you write down that comes quickly and easily that is the most accurate. Don't worry if you feel, see, sense or "know" stuff that seems mad. Images of things that make no sense, like trapeze artists, might just refer to the fact that the person in the story is describing her marriage as "on a tightrope." The more you do this exercise with magazines, the more you will come to understand how your psychic self works. It's common to get things in code!

HOW TO STUN AND AMAZE YOUR ENGLISH TEACHER – OR YOUR BOOK CLUB

If you're studying English at the moment, or if you're in a book club you can use your psychic ability to come up with insights in your essays or group discussions that will leave everyone with their jaws hanging open. If you're a student, this is not a shortcut to an easy 100% result for your next exam. You will have to do the study as well. But with your psychic abilities switched on, you should be able to deliver something extra special.

If you have a set book for English, tell yourself that you are going to turn it into a movie. A mind movie! You will need an hour for this meditation, which should be done as soon as you have put the book to one side or finished a chapter. Put on your psychic sleeping bag, which you've learned how to do earlier in this chapter. Now tell yourself that you are going to try on the costumes or clothes of five of the characters you are reading about. You should have descriptions of these clothes from the book itself, but if the author has been skimpy on details, you can create the wardrobe you feel is right for that character.

Try on the costumes or clothes of each character in turn, beginning with the one you liked best, graduating to the one you liked or identified with least. As you "wear" their clothes, make a point of sensing what they are feeling and thinking. What do they fear? What do they love? How do they eat their food, fast or slow? Get further into the character by really feeling their clothes on your back. As you become each character in turn, ask them how they feel about the way their story in the book is developing – and how they really feel about the other characters.

Remain in this meditation for as long as you like. When you have finished your last wardrobe change, get up, have a cup of tea, or just shake yourself out of it, and make notes about everything you experienced, felt or just "knew" during the exercise. The more you do this, the more deeply you will connect to the book, and the characters, which could take you from a B minus to an A plus

Throw a psychic party

You will need really good friends for this party, but also an equal number of strangers or acquaintances you don't know very well. Why? Because you are going to share your psychic gifts and "read" each other, based on your watches and your jewellery. If you don't wear either, bring something else personal to the party, like a favourite pen or ornament.

Once everyone has arrived, throw all the watches, jewellery, and other objects into a big bag or container, and get each person to pick something up in turn. Obviously, if you just happened to score your best friend's watch, you might want to put it back in the pile and find something else belonging to one of the guests you don't know. Otherwise, your intimate knowledge of your best friend's love life could get in the way of a truly psychic reading!

Taking it in turns, each person closes his or her eyes, really "feels" the object in their hands, and then starts making comments. This can be really funny, or it can raise eyebrows all over the room. The main thing is a warm, friendly atmosphere. You are all here to test your psychic knowledge, not to freak each other out! Once the speaker has finished dishing out his or her insights, the real owner of the object can be revealed – and you can all discuss just how close the object reading came to the truth.

This works because jewellery or watches, in particular, carry the vibration of the owner. Sometimes information which makes no sense to the owner will have another explanation, though. Antique jewellery may indeed have an imprint, but it could belong to someone who died 100 years ago. So, with the best intentions in the world, a friend at your psychic party could actually be giving a reading for the original owner, not the baffled person on the couch opposite.

Psychic TV news

For this exercise you will need to do a special meditation before you are allowed to switch on your personal psychic TV and watch tomorrow's news. Relax your body, either by sitting or lying down. Count backwards from ten to one, seeing yourself walking down a long flight of stairs. See your TV set in front of you. You can choose the colour and shape. It might even be an old 1960s model in black and white! Then follow these steps:

* Tell yourself you are now going to see your personal psychic news reader. Once again, you get to choose the age, gender, personality, and features. Are you watching the 7 p.m. bulletin with a Chinese

sage, or a red-haired man with freckles and a red tie?

* The first bulletin is ready to be delivered. This will be something about your past. Listen carefully. What are the headlines? What kind of report is it? Make a note of it and come back to it later, after your meditation is over.

* Keep walking down more stairs. You can count a further 20 stairs this time. Your psychic newsreader is now going to give you a bulletin about tomorrow. It may come in words or pictures. Make a note of it.

* And now, the news in detail! Climb down 10 more stairs in your imagination for the final, full news report. Your newsreader is now going to go into quite a lot of depth about tomorrow. Once again, note anything which comes through. And how does your newsreader's voice sound? Optimistic? Pessimistic?

When you wake up and shake up from this meditation, write down everything really quickly. With a little analysis, you should be able to make sense of the first report, which was your past. Or perhaps your newsreader came right out and said everything very clearly. By this time tomorrow you will be able to check up on the accuracy of the two other bulletins – the main headlines, and the in-depth report. If you find it works, keep practising. In time, you will be able to switch on your psychic TV to do news headlines about next week, next month or even next year!

Are you supersensitive?

Everyone is psychic, but some people are strongly psychic, which means that if you are, a lot of the exercises in this book will come easily to you. In addition, if you think back to your childhood, you might remember funny incidents or unusual things about yourself which you've taken for granted – until now. Did you ever sense things about people, especially teachers or family, without being told? Have you ever seen a dead animal or person as if they were still alive? These are all signs that you are supersensitive. Living with this level of ability is a challenge. If you are supersensitive already, here are some things which will help you survive!

Remember that too much noise or violence is bad for you. This particularly applies to films and television. If you are in tune with your psychic self, you may have stopped watching X-rated films or violent news reports or distressing scenes on TV some years ago. If not, you may want to monitor how you feel when you are exposed to this kind of stuff. If you regularly get shaken, upset, or feel exhausted or even depressed, you don't need any more signals. Many people in our world are totally numb to horrible stuff on the big and small screen, because it's been pushed at them for so many years that their sensitivity is very low. If you are extremely psychic, however, it will be better for your peace of mind if you avoid anything with guns, blood, or screams.

People who get off the phone and leave you feeling exhausted, or those who seem to bring out your gloomy side, are not good psychic company. Because you are supersensitive, you may find that you absorb other people's needs and feelings like a sponge. The plus side of this ability is an incredible accuracy in spotting problem people – even when you are introduced to them for the first time. Is someone smiling and being polite, but somehow turning you off at the same time? This may be a sign that your psychic antennae are quivering, and giving you strong feelings that this person is a negative influence.

THE SIXTH SENSE HAS NOTHING TO DO WITH THE SCARY MOVIE AND EVERYTHING TO DO WITH YOUR NATURAL ABILITY TO MAKE THE RIGHT DECISIONS.

The overall effects of being so sensitive can be quite difficult, though. You are going to encounter people who want to lump all their problems onto you, moan or whinge to you, or even play little games with you. This is something which should bounce off you, but unless you make a special effort to put on your psychic sleeping bag each time, repeated exposure to these kinds of individuals could leave you feeling permanently tired or depleted, without knowing why.

What do you do about premonitions, especially if world events are involved? One of the first things that many supersensitive people experience is an awareness of forthcoming tragedies or disasters. Later on, this seems to change, and the dreams or scary visions stop. It's almost as if the negative events are easier for your psychic abilities to pick up on! In the meantime, though, you need to find like-minded people to share your feelings, and perhaps to help you sort out the next step. It's quite true, the police do work closely with some mediums and psychics, and so it's not impossible that your premonition could be put to good use. Nevertheless, you need to start from a solid base, and preferably attach yourself to a group like BAPS, the British Astrological and Psychic Society, or the Australian Psychics Association, or The Journey Within, in America (PO Box 1413, Clifton, New Jersey 07015). Check out the website www.awakenone.freeservers.com for more resources.

Your inner psychic jukebox

Here's an easy way to keep your psychic abilities fresh and power-ful, without driving yourself crazy. Basically, you need your own jukebox! Every time you meet a situation or person which you need psychic insights on, just check the songs that drift into your mind. With practice, you can develop an amazing ability to accurately assess any set-up or individual, just by tuning into the songs you are picking. The lyrics say it all. So does the mood of the song. Want to know more? Here are some real-life examples.

Jackie heard a guy called Colin was interested in her. He seemed nice, and he was quite good-looking, but every time the subject of Colin came up she found the old Frank Sinatra/Sid Vicious song, "My Way," coming into her head. In a few months she got to know Colin a lot better. It turned out he was a complete control freak, especially where girlfriends were concerned. Her inner psychic juke-box had been spot-on!

Marcus was determined to book a trip to New Zealand so he could catch up on some skiing and bushwalking. Every time he checked out airfares on the internet, though, he kept thinking about the Madonna song "Spanish Lullaby." Marcus ignored it, but a few weeks later he wished he'd listened. Before he knew it, he'd fallen in love with a Spanish girl backpacking around Australia, and so his New Zealand holiday had to be canned for a trip to Barcelona instead. He lost his deposit! Marcus also had other Spanish clues and signals around this time, so now he's learned to tune into his psychic jukebox more closely.

Jessica couldn't get the old classic song, "Fever" out of her head. She woke up with it, heard it on the radio, and even found herself whistling it while walking down the street. A few days later, she packed for a trip to New York, but skipped the health insurance. Bad move! Within hours she had picked up severe flu from the air-con-ditioning on the aeroplane and, you guessed it, within days she was running a high temperature. Sometimes your psychic jukebox is the best warning system you'll ever get.

Helping your sixth sense take off

The sixth sense has nothing to do with that scary Bruce Willis movie, and everything to do with your natural ability to make the right decisions. You were born with it, and it's just a question of living naturally and easily with it, and also coming to use it as a much-loved tool. You make decisions about your future every day, and you often use some pretty dubious tools to make those decisions. You might not think about it, but how many of your choices are based on these things?

* Past bad experiences, and your fear or anxiety about repeating the risks.
* Lucky past experiences, and your faith that you'll get lucky again.
* What your friends tell you to do.
* What your parents tell you to do.
* What you read in a magazine last week.

Blending common sense and sixth sense

Wouldn't you rather make your decisions, especially the big ones, using other abilities as well? Prejudice or vague hopes are not a good basis to make choices with. And every culture and nation in the world has a set way of using the sixth sense to guide them forward. Native Americans have special techniques, and so do Australian Aborigines. Here's how you can learn to live with sense number six, without driving yourself too crazy.

Firstly, don't talk about it all the time or use it to make yourself seem more mysterious or interesting to other people! It's like big-noting your ability to taste food. Why bother? The more natural and casual you are about your skills, the more easily those skills will blend in with the rest of your personality and your life. Even when you pick things up psychically – perhaps with songs on your inner jukebox – you don't need to make a big deal about it. Just tune in and pay attention, privately.

Expect to be given repeated messages and clues about situations and people, and you will be. In time, you'll just come to "know" what the truth actually is, as an incredible blend of coincidences, strange twists of fate and other signs and signals pointing something out. Let's just say you're choosing between two jobs, for example. One is in a hair salon, and the other is in an Italian restaurant. Over the course of a week, you might find you develop a real distaste for garlic (your sixth sense of smell is "sniffing out" a problem). You may also hear Italian opera on the radio, and find that it grates on you. In the space of a day, you might meet two people who have worked in Italian restaurants and had a bad time. Maybe you'll also get songs like the theme from Hair, on your inner psychic jukebox, reminding you of the hair salon option! Clusters of psychic hints and messages are a sure sign that something is going on, and you need to listen. Experiment. After a few months, you'll come to work with these cluster clues without even thinking about it, and as a result, you'll find yourself automatically and easily making the right decisions.

There are usually three warning signals with any situation or person where the message is "Don't go there." We don't know why it happens in threes, but it seems to be a rule of life. Maybe you're thinking about investing all your hard-earned cash in an ostrich farm in Peru. On day one, you lose your cheque book, which means you can't pay any money out for at least two weeks. On day two, you meet a person who is allergic to ostrich feathers. On day three, your email goes down, and all your communication with Peru ostrich farmers disintegrates! One obstacle could be just a passing glitch. Two obstacles need careful attention. Three, and we reckon you should definitely think about it!

Start a psychic art book

Some people are really gifted at drawing, others can't even come up with a picture of an orange unless they have a peanut butter jar lid to draw around first. You could be pleasantly surprised at your ability to create sketches when you are in a special psychic meditation, though. If you start your own art book, you could not only develop your abilities as an artist, you could also end up with a fascinating pointer to the past, present, and future.

Begin by protecting yourself with your psychic sleeping bag, and then relax completely as you visualize seven colours washing over you. Begin with violet (also known as lilac) which is a beautiful sugary pink-purple. Then graduate to very dark purple. Move to turquoise blue, to the point where you can feel it flooding every pore. Your next colour is sparkling green. Finally, meditate on yellow, orange, and red.

Pick up the pen and write down the name of a question you have. Here are some basic questions which work for everyone:

* Where will I be in five years' time?
* What is (insert guy's name here) really like?
* What will next month bring?

Start doodling without trying too hard. Just grab the pen and start drawing whatever comes into your mind. You may want to put in particular objects, or words, and numbers. Using colour can really help. The idea isn't to be the next Leonardo da Vinci, it's really to use your intuition to inspire you to draw psychically. The pictures or images you end up with should, in time, reveal truths about your question. Test yourself continually and make notes on your progress. In this way you'll come to rely on your psychic art book as a regular part of your Goddess toolkit, and if it works for you, there may come a time when you are using it on a weekly basis. This technique isn't for everyone, but for some people, it's the ultimate way to peer into the hidden truth about people and situations.

Spooky cats and cosmic dogs

Did you know that animals are becoming more psychic? After thousands of years of living with us humans, they are beginning to learn special techniques for snapping up the best dog or cat food, the nicest cushion by the fire, and the most affectionate lap. Even people who are sceptical about the sixth sense have to admit that animals have a certain something. If you want to develop a really good relationship with your animals – cats, dogs, and horses seem to respond best – then try creating a more psychic connection with them. Have you ever seen the Gary Larson cartoon from The Far Side that shows a man talking to his dog while his dog thinks "Blah, blah, blah?" That really highlights how unequal most of our animal communication actually is. A pet will pick up your irritation, or your stress, but not the information about spilling chumpy chunks of dog food all over the kitchen floor. The same thing happens when you "instruct" your cat not to bring any more dead mice into the house. It makes you feel better, but all the cat is receiving is a psychic twitch about your anger.

The best way to get through to cats and dogs, and also horses, is when they are relaxed, after they have eaten, or when they are sleeping – but not when they are in a deep-sleep state. You might feel a bit silly introducing yourself to your animal after all these years of non-communication, but you've got to start somewhere. If your pet is extremely psychic, at the first silent "Hello" that you send, he or she may wake up and be on full alert. If not, though, don't worry. The message should still be getting through!

After hello, move on to a few compliments. Tell your animal good things about himself or herself. Pets rarely receive this kind of feedback, unfortunately. Human owners spend a lot of time pointing out the errors of their ways, but they appreciate loving attention as much as we do. Shamelessly flatter your cat, if you think he or she will like it! Only then can you move onto slightly more tricky areas of communication. If you really don't like the way your dog barks at cars, now is the time to point it out. Promise the dog that you love him or her, and that there will always be food and a warm bed, but be firm about the barking. You don't have to use a lot of words or make it a complicated message. Dogs and cats respond to short, simple stuff. If you telepathically send a picture of the car, and the message, "No bark!" that should work. The more you do this, the easier it will get. As in the real world, pets need to be repeatedly told or asked, until they get the message.

Cats and dogs can already show you clear evidence of their psychic ability. For a start, they commonly know when you are coming home. If you are late, or have been away on holiday for a while, they can even time it to the minute. Pets also know when you are going away. They may disappear themselves (just to make a point!) or even mess on the carpet. This stress reaction is hard to understand. After all, you haven't told them you're going! Animals rely on you for their food, though, so even a temporary departure can make them nervous, and it's in their interests to pick it up using their sixth sense. This is a good time to reassure them, using your psychic ability to send the message, that they'll be OK in your absence, and even giving them the date you expect to be home again.

How not to be psychic!

Here are some classic ways to shut down your psychic ability, or make it impossible for yourself to use your sixth sense. If you've ever wondered why you're not getting anywhere with your psychic powers, or why you have them sometimes but not others, this list may provide some clues.

* Being around a lot of noise is a bad idea. Noise addicts typically don't know they are creating so much volume in their lives, either. Do you walk into a room, put on a CD, and then switch on the TV to see what's on? Do you pump your stereo and always use the bass, even when there's no bass in the music? Is your personal stereo always on the highest volume, and do you crash saucepans around in the kitchen? Too much noise in your life is frequently a way of making sure other people notice you, believe it or not. It's a way of being at the centre of attention. Noise can also make your life feel full, even when it's essentially you who is so empty. A lot of loud music, or radio, or shrill alarm clock noise, can actually distract you from the real mission of getting to know yourself better – and facing whatever is so hollow inside you. Whatever motivates you to be noisy, remember two things. First,

it drives other people – and animals – crazy. Second, it totally shuts down your psychic ability. You will only get very weak, diluted results from any of the experiments in this book if you live a life which consists of garage music for breakfast, talkback radio for lunch, and blaring TV news for dinner.

* Being time-poor is another way to shut down your psychic gifts. If you don't have time to meditate for even ten minutes a day, what are you doing, Goddess? Ten minutes can sometimes be enough to kick-start your sixth sense, and you should be able to squeeze it out of a normal 24-hour day. If you are constantly stressed, rushing, speeding or racing then you will make it very hard for yourself to use any other sense except one – the panic sense!

* Being sceptical or doubtful is healthy, as you need to know the difference between truth and reality when you start to live as a psychic person. Everyone needs a bit of common sense and a reality check. That's why a lot of the exercises in this book require you to check, test and grade yourself – and give yourself time, so that you really know you're the real deal, psychically. Too much pessimism or cynicism, though, and you will shut your psychic gifts right down. This can also come from the people around you. Stay open and trusting, but keep your commonsense radar switched on too.

How to click with people psychically

Did you know how much rhythm and speed has to do with getting on with people around you? This especially applies to your family, your housemates, or anyone else you live with. It also applies to people you see every day, like those you work with, or study with. To really get along with everyone, you can do a simple tuning-in exercise which connects you to their personal rhythms.

Some people need space – particularly personal space. Some people need you to talk to them more, others prefer longer silences. Some people move quickly and are impatient, others love to take their time. Everyone has their own needs and preferences, and if you "match" them, even temporarily, you will find everything becomes easier.

Breathe into your solar plexus, around your belly button. Pay attention to that spot on your body. What is your basic gut feeling about the person in front of you? Do you get that they want to eat their lunch in silence today, or are they stressed out about something? Are they tired? Do they have a burning issue they need to discuss with you, but they don't know how to start? Are they thirsty? Hungry? Bored? Do they want to take their time today or are they in a panic? The more you can "read" other people's personal rhythms, the more you can fit their prescription, and they may not even know what you're doing. People who are in careers where extreme sensitivity is necessary, like counsellors and caregivers, do a lot of this gut-feeling adjustment quite naturally. The rest of us have to learn it, but it can make a big difference to your comfort zone, and other people's comfort zones too.

We all assume that other people are exactly like us, but they're not! If you breathe into your solar plexus, and tune into what's required, you'll find you have better relationships on all levels – with your family, friends, love bunnies, bosses, teachers, clients, or colleagues. This is really what being psychic is all about. It's not only there for you to predict your future, or get extra insight into the present. It's not even there for you to make the right decision about your next holiday or job. This amazing tool, which every Goddess on the planet has, is ultimately there to help us get along with each other more easily.

Try it when you're in separate rooms in your house or flat. Of course, you can hear someone else in the next room – a friend watching TV, your mother cooking, your father washing up – but check in with your solar plexus to see what's really going on out there! Is your mother fighting off a headache, and would she absolutely love it if someone offered her a cup of tea? Is your friend watching the news, but actually worrying about her boyfriend? Is your father in a mad rush tonight, and will your own go-slow schedule mean you're out of sync? Subtle and small details are the keys to clicking with other people's rhythms.

A lack of sensitivity, for the same reasons, can be disastrous. Have you ever wondered why lovers move in together, then break up – despite the fact that they were crazy about each other before? Have you ever been baffled at the way share accommodation situations disintegrate into total nightmares? Do you feel like you'll never get it right with your family, even though you all mean well? The answers to all these questions lie with sensitivity. A lack of it can throw you way out of sync with the people you work or live with, and that can be enough to unsettle rhythms and atmospheres to the point where tension becomes too much. This is the case even when you've all got a million things in common! Who knows, you might just have found the best use for your psychic powers yet – and it's just a simple matter of tuning into others.

Energy Cleari

The space around you is one of the key indicators to what's going on in your mind, and therefore your life. We're all busy and it can seem at times like it's time-consuming and unnecessary – and hard! – to keep on top of the mess that all too quickly accumulates on our desks, in our cars, bedrooms, bathrooms and so on. It's easy to rationalize and give other things priority: our working life, social life, love life and just about anything else that really prevents us from staying in to just sort things out. At first glance, cleaning and clearing things may seem boring, but there's a whole new way to look at these mundane tasks, which lifts them to a level of ritual and imbues them with a wholly fresh and spiritual dimension. As a Goddess you should know that everything is spiritual anyway, so the thing is to see the sacred in the mundane (which is the essence of being Zen) and consciously be aware of the finer nuances of all that is energetic.

Clear the deck(s)

There is a lot of value in devoting time and creating the mental space to clean and clear as a daily ritual. It may sound suspiciously like we're telling you to get back to the days of being a house-proud 1950s woman with her shipshape home, but this is not to say that it's necessarily regressive. It is, in fact, a progressive way to stay clear and focused, especially in the face of the increasing pace of modern life. Some Goddesses may even think it's old-fashioned to care about being fanatically clean and organized, but when you haven't much time and you need to make certain things happen, who needs to muddle through a muddle? Get organized and put some discipline into this part of your life, and we guarantee you, you'll truly be a modern woman who's right on track. What's the point of being fussy? We believe there is a major one and it's all to do with your "head space." So, the equation for this chapter is: Head space = Home space.

Once again, we're dealing with energy and the message this time is that you can change things in your mind by changing the energy in your physical environment. Being a fully evolved Goddess in any capacity will be much more difficult if you don't have some sort of a handle on energy in general, and the best starting point is within your personal sphere. We are big on taking charge of things; being pro-active in every area of life is our mantra! We also believe that if you really want to experience seismic shifts in your reality, then you need to focus on and be aware of the impact your immediate spaces and environments have upon you. These may be in your home, in your car, your office, or even your local community.

Your environment has amazing relevance to how you are truly feeling and where you may find yourself at any given point in time, but you need to notice it and be aware of it at all times,

SPECIAL GODDESS CULTURAL TIP

Cleaning is an essential part of the religion in many cultures. In the Hindu culture of Bali, for example, the sweeping of the ground and subsequently making offerings to the Gods is a daily ritual that is faithfully observed. To the Balinese, the cleaning and clearing of the old energies (dead leaves and debris) is "bhakti," which means it is a devotional manner of worship that cleanses the area to receive the fresh energies from the Gods.

and then allow it to give you the clues you need to act. Energy needs to be fluid and, like your body, your surrounding physical spaces are potential repositories for energy that is either stagnant or blocked when it should be free-flowing and harmonious. It's simple to feel the energy in an environment and we all assess the energy levels in other places constantly, however, we may no longer have the same level of awareness about our own environment. The reason for this could be that we're too close to it, or somewhere along the way we lost the ability to be objective about it and to understand how it's not working or serving us any longer. So, young Goddesses, you'll simply have to take those rose-coloured (Gucci) glasses off! It's the same reason certain cafés, restaurants, and public spaces are evergreens – people gravitate towards them all the time – while others can't seem to get any momentum. It's just an energy thing. It's also common sense that if you have a fresh, clear environment where the energy is light and the vibrations are right, then you'll be able to personally manifest more of the same.

Notice how the energy is flowing in the spaces around you and then you will begin to see where you may need to make certain changes or do some fine-tuning in order to keep your life moving in a positively directed way. You will begin to see the results of your own power if you take the time and put the maximum positive energy into clearing and sanctifying the space around you. It's all about you and your attitude to rolling up your sleeves and getting into it.

Goddesses . . . start your vacuum cleaners!

Energy clearing is work

A word of warning for all those Goddesses who are gleefully rubbing their hands together and thinking this is by far the easiest route yet to personal power. Firstly, it is not easy – more often than not energy clearing and shifting is the most time-consuming of activities and requires considerable dedication and commitment. Like anything that results in long-term change, it takes real effort. It does not necessarily happen overnight, and although there are ways to start small while still giving you a real sense of progress, generally it can be very hard work indeed. Secondly, it can be quite an emotional process – so keep those tissues handy! You are releasing a lot of stuff that you've held on to for a variety of reasons (and only you know why) and, while it may certainly be cathartic and nostalgic, it can sometimes be upsetting. So be prepared, and be brave, and you won't regret letting the past go, especially when you realize that, done properly, you're making room for many more wonderful new things to come into your life. Thirdly, once you've started, you need to keep it up to achieve real and lasting results. Energy clearing is not a thing that you do as a one-off. It's an ongoing task and a personal commitment to keeping things moving and maintaining a freshness and vitality in all areas of your life.

So with that (small!) caveat in mind, what follows are our best tips ever for tackling all the difficult or no-go zones. It may sound basic, but the best way to start is by making a list, which is daunting, especially when it's long! Here's a true story by one of our Goddess friends about her own personal energy clearing journey...

SPECIAL GODDESS ANECDOTE
A Goddess friend went through a major life change in her mid twenties. Dissatisfied with her job, she resigned. Dissatisfied with her live-in partner, she told him she wanted to break up. She then put her house on the market and, without examining much, stashed the entire contents of her life into (beautifully) labelled boxes which then went into a shipping container in a commercial storage unit in a far-flung suburb. With her remaining possessions now squeezed into two suitcases she moved to Paris, where she followed her dreams in the fashion industry. She set up a flat and kitted it out from top to bottom. A brand new bed resulted almost instantly in a new relationship. A new library of art books resulted in new directions creatively. New music and fashion purchased on trips to London resulted in a whole new outlook. Our Goddess friend had never felt better, and for a long time she never looked back.

A decade later, and now in her mid thirties, she decided it was time to go home. So she packed up her Parisian base and shipped a mass of (beautifully) labelled boxes back home. She then bought a new place and had all her boxes shipped to it from her storage unit. Coupled with the Paris boxes, there were over one hundred boxes in total. Our friend had forgotten how much stuff she had and, after an initial freak-out, she then (somewhat shakily) began the task of sorting out, box by box, the sum total of her life. She gave linen away, pared down on crockery, cutlery, and kitchenware items. She threw out old clothes, had blankets cleaned and repaired, eliminated excessive decorative objects, and sold art to which she no longer related. She tossed out and tore up old documents, letters, photographs, postcards, and memorabilia, some of which she had held on to for thirty years. She recycled with the zeal of a TV evangelist. She was on a mission and she wasn't going to stop.

She then went through all her Paris possessions with the same level of ruthlessness and whittled them down to the most essential, the most beautiful, and the most useful items. Anything broken was either repaired or ditched. She gave many presents to friends and their children and bagfuls of goodness-knows-whatnots to charities. She sold unwanted furniture over the internet and to second-hand dealers, and bought new pieces with the proceeds. She advertised a garage sale and converted her old vinyl records and paperback books into cash, which she then used to buy new books and CDs. She renovated. She cleaned. She chucked. She left no box unopened. She took six months.

When she finally came up for air, our friend had a flat she could move into, that she could also live in and – most importantly – grow in. Every single object was one that she loved or felt good about. It was a revelation. She felt lighter than she had ever felt in her life. She began to expand her home business and a new boyfriend wandered onto the scene. She had done it tough – cried on countless occasions over the old love letters, photos and diaries, parted with hugely sentimental things – and come out of it clearer and more focused than she had ever been in her life. As she put it: "I had to let go, to let in."

Spring cleaning – doing the tuff stuff

It's not called spring cleaning for nothing and there are good reasons why the season for renewal and rebirth is the best time to pull on those rubber gloves and stock up on garbage bags. If you want to have a hot summer, we suggest you get busy in the months beforehand and really get into your personal energy clearing programme. Now we know it's a major challenge, but you have to look at all of the large items and spaces in your life and check whether or not the energy needs to be cleared. It's always easier to put it off, but once you understand about blockages and energy systems, you'll be keen to stir things up – or at least remove what you don't need: the negative stuff – and see what the Universe sends you after that. Think of it as the big payoff for a hard job well tackled. It's also interesting that many Goddesses do a big purge and then they discover that they need to move house – all of a sudden the energy where they live no longer suits them – or that they need to change careers or even cities. There are many upsides to being consistent with your cleaning and clearing your space. If you do a few hours each week, you can accomplish a lot that seems insurmountable at first glance in a couple of months. If you then continue to stay light, then it's always a much less onerous task to make changes of any sort in your life. If you're not burdened by excess baggage, you'll always be ready for whatever excitement is coming. And more importantly, you'll be able to act on it.

Goddess Earth care

Taking care of the environment while you energy clear and clean must be a priority. Being responsible for the Earth while you are being responsible for your own small part of it is an essential part of truly being and worshipping the Goddess. How you recycle and throw things out is as important as doing the clearing in the first place. It shows you care about the planet as a whole and that you're not prepared to trash another part of the world just to improve your own life. Whatever you do sends out a beacon to the Universe, so try to throw out things where they can be recycled, or at least appropriately disposed of. That old rubbish dump that you never have to eyeball is no excuse for not being a responsible Goddess. The same goes for chemically based cleaning products that magically go down the drain and yet end up in the oceans, which are the lifeblood of the Earth Goddess. We recommend using natural and/or environment friendly products for all your home cleaning and energy clearing activities.

Earth Goddess – Nature rules

The following ideas are some simple, effective, and inexpensive cleaning recipes.

For the fridge: Warm water and vanilla essence to wipe down the inside surfaces.

For the kitchen and bathroom: Bicarbonate of soda and vinegar for mould.

For wooden floors: Warm water and a capful of kerosene. Do a final mop with warm water, this time adding a dropper of lavender oil instead.

For drawers in the bathroom and kitchen: A couple of bay leaves in each drawer and cupboard.

For bathroom/shower tiles: One cup of vinegar in a bucket of water.

For stainless steel benches: Methylated spirits on a kitchen paper towel is more effective than chemically loaded commercial stain removers.

For the inside of wardrobes and closet surfaces: Warm water with a dropper of lavender or lime oil.

Glass windows: One tablespoon of vinegar in two cups of water. Use a spray bottle.

For mouldy or mildewed surfaces, such as walls and ceilings: Two parts warm water to one part vinegar wiped over the surface a few times kills the mould spores. Alternatively, mix 1 part borax, 2 parts water, and 1 part vinegar in a spray bottle. Borax inhibits the growth of mould, so wash down the walls with the borax solution as well. The most important thing to remember is to keep things dry and to keep the air "moving" and fresh. Bacteria, mildew and mould cannot live without dampness and still air.

Furniture: Create your own polish – three parts olive oil mixed with one part white vinegar or two parts olive or vegetable oil with one part lemon oil.

Basin and bathtub cleaner: A sprinkle of bicarbonate of soda followed by a hot water rinse gets rid of germs. Or use a non-chlorinated scouring powder.

Lime in lavatory basin: For encrustation of lime and other minerals, neutralize it with vinegar and then brush it off.

All-purpose cleaner: One part hot water, one part liquid soap or borax. Add a squeeze of lemon juice or a splash of vinegar for heavy dirt. (There is no ammonia in this recipe and it cleans as well as commercial cleansers without causing problems such as respiratory ailments and skin reactions.)

Disinfectant: To reduce germs on large surfaces, use half a cup of borax dissolved in one litre hot water.

GENERAL BASIC SHOPPING LIST

These are cleaning products that are as close to being natural as possible:

* Bicarbonate of soda
* Salt
* Distilled white vinegar
* Lemon juice
* Liquid soap
* Borax
* Lavender oil
* Lime oil

TOP SPACES TO BE CLEARED IN SPRINGTIME

* The garage
* Storage sheds in the garden and around or under the house
* The top of your wardrobe
* Your home study or office
* Filing cabinets
* Suitcases full of old clothes
* The hall cupboard, linen closet
* The bathroom cabinet
* Commercial storage
* The attic or roof storage area

* Any place you're keeping boxes of things (at your parents', friends', or ex's)
* Under the bed
* The fridge and oven
* Under the kitchen sink
* Any storage units (trunks, chests, baskets) where you've just been stashing stuff
* Your car

Goddess tool box for raising positive vibrations

Once you've cleaned the space, then you can clear the space to raise the energy. Knowing how keen you must be to get started (!), we will begin by setting you up with all the right tools. Every Goddess needs a working toolbox to tackle the areas in and around the house and the body that need to be cleared. We recommend you gather your resources before commencing any clearing, so you can complete the task and energies are not left literally hanging around, unfinished. There are things you need for clearing as well as objects and items for balancing the energies in the room or area after clearing it. It's all about first neutralizing, then raising the vibrational level in your environment, and thereafter maintaining it.

Herbs

Herbs are powerful cleansing agents and there are a few that stand out for our purposes. These herbs can be used in leaf form and burned, or added to a handful of sea salt crystals to make a mix. They can also be put into a small pouch and placed strategically on window ledges and near main doorways.

Sage: One of the primary and most commonly used tools for clearing your space is sage. Sage has been used for centuries in ceremonies and rituals in cultures around the world, such as Native American, indigenous Australian, Tibetan, and Chinese. There are two main types of sage, common garden variety sage and white sage (grandfather sage). White sage is the most powerful because it has denser smoke, which helps to lift the energies more effectively. We recommend white sage for those heavy-duty jobs, such as your new flat that previously housed tenants from hell!

Rosemary: Rosemary is cleansing, purifying, and strengthening. Perfect for the bathroom!

Basil: Basil is powerful for opening the heart chakra and staying receptive to universal energies. Basil is good to use in the bedroom – you'll enjoy those vivid dreams too …

Bay Leaves: Bay leaves are excellent for warding off negativity. Special note: They're also great for warding off cockroaches, which for some Goddesses is the same thing!

SPECIAL CLEANSING RITUAL FOR THE BODY

Using three leaves of white sage, removed from the stalk, burn each leaf individually in sequence in a heatproof bowl. With a feather, disperse the smoke over your body, moving from the feet region upward to the top of your head in a rotating, circular motion. This ritual helps to release from your aura any negative thoughts or incidents and prevents these from penetrating the physical body's energy centres (chakras). This ritual can be done daily if necessary, and is particularly helpful during periods of high stress, such as during exams, or for Goddesses suffering from post-traumatic stress syndrome, such as after a car accident or after a relationship breakup.

Feathers

The feather is used in energy clearing and energy raising rituals for a number of reasons. The feather is a symbol of the soul, because feathers come from birds, which are living entities. Native Americans believe that feathers retain and emit – to whoever carries or uses them – the energy of the bird they have left, and therefore they are precious gifts for ground-dwellers. Feathers can be used in cleansing rituals to assist in smoke dissipation and to spread the vibrations and carry them higher – literally lifting them up. The feather itself shifts the energy, clearing blockages in the body or in the home.

Incense

This is a Goddess toolbox essential! Incense has been used for centuries in cultures and ceremonies throughout the world. The use of incense brings a sacred element to any space, adding texture and fragrance. Incense is to carry your prayers and invocations to the Gods and to purify a space, removing any unwanted energy and promoting consciousness vibrations in its stead. The atmosphere that is created by burning incense can transform an ordinary room to your own personal mystical temple. The smoke lifts the energy that may be obstructing the harmony and happiness you deserve to have in your life. The fragrance of the incense affects the senses directly and it can change the way you (and others in the space) emotionally react. Incense can automatically lift your personal energy levels.

As the smoke from the sticks clears and raises the vibrational atmosphere, you will sense the energy shifting. Natural incense recipes are composed of aromatic gums, resins, and other scented substances, such as oils and herb-based extractions. With the wide variety of incense available now, you should be able to find many different types to suit your specific purposes. Some are calming, others are mood-lifting, healing, or meditative, for example. They usually come in sticks or cones and are slow-burning. You can make your own, although ready-made incense is easily obtainable in most metaphysical/alternative shops and health food stores these days. The main thing to check is that the incense is naturally made.

Salt

Salt has been used for centuries in many cultures as a primary absorber of negativity. Because it is derived from the sea and from river and lake systems, it holds a special place in rituals all over the world. From the ancient superstition of tossing spilled salt over one's left shoulder (left side of the body to avert the evil eye from causing disruption) to warding off bad luck for Pagans from the Wiccan

GODDESS HOT TIP!

As with any material that is a potential fire-hazard, please be certain to exercise care and practise standard fire safety precautions when using incense or other flammable items in or around your home.

You can create a shrine (see the Magic and Rituals chapter to learn to create a Goddess altar and shrine) and conduct your own rituals using incense, candles, and other relevant items. Incense is also lovely when placed in garden pots or flowerbeds. Some avid gardeners and outdoor barbecue queens swear by the anti-mosquito effect this has! One time-saving technique for busy Goddesses-on-the-run is to light a stick or two of incense and simply walk the boundaries of the house or room waving the sticks from the floor up to the ceiling to disperse the smoke and give a quick-fix energy boost. This is a great tip to raise and clear energy, especially if you are the Goddess/Hostess-of-the-moment and you have guests about to arrive on your (hopefully, energy-cleared) doorstep!

tradition, salt has been traditionally used to neutralize negativity and to break hexes. The ocean is nature's greatest cleanser and sea salt is a wonderful preserver with antiseptic properties. In clearing the energy in the home, Goddesses can prepare the corners of any room by dusting, vacuuming, and even "clapping out" (see "Aboriginal clap sticks" below) the corner, and then placing sea salt in each one. Another method is to dissolve the salt crystals in a bowl full of water at room temperature and, with the right hand, flick or splash small amounts on the walls in each corner of the room you wish to clear.

Sanctified water

Sanctified or sacred water is water that is specially prepared and blessed for a particular task, such as clearing the energy in a room or on a pathway (this works in a garden too). Put the water into a clean glass, crystal, or ceramic bowl (note: Do not use plastic bowls for sanctified water as they are unable to be cleaned properly and they retain energies). Draw your index finger through the water, first vertically and then horizontally. This is the blessing movement. As you do this, ask the Universe to bless and purify the water for the task you have in mind.

Bells

Sound is one of the most frequently used energy lifters in cultures throughout the world. Chanting and bells are used in religious ceremonies throughout the East. Music and singing are used in all cultures and religions, even though many people are probably less formally religious than in the past. You only have to think about the effect on your mood of putting on a soothing CD. Bells are very effective clearers and have a restful and calming effect on the spaces in which they are used. Tibetan bells are very popular and can be bought quite easily at markets and from Asian general stores, as well as alternative or new age shops.

Aboriginal clap sticks

Another powerful way to incorporate sound and rhythm into your energy clearing activities is to use Aboriginal clap sticks. These are thick, carved wooden sticks which are used in the ceremonies and corroborees of indigenous Australians to summon the spirit world. Clapping out a corner is a great way to shake up the energies and really get things moving in a specific area of your home. If you have an interest in or any knowledge of the ancient Chinese art of Feng Shui, you may wish to use the wooden clap sticks as a powerful energy raiser for clearing the particular area that corresponds to the wood element or direction in your home.

Drums and cymbals

Once again, these are wonderful additions to the Goddess toolbox as they are energy field "shifters." The drums carry the spirit of the Earth Mother in the Native American tradition, and are excellent for building vibrational levels where there has been negativity such as illness or an argument. Drumming rhythms work on the subconscious by inducing a trancelike state of altered consciousness, similar in nature to the effect that deep meditation has on the brain. By maintaining a tempo that gradually increases in intensity, mental energy can be lifted and shifted to bring about a parallel change in the physical atmosphere of a space.

Once again, for those Goddesses who are interested in or who have a knowledge of Feng Shui, cymbals are extremely beneficial for areas of the home which correspond to the metal element. Their sonic resonance is very soothing and "finalizing" as an energy sealer for a room that has been cleared. We really like the small Tibetan cymbals which can be used on each hand between the forefinger and thumb as these produce a particularly sweet-sounding resonance that is not too dominating for smaller spaces. Perfect for a tiny bedroom! The size of the cymbal is a matter of personal taste, however, we've noticed that it sometimes seems as if the room dictates what would be best for it – some cymbals just don't seem to work for no apparent reason. We have therefore concluded (from various field tests!) that in these cases size really doesn't matter and you just have to go by the feel!

Rattle

Rattles come in many forms – some are gourds (African) and some are made up of wooden bells or hollow pieces containing seed pods (Native American). According to one of our global Goddess gurus, Denise Linn, the rattle is an excellent complement to a drum and is great to finish off an energy clearing ceremony. Denise believes that rattles create a very gentle energy field and they can be used to "seal" a room after

SHA ENERGY – THE BAD STUFF!

In Feng Shui, sha energy is the opposite of the desirable, free-flowing, and health bringing ch'i energy. Sha energy is energy that is blocked or stagnant. Problems in a particular part of your life can sometimes be an indicator of sha energy and remedies are then called for. Leading Feng Shui expert, Lillian Too, is the author of many books on this extensive subject. We recommend that all Goddesses who wish to investigate the finer details of this fascinating science refer to any of her books.

the energy has been cleared, thus affording greater protection from other unwanted energies. In her highly practical and meticulously researched book, *Sacred Space*, Denise describes specific Native American techniques for blessings and for using rattles for maximum energy-lifting effect. We recommend to all Goddesses who wish to know more about this fascinating subject to read *Sacred Space* (see the Goddess Library for details).

Oil burners

Aromatherapy is becoming increasingly popular and oil burners can be used throughout the house or office to raise or clear the energy. There are a wide variety of oil burners available today, and even general stores now carry a range of attractive designs. Gone are the days when you had to use those tiresome and porous terracotta burners which soaked up all the oil before it even had a chance to burn! Oil burners are particularly useful on your desk to increase your powers of concentration (jasmine oil), or in the bathroom to help you to relax while taking a bath (lavender), or even in the bedroom to spice up your love life (ylang ylang). One of our Goddess friends, who has four-year-old twin boys, swears by burning lavender oil in her kids' playroom to keep them from getting out of control (and driving her nuts) while they are playing.

To use a burner, always put water into the dish first and add a few drops of the oil to the water before lighting the candle underneath the burner. Make sure that you top up the water and oil as necessary as drying out is a potential fire hazard. As ever, Goddesses should practise safety first. There's not much point in burning the place down just to clear the energy!

Fragrant room spray

Increasingly popular, fragrant room sprays are, like fragrance or perfume for the body, a highly personal choice. They can be used as the final "kiss" at the end of an energy clearing exercise, much the way you would use fragrance at the end of your beauty ritual, before dressing. Among our favourites are the range of room sprays available from Shanghai Tang and from Crabtree and Evelyn's light as air "Freesia" room spray.

Vacuum cleaner

We won't insist you stay in the realm of the non-technological in order to do your energy clearing rituals. A good high-suction vacuum cleaner works for us every time! They are excellent for cobwebs, which are said to trap the negative energy, and for de-dusting hard to reach corners and, most importantly, indispensable for cleaning under beds, sofas etc. You must, however, toss out the bag or clear it after every major energy clearing exercise. This is really important, because what is the point of sucking up the stagnant old energy if you then leave it sitting in a cupboard? Keep a good supply of bags on hand so you can chuck out the used ones with impunity.

Basic Goddess energy clearing ritual

There are many ways to clear energy in an environment, and there are many books detailing elaborate purification and energy clearing rituals from other cultures. These work, but we also believe you can be a bit free-form with your clearing rituals. Create your own methods and order of activities, which feel good for you, and use the tools that are available to you. Once you've read through the chapter you can decide which tools you'd prefer to use. You may wish to use "sound" to do your clearing work with, say a rattle or bells or by running your (slightly wet fingertips) around the edge of a crystal bowl. We recommend that you design your own rituals according to what you feel would be the best for you. Maybe you just want to vacuum the whole area, sing a little song, and throw some salt crystals about. Whatever! As with anything, the main thing about clearing rituals is the intention. Your intention is purely the state of mind you beam out to the Universe. We stress that there is no single ritual that can clear an environment or change the vibrations if the energy or the right intention isn't there to clear it.

New Year's Goddess special affirmations

Make it a fresh start in the New Year, but with a twist this time – it's not about trotting out those boring (same) old New Year's resolutions. Forget about the resolutions to lose weight, use your mobile phone less, or give up smoking (although you really should!). Instead, use the New Year's energy to space clear and make affirmations, and then see what comes up after you've done it. Resolutions may be a cliché, but there is a basis for them. The New Year is a powerful time on the planet. There is so much collective thought energy surrounding it and this means it is that much easier to engage with and harness this energy for your own special Goddess needs. The New Year period is the only time of the year where the global energy is actually pushing everyone to create a new slate, to have a new experience, to choose a new path, or to

BASIC ENERGY CLEARING METHOD

1. Take off your shoes before beginning the ritual. If you don't like going barefoot, wear cotton socks – the main idea is to "ground" yourself to fully connect with the earth while you work.

2. Walk the perimeter of the area and try to feel where the energy seems to be blocked. The blockage may even be visible to you. And you may need to move items out of the area in order to feel the energy. Meditate on what you want to achieve by doing this clearing ritual.

3. Starting with that spot, sort out the items in the room which are cluttered or have sha energy and keep going till you feel the energy shift.

4. Thoroughly cleanse and vacuum, mop and polish the floor and all surfaces or items in the space. Investigate the insides of drawers, cupboards and storage units and clean them out.

5. Take out the unwanted items for correct and final disposal (see note below) and try to replace them with new sacred objects, symbols and talismans that empower the fresh space.

6. Move around the space to break up any remaining energy blockages.

7. Light a candle in each corner, or wherever it feels appropriate.

8. Burn sage, herbs, or incense (see Goddess tool box page 279) and place a few sea salt crystals in each corner of the area you are clearing.

9. Chant or make sounds with bells, drums, and rattles to restore harmony to the space.

10. Make clear affirmations to the Universe for the new energy you wish to come into the space.

Note: When we refer to "final disposal," we mean that you should take the unwanted items, for example, bags of clothing, to their final destination. There is no point clearing from one part of your space and leaving the old energy still hanging around your home. Aim for completion. Just be certain to take the stuff out and away from your home!

go on a new journey. It comes on the heels of the solstice (around Christmas time) and regardless of the general hype around it, you can and should plug into it and work with this collective energy for your own private and personal advantage for the year to come.

Decorative objects and talismans

Objects that are symbolic can be placed in the home to maximize the energies of the inhabitants and radiate energy throughout the space. They can be objects which are hand crafted, old or new, or they can simply be objects found in nature. A talisman is a charm, amulet, or figure to which specific powers, effects, and benefits can be ascribed. For example, talismans that are worn on the body as jewellery can contain crystals that have certain properties for healing and protection. The same applies to objects for the home.

Objects become talismans when they have had a power conferred upon them by cultural, religious, or personal means. For instance, you might be walking on a beach and come across a perfect double-sunrise shell. At the moment of discovery, you may have been thinking of your relationship. The object then has meaning and significance for you personally (call it a universal sign, if you will) and could then be used in the relationship corner of your home to increase and solidify the energy around your relationship. Shells, pebbles, feathers, seed pods, driftwood, coral, leaves, and sand or earth are excellent grounding objects and bring positive earth energy into your personal space.

ALL SPACE IS SACRED

Other more traditional talismans, such as the cross, have their own more universally acknowledged talismanic power. Likewise, pyramids, triangles, and pentagrams have power, which can be invoked without you necessarily having to confer any meaning. Statues of the Buddha (compassion and serenity; also used in Feng Shui to reduce overpowering sha energy), Kwan Yin (the Chinese Great Mother Goddess), the yin/yang symbol (representing heaven and earth and the duality and flow of the life force or source of universal energy) are other well-known symbols. Placing these in a prominent position in your home and keeping them well lit and dust free is essential to maintain their energy field at an optimal level. Adding small offerings, such as placing fresh flowers on the Buddha or Kwan Yin, or lighting votive candles under the cross (for divine protection), are other ways to honour symbols and talismans whilst invoking their powers. Having pairs or groupings of objects is another way to enhance and strengthen their properties.

The mandala – symbol of eternity

Well, it's not the name of a fancy cocktail! The mandala is one of the oldest symbols known to the spiritual traditions of the East. Traditionally either a circle design or square combination of symbols, a mandala can be painted on a flat surface or carved into a three-dimensional relief. It is one of the most powerful sacred symbols of all. The circle has always been associated with completion, unity, and wholeness, and accordingly is representative of the shape of the Universe as well as its divine perfection. The square mandala is representative of balance. Concentrating on a mandala is an excellent aid to meditation practice as it reflects the passage from one state to another, representing the transformation of the personal to the universal, the material to the spiritual and, ultimately, momentary transience to the eternal. As they are energy centres, each chakra has an associated mandala. Mandalas are beautiful objects, invoking the power of the infinite in your home.

Animal totems

Native Americans use animal objects and figures to invoke the individual properties of particular animals that hold significance for their family or tribe. For the Native Americans, all space is sacred and every square inch of the planet holds a unique energy connection to all that is living. All animals are fellow creatures walking alongside them, and should be honoured accordingly. Animals exhibit patterns of behaviour and habit, which hold invaluable lessons for how we humans should live. Each animal totem represents one overriding or major lesson. For example, the turtle is the oldest symbol for the earth. It is the embodiment of the Goddess energy as it symbolizes the mother of all things. The turtle also symbolizes protection and healing, and is the actualization of the creative source. The placement of a turtle in the centre of the home is an excellent method of producing grounding energy as well as creating stability and abundance in the home.

Space claiming

There comes a time in the life of all Goddesses when being in someone else's space becomes a necessity. There can be different reasons for this, but they all require you to adjust in some way. You may need to for work purposes – particularly if you go to work in the corporate world. It may be for personal purposes, such as hanging out at your boyfriend's or friend's flat, or even for play, such as when you travel and stay with someone, or perhaps you're in a band which

Below is a list of some animal totems and the major life lessons they represent.

TOTEM	LESSON	ENERGY FOCAL POINT
Dolphin	Life force	Breath energy
Eagle	*Great spirit*	*Connection to the divine*
Snake	Transmutation	Life–death–rebirth cycle
Dog	*Loyalty*	*Protection*
Wolf	Teacher	Intuition and wisdom
Butterfly	*Change*	*Self-transformation*
Horse	Power	Physical power
Frog	*Cleansing*	*Soul*
Swan	Grace	Awareness/healing
Lion	*Leadership*	*Heart*

practises in a band member's garage. It's hard to be creative, productive, or relaxed if the energy of a space isn't conducive for your purposes. So, if the vibe of a particular room or place isn't doing it for you, you may need to quietly shift the energy field in order to be able to coexist within the space. There are a few ways to gently enhance your own energy field in the face of someone else's dominant one.

* Use affirmations. Mentally ask the Universe to allow you to enter and function in the space to your optimal capacity; mentally affirm that you are looking forward to achieving positive things by being there.
* If you get a moment alone, clear out rubbish or other residual energy from waste bins, the tops of conference tables, and wipe off the scribbles on the whiteboard etc.
* Restructure the seating arrangements to reflect the group energy that you desire, removing extra chairs so that there are no "invisible" personal agendas present.
* Light incense, if it is allowed, or arrange for an oil burner to lift the vibrational levels and clear the previous occupants' energy from the room.
* Adjust the lighting where possible to be more intimate and friendly – no one emits their best energy under harsh fluorescent overhead lights.

- In a hotel room, light a candle and incense, then bless the room for the safety and protection it will give you. Walk the boundaries of the room and wave the incense stick throughout.
- Organize fresh fruit, flowers, and jugs of iced water and lemon or lime slices for vitality in a conference room or creative space.
- Play some music that is soothing and calming to neutralize the "words" that may have been emitted in the space before you entered.
- Freelance or casual employee Goddesses, who have to work in some grotty back office or busy corner, face their own challenges. Where possible, try and sit with your back to a wall, bring your own small oil burner and some crystals for energy balancing, and bring a fresh flower with you to the office each time. Claim the space as yours!

Special Goddess ritual
CLEAR YOUR LOVE CORNER!

Move all the furniture out of the love area in your bedroom. To establish the correct area, you may need to refer to one of our Feng Shui references (see Goddess Library). First, move all items and furniture out of the corner: you're starting over! Take your ever-trusty and faithful vacuum cleaner and thoroughly vacuum this whole area. (Remember to make sure the vacuum has a fresh bag when you begin or is clean and empty inside, and also to then remove the bag and throw it away afterwards.) Next, if there are wooden floorboards, mop the floor and skirting boards with warm water, adding a few drops of lavender oil to the water. Take a small amount (a few pinches) of sea salt crystals and place them deep into the corner.

A TRUE GODDESS LOVE STORY

A Goddess friend who wanted to attract her soul mate did a series of cleansing and energy clearing rituals on the love corner of her bedroom and her home. To augment her cleaning and clearing strategy, she opted for two powerful symbols for each area. In her bedroom's love corner she placed the classic "bed-in" photo of John Lennon and Yoko Ono, when they were famously photographed in bed at the height of their love affair; and in her home's love corner she placed a traditional painting of a Balinese wedding. Within a few weeks of doing the cleansing and regularly burning incense in each corner, she had met – in her words – "the man of my dreams" and, what's more, she didn't even have to go anywhere as he came right to her front door!

Light a sage smudge stick (these can be bought at your health food store) or incense. Move the smoke around the area until you get the sense that the energy has shifted. Then, take a rose quartz crystal (refer to Crystals, Oils, and Remedies for a cleansing ritual and reprogrammeming for your crystals) and place it in the corner. Wipe down the furniture and move it back into a pleasing arrangement. Affirm to the Universe that love is all around you and that you are open to and ready for love in your life.

Special Goddess herstory note – the day of love

In Turkish mythology, Fridays are called "muhabbet gunu." That's Turkish for "day of love, affection and friendship." Well you knew Friday was loaded and not just in reference to those last-minute dates at the local bar! Over the eons it has become customary in Turkey not to do any housework on a Friday until after 1 p.m. If you clean or do household chores at any time before this, it is believed that you risk sweeping "love" outside your home...so now you have a real excuse to procrastinate on that gritty bathroom sink! Tradition has it that Friday mornings are a powerful time to "energetically cleanse" your home, for instance, by burning dried olive leaves. It's also a good time to dabble in some good old-fashioned fortune-telling. Now you can make Friday mornings a time to feel love and give love from within and without – and plan that date with the cute guy on the second floor!

Sacred shrine

A shrine is yet another way of bringing the sacred into your daily life. Your sacred shrine should be a place of serenity, but it can be almost anywhere that you feel it. Anywhere you can read, write, paint, or create whatever you need or desire. Having a shrine deepens our sense of self and of being; shrines give new energy and vitality to our homes. They are easy and fun to create, and they have power-ful effects on us through their subtle energy. Shrines connect us with the divine. A home shrine is a sacred space in the midst of things – reality in all its messy glory – and it reminds us that spirituality is not separate from everyday life, but is truly an essential part of all aspects of living.

The dictionary definition of shrine is as general as "box, coffer, cabinet, or chest" or as specific as a "place where saint's relics are preserved." Shrines create a sacred space, a place of spiritual mag-netism, beauty, and joy. A shrine is similar to an altar in so far as they are both sacred spaces – the difference is that a shrine is a place that doesn't need to be moved. It's a place that is permanently erected for the purpose of its sacred meaning to those who create it. Some shrines have been in the same place for centuries. For example, there are permanent shrines to the Goddess scattered all around Europe. The other point of difference is that shrines are sacred places used solely for honouring the deity or Goddess, not for affirmations, magic or ritual work – altars are best used for that purpose.

The easiest way to have the Goddess in your everyday life is to have household shrines. Shrines can be very simple, such as a simple bowl with a candle nestled inside, to something far more ornate. Your shrine can be either a reflection of your personal style or created especially for a Goddess or deity that you are honouring.

Prayers can be said at the shrines every day. When we pay daily homage to our chosen Goddess, we are creating our own sacred ceremony which we can do alone in our own format.

> An altar is a sacred space that, connects us with the earth and heaven.
>
> Denise Linn,
> *Altars*

Upon waking, go to the shrine and talk with your Goddess. You can use this time to ask for guidance or outline specific needs that either you or your family may have, for example an exam, a situation at work, an issue with another person. At the same time as you are asking for help or guidance, thank her for all that she has blessed you with to date and for the chance of another day to live fully and vitally on the earthly plane.

How to create your own special shrine

All you need is imagination and a few special items. A good place to start is thinking about what means something to you personally and what brings you joy. Crystals and talismans are great, so too are jewellery and photographs, cards or natural objects, such as shells and feathers. Go wild, young woman, and express yourself! If you feel at a bit of a loss in terms of knowing where to start, use the tool box which begins on page 279.

Goddess decorating tip

Next time you go to your favourite local Thai or Asian restaurant, check out the dedicated shrine nearly all of them have mounted on the wall, usually near the service desk. It will almost always be prettily painted, lit up with coloured lights, and contain figures, such as a Buddha, photographs, flowers, and burning incense. One of our Goddess friends, who is a bit of a bower bird, found a shrine from an Asian restaurant (she thinks Chinese) that had been dumped on the side of the road. She cleaned and fixed it up – all it needed were a couple of new light bulbs – and once it was in perfect working order she mounted it in her kitchen (in her reputation corner) where it is a focal point of conversation!

A shrine can be placed anywhere in the house or garden. The mantle of a fireplace is often a favourite place to put your pictures of family and friends and other treasures.

Table tops, especially ones that are in a corner somewhere, old chests, window ledges and wall niches are great for flowers, shells, and natural objects. Specially made platforms that are wall mounted are another way to create a focal point.

GLOBAL GODDESS GURU TIP

Jean McMann, in her beautiful book Altars and Icons, describes how ordinary objects or arrangements become dynamic when given extra attention and significance. She says that arranging treasures and knick-knacks is a form of "sacred play."

Special days to make a shrine

* Birthdays and other special days that mean something to you.
* Holidays, such as Easter, Christmas, or Halloween.
* The solstice, the new moon, New Year's day.

It's easy being a [green] Goddess

As with a shrine positioned in a garden, having a garden itself is a wonderful way to celebrate the abundance of nature in our everyday world. Gardens are sacred places of nurturing rest and idea creation. Simply stepping into a garden may instantly transport us into another realm. Gardens invite us to actively participate with nature. They allow us to symbolically take out time from our busy lives and they draw us back again and again to pray, play, or just relax. If you're into Zen, gardens are the perfect microcosm of the Universe through which to practise raising levels of awareness and concentration.

The great outdoors can also be used to create a magical space – it could be time to exercise that green thumb! A fish pond or a reflection pool, or even just a pretty corner of the garden that you dedicate for the purpose, are all ideal. If you have a two-feet-long "juliet balcony" on the umpteenth floor of a high rise, then pot plants work just as long as you water them and don't let them die! As always, what counts is your intention to create and maintain the space.

Clear your garden regularly for the season and don't forget to manage your weeds and your pests! The mantra here is snails are killers! (We do make a slight exception for caterpillars, though, because they bring the all-important "change" energy of the butterfly. Relocate them if you can.) Remember, just because it's outside the house, it's still your space and therefore it reflects where you are spiritually. Are you tangled up in toxic weeds, or are you free to reach the sun and rain? Do your plants get adequate water and drainage? Are they thriving or dying? Check out those sad-looking, half-empty pots on the veranda or deck. There's a lot to do, isn't there? Hmmm, it could be a bit scary if you don't get onto it pronto!

Parks can also provide us with our essential connection to nature. Whether it's a local park, National Park or a green space somewhere in a city, parks give us a source of peace and the renewal that we need on a daily basis. Parks offer solitude, an unspoiled place to walk, and a restful source of energy exchange between nature and us. They remind us of our essence and they inspire us to get back to it.

Shielding process to protect your space and environment

The following process allows you to invoke a protective covering as your own personal energy shield. Used daily, it supports balance and harmony. Clearing the aura before shielding is very important.

Clearing your aura

1. Rub your hands together several times. Feel the energy build between your hands: you will soon feel them becoming warm.
2. Rub your third eye (found between your eyes, just above your nose) and as you do, say, "In the name of Goddess Mother Earth, Father Sky and The Divine."
3. Rub your hands above your head and down your arms, front, and back, reciting, "I cleanse my body, I cleanse my soul." Say this three times.

Creating a protective shield around your body

Once your aura is cleansed, you can create a protective shield around your body by following these steps.

1. With your eyes closed, stand with your arms beside your body, hands facing upwards. Visualize yourself being covered with pure white light, feeling the white light penetrate every cell of your body.

2. See a violet flame rising from your feet, up and around your whole body, swirling and transmuting all negative energy. As it does, make this statement, loud and strong, "Goddess and Lord God of my being, anything that has entered my auric field, my body or my life, that is not here in love and light and service, I ASK THAT IT LEAVE ME NOW."

3. Finish by saying, "And so it is."

Feng Shui

Feng Shui – it's so complicated we can't even say it. Feng shoe? Fung shway? Feng shway? A Chinese friend says, "fung shway" so we're sticking with him. Just when you thought you knew how to pronounce it, though, you soon realize you've got other stuff to think about – like the four versions of Feng Shui! There's Eight Directions, Eight Houses, Flying Star, and Form. Some Feng Shui experts use a compass called a Lo Pan to tell you what should go where while others don't. A few people also use Chinese astrology, also known as Nine Ki, to help them tell you where to put your bed, and what time to start the Feng Shui process, because if you're not in the right astro-phase, it may not work! Then there's the simple Feng Shui system which only uses a grid of nine squares called a Ba Gua. No compass, no birthdate calculations – but no results either according to some. In the middle of all this total confusion we ask, "What's a Goddess to do?," especially if your mother keeps putting an ironing board in your love corner or your parents move all your furniture into the hallway. Goddesses, we're going to give you the very basics here and if you want to delve deeper into this amazing topic, there are a number of excellent books out there for you to look at. We've listed a few that we think cover it best in the Goddess Library.

Feng Shui is the ancient and traditional Chinese philosophy and science of object placement and energy called Ch'i. It creates harmony and good fortune in one's internal environment. It's known to Indian culture as Prana. You can call it life force. You can't see it, but it moves like wind or water (yin and yang). Sometimes it's too fast. But it's even worse if it's not moving at all. Like stale air or stagnant water, Ch'i that is stuck can also make you stuck in your life.

Feng Shui teaches us to live in such a way that we do not disturb the harmony and flow of these energies (yin and yang). We can learn to bring into balance and harmony the flow of natural energies, in particular the life force through cleansing, clearing and beautifying one's personal space, and the arrangement and placement of objects.

Cutting Ch'i is another important concept. This makes the energy around you swirl crazily inside your home. This can make you feel confused, and if you're permanently around this Cutting Chi, you may even become ill. What causes the dreaded C.C.? Sharp corners. That's why Feng Shui fans hate to see you sleeping under a beam, or an electric fan. As a rule of thumb, you can do your own instant Feng Shui, just by making sure that your bed, or your favourite chair, isn't in the line of fire of anything pointy. If you could see the energy with your eyes, especially around the sharp point of a table, or the edge of a wall, it would be zig-zagging all over the place. Think round, curvy, free and easy to go with the flow!

GLOBAL
GODDESS
CULTURAL TIP

In Mexico, the first day of November is known as the "Day of Dead," and it is a special day for celebration and worship throughout the country. This day is also observed in parts of the American southwest region. Ancestors are honoured with feasting and festivities. Upon the altars constructed in homes, families will place flowers, gifts, and the favourite foods of a deceased relative. This is also common in other Latin cultures, such as in Cuba where the people make offerings to their ancestors in their home shrines on a regular, if not daily basis.

Power up your gadgets!

Energy can get stuck in computers as well as bedrooms or bathrooms. If you haven't taken a look at yours lately, it may be time to do some serious trashing. Following the rules for energy clearing is the same as for objects and rooms – before you "design" the space around you, it's crucial to get rid of the rubbish first. Your computer could well be a graveyard of unfinished letters, assignments that you can't get round to facing, project ideas that are now well over a year old, or computer games that, frankly, you got free with your original purchase but never play. If you're really nervous about losing things forever, drag them into the trash and leave them there for a month, then drag them out again to make a final decision. The golden rule for energy clearing/energy production is a simple question to yourself: Energy up or energy down?

Every time you eyeball something on your computer, ask yourself this question aloud. If it's energy down, you know what to do! The more space on your computer, the more space you will have to live your life.

De-junk your handbag

We sleep for one-third of our lives, but the typical Goddess also lives out of her handbag for another third. If you empty yours out on the table now, though, what would you find? This is what our friend Harriet discovered:

Two squashed tampons
An address book with scratched-out names
A comb full of hair
Old bus tickets
Cacky old lip-salve with bits of fluff stuck to it!

You get the idea. Energy has to flow through your bag the same way it has to flow through your computer or your bedroom. Apart from anything else, if you have to chuck everything out onto the pavement every time your mobile phone rings – in order to find it – then you're definitely holding yourself up.

A good way to trick yourself into having an easier, more organized life is to switch to a smaller handbag. Or, if wads of paper are really essential to your job or studies, to go for a briefcase plus a smaller handbag.

The cash in your purse is a good place to start. If you lug around tons of small change, ask yourself just how long you think you've been carrying it. If five-pence pieces get relegated to the back of your purse every time, chances are you could be constantly dragging the same half-kilo of change around for months. Stick to the big stuff and there could be more of it in your life!

How fast should you expect results?
The law of circulating energy says that as soon as you make room for something new, it will arrive – but with perfect timing for you and everyone else. If you are desperate for a new job, a lot of cash, or a new lover, the wait that occasionally follows your Feng Shui frenzy could seem annoying, but don't worry, the Universe is timing it – not you! Once results have fallen into place, you'll see exactly how things came for you, and those around you, at exactly the right time!

GODDESS BEAUTY NOTE

Epsom salts can be put in a bath for a wonderful mood lifter and aura cleanser. They are excellent for clearing energy blockages in the body to detoxify, leaving the skin soft and the circulation lifted. Pour half a cup into a slightly warmer than room temperature bath and soak in it for as long as desired. Try it on a waning moon (the best time for a detox) or the full moon (to enhance beauty!)

Global Goddess Guru: Simon G. Brown

Simon G. Brown is trained in Oriental medicine, philosophy, and design. His clients include Boy George, British Airways, and The Body Shop, and he is the author of Thorson's *Principles of Feng Shui*. We sent him some e-mail (or should that be chi-mail?) questions about the perfect Goddess bedroom, and this is what came back:

Simon, can we ask you what colours work best in a bedroom? Is a girl crazy to want candy pink pillows?

'It depends on what you want to achieve. Candy pink is associated with romance, pleasure, and fun. Brighter colours such as red, yellow, and orange are good for being more dynamic and outgoing, whereas pale green, blue, or cream help you feel calm and get to sleep.'

Goddess Guru, the question we are all dying to know is, where should we put our beds? Is it true that having your feet facing the door is out?

'It is most important to find out which direction the top of your head points in bed as this will have the greatest influence on the way you feel. South is calming, southeast motivating, east energizing and good for waking up, northeast for being creative, north to feel expressive, northwest to improve the quality of your life, west for romance, and southwest for wisdom.'

Simon's Feng essentials:

* Put a pair of candles in a safe place in the north or northwest part of your bedroom for friendships.
* Place a water feature in the east or northeast part of your bedroom to feel more enthusiastic, ambitious, and confident. This is also good for self-esteem.
* Plants will help keep the atmosphere clean and bushy plants will absorb sound, creating a more peaceful atmosphere.
* Try to arrange your room so that no corners point at your bed. If this is not possible, put a plant in front of the corner or hang a piece of fabric over the corner.
* Use pure-cotton bedding and bed clothes as synthetic fabrics can build up a static charge of electricity that can interfere with your own electro-magnetic energy.
* Move any electrical equipment as far from your bed as possible.
* Keep images that put a smile on your face and help you get through life's challenges in your bedroom. These could be people you admire, a lifestyle you want for yourself, or reminders of good times.

SPECIAL GODDESS CULTURAL ANECDOTE

The Hindu island of Bali in Indonesia has several acknowledged streams of naturally holy water. The name Bali means, "Island of the Gods." This holy water is used to worship the various deities of the culture, for example, Vishnu and Shiva. One of the major sources of this spring water is at the ancient water palace in Karangasem in the northeast region. The water flows from Lake Batur, which is located at the foot of the still-active volcano Kintamani, into a system of mineral pools. This system is called Tirta Gangga, which iterally means "holy water," with "gangga" referring to the sacred Ganges river in India. Priests come from all over Bali to fetch the holy water for the special ceremonies and cleansing rituals that are such an important part of the "bhakti" or devotional aspect of Balinese culture. Folklore holds that the most beautiful women in the kingdom used to come and bathe in the pools as the waters were said to make them more beautiful if they bathed in them under the full moon (purnama). The Raja who lived above the pools used to then select the most beautiful of these women as his concubines.

Goddess grounding ritual

This is a great ritual for those Goddesses who have super stressful jobs requiring them to interact with a large number of people throughout their working day.

This very simple ritual helps to prevent you from dragging in unwanted energies as a result of your interactions. It is a process designed to literally "earth" you, so that when you re-enter your home at night, you are once again neutral. Your home is then always a sanctuary and will remain free from the chaotic energies sometimes associated with the outside world. We believe that prevention is always preferable to cure, so here is a suggestion for you to try.

GODDESS TIP

An ordinary compass from a hardware or camping store can help you work out the direction in your bedroom.

Keep a sand box by the front door: Take a shallow wooden crate or low-sided wooden box of rectangular shape and fill it almost to the brim with sand from your favourite beach or, if you live inland, take pebbles or earth from the nearest bush or desert. The idea is to remove your shoes before entering the house and place your bare feet in the tray. Wriggle your toes deep into the box. Visualize and feel unwanted energies draining from your head through your body, out your feet, and into the box. Stand there and affirm that you are home again and safely in your space, thanking the Universe for its support during the day.

MOON GODDESS CLEANSING TIP

The best time to detox or clear energy is on a waning moon, so that you are ready to receive the new energies that will come in on the new and full moon. Some energy clearing practitioners, such as Karen Kingston, also recommend not clearing whilst you are pregnant, menstruating, or have an open wound. Karen also recommends a shower or bath before performing the ritual. We would add to that that you should bathe afterwards as well.

Car energy clearing ritual

In dream analogy, the car is representative of the body, so it pays to respect the connection between how your car is running and how your body is also travelling. Keeping your car spotlessly clean is a prime method of affirming to the Universe that you are also maintaining your physical vehicle – your own body.

Wash, polish, and spot detail your car, including windows and tyres, on a regular basis. Vacuum thoroughly throughout and use cotton buds or q-tips for those little cracks that seem to gather all sorts of nasties, such as sand, hair, and those annoying chewing gum wrapper ends.

After vacuuming, wave your hands through the air from the driver's seat right through to the back section. You can enhance your car energy by burning incense (carefully!) and waving the smoke through as per the feather ritual, for example. We also recommend room sprays be kept in your glove box. There is a new aromatherapy product we love – it plugs into the cigarette lighter (a far better use for it!) and

SPECIAL TIP FOR GODDESSES

When you are taking any elements from nature, always remember to leave an offering. Leaving a strand or two of your hair is an acceptable symbol of your gratitude.

you insert pads that have been soaked in certain oil blends. We also have Buddhas on our dashboards (excellent for reducing, if not eliminating, road rage!), feathers, sandalwood mala beads, and dream catchers. When your car is your office, you may as well make it your sanctuary. Finally, spray the whole car with the room spray and close it up – you're done!

Mind Miracles

The Goddess in the pole position of life is the one who has truly learned to master her mind and who can create apparent miracles at will. This Goddess at-the-wheel-of-life has understood the true nature of mind clutter and controls her impulses, swiftly rejecting distractions and bypassing confusion as effortlessly as chiffon glides across skin. The calm and ethereal Goddess who has learned how to maintain composure whilst still being busy or creating in a whirlwind is always one to watch – and there will always be people who want to watch her! She is one who has realized that the Universe lies within her and as the captain of her own ship she must set a clear course.

Indeed, operating with as much clarity as possible must be a prime focus for any Goddess worth her (energy clearing) salt. So in this chapter we look at the power of the mind in manifesting what you truly want. You'll soon be able to manifest more than the occasional miracle or two! We will discuss creative visualization techniques – where you see the picture in your mind and then reap the reality – and how to market your intentions to the Universe using simple methods that send a clearly stated message. We call these mind miracles. It's the art of using your mind to literally create miracles.

In addition, we'll also look at how you can rid yourself of your old thought habits by starting your own mental rewiring programme. We'll discuss how you can do your bit for the world, humanity and the community you live in. In short, we'll give you the equivalent of a jump-start to using your mind as a frontline tool in life. It's the most readily available and effective one you have. So, sharpen up your imagination and dust off those shelved dreams: there's a whole new reality coming right at you . . .

Your universal intention

Before you leap into visualizing and manifesting those designer shoes or whatever it is that you have your heart set on – we hope this also includes the odd request for world peace and reduced ozone depletion too – it is very important to remember that whenever you ask the Universe for something and imagine a new reality for yourself – which is exactly what you are doing when you use creative visualization techniques – you must be aware that you are sending out a major invitation by thought wave. Every thought you transmit is a beacon for all of the individual elements to begin lining up for the delivery. If you send out mixed signals, that's exactly what you'll get in return.

If things are coming into your life inconsistently and chaotically, it's a dead cert you have to go back to the drawing board to clear it off and start again. This is why you must set and send out your thoughts clearly, so that what you say you want is what you'll get. Goddesses should be very aware that thoughts are "beings." An emitted thought is not just purely a creative facilitator. It has a life, even if you believe it never left your brain – sorry, honey, but it did. For better or worse, you have created something. And that will always have ramifications. As the saying goes, "Where the mind goes, energy flows."

Below is the golden rule for all Goddesses who are practising our creative visualization techniques for mind miracles, or indeed for any of the other methods described throughout the book:

Whatever it is that you desire to occur, you must want it for the highest good of all concerned – for the universal good.

Global Goddesses unite!

Which brings us to your higher purpose on this planet. You have incarnated at this particular time and in a particular part of the world for a purpose in this life. As a divine instrument of the Universe, God, the Infinite Intelligence or the Source – call it what you will – you have a responsibility to figure out your higher purpose and your destiny, which serves that purpose. If you have as the primary goal for your life that you want to give back to or help the earth through its evolutionary process, then you have truly tapped into the highest purpose possible. With such a universally positive aim, you will find that all of your desires, whether material or spiritual, will truly be manifested.

For those Goddesses who think that's easy enough to do, it's actually more than an idle thought that you have from time to time – you have to deeply feel the need to contribute and be willing to put that first, above all else. Lip service to the cause simply does not work. By acknowledging your role here on the physical plane as being a supportive one, and by being willing to engage your creative endeavours to that end, you are absolutely sending out a message to the Universe that you deserve to be supported in achieving your own personal goals and desires. Your intentions then have purity and a singular beauty, which in turn, pulls in more of the same energy. We'll talk later in the chapter about how you can make this a reality in your life by committing even the smallest acts of generosity regularly. There are many ways to be a positive force for universal good.

What's really on your mind?

If you say to yourself that you want certain things but, at the same time, in the back of your mind there is a more dominant thought such

LETTERS OF INTENTION

As a little exercise to get you going, write a letter of intention to the Universe. In it describe all of the things you would like to see positive changes to in your lifetime. State what you are prepared to do to serve a higher purpose and how you see yourself being a contributor to the welfare of the planet while you are here. Then list all of the things that you would also like to see happen in your personal sphere. You can list anything at all here – better relationships, more creative output, a new place to live, a more satisfying career... put it all down. Then date it and seal it. Put it under your pillow for the first night and, thereafter, keep it in a safe place. You can even forget about it and come back to it in a year or two to see what has happened since you wrote it.

WE BET YOU'LL BE AMAZED...

as, "But I don't really deserve it [because of xyz]," then obviously the dominant thought will prevail. Now here's the catch: This dominant thought may be a conscious or a subconscious thought – one which is so deeply ingrained that you're not necessarily aware of its existence, let alone its effect. Subconscious thoughts can completely sabotage any consciously expressed thought if they are in conflict. These may include strongly held beliefs about yourself, which are usually the result of old conditioning from childhood or from assumptions by others. They are often in play when we have agreed to see ourselves in a certain way, and are most often based on second-hand observations by others that we have simply taken on board.

We should always closely examine any observations others make about us to see if there is truth in them, and in this way we discover for ourselves who we really are. Both conscious and subconscious thoughts can play havoc with even the most meticulous and well-planned visualization. Creating mind miracles is not a passive exercise in wishful thinking – rather, it's active work that requires dedication and a bit of perseverance to obtain major results. It is part of the role of this chapter to alert all Goddesses to the potential mines on the playing field prior to commencing any creative visualization.

Goddess – know thyself first!

To fully prepare for creative visualization and to create mind miracles, you must know yourself and ideally have some idea of what your destiny is on the earthly plane – you must try to establish the true nature of your personal mission. You therefore need to know your own true nature as well. The reason for this is that you will be much more focused in your planning process if you have some idea of where you want to go and what your personal milestones are going to need to be in order to arrive. Hopefully, by the time you get to this chapter, you have checked out your full astrological and numerological profiles, been in touch with your inner angel and spirit guides, and examined the life lessons offered by the tarot. Hopefully, too, you are buoyed with positivity about both your star qualities and the limitations you need to work on and overcome to really start to make progress. If you've done the work, you'll be well placed to examine an array of conditioned assumptions about yourself which are both positive and negative.

The power of your beliefs is immense – beliefs can be constructive or destructive. Beliefs, wrongly or rightly held, have enormous influence on your relationships, your health, your career – all areas of your life are a reflection of the beliefs you hold. The task for every Goddess is to understand what beliefs you are holding and to remove and replace those that are – literally – holding you back. And once you've nailed these, you'll be ready to make a request of the Universe that will be the most effective and the most personally appropriate for your journey.

The Goddess checklist

Your 21st Century Goddess Profile is a checklist for you to compile a personal overview to help you see yourself as the Goddess you really are and to ferret out those negative thoughts before you ask the Universe for anything. Obviously this is only a rough list to guide you – it's not meant to be exhaustive. And you may have plenty of other stuff to write down, especially if you've been on "the path" for a while, so feel free to add other relevant information as you go.

Do try to keep it simple though – it makes it a lot easier to glean the gems if you avoid too much detail. Just try to be as honest with yourself as you can be. This is a very useful exercise that is solely for your benefit – no one else has to see it. Now, grab a pen and some paper and get cracking!

OK. So you will now have a piece of paper with all sorts of things written on it. Can you see any positive or negative trends throughout? These are the key indicators of the belief system you hold about yourself and are therefore influential in the success or otherwise of any creative visualization project you undertake. You need to be very clear where any negative programming exists and systematically

YOUR 21ST CENTURY GODDESS PROFILE

1 **Personal Goddess** _____
   Positive aspects _____
   Negative aspects _____
2 **Astrological sun sign** _____
   Positive traits _____
   Negative traits _____
3 **Astrological moon sign** _____
   Positive traits _____
   Negative traits _____
4 **Ruling number** _____
   Positive aspects _____
   Negative aspects _____
5 **Personal year number** _____
   Meaning _____
6 **Current phase of life** _____
   Write a brief paragraph as to what stage you feel you are at in your
   life. For example, where you are at in school, whether you're moving
   out of your parents' home, engaged to be married, going back to
   university, starting a new job, or undertaking a career change.

   _____
   _____
   _____

7 **What would your friends say about you?**
   _____
8 **What would your family say about you?**
   _____
9 **What would your partner say about you?**
   _____
10 **What do you think about yourself?**
   Positive personality traits _____
   Negative personality traits _____
11 **Do you believe you can be successful?** List the reasons why or
   why not _____
12 **Do you consider yourself a successful person?** Describe what
   success means to you _____
13 **Do you mostly get positive feedback** and support from people
   when you try to do something or say you want something? _____

replace such beliefs with positive affirmations. The key to the whole thing is to re-write all of the negative beliefs you hold about yourself by discovering what they are and then rephrasing them into positive beliefs.

Creating new affirmations for positive change

One of the major barriers to success in creating mind miracles is the inability to turn off or change the dialogue or voice of the inner critic. We all have it to a greater or lesser degree, however that's just our conditioning trying to control us through the ego. The ego does not want you to surrender all of the habitual thought patterns that allow it to remain in control and keep you in the trenches. Successful people in life have learned to tune out this nagging and doubtful cynic who says, "You can't," or "You shouldn't," or "You don't deserve that." They have learned that the Universe really wants us all to have everything, which is Ab-Fabulous, so any other noise coming over the wires should be regarded as static, which is exactly what it is . . . and exactly what it creates. The universal voice is harmonious and beautiful. It is positive and life-affirming. The universal voice creates, it does not destroy. It's the real voice to listen to.

Creating affirmations that are in alignment with the universal voice is very powerful and will create breathtaking changes in every aspect of your life. Whatever you put energy into will bring forth the same, so putting energy into creating a new positive inner dialogue will have profound effects on all aspects of your life – your relationships, your health, your material wealth and, most importantly, your spiritual enrichment.

AFFIRMATIVE ACTION!

Look at the list that you have compiled about your belief systems. Write down your goals in order of priority. Be as specific as you can be. Next, re-write any negative feelings you have as to why you believe a particular goal may not manifest for you, replacing them with a positive affirmation(s) that reflects each of the goals you intend to manifest.

An example: Let's say you would like to have total financial freedom, where you have an income stream which you created, that keeps coming until you no longer need to work. If you hold the negative belief that money will never come to you because it never has in the past and/or you don't come from a monied family so you have a hard time believing financial freedom is possible for you, then you could rewrite that belief as follows:

Money comes to me as I need it.
I always have money and there is even more coming to me in
*   the future.*
I am worthy of being wealthy because I believe in abundance.
The Universe is abundantly wealthy and because the Universe
*   is also within me,*
I am abundantly wealthy.

Note: Affirmations should always be in the present tense – that means, think of it as if it is already occurring, until it actually does!

Goddesses, you need to truly believe in abundance before you can attract it – and hold on to it. It's all about reaching your goals, however small or grandiose they may be. No matter what the end goal, it is very achievable if you practise affirming your intentions and then carry out the visualization techniques to support your intentions. You

HERE ARE SOME AFFIRMATIONS TO GET YOU STARTED

I am a child of the Universe and I am connected to the infinite intelligence that allows me to create anything at whim.

I am abundant and I believe I deserve all that the Universe wishes me to have.

Success comes easily to me.

I am able to use my energy powerfully for my own creative expression.

I am beautiful in every way. The Universe reflects my own beauty back to me.

I am perfect right now for the task that is before me.

I am a success in life because I have learned from my past life lessons and I have an amazing future ahead of me.

I am lovable. I am loved. Love is both within me and all around me.

I have no fear. There is no need. I am positive that everything is for the best.

I love my body. It is strong and free. It helps me to achieve my goals in life.

I am responsible for my feelings and I honour myself by being honest with others.

You get the general idea. The whole point is to be creative and to say the thing that really goes to the heart of where you want to be, by phrasing it in the here and now.

need to believe that you absolutely and positively deserve to have it – whatever it is that you want – and that you can have it. And also that you deserve to keep it. Believe it or not, for most people this is very hard to do, and for a variety of reasons. This could also be the reason why some people win the lottery (what we'd call a successful creative visualization project!) and then lose all of the money and end up having to go back to their old lives with very little to show for what they had won.

The Rule for Goddesses here is: If you want to earn it, first you have to learn it.

The Universe itself is infinitely abundant, and so there is plenty to go around. You just have to know how to affirm the concept of abundance until it becomes second nature and therefore your reality. This is a part of the work that needs to be done until you have successfully rewired the old grey matter into agreeing with your new stance. We are huge fans of affirmations – as they hold the key to positive change. The best way to eliminate a negative quality or situation is to focus on the opposite positive quality or the preferred scenario. Whatever you focus on gives it energy, so you may as well make whatever it is positive. After a time you'll find that what you wanted to be rid of has transformed into the thing you were focusing on. It's all in your intention from the outset, so you'd better make it good!

THE RULE FOR GODDESSES HERE IS:
If you want to earn it, first you have to learn it.

DIY Affirmations

On page 309 are some further examples of affirmations that can be done either before or in tandem with the creative visualization techniques that we will be exploring. These are a guide only, because we have found that often the most powerful affirmations are ones that each individual designs for herself. It's all about YOU and creating what you want, so why not be creative from the start? In this way the affirmations you create are then uniquely powerful for you alone. It's all about continuing to appreciate and affirm your own individuality and your own unique mindset so you can manifest your own desires in the strongest way possible.

Special tip for thinking Goddesses
(or Goddesses who think too much!)
Affirmations can be used alone or in the context of a meditation. They can be intoned as a mantra (a phrase which you repeat or

chant over and over until you produce a lyrical, tonal sound and a continuous looping effect). Meditation is a heightened form of concentration which can be a very calming and powerful method of rewiring yourself for positivity and enhancing focus on any goal. For Goddesses who have never meditated or chanted before, at the end of the chapter you will find a section describing a method of meditation and a simple mantra.

Opportunity knocks . . . or did it?

Now this is where all good Goddesses have to put on their detective caps and start being super sleuths on their own lives. That's right – it's no longer on the weird neighbour or the loud couple down the road, it's you shining your own heat and light on your own life. Sounds spooky? Well, it is, kind of. Once you have visualized something and affirmed it to the Universe, the elements will begin lining up to deliver it, as we've mentioned. Now what this means is that the right person or the right situation will present itself and it may only be a preliminary to get you into another scenario which will really be where you're meant to be – and there can be a gazillion permutations and variations on how things happen. The point is, you have to be ready. Ready to recognize the opportunities that are about to pour in.

STRATEGY FOR
CREATING
MIND
MIRACLES
Think it.
Write it.
Say it.
Repeat it.
Twenty times
(or more).
Believe it.
Receive it.

The main trick is that you have to notice signs and what seems like strange coincidences when they do start occurring. Then you have to listen to your heart (sometimes you have to ignore what is going on in your head) and tap into your deepest gut feeling on whether this is a significant thing for you. Instinct is the key indicator, along with your heart. This may sound obvious enough, but many's the Goddess who almost got what she wanted and then dipped out because she didn't recognize the opportunities that were being presented at the right time. It's very important to remember that you have to be in the right mind for things to come in at the right time.

Creative visualization:
TWO HANDS FOR BEGINNERS!

Now that you've had a bit of background and insight as to your personal motivations and potential self-sabotaging thought processes, it's time to get going on a few hands-on techniques for manifesting

SPECIAL GODDESS SIGNS AND OMENS CHECKLIST

* **Phone numbers:** Numbers that you can never seem to remember for some reason. These could be a sign that you're not meant to be calling that person or place.

* **Number plates:** When you notice a number plate for some reason, look at the numbers and the letters – is there any meaning for you in them?

* **Television shows:** When you feel compelled to turn on the television and you happen to channel surf onto a show, then there's some connection for you to make, particularly if you don't watch it very much. Take notes!

* **Films:** Particularly when lines resonate strongly. When Julia Roberts says to Hugh Grant in *Notting Hill*: "I'm just a girl, standing in front of a boy, asking him to love her," a Goddess friend of ours decided to be brave and declare her feelings to someone who she'd been in (unrequited) love with for years. As a result of her motivation, she ended up marrying him, just like the happy ending in the film (aw shucks!). No apologies from us on this one – we LOVE happy endings.

* **Coincidental meetings with people:** You maybe thought about calling someone or meeting them and then you literally bump into them in an out of context situation. You either have something to impart to each other, or it could be one-way. Listen or speak up!

* **Being in a particular place when something major happens:** You were meant to be there for a particular reason – to make some sort of connection with your destiny.

your heart's desires. There are many time-tested methods available, so we'll run through a few of the most popular versions.

Visual mapping
CREATING THE ULTIMATE DESIGNER LIFE

A personal favourite of ours, the time-tested method of creating visual maps is popular and usually highly successful. Visual maps can be either word or image-based. We have found that people invariably fall into two camps: those for whom a word trigger is more effective in order for them to visualize something, and those who pre-fer to see a direct image in order to focus on the goal they have in mind.

Words are powerful. For certain types of people who are more conceptual (or perhaps more left-brained!) in their orientation, they

* **The six degrees of separation:** This theory was coined in the United States by psychologist Stanley Milgram and it posits that between every person in the world there are only five others linking the two of you. One of our Goddess friends was a huge fan of a particular rock star and she arrived in New York determined to meet him. She had thought about it a lot and finally she manifested it. Within three months a new friend whom she had only just met invited her to an album launch, which ended up being his. Of course she more than got to meet him!

* **Jobs that don't work out or interviews that you don't get the call-back for:** You weren't meant to get it or the company wasn't going to be the right vibe for you. Something better is coming. You'll have to check in with your heart space to figure out what it is you're not yet getting though. Maybe you're not meant to work for someone else; maybe you're meant to work for yourself in order to make your dreams happen.

* **Missing the person you were supposed to meet and then meeting someone else as a result:** The person you meet may end up being the right person or better person for you to meet for whatever reason.

* **Coincidences of every kind:** Pay attention, for they are potential turning points to your destiny.

This list is a start, but YOU have to do your own detective work. Let's face it, the Universe wants you to succeed, but it's going to make you do a little work to get there . . .

can be a more effective means of creating mind miracles. Below we have compiled a list of categories to help you figure out the areas that you may wish to focus on. For each category you can write down your goals and add any keywords that may be associated. Do it in your own words for you are now the author of your destiny!

Create a visual map that is word based: On a blank piece of paper, write down the list overleaf, using coloured felt-tips, crayons or pens. (It may be easier to start off in pencil and use a rubber until you have the proportions you need, then go over the outlines with the colours later.) This is only a guide – you can add or delete or as you see fit – but we prefer to use all of them because it is more effective when you work on a holistic overview. It's all about balance (that and being a well-rounded Goddess). The other reason why it makes sense to do the whole list is that it's not much good bringing in the partner of your dreams if, for example, you haven't got your health or your financial stuff in order and you're not really happy in your job. Give yourself the best chance by asking for everything you need, at once!

* Health
* Life/general
* Spirituality/esoteric
* Skills/hobbies
* Financial/money
* Lifestyle
* Community
* Travel/culture

* Physical fitness/body
* Love/relationships/family
* Education/mental
* Sport/activities
* Home/environment
* Career/work
* Rest and relaxation
* Experiences

Once you have written out the headings on this list, write next to them a few key words that will be your trigger words for the topic. Opposite is an example done by one of our Goddess friends, a writer by profession. This is a fairly safe visual map and you can go a lot wilder if you want (don't be afraid to go there). No one can limit your imagination but you. The word triggers our Goddess friend came up with for her visual map are realistic, occasionally whimsical, practical, creative, and often very specific.

SPECIAL GODDESS AFFIRMATION

I am infinite.
I am pure potential.
I am deserving of
all that is beautiful
and limitless.
I am lovable.
I am loved.
I am successful.
I am powerful.
I am.

The next thing to do is write your trigger words in "list" form and put a coloured bubble around each list, highlighting the category in a contrasting colour. If you have a computer that will do graphic design, you can make it very funky and colourful indeed – try adding your own personal symbols for each category and bolding out the key words.

Cut out each bubble and stick it down onto the white cardboard in a circular format starting with LIFE as the bubble in the centre and the others radiating around it. Pin it up in your study or a private place where you'll see it constantly – inside your wardrobe door is a great place to stick it. You could also draw it on a whiteboard (as long as it won't be erased until you've manifested your goals!).

Another technique is to write each category and word trigger on a separate page and bind the pages together. You can keep it next to your bed (read it before you sleep and upon waking) or in the car (now you know what to do while you're waiting in traffic – less road

GODDESS WORD TRIGGER EXAMPLE

Life/general: Active/exercising my free will/fun/full/peaceful/dynamic/ variety/social/integrated/balanced/parties!

Health: Allergy-free/strong immune system/clear head/improve memory/no flus or colds/high-energy levels/yeast-free diet/better bounce-back capability.

Physical fitness/body: Renew gym membership/increase body tone/ reduce hip line/stronger thigh muscles/flatter stomach/better posture/increase lean muscle mass/reduce body fat percentage.

Love/relationships/family: Soul mate/new life partner/closer platonic friendships – male and female/more male friends in general/new baby next year/closer ties with brother.

Spirituality/esoteric: Practice energy clearing/regular visits to ashram/ read more books on spirituality/meditate daily for 30 minutes/create shrine in bedroom for meditation/spend more time in nature.

Education/mental: Upgrade software skills/memorize affirmations/pass lifesaving exams in top 10%.

Skills/hobbies: Make quilt for new bedroom/learn to scuba dive.

Sport/activities: Enter local doubles tennis competition in summer/go to the beach more.

Financial/money: Increase savings balance/invest in share market/establish superannuation fund/find investor or business partner for agency.

Home/environment: Paint and decorate spare room for guests/buy new house in the inner city within 3 years: two bedroom terrace/pretty English-style garden/city skyline views/private and quiet.

Lifestyle: Work out three times per week/Monday off every second week/weekend away once a month/eat at home more/one 4–6 week overseas holiday per year.

Career/work: Increase freelance copywriting assignments/win more corporate and advertising clients/increase word rate for editorial work

Community: A charity walkathon in your area/donate clothing to charity/ volunteer to help at local retirement home.

Rest and relaxation: Go to bed earlier and get up earlier/do yoga/read more novels/fortnightly massages.

Travel/culture: Visit India/Alaska/South of France within next ten years/attend the theatre more regularly/attend at least one art exhibition per month.

Experiences: Swim with dolphins/scuba dive in the Maldives/climb Mount Kilimanjaro/see the perfect sunrise on the Pacific Ocean and the perfect sunset on the Indian Ocean/drink champagne at dawn on New Year's Day every year/go camping for a month in the national park/meditate at the edge of the crater of the volcano on Maui, Hawaii.

rage too; an added bonus!). Laminated pages last longer if you like the booklet idea. You can even do it in a school exercise book. The idea is to look at and read it repeatedly, until you know it by heart and it is imprinted on your brain. It's all about focus and repetition for the best results.

Note that time-specific requests also have a role to play. It's absolutely fine to be day, month or year specific in relation to a certain thing that you want to happen. Sometimes, however, you may not be able to quite envisage when something should occur, and so you might decide to leave it up to the Universe to bring it in when the time is appropriate. As you begin to achieve certain goals, you will become clearer on the time frame for those that may have been somewhat vaguer.

Images "R" Us! For those Goddesses who relate more strongly to an image-based visual map, it's the same process. Creating a collage of images and graphic symbols that inspire and affirm your goals is another highly effective method for creating mind miracles.

You will need a variety of magazine tear sheets, postcards and (personal) photos to cover the subjects listed: Get those scissors working. Stick the images you've chosen into an arrangement on the page. Don't worry if you think you're not artistic. Remember: You are an artist of life, so anything goes!

You can add to word triggers with images or substitute word triggers with photos and pictures etc. A layered combination of words and images is usually what most people find works best. You may wish to have one image for each category which best epitomizes your goals. Or you may have a number of images where elements of each speak to you. As we've said before – it's entirely a personal choice as to what works best.

REMEMBER IF YOU CAN SEE IT, YOU CAN HAVE IT!

Flat cardboard collages are fun to make as well as being stimulating to gaze at and meditate upon. If you really need to work with a lot of images, however, buy a scrapbook and fill it up. Alternatively, you can bind your individual category pages into a portable book format. Then, if you need to make changes, all you have to do is take out the old page and replace it. Some people have each page laminated, which allows them to sit better and last longer.

You can frame this collage and then put it above your desk in your home office or study. Another alternative is to frame, or laminate it and hang it in the kitchen area of your home. The kitchen symbolizes wealth and prosperity in the home – it is also an area in the home where you go frequently and, you will therefore, see it all the time. Another great place to hang your visual map is in the bathroom area. This is a strong energy centre for cleansing and renewal, so it is also a powerful place for manifesting. The bathroom is where we are more "inner directed" and in a safe, private environment. This makes doing the affirmations easier. In the end, though, it's all personal choice – just be sure to put it where you'll see it last thing at night and first thing in the morning. LIFE IS...PICTURES!

Changes: Two, three, four …

People change and so do their desires. It's part of the ebb and flow of life and it occurs naturally over time or in the wake of a particular event. Goddesses should be objective (at the least) and ruthless (at the most) in reassessing and re-evaluating goals on a regular basis. There is nothing to fear from change. It's healthy and it shows you're not too attached to your goals. Changing a goal because you've outgrown it or it has lost its appeal is smart. Hanging on to something that is no longer your highest desire makes no sense. You just have to be vigilant with yourself and force yourself to constantly check in with what you are feeling and what is going on in your life at the time. It's all about change and adapting to it. You also have to be on the lookout for conflicting goals. You can't very well be a famous travel writer and not want to fly.

Goddess story from the frontline

One of our Goddess friends in her late twenties always had particular goals for her life that she had been working towards when, just before her 28th birthday, her father died unexpectedly. Her mother had died when she was in her early teens and her father's untimely death brought home the realization that all her life she had been trying to make up for the loss of her mother by being a good daughter for her father. She had set herself goals that she thought would reflect that to him. Her dreams included wanting to be married and have a family, and owning a nice home in a "good" area. She spent several months in deep grief, contemplating all of her past, and she gradually came to understand that she had never really allowed herself to want what she really wanted for herself. For the first time she was able to see that her old desires and dreams were not really hers. She was sad at the fact that neither of her parents had ever seen her with the partner she truly loved or with children. However, beyond the sadness, reality was calling.

Slowly she began to recover and a year later she had moved out of her old flat where she lived in Orange County, California, put all of her possessions in storage and bought herself a ticket to New York. In the spirit of her new mood, she changed her career entirely from one that was science-driven and research-based to enrol in a liberal arts degree at university. Her new life consisted more of making friends of both sexes without any prerequisites in mind about marriage or having a family, or owning a house. Within a few years, however, her inheritance came through, which enabled her to buy a small walk-up property in downtown Manhattan and she met and moved in with someone she'd met through her studies. By letting go and following her heart, by accepting change and by being prepared to put her faith in the Universe, she eventually did get all that she had dreamed of for her life.

A little note about attachment – it's all about surrender!

The great thing about creating mind miracles is that once you have put it
(a) down on paper and
(b) communicated your intentions to the Universe, you can then
(c) relax!

One of the key things to being successful in your quest is to not be attached to the results for which you are hoping. You've got to let your desires and intentions float out into the cosmos unimpeded so the Universe can get to work and do its thing without you holding on to your request like a limpet to a rock. It will happen, but you don't need to be obsessive about what the end result will be. In other words, you need to develop trust that the Infinite Intelligence knows exactly what it's doing. Which it does.

When we speak about repeating your desires and looking frequently at your visual maps and so on, you should remember to do it with what Buddhism speaks of as "non-attachment." Non-attachment means you are open to a result that is solely for the highest good of all concerned. This means that if a better goal is manifesting as a result of other forces (or other desires that you have), then you will bring in something possibly even better than what you imagined or envisaged. It means that you are protecting yourself from being obsessive and you are respecting that while you've done as much as possible to prepare yourself creatively, you ultimately surrender to the wisdom of the Universe and you allow the Universe to be the best guide for you. It is. Trust it.

Mind body spirit – the holistic trinity

So far we've been talking about your conscious and your subconscious mind. In this section we switch the focus to the body, and then we'll look at your spirit in the meditation section. The body and the mind are very similar in that the more they are conditioned, the better they will respond. If you're not in tune with your body and your spirit, it's going to be that much harder to define, let alone to achieve, your goals. The body is your carrier on the road to any of your future successes, and it is important to optimize visualizations in all of your categories by making sure "the carrier" is in tip-top condition for the long haul. Like anything, the best results are obtained (a) by starting early and (b) by doing it regularly. The great news is that with regular imaging, you can use visualization to reconnect you to your physical body and to steer to it good health, vitality, stamina and a consistently high level of energy.

The body

The body responds to the commands of the mind, and it would be harder to find a more dramatic example than that of the practice of "pointing the bone" that occurs in the Aboriginal culture of Australia. If the tribal elders so decree it, the bone is pointed at one of the members of the tribe, and they die. They die from the deeply held belief that this is irreversible and fatal. They would have to reverse their entire belief system to avoid their fate, however, few are able to do so.

Likewise, wellbeing and its opposite, illness, are a combination of the same deeply held beliefs, attitudes, thought patterns, and emotions. Channelling these into a positive force leads to wellness and channelling the opposite negative force results in illness. Wellness and illness can therefore be seen as flip sides of the same coin.

Humans are endlessly creative – this we know – yet many of us are still not taking responsibility for our negative creativity: Illness or lacklustre health. You can heal yourself with a relentless mental attitude of health and fitness, by being unable to imagine yourself as anything other than healthy and fit. That, in combination with total body awareness, consciously noticing when you have problems, even small ones, and trying to tap into and understand the cause of them, will keep you in tune. You have to listen to your body, really pay attention to it and what it's telling you.

Like the physical world around you, your body is a reflection of what's really going on for you. It holds the key to your progress. If you ever become ill, then you must switch your focus to the positive and concentrate on being strong and healthy. You need to give your body what it needs. The body has an incredible ability to bounce back, so if you give it what it needs – good nutrition, water, rest and exercise, as well as positive healing affirmations – you'll see results in a short time. The best affirmations for healing the body and long-term wellness are to be found in Louise L. Hay's seminal book *Heal Your Body*. We recommend all Goddesses keep this book handy. It will help you with any healing work.

If you see yourself as less able-bodied, you'll become so. If you believe you're getting older, you will. If you think you'll catch a cold, you've already emitted the thought and that's what will happen. If you believe that you can't lose weight, you won't. The rule is that wherever you put heat and intensity, something will start to cook! On the other hand, if you want to truly glow and to be a beacon of good health, put vision – strong, powerful mental images and positive thought energy – into every aspect of your body, and in time you will produce a wellbeing that is truly lasting.

Meditation
TAKE THE TIME TO TRAIN YOUR BRAIN

And now it's over to your spirit. We've discussed how your thoughts contain energy and how they "create" once they are emitted from their initial source in your brain. Thoughts are simply energy which moves from the mental plane into the physical plane. The concept of "thought drift" is one which can then be seen in a new light as a result of understanding what our thoughts are in fact doing – and what they are potentially capable of doing. You know how, without even being aware of it most of the time, you seem to just drift from one topic to another in your mind. It happens when you're tired or when you're idle – meaning, not focused on a particular task – when you're waiting around to catch a bus or sitting in traffic or sometimes even just before you go to sleep. Thought drift is aimless – thoughts which flow without a clear direction.

Meditation is a very important part of preparing yourself mentally and creatively to pull in the universal energies that will serve you best, and the way to do this is to direct your thoughts in a focused and positive manner. Goddesses who want to be powerful in their lives and manifest their unique destiny need to get a handle on thought drift and take charge of it. Thought drift frequently contains many negative aspects which are part of the subconscious and undermining inner dialogue that we've discussed. Reducing thought drift is a priority if we are to take control of our mind and not let it run us. We need to run it! And while it's a definite challenge to control what seems like the endless stream of dialogue rotating around our oversaturated brains, Goddesses who want to manifest mind miracles will be better prepared to step up to the plate if this is made part of their daily routine. Meditation is a means to this end.

Meditation is an ancient practice that aims – through deep concentration, breath observation, and relaxation of the conscious mind – to reach the state of calmness and "thoughtlessness" that lies between consciousness and deep sleep. When you train your mind to be still by meditating, you can go beyond thought to an awareness of your real self – the real essence of you. This will also help you to define who you are and, therefore, what you really want. It's a truism that if you don't know what you want then you're not going to get what you want. Meditating puts you in touch with that part of you that will allow you, from that still point within you, to discover what will really rock your world. Meditation reconnects you to your spirit, and is essential for your ongoing development and for understanding who you are and who you might become. It may take a while to find your centre, so you need patience too – lots of it! But we promise you (and we don't make promises lightly) it will definitely be worth it.

Meditation has many add-on benefits too – reduced stress, increased focus and concentration on tasks at hand, improved quality of sleep, increased memory capacity, more energy, enhanced feelings of calm and peacefulness, greater feelings of contentment and happiness, and a more positive outlook in general. Who wouldn't want this list to be a permanent part of their life?

Special Goddess meditation

For those Goddesses who have never meditated or even heard of meditation before, you're in for a treat. One myth to dispel: It's not a silly or boring

THE GOLDEN GODDESS VISUALIZATION

Goddesses who want to "go for the glow" need to affirm and visualize their body glowing with radiant energy, performing magnificent feats of endurance and, most of all, having fun. This can be done last thing before bed, or at any time during the day when you are doing something physical. Tell yourself throughout the day how much you love your life, how much fun you are having right now, how great it is to be healthy and strong. See yourself glowing golden from head to toe, with shiny hair and luminous, fresh skin. See yourself as being in perfect health and awash with golden radiant light. Tell yourself that you are moving towards ultimate health, in every respect. To be effective, these affirmations have to be made in the present – right here, right now – so they will manifest in the future. Become the Golden Goddess now!

pastime for people (read hippies) who do nothing but hang around in ashrams all day, even though that's kind of what it looks like. Well, actually sometimes meditation looks exactly like that, because meditation is basically the art of doing nothing – or, more accurately, thinking nothing – because you can do a very effective walking meditation or chanting meditation and these can also achieve excellent results.

And it not only happens in ashrams, it happens in gyms, offices, and homes all over the world. People from all walks of life and cultures meditate. Some of the most successful entertainers and business people in the world – Oprah Winfrey, Sting, Tina Turner, and, of course, the newly spiritual girl, Madonna – meditate. Children in schools in certain parts of Asia meditate as part of their daily routine. Meditation gives a tremendous boost to your powers of concentration and focus. If you are trying to create mind miracles, you'll send out a clearer message and you'll get a better result from any visualization practices if you learn to meditate and do this in conjunction with affirmations and imaging to maximize your chances of success.

A special Goddess meditation specifically for creating Mind Miracles: This is the breath observation method, and it will get you into the zone. Choose a time when you won't be disturbed. This is your precious time!

Take off your watch or set an alarm clock for a few minutes time. Get comfortable by either sitting on your bed with your feet on the floor or sitting on the floor with your legs in a crossed position and your spine against the wall for support. You can even sit on a chair or, if you prefer to, lie on the floor. Whatever feels right for you.

1. Breathe in through your nose with your mouth closed.
2. Leave your eyes either half-open and focused on one point in the room or, if you prefer, you can close them fully.
3. Continue to breathe through your nose until you feel the breath go all the way to your stomach, and then breathe out the same way so you can feel a kind of "loop" pattern in your breathing.
4. Don't follow any train of thought (we know this is hard but you have to try) and if any thoughts arise, let them fall away as you return your focus to your breath.
5. The thoughts will continue to come – the trick is to learn to ignore them. They have no place for you right now because they are only serving to distract you from your mission to find your true essence.

If you find you have too many thoughts, practise running an affirmation over and over in your mind. For example: "I love my life. I am happy and contented. All is well in my world." You can change the affirmation to reflect each of your chosen categories. Rotate these throughout your meditation, or alternate each meditation with a new affirmation, so you cover all the areas in a balanced way.

6. Be still, don't fidget, and really try to control any excess body movement. Focus.

7. Do this for as long as you can. You can start with a few minutes and work up to longer periods. Do it first thing in the morning when you're fresh, and then again in the evening before you go to sleep.

You've got to have faith
THE POWER OF PRAYER

You can do your bit for anyone you know who is going through a rough time by praying or affirming that they will come through whatever it is they're going through. You can be a conduit for change on their behalf and they never even have to know that you're doing it. Sending them positive vibrations in the form of thoughts that affirm they are coping well and that they have the strength to get beyond their current dilemma will assist their passage. You can also do this for someone you know who is unwell. Obviously they have to do their bit – you can't cure them by yourself, but you can boost their mental strength vicariously by praying and affirming their recovery, so they have an increased ability to heal.

THE MORE YOU MEDITATE, THE GREATER THE RESULTS – BUT YOU HAVE TO DO THE WORK.

The beauty of affirming prayer is that it is a third-party meditation and as the Universe hears all thought, it can only go out into the ether and come back multiplied. Calling on your essence and channelling it into positive causes in line with a higher purpose is extremely empowering. It gives you a chance to contribute directly to finding solutions. The Universe often signals actions that need to be taken, and you will feel these intuitively. Never underestimate the power of your visions and prayers. You really can have an effect and you really can make a difference. You can do it for world peace, to help save the environment, to make your local community stronger – there are many ways to visualize and affirm that which you desire for the global good ... so, it's all good.

Mind miracles for busy Goddesses

Here are our top tips for those Goddesses who haven't got time to do the hard yards of making collages or word-trigger visual maps, but who just know they deserve the glory anyway!

* Put a postcard of that beautiful and unspoilt Caribbean beach you're determined to see for yourself in a frame by your bedside table.

* Type out an affirmation of what you want (a specific goal, such as pay rise or new attitude) and tape it to the front of your diary where you'll see it every day.

* Cut out a photograph of a healthy and fit body shape and stick it onto the fridge with a magnet and a shortlist of your fitness goals.

* Make a tape of your category affirmations or burn a CD to play in the car whenever you drive anywhere – intersperse the affirmations with some soothing meditation music.

* Leave a magazine lying open at the page showing a beautiful home, view, or role model, where you will pass it all the time when you're at home.

* Attach a Buddha to the dashboard of your car to make you calmer whilst driving – you won't feel like swearing at another car when the Buddha is in your face – and be inspired to be more compassionate and to practice loving-kindness throughout the day.

* Write yourself a positive beauty affirmation and put it on your bath-room mirror so you can practise being more appreciative of yourself every day when you deal with your reflection.

* Always carry a £50 note in your purse. It's not to be used under any circumstances, even if you are experiencing temporary cash flow problems – it's to remind you of your permanent, natural state of abundance.

* Create a computer screen saver which scrolls an affirmation across your screen by way of a daily greeting. Repetition really works wonders.

* Programme your mobile phone to greet you with a cheery message rather than a brand name when you turn it on in the morning. One of ours reads, "Life is Beautiful."

* Leave an inspiring biography on your coffee table, where you'll see it all the time and guests will pick it up. For example: *Catherine: Intimate Portrait of a Champion* (by Cathy Freeman, Australia's famous aboriginal Olympic Gold Medallist runner) would be an ideal book to leave lying around if you're an athlete.

* Put up pictures in your office of you and your work colleagues having fun together – this can assist in maintaining and building feelings of friendship, teamwork, and solidarity between you all, even when the going gets rough.

* Write yourself a cheque for what you think you deserve for your creativity (see "Wealth Creation Hollywood-style" overleaf).
* When you wake up in the morning, place your right foot on the floor first. Silently affirm to yourself that, because today you are starting off on "the right foot" and you are going to put your best version of yourself into the world, it is going to be a fantastic day.
* Keep a role model(s) or mentor in your mind all the time. Many famous people have other famous people to inspire them. Pop icon Britney Spears cites Madonna and Oprah Winfrey as her role models. With images of those women in her mind, Britney will be in the public eye for a long time to come.
* Write yourself a checklist of the qualities that you would like in your partner or soul mate. Be as specific as possible – if you want the person to speak three languages, say so!

Be the girl who asks the Universe directly for what she wants – if you do, you'll get what you need.

Special Goddess banking

Write yourself a cheque as if you were paying yourself what you truly believe you are worth and that you deserve. Now, obviously, it depends on the arena that you're in – in other words, if you're a publicity assistant for a trendy magazine you are being wildly unrealistic putting £5 million as your goal salary if you want to stay at that job! Perhaps you could generate a pay rise for yourself by visualizing that you can contribute more and that contribution is worth, say, another £5,000 on your gross salary. So you could write a cheque for that amount, date it for six months' time and put it in your wallet. Now the hard work begins: Organize new sponsorship deals for the magazine or other forms of revenue and profile-raising activities that will be impossible for anyone to ignore. One way or another you'll get your raise – you may even need to be headhunted – but if you are worth it and believe you are, then one way or another you'll get it.

Mobile mantra mix –
POSITIVE VIBRATIONS WHEREVER YOU ARE

Mobile phones are handy little tools for those techno Goddesses who want to re-programme their brains while they move around. Apart from the programmable daily greetings that can be used so effectively for affirmations and positive vibrations in general, you can practise sending friends beautiful messages that uplift and inspire them to help them get through their day, no matter what's going down!

Here are some examples to get you started:

* U R BEAUTY-FULL
* U HAVE LOTS OF FRIENDS
* U R PERFECT 2

* IT'S ALL GOOD!
* SUCCESS BECOMES U
* U RULE!

If you have a friend who's pretty good on text messaging (SMS) then take a week where you send each other positive affirmations in support of your individual goals.

Swap lists, and for seven days straight send at least one affirmation on the list to each other twice a day. This is a great and unexpected way to receive your affirmations and move towards your goals, even when you're frantically busy. We say a week because that seemed like the maximum commitment that was reasonable, but if you can find someone who is prepared to swap messages for a longer period – say a month – then go for it. There's no excuse then!

WEALTH CREATION HOLLYWOOD-STYLE!

Hollywood folklore naturally abounds with both good luck and hard luck stories – they don't call Sunset Boulevard "The Boulevard of Broken Dreams" for nothing – and many's the star who used to be the checkout chick or the local bartender. Some of the best and brightest stars in Tinseltown gave themselves and their careers a head start just because they used their noodle better than the next actor, comedian, or rock star. They know how to visualize, and a few have developed their own methods to do this.

Top entertainer, comedian, and general loony tune Jim Carrey is one who used a creative visualization method for creating wealth in his career. When Carrey first moved to Los Angeles as a struggling stand-up comedian, he wrote himself a cheque for US$10 million which he decided was going to be his pay check for a feature film in which he would star, sometime in the future – he didn't know when. He then continued on his way from one small live stand-up gig to another, then television beckoned, and finally film roles came his way. His natural physicality lent itself to weird and comic roles, and on film Carrey found his niche. Eventually he reached his life goal when his movie, The Mask, blasted its way onto the top of the box office the summer it was released and continued on to worldwide success. His reported pay check? US$10 million.

GLOBAL GODDESS GURU TIP

In Shakti Gawain's classic and insightful book Creative Visualisation (see the Goddess Library) she has a trick for turning a daily routine into a beauty ritual. Shakti's tip is to take a hot bath or shower to thank and affirm the beauty of your body. It's great for raising self-esteem, if done on a regular basis. The idea is to visualize the hot water healing, calming, and invigorating your entire body.

At the same time that the water is running over you, you imagine any health or other problems being washed away, so all you are left with is your true radiant self, shining brightly from within. Affirm how strong, firm, and healthy your body is. Help your body do its best work by giving it pictures of its purest potential. Thank your body for its service and for all of the hard work in getting you to this point!

You've got (voice) mail . . .

And while we're on the subject of cool visualization hints for techno Goddeses – and taking a leaf out of Bridget Jones' Diary (admittedly with a bit of a twist) – you can even use your own voice mail for positive growth. No obsessions over empty dial tones here: Call your own phone number and leave your affirmations as a recording on the voice mail. At least you'll have a real excuse to ring up and check your messages (hit the repeat button as many times as you want for the best results) and you never need to worry about not getting a phone call again. Use it to deal with pressure situations at work, improve your self-esteem after a break-up, lose weight, and feel good about yourself, all day long. Sometimes hearing someone else's voice on the message makes it even more powerful to listen to. If you think this works better for you, ask one of your friends to record the message.

Brain storming
WHILE YOU WERE SLEEPING . . . YOU GOT AN A+

This is something we learned as students – we used to record a cassette tape of our study notes and then we'd play the tape while we fell asleep. The idea was, subliminally the brain would be taking in information even when we were exhausted from over-studying! We all passed, so we have to say it must have done something, but the act of making the tape is in and of itself very helpful to achieving your examination goals. Try this technique, too, with your affirmations and category goals.

If you are a student, make a tape recording or burn a CD that contains your positive, confident intention to do really well in the examination(s). See the result you desire at the top of your exam paper and your overall results. Know that you can have any mark you desire if you expect you can pass at that level. Visualize yourself in the examination reading the questions and writing the answers confidently and quickly. See yourself calmly finishing the paper with plenty of time to check over your work and correct any omissions. Practise exam papers over and over until you can do them within the time period required. Better still: See yourself having the most fantastic holiday ever having attained such brilliant results. Think frangipani, island paradise, palm trees, coconuts and perfect sunsets — now there's a good reason to swat!

Write your own references and report cards

Another great tool for projecting yourself into your desired reality is writing your own references, report cards, and letters of introduction. This can be very therapeutic in that it forces you to acknowledge all of your various strengths and skills. Write the glowing reference that raves about your performance at a particular job or role, how well you are liked by your co-workers, how much you contributed as a hard-working team member. Stick it in the front of your work diary and read it first thing every morning when you sit down at your desk. If you're a student, write your ideal report, giving yourself the comments and marks that you would like to see on your real report card from your teachers or lecturers at the end of the semester.

Another technique for acknowledging yourself in a positive light, especially before a job interview, is to write a letter of introduction in the third person, as if you were recommending yourself for a particular position or role that you are applying for. See yourself in the job that you want. Say all of the things that you want to project towards your interviewer or personal referee. If you can see yourself as being enthusiastic, willing to learn, personable, punctual and passionate, then the whole world will too. And you'll definitely get the job.

Mind-movies
WRITE, DIRECT, AND STAR IN YOUR OWN LIFE!

This technique is fantastic for those with a cinematic bent. We've discovered that while some people feel more comfortable with a single 2-D (two dimensional) image in isolation, some of our Goddess friends are movie buffs who are equally comfortable seeing images both in 3-D and in sequence.

For these Goddesses who prefer to glow in the dark, we suggest you take one of your favourite movie scenes, where something that was particularly poignant or powerful for you was taking place. Now take Cameron Diaz or Julia Roberts out of the scene and imagine it's you in their place ... see yourself saying the lines, acting out the joy, rage, sadness, or whatever, and feel all of the emotions that roll through you as that happens. See the actor(s) who are in the scene responding to you, using your name. You can even add to the script if it serves one of your category goals, or your higher purpose. Do this with as many different films as you need. Try and find a scene for each of your goal categories that gives you a "reel" life version of the events that you would like to happen in your own life. Better yet, write your own screenplay with the characters as people from your own life (your soul mate, current boyfriend, your boss or your family) and have everyone speak the lines you'd like them to hear and that you would like to hear from them.

This is a particularly healing visualization method, which will lead you to being more assertive and feeling stronger about your relationships and your ability to deal with difficult scenarios, such as conflict-resolution. Go on, make it happen, we dare you to . . .

The yellow rubber duck test

If you would like to test yourself – and us! – please take our yellow rubber duck test. This is a simple exercise to see how your powers of manifestation are progressing. The idea is to hold the image of a yellow rubber duck in your mind for a minute or so and to see if you can manifest one within a 24-hour period. You can't cheat and simply go where you think they might be, you are meant to just go about your normal business and see when and where they show up. This is the key to it, because it will let you know how quickly you are able to make things show up in your life. And once they do, it should absolutely confirm for you, once and for all, that if you think it, it will come.

MAGIC MANTRA SAY IT MEAN IT WATCH IT HAPPEN.

One of our Goddess friends took the test and was amazed at how many she manifested in one day after doing the rubber duck visualization. Flying around doing her usual Christmas Eve shopping whirl, our Goddess friend came upon her first two rubber ducks floating in a lily pond at her local nursery. She then went to her sister's new flat in the evening for Christmas Eve drinks and in the bathroom there were six rubber ducks of different sizes sitting in a row on the edge of the bath. The next day at the family lunch she pulled a Christmas cracker with her father and a small yellow rubber duck on a key chain landed in her lap! A grand total of nine rubber ducks in 24 hours! Not bad for someone who was a bit of a sceptic either – she says it sounded so ludicrous because they are a bit out of left field – she couldn't believe she'd be able to manifest even one. To this day our Goddess friend has her house keys on the rubber duck key chain and she swears it reminds her to hold fast whenever she feels as though she's losing faith in her own vision. She now calls it her "key to the future."

Blues busters

We all have days when we get down, however, for some people it's a recurring theme. In *You Can Heal Your Life*, Louise L. Hay describes depression as being anger you do not feel you have the right to have, and so it is turned inwards, at the self. Depression is an illness – it truly is dis-ease, and it can be acute (temporary) or chronic (long-term).

Affirmations of self-worth and self-love assist in the treatment of depression. For those Goddesses who are in need of a real lift, here's a wonderful visualization. Do it as many times a day as you need, and let your mind float way above the melee...

Imagine: You are in a hot air balloon. The balloon is brightly coloured and you are standing in the basket with the balloon's cylinders firing, ready to lift off. In preparation for lift-off, you check your sandbags, for these are the key to maintaining altitude and consistent speed on your journey. You label each of the sandbags with red paint: sadness, anger, rage, jealousy, resentment, bitterness, injustice, pain, grief, a situation, an obstacle, irritation, annoyance, misery, stubbornness. Label as many or as few as you feel you need to.

Now see the sandbags lying in the bottom of the basket. Once you feel you are ready for lift-off, let go of the anchoring cord on the balloon. As the balloon begins to rise, pick the sandbag that is most appropriate for your current mood and toss it overboard. Feel the instant lift of the basket. You are lighter! Visualize the bag falling onto the earth below you and splitting apart, spilling the sand which then blows away into the ether. Do this for each of the bags until you feel as light as a feather, and then peacefully and serenely drift in your balloon into a beautiful sunrise or sunset.

Winning ways
HOW SPORTS STARS GET TO THE TOP

Ask any successful athlete or sporting identity about the importance of being able to "see" themselves winning a particular event in their chosen sport before the event, and they will confirm that it is a major part of their preparation process. Coaches and mentors all provide visualization reinforcement beforehand, however, the athlete has to personally overcome whatever fears and limitations he or she has within. There are many barriers for athletes to overcome in order to not merely line up at the starting blocks but to realize their vision and end up with the trophy, having crossed the line first.

Tiger Woods rocked the golfing world with his unprecedented winning streak in golf. His successes would have been incredible enough for a professional golfer to achieve even in the mature part of their career, but that Tiger has had so much success and at such an early age (he's in his early twenties) is the most staggering fact to those in the sport. Woods is really only just getting started, and already he's rewritten the record books! What most people who heard about his successes may not know is that Tiger is a great believer in the power of visualization and is reported to spend up to four or more hours per day visualizing his strategy on the golf course. He sees every shot, playing it over and over in his mind before the event, and he strategizes how he needs to play on a particular course or for a particular event. To spend that much time residing in one's own mind – and specifically setting up images – is true dedication. That it so intensely enhances a natural practical skill set is testimony to the power of pictures in releasing mind miracles.

When 400 metre-sprint star Cathy Freeman was recently inducted into the Living Legends Hall of Fame, she was asked why she didn't cry after winning the gold medal at the Sydney Olympic Games. For those Goddesses who did not witness that classic moment in sporting history, Freeman simply sat on the track and looked around her, catching her breath! The presenter was curious about Cathy's rather unexpected reaction, perhaps thinking that she would have been more emotional at the realization of her long-held dream. Freeman paused for a second before replying, "I think because I had already experienced it [winning the gold medal] in my mind so many times, it was so familiar to me." Winning that gold medal had been the image she had held in her mind for so long that, by the time she ran the final, it almost came as no surprise. Cathy knew exactly what she had to do to be the one stepping up to centre place on the podium. Basically she was certain that she deserved to win. This is the mindset of a winner. And the principle is exactly the same for world-class athletes as for anyone who is trying to achieve something – believe it!

> If you want to win, you must expect to win.
> Basketball coach,
> Dean Smith,
> to NBA star,
> Michael Jordan

We can learn a lot from the preparation, dedication, and perseverance of sports individuals because their lessons are common to us all. They are simply more dramatically played out in very specific situations. Sporting achievements are graphic examples of the effects of visualization and the power of mental energy.

All Goddesses who love to play should pay really close attention to the lessons they hold for everyday life.

How a split second...
MAKES ALL THE DIFFERENCE IN THE WORLD

Superstar athlete Cathy Freeman, has been visualizing for a long time in her career, and it has taken her right to the top. In the book *Catherine: Intimate Portrait of a Champion*, Cathy Freeman tells of how, in January 1996, she wrote the number 48.63 on a piece of paper at a time when her personal best for the 400 metres was

49.59. In her words: "I set goals and then take action to achieve them. Writing things down helps to steer me in the direction I want to go. In July of 1996, I wanted to go to Atlanta and record this time. I stuck that piece of paper on my bedroom mirror and every day I visualized this. I believe if you want to fulfil your goals, you must clearly establish and define them." In the Atlanta 400-metre Olympic final, Freeman broke both the national and Commonwealth records at a personal best time of . . . you guessed it: 48.63.

Congratulations – you made it!

The final part of the visualization process is to celebrate your successes. It's important to give yourself positive feedback to acknowledge and celebrate yourself. You are the miracle worker and you need to allow yourself the time to reaffirm the abundance and miracles that you, personally, have pulled in with your own positive energy. If you have realized your dream, whether it is a house that you've bought and renovated, or the business you've started from home, plan a moment to thank your personal cheer squad – the Universe and yourself – for having the vision in the first place!

Dreams

You are lying on a beautiful, long beach with waves of crystal blue-green water crashing on the shore. You are sipping a cool drink and the sun is beating down on your tanned, finely honed body. A tall, dark, downright beautiful young man stops to talk to you. You cannot see his face, but you know that he is familiar. While he is telling you something, you look up just in time to see a pair of dolphins playing in the water. As you watch, somehow, the scene changes and all of a sudden the sound of the ocean becomes eerily silent.

Your mysterious stranger has disappeared but your mother waves to you from further up the beach. A sense of foreboding creeps over you and you see in the distance, a tidal wave forming. The water by the shore has virtually disappeared, stranding the two dolphins. You are torn between running away and trying to reach the dolphins to save them. You can't think, you can't scream, you can't move a muscle.

You wake up.

The power of dreams to play out our deepest fears and pleasures has been closely examined during the 20th century, starting with the thoughts of Dr Sigmund Freud and developed by Carl Jung and other great thinkers of the century. Freud called the interpretation of dreams the "royal road" to the discovery of the unconscious – which everyone can travel to discover the truth of unconscious processes for themselves.

We spend about one-third of our life sleeping and part of that time is spent dreaming. Basically, dreams are our method of relaxing and letting our minds drift away to a distant world. While dreaming, we interact with people, places and objects. When asleep, our brain does not have to deal with the outside world, and it is believed that our brain is more active and more attuned to our self conscious, as well as the universal conscious, during sleep than when awake. Hence, our dreams may reveal things our conscious mind is incapable of interpreting or too busy to focus upon.

We have put together a chapter on dreams, focusing on how to work with this fabulous resource to help you develop your Goddess-given psychic talents. Astral travel, discovering information about your past lives, and banishing nightmares are possible through dream work. We have also given some invaluable tips on interpreting dreams and making a magical dream pillow, which can be used to enhance psychic dreams and stop nightmares.

> Dreams give real experiences in the spiritual world.
> Dreams provide a symbolic picture of current conditions in our lives.
> Dreams offer contact with God.
> Dreams instruct us in a lesson.
> Dreams present a solution to a problem.
> Dreams give us a glimpse into the future.
>
> **Edgar Cayce**

How do we dream?

When we dream, we are in an alpha state. You may have heard the term "REM sleep," which stands for rapid eye movement. This is the period of sleep in which the brain produces predominantly alpha brainwaves that create a state somewhere between being awake and being asleep. REM sleep is actually a very active state, and it occurs at 80–90 minute intervals. We experience about five REM states a night, which means there are plenty of times when we are able to dream.

In dream sleep we have the opportunity to resolve our psychological problems. When we have unfinished issues, our dreams act as a way for us to uncover what's going on. Other dreams are the residue of our day, memories, or wishes that haven't been fulfilled. By dreaming about these things, we have an opportunity to complete or to understand what these images want us to know about ourselves.

Through research in the 20th century, the following facts have been discovered that are useful to understanding 21st century dreams:

* Most people dream in colour.
* Dreams are visual in nature. Taste, smell, and touch usually seem to be deactivated.
* Dreams are more often disturbing and unpleasant than pleasant.
* The most common setting for dreams is indoors rather than outdoors.
* Dreams usually involve motion and action.

Our dreams can only produce these images if we have a connection with them on a deep level. Things that our waking mind might dismiss as trivial are able to pursue us in our sleep. In fact, as nothing is by chance, it is important for us to realize that these images are indeed significant for us. And nothing goes unnoticed.

Many people believe that their dreams can predict the future. When we have negative or frightening dreams, we may become anxious about the future. Alternatively, when our dreams depict something we want to happen, we become hopeful that the dream will come true. Most dreams are not prophetic but are psychological or spiritual in nature; their primary function being to help us live to our fullest potential in the present.

Why do we dream?

We dream to heal any imbalance that we may not be aware of, and to guide us to areas of our life that need attention and to suggest action we might need to take. If the messages in dreams are constantly ignored or blocked, then we may develop physical or psychological problems. More importantly, our dreams show us what has caused us to be the way we are. With this knowledge, we can address the cause rather than the symptoms of an illness or problem.

Dreams also have a spiritual dimension and guide us by indicating abilities we have, latent or otherwise, and may help us work out what talents we need to develop. Dreams of this nature also tend to indicate or give us some form of a clue as to what prevents us from developing these abilities further.

Dreams come from your soul and are intended to help you progress in your life's journey. When we sleep, the physical world is on hold, giving your soul the opportunity to have a dialogue with your higher power. Dreams help create a bridge so we can get a glimpse of what our subconscious is really doing.

Working with your dreams

What do dolphins mean to you? What about tidal waves? There are a hundred and one books on the interpretation of dreams, ranging from those that give "set" meanings to those that blithely state that if you dream of spiders you will be lucky the next day. We like to approach dreams in a way that goes beyond dreams being simply superstitious omens and to encourage you to take notice of the images in your dreams.

Ultimately, the person best suited to analysing your dreams is you, although it might take some serious thought, a hefty measure of honesty and a session of hard questioning to winkle out what a dream image may mean to you!

Dreaming about a certain object may have very different connotations for different people. For instance, a white horse may mean one thing to a person who likes horses, and a far different thing to someone who is scared of them. So, a book with "set" meanings may not work well, although a number of dream symbols usually have some form of universal interpretation that can help indicate what issues you are dealing with in your life.

> If the dreamer does not get the message, or if the conscious mind does not get involved with the dream content, the unconscious mind will keep sending up the same materials until they are noticed. Dreams are repetitive in their content and message. We are given many opportunities to pay attention and to get involved on the conscious level with the materials coming up from our unconscious.
>
> Carl Jung

A dream diary or journal is one of the best tools in starting to learn about the way your dreams work and it can help you divine some clues on how you can tap into your own subconscious power through dream work.

Keeping a dream diary or journal

The important part of a dream is what the dreamer remembers upon waking, whether it is a picture, an emotion, or a particular situation. Often the meaning of remembered dreams isn't clear or doesn't make sense. Dreams are at times like a picture puzzle, and assembling the pieces to make sense is what dream work is all about.

Get a notebook, diary, or journal that you can dedicate solely for recording your dreams. Make your dream journal look special and feel beautiful by decorating it with pictures, fabrics, beads, or any other things that makes it uniquely yours. Use feathers as a bookmark, or you could even lightly spray the journal with an appropriate essential oil blend, such as lavender or rose.

Keep the journal by your bedside, with your pen at the ready. When you wake up – whenever you wake up, even if it's the middle of the night – jot down as much of the dream as you can and don't forget to date it. As memories of a dream usually begin to self-destruct in about ten seconds, it is critical that you write down what you remember seeing in your dream as quickly as possible. Don't dwell on the detail – just describe what you still see or feel. See the next topic about how to recall your dreams.

DREAMING HAS A MEANING, LIKE EVERYTHING ELSE WE DO.
Sigmund Freud

Make a point to also tell someone about your dream. A lot of cultures encourage the telling of dreams. Start doing this with your family or friends. Others may see your dream differently and may give you some insights you are unaware of, but remember: It's your dream and even if what the other person is saying sounds OK, still leave room in your mind to work out your own interpretation.

It's also useful to keep a small notebook with you during the day, so you can jot down pieces of the dream as they come back to you the next day – you may find that something that happens during the day will remind you of something in your dream. Scribble it all down!

As soon as you have time to examine the dream more closely, look for repeated symbols, familiar patterns, cycles, or progressions that echo real-life situations. You may find that you come up with a list of symbols that seem to connect in a particular way in your dream. You may then refer to a dream dictionary. Also note down any thoughts about what you think your dream has to do with.

Some dreams are very literal and it's easy to discern their meaning. Others are rich in symbolism, which can take time and effort to decipher. See later in this chapter about how to put together your very own dream dictionary.

Tips for sorting out dream information in your journal

The importance of keeping a dream journal cannot be overestimated, as it can really help you understand your life's directions or your real concerns. Here are some suggested headings you may wish to use in your dream journal:

* **Day and date:** Are you having sequential or serial dreams?
* **Time:** Are you dreaming at around the same time?
* **Numbers:** Were there any numbers in the dream?
* **Atmosphere:** Did it feel cold and icy or hot and stuffy?
* **Mood:** Was there a sense of fear, or were you nervous?
* **Symbols or objects:** Did you dream of a particular shape, object, or symbol?
* **Journey or travel:** Did you go to a familiar place or was the location totally foreign to you?
* **Colour:** Did any particular colour seem significant in your dream?
* **Conversations:** Did you talk with anyone? What did they say? Did you know them?
* **Previous associations:** Did the dream include anything similar from other dreams?

Tips for remembering dreams

The most important thing about remembering your dreams is that you actually want to recall your dreams. If you believe you can, and you instruct yourself to remember your dreams before falling asleep every night, you will.

Your brain is like a child, it won't always do what you tell it to do, but most of the time it will. Telling our brains to recall a dream is, in effect, reinforcing the fact that we believe that dreaming is important. When we focus our attention on a task, the mind will follow. If this tactic at first doesn't work, don't get discouraged. It may take a few tries. Just be patient with yourself and keep trying.

After instructing yourself to remember your dreams upon waking, reinforce your intention by placing your dream journal and a pen that works close by your bed so that you do not have to move much in the morning to get ready to record your dreams.

When you first wake, lie very still and allow your dreams to flow into your consciousness. Have a pen in one hand and the journal in the other and immediately write down everything you remember in your dream journal.

If you don't remember the entire dream, write any fragment you recall. If nothing comes to mind, ask yourself what feeling you woke up with, and write that down reminding yourself that your dreams are important and that everyday you will remember more of them.

Like anything worth the effort, recalling dreams takes practice. Every morning you will find that you will remember more. Dreams need your attention and awareness, and you will be surprised that you do get some interesting solutions to your life issues through dream work.

As you become more proficient with dream work, you can go one step further and ask a question in the evening that you wish to have answered through your dreams.

It is well documented in sleep laboratories that a question asked in the beginning "twilight" stage of sleep seems to penetrate through the brain's "facts file" during the later stages of sleep, bringing a direct answer to mind upon waking (see later in the chapter).

Over time you will come more and more able, using your heightened recall abilities and your dream journal, to capture the answers to your questions through your dreams.

Creating your own dream dictionary

As you continue recording your dreams, you may find that you build up a distinctive list of symbols that seem to recur in your dreams, together with your discoveries about what these symbols appear to mean. This is the start of your very own dream dictionary. Over time you will be able to add to this initial list of symbols, and modify the meaning of some of them in line with what you know they signify for you personally.

LEARNING TO UNDERSTAND OUR DREAMS IS A MATTER OF LEARNING TO UNDERSTAND OUR HEART'S LANGUAGE

Ann Faraday,
The Dream Game

To get started with creating your own dream dictionary, make notes at the back of your dream journal of some of the common themes and symbols that we have selected in this chapter. Choose only those themes or symbols that feel relevant to you. Do you remember dreaming about having sex with an ex-boyfriend? Do you get recurring dreams about your teeth falling out?

Do you remember the circumstances in your life when you had those sorts of dreams? If you don't recall, a personalized dream dictionary will help you record any relevant life situations that may have prompted your subconscious mind to come up with a particular symbol.

Other things you can record alongside each dream image include any other thoughts, feelings, or impressions about the symbols – for instance, is flying in a plane a scary experience for you or do you find the thought of bungee jumping exhilarating and fun?

Continue adding themes, symbols or images to your list as and when they occur in your dreams. Recording your own interpretation of these symbols will, in the long term, give you more awareness and insight into yourself and your daily concerns.

What did that mean?
YOUR CRAZIEST DREAMS DECODED

Have you ever had a dream that has stayed with you and you haven't been able to resolve what it means? Well the best solution is to not always work out the dream, but to feel into it, contacting that part of you that does know. Just let it go – forcing anything will prevent you from knowing what the dream is really saying to you. Trust that sooner or later another dream will give you some more information.

Frequently there is what is known as dream distortion. It is what makes a dream seem strange and unintelligible, and it is what makes it hard to interpret dreams. Dreams use symbols, some of which we understand, but the meaning of others will need to be uncovered through asking what the image or item means to you.

> A dream is a spontaneous self-portrayal, in symbolic form, of the actual situation in the unconscious.
> Carl Jung

While the symbols and images that appear in dreams may mean different things to different people, some symbols also represent common archetypes – meaning representations of thematic figures within society, such as legal or political authority, religious icons, parents – that we relate to on a very deep level.

The following top ten themes and a list of some common images will introduce you to some of the more common interpretations of these symbols.

Our top ten dream themes!

If you thought you were the only one to dream some pretty weird stuff, well, it may surprise you that a great many other people have dreams that feature the same type of weird things.

Ever dreamt that you were flying effortlessly through the air or that a madman looking very much like your boss was chasing you around a city street armed with a sharp axe? Well, you may not be alone.

Here are some of those "weird" dreams – in fact our top-ten themes – and suggestions about what they may mean for you. Use this as a guide to inspire you and to encourage you to find out more specifically what these images may mean to you.

Actor or famous person: Sometimes dreaming about a famous actor or actress may be a wish-fulfilling dream, or it could hold an important message about you. We admire celebrities and may wish to have some of their characteristics. Consider the personality traits or any other trait that attracts you to that person. This will help you figure out why you are dreaming about him or her.

Being chased or unable to move: If you're in a situation in your dream where you need to move and you're either frozen on the spot or have no control over your limbs, ask yourself the following questions to provide some insight into why you might be having this type of dream:

* Is there anywhere in your life that you feel stuck?
* Are you unable to move away from a job or relationship?
* Is someone around you holding you back?
* Are you holding yourself back?

If you dream you are being chased, maybe you are running away from or trying to escape things that symbolize your own negative habits. Ask yourself both of the following questions:

* Who is chasing me?
* Why are they chasing me?

If a stranger is chasing you, you may find that this represents your unconscious attempting to make you aware of your negative nature. If you are doing the chasing, you might be expressing some aggressive feelings toward others or your dream may indicate that you may be pursuing a very difficult goal. (See also the entry for "Running" later in this chapter.)

Ex-boyfriend or girlfriend: Individuals that have been an important part of our lives not surprisingly continue to take up a part of our mind and heart. It is impossible to shut a lover out of our thoughts and feelings just because the relationship has ended. You will continue to dream about your ex-girlfriend or boyfriend until you let go, which will happen once you learn the lessons they were here to teach you.

If you did not want the relationship to end and you wish you could get back together, it's important to understand that dreaming about your ex-partner doesn't predict a future involvement with that person – it may simply be a wish-fulfilment dream.

Falling: Experiencing this sensation in a dream usually represents underlying fears and feelings of inadequacy and helplessness. Falling indicates a loss of emotional balance, or that you have control issues. Are you fearful of letting go? You may need to address your primary fears, current difficulties, and any situation that seems to be on a downward spiral, especially those situations that seem outside of your control.

Falling can also represent a lack of self-confidence, especially if you fall down in front of other people. This dream situation can indicate that you feel something in your life is unsafe or uncertain.

Alternatively, you may need to ask yourself whether you are over-confident – perhaps your ego is running the show, and this is a warning to step back and listen with your heart.

Some people believe that, if you keep falling in your dream and don't wake up, you will die at the point of impact. This is not true – you will simply wake up out of fear, not because you're in danger of dying.

Flying: Some people believe that flying in a dream can be an actual out-of-body experience (see later in this chapter about astral traveling and how to deliberately have an out-of-body experience). An out-of-body experience is when a part of us actually goes to places on the physical or inner plane.

Native Americans, Hindus, and Tibetan Buddhists believe that the ethereal or psychic part of our body can detach from our physical body and travel great distances. This part of us can even fly into other dimensions, which certain mystics refer to as the astral plane, to learn from advanced souls – sometimes referred to as teachers or masters.

Flying dreams can provide a wonderful way of feeling free of your body – you can go anywhere or place, even to your lover's bed.

Carl Jung's idea was that in a flying dream, we are expressing our desire to break free of restrictions and limitations. We have a desire to be free and above all difficulties.

Flying represents freedom from earthly concerns, the desire to escape, and may indicate a wish to avoid dealing with something that is difficult. Dreams of flying might also indicate that you need to see a problem from a distance, or that you need to see what's up ahead.

Flying by yourself in a dream also indicates that you have a strong mind. Flying with a guide indicates that you have the ability to project your mind into the spirit world and communicate with spirits.

Nudity: In a dream, nudity suggests vulnerability and exposure. Are you very guarded and unwilling to let people see the "real" you, or are you feeling embarrassment as a result of a mistake? Dreaming you are nude may also be a way your subconscious is encouraging you to become more open with your feelings and more accessible emotionally. If you dream that you are naked inappropriately, such as in a public place, is there a part of you that needs to be rebellious, but you fear that people may not accept you for who you really are? Dreaming about being naked in public usually leaves us feeling disturbed after spending most of the dream feeling embarrassed, ashamed, or odd. We sometimes spend most of the dream dashing around trying to find something to put on or with which to cover ourselves. And what's really strange is that the other people in this dream do not seem to either notice or care if we are nude. Only very rarely do we wake up feeling comfortable about being nude.

Parents: As an archetype, the father represents the protector, lawmaker, the head of the home, the ruler. He may appear in dreams as a wise old man, a king, or any figure that represents a paternal form of energy. The father also represents the expressive, creative, protective, and active part of us while the mother corresponds to our receptive and nurturing side.

The archetypal mother is a force that urges us on and inspires. Often the knowledge she holds is intuitive and can't be expressed in words – she may also be symbolized as the archetypal primal Goddess.

Dreaming of a father figure may indicate that you need the help or advice of this paternal symbol, or that you need to become more self-reliant and confident, that you can depend upon your own resources or ideas. This type of dream may even indicate that this process is already happening.

When you dream about your own father or mother, you are expressing feelings and concerns about them that you usually cannot express in daily life in a safe way. You may live away from your parents or they may have died, so dreaming about what needs to be said, helps to heal what needs to be healed.

Dreaming about one or other of your parents or of a father or mother-like figure may also mean you are trying to resolve the male and female sides of your personality or self. When these two sides of your personality are interacting well together, we can achieve balance and a sense of awareness that leads us to experience peace and productivity.

Pregnancy, babies and birth: Dreams about being pregnant usually indicate a new project. Giving birth is the most creative act, and in a dream it generally means something new is brewing.

If there are newborns in your dreams, you can assume that they represent you. You are the baby and the dream is telling you something about your development in a particular area. At times of great change or renewal, a baby may appear in a dream to represent your potential or a new beginning.

> A mother knows exactly how to push your buttons because she is the one who installed them in the first place!
> Phyllis Crystal,
> *Cutting the Ties That Bind*

Women who are pregnant commonly have dreams about giving birth. It is simply the mind trying to cope with a significant anxiety-provoking event. If you are not pregnant, this dream could symbolize new beginnings or the potential birth of new ideas or ways of living. It could also represent the start of a new stage in life.

Sex: Having sex in a dream indicates one of two things. The first and most common is that the dreamer needs to become more intimate with their male or female side. The dream usually indicates that there is a need for both the male and female sides of the self to share closeness in an uninhibited way. This sharing restores a balance to the dreamer that they were repressing.

Another reason to dream about having sex is to heal the dreamer of the fact that they are currently not having sex with their partner. In this case the dream attempts to heal the stress. If you are having sex with another woman in a dream, this is a healing device intended to put you in close contact with yourself (the same applies to a man dreaming of having sex with another man).

If you dream of having sex in public, it is an indication that while you are with yourself in private you repress your feelings in public; your subconscious is asking you not to be afraid of being honest with yourself in front of others.

A sexual dream may be about physical pleasure but it may also be about power and control. It may be a form of wish fulfilment.

In the case of having intercourse with someone you admire, you may actually wish to be more like them, or you may want to connect to certain aspects they represent to you. Usually it is not a prediction of things to come in the near future.

If you are watching other people having sex, it is a reflection of your emotional and mental concerns about sexual performance or interaction.

Teeth falling out: Dreams about teeth falling out are quite common and are associated with the fear of losing something, perhaps someone valuable to you. This type of dream can be triggered by a number of things – a physical problem leading to an inability to have children; feeling incapable of raising a child; having children who are ready to "leave the nest;" wanting a child when your partner doesn't.

As teeth can symbolize change, dreaming of them can sometimes mean that you have decisions to make and don't want to make them. It can also indicate that you are in a situation where you cannot assert yourself.

Other common dream images

Dreams are created by our own thoughts (conscious or unconscious). The mind that created the dream also knows its meaning. The following list of common symbols gives some suggestions as to what these images may mean to you.

Bathroom: Dreaming that you are in or using a bathroom may suggest that there is a need for emotional and psychological cleansing. You may need to get rid of some emotional and psychological baggage. The bathroom is a good dream symbol. Consider all of the details in your dream, and make an effort to cleanse the mind and spirit, particularly by letting go of any negative or otherwise unproductive thoughts.

Colours: Colours are symbolic – we communicate and relate ideas with colours, and they can also represent a form of energy in your dream. The meaning of the colours in your dreams depends on the meaning of colour in your daily life, however, here is a list of some of the usual associations that colours have.

* **Black:** Feelings of depression, sadness, or despair
* **Blue:** Spirituality, optimism, positive thoughts, or communication

* **Green:** Money, jealousy, health concerns, or a feeling of love
* **Red:** Passion, sexuality, a feeling of anger, or a warning
* **White:** Purity, transformation, cleanliness, or dignity

Death: Death is usually a symbol of some type of closure. It may imply an end to one thing and the beginning of another. Death dreams usually have a positive symbolism.

If you are the dead person in your dream, it could imply that you would like to be rid of all of your worries and struggles. Dreaming about the death of someone you care about may be an expression of your fear of losing him or her. Dreaming that one of your parents died may express fear of loss, but it also may be an unconscious valve through which you release anger and other negative feelings.

Drowning: Dreams of drowning suggest that unresolved emotions, or old issues are overwhelming you. It may imply that a release of the old is necessary to begin anew. This dream serves to encourage us to embrace and effectively cope with problems in life.

Fire: Fire can be a deeply spiritual symbol representing transformation and enlightenment. It can also represent danger, anger, passion, pain, or fear. Is the fire in your dream destroying something or someone? Are you currently engaging in negative behaviours or knowingly making destructive choices? Dreaming of fire may be a warning to encourage you to change those things in your life that may prove to be dangerous to you.

Friends: These are individuals who are emotionally valuable to us and through whom we learn a lot about ourselves. Dreaming of friends is more than likely an attempt by your subconscious to bring up uncomfortable feelings that you may have about yourself or others. What are the qualities of these friends? Is there anything you need to say to that friend or that you want to hear from them?

Always remember that sexual dreams, in this case involving a friend, don't always have a sexual meaning.

House: Houses usually symbolize our emotional and psychological selves. All of your experiences, stages of development, and parts of your conscious and unconscious life may be represented by a house in a dream. Explore your "dream house" to learn more about yourself!

Intruder: An intruder breaking the law or breaking into your house may be representing an unconscious part of your psyche. The intruder may be a symbol of your feelings of guilt and or of some self-indulgent behaviour. If you had a fearful real-life experience, this dream may be reliving that experience, hopefully, allowing you to process the fear you felt in real life.

Man: A man, particularly a father figure, could be interpreted as the creator or destroyer. At times, a strange and ominous man in men's dreams could represent their "shadow" or their negativity – the darker side of their personality. Carl Jung called the "strange man" in women's dream the "animus," representing autonomous, unconscious energy, and he plays a vital role in letting the women obtain a deeper understanding of themselves.

Marriage: Usually experiencing a marriage in your dreams represents the coming together of all the various parts of yourself – feminine and masculine, spiritual and rational. Marriage in a dream is an affirmation and an encouragement to continue growing in self-awareness until you are transformed. If you are not married but would like to be, dreaming that you are being married, could well be a form of wish fulfilment.

Rape: Rape is a deeply personal violation. Dreaming of it suggests that you may be feeling robbed of choices or negated as a human being. In a dream, rape has very little to do with sex. It is about power, control, and anger. If you are a rape victim, the traumatic nature of this experience may cause you to have a dream like this from time to time as a way of helping you process the experience.

Running: In the dream, are you running in a competition or are you running to or from something? If you are simply running, it may be an indication that you need to slow down. If you are competing, consider your current challenges. If you have won a race, your unconscious may be expressing confidence. Running also symbolizes your energy levels. Are you running on empty? Do you have the strength to get through life?

Tidal wave: Tidal waves suggest a period of emotional upheaval, anxiety, and stress. Giant tidal waves in your dream may be symbolic of current emotional unhappiness and psychological stress, threatening to destroy or uproot you. Ask how much strength you have to ride out this situation. Also note whether, in the dream, you are consumed by the wave, or do you survive the ordeal?

Water is a very powerful and deeply spiritual dream symbol; large bodies of water represent our unconscious minds and soul experiences. Water symbolizes emotions – rough, smooth, clear, and murky.

Tips and techniques for enhancing your dream work

Travel cheap – learn to fly

There are two ways you can experience flying without using an aeroplane! One way is through programming your dreams to contain a flying sequence. The other way is through the experience of astral travel, when your spirit or an etheric part of you leaves your body and sets off on an adventure on either the physical or spiritual plane.

This can occur naturally through your dreams and you may already have experienced feelings of your body floating through time and space. When we sleep, we sometimes feel free of our body as the etheric part of it leaves, to rest, explore, or travel to certain inner or spiritual planes, such as a place that contains our Akashic records. These records are said to hold all the information about the Universe and each person's "soul purpose," as well as important stuff about our past lives and present or future events.

Spirit or astral travel can also occur naturally when our etheric body decides that it needs some "time out" to reconnect with the greater energy of the Universe. This may occur during traumatic physical events such as a life-threatening accident when the spirit, somehow finding it hard to stay in the body, leaves it for a while until it is safe to return.

It is a very good idea to allow our spirit to access or reconnect with its nature. This is especially important in helping us hone our intuition and our ability to access our subconscious through dream work. Astral travel can help us bring back some important insights – treasure – so that we can progress in our psychic or spiritual development. Knowing this, over the centuries magical practitioners have developed rituals and techniques so that they could consciously travel to the astral planes. We have developed the two rituals overleaf to help you to do something similar!

Ways of dealing with nightmares have been developed since ancient times, with each culture producing different ways of protecting themselves from this disruptive type of dream. The Native Americans devised dream catchers, circular webs made from natural fibres and decorated with beads and feathers. These are designed to snare nightmares and give the dreamer protection while sleeping. Herbs, crystals, spells, and the making of dream pillows have also aided people in getting restful sleep without nightmares (see later in this chapter).

By the way, don't be frightened by astral travel – you are always in control – we never completely leave our bodies as we are connected by a cord that holds the spirit so it can find its way back to the body.

If you want to be able to experience flying, either in your dreams or when you are conscious, you first need to learn to relax your body. The reason for this is that before you can fly, you actually have to experience being fully present in your body.

Most of us don't really know what that feels like, because usually we live in our heads, or in a time that is in the past or the future – anywhere but in our body in the present! By doing this we forget to honour our body and undermine our ability to be fully integrated beings.

After repressing it, denying it, hating it, and altering it, we are discovering that in denying the nature of the body, we set limitations that may prevent ourselves from experiencing our wholeness. Gradually, if we integrate and honour the body, mind, and spirit, we can create within ourselves a sense of balance, peace and happiness.

Step one: A ritual to heighten your awareness of your body

This ritual is designed to help you become aware of the boundaries of your body. Once you know its boundaries, it will be easier for you to let the body go in your dream and feel it fly. Do this exercise for about 10 minutes each day for a week.

Wear comfortable clothing and lie on the floor or bed with your arms and legs open, like a star, and your head supported by a pillow. Close your eyes and take a big deep breath, exhale, and then take another deep breath, breathing right down into your stomach.

Next, focus on your breathing. Are you forcing it or are you breathing without effort? If you feel a bit strained, you may be holding onto feelings of stress or anxiety.

Become aware of your feelings. Are you feeling relaxed and comfortable, or are you feeling uncomfortable or worried? If you are feeling stressed or anxious, visualize that with each breath you exhale, the stress and worry is leaving your body. Continue this visualization until you feel that you have fully released your troubled feelings.

Now, bring your awareness to your feet and breath into them. You can do this by simply visualizing that you can direct the breath towards that particular area of your body. If done with intention, you can actually feel the coolness of your breath flow into that part of the body.

Once you have breathed into your feet, move them and wiggle your toes. Next, bring your attention to your ankles, lower legs, and knees, and breath into these areas. Continue to move your attention up and down all parts of your body until you have made a connection with your entire physical body.

If you want to experience a sense of flying in your dream, do this ritual before going to bed. Once you feel relaxed and that you have connected with all parts of your body, ask your subconscious to grant you your wish of feeling how it is to fly and be free within your dreams tonight.

Alternatively, incorporate this ritual into the "out of body" ritual below in preparation of some conscious astral travelling!

Step two: Out of body ritual

Before you begin this ritual, take a bath using essential oils that calm the body and mind, such as lavender or marjoram (see our chapter on Crystals, Oils, and Remedies).

Remove any unwanted energy in your room by smudging the space with a smudge stick or a stick of your favourite incense. Once you have prepared yourself, do the "awareness of the body" ritual (described opposite), until you feel relaxed.

Now bring your attention again to your breath. With each breath, let go of your body, focusing only on your breath. You may start feeling yourself going deeper into a trance. You will start to feel other sensations, like you are floating – maybe you can't feel the bed, or even your own body. Do this for as long as you can or like. When you are ready to return, gently arrive back in your body by moving your feet, hands, and head.

Once you feel it's OK, write about your travels in your journal. Even if you don't think you have travelled, write whatever comes to mind. As you become better at it, you can go and visit where ever, whatever, whomever you want. Just remember: It's all in the breath – breath is spirit, and

My belief is that the body is a very sacred place and that the reason for the soul and spirit connecting to it is because it's a privilege to be able to feel what it's like to be human. It's hard work being human – there is a lot of pain and heartache – but on the other hand there are some wonderful feelings that can only be experienced by the body. That's why the spirit and soul are here – to learn.

when you become more aware of the breath, you touch your spirit. Allow its energy to guide and support you. The energy of the spirit is amazing, so use it wisely.

Make sure your intention is to relax rather than have an out-of-body experience. If you push it, you will miss the experience. It's also easy to fall asleep when you're beginning this practice. You may have to do it a few times before you're able to stay in the experience.

Carl Jung said that the unconscious is not necessarily smarter, but that it holds different information than our conscious mind. It enables us to see things that are at times difficult to understand and admit.

How to beat your nightmares

A nightmare is any dream that wakes you up because it is frightening. Nightmares are a direct result of overwhelming feelings of fear and help-lessness, or are a result of a deep-seated trauma that you haven't been able to resolve. If a person cannot handle a situation or event, or has guilt-based conflicts, they will bury it within their unconscious.

However, these powerful negative feelings don't just go away – they sit there, and we develop ways of coping. Sometimes this is why people drink or consume drugs, numbing their bodies so they escape their worries and problems. But you will find that these people will also have compelling nightmares, such as being chased or that they are being physically threatened, or they will develop phobias, extreme anxieties, or obsessions.

Spell for banishing nightmares

Gather together the following ingredients to make a powerful anti-nightmare a herbal pouch – that you can tuck under your pillow to prevent the recurrence of your nightmares:

* A piece of paper with a short description of your nightmare written down
* 4 cloves
* Pinch of ground basil
* Pinch of ground sage
* 2 drops of lavender essential oil
* White or cream cloth about 20 cm (8 inches) square
* A length of white ribbon, long enough to securely tie the pouch.

Place the piece of paper and the dried herbs in the centre of the cloth. Add the drops of oil and gather the corners of the cloth (like a moneybag) and tie it securely with the ribbon. Place the pouch under your pillow and sleep with it there until the nightmares go away. You might like to refresh it with a couple of drops of lavender oil every so often.

CARL JUNG CALLED THE NEGATIVE FORCES IN DREAMS THE "SHADOW"

If your nightmares continue for an extended period of time, consider obtaining professional counselling as you may be dealing with some serious issues.

Making a magical dream pillow

Use the following dream pillow to activate the unconscious mind, enabling it to understand your dreams or to see into the future. It's most effective in the week leading up to a full moon (the end of the waxing phase) and during the night of the full moon. Gather together the following items:

* A handful each of dried mugwort, star anise, nutmeg, lemon balm, bay leaves, rose petals, mint, cloves, and laurel leaves
* 6 drops each of lavender and frankincense essential oils
* A square blue-cotton pillow or small blue bag about 20 cm (8 inches) square.

Place the herbs and oils in the bag. Place your dream pillow in or under your normal pillow. Other magical herbs to use in other dream pillows include the following:

* **For pleasant dreams:** Anise, passionflower, gardenia, skullcap
* **To halt a nightmare:** Bay, vervain, sage, dandelion
* **For restful sleep:** Chamomile, marjoram, lavender, peppermint, valerian
* **For psychic dreams, astral protection:** Mugwort, jasmine, marigold, rose, onion, lemongrass
* **To dream about your lover:** Yarrow, lavender, jasmine, rose, mugwort.

These combinations can also be useful in dream pillows:

* **To ease depression:** Thyme, St John's wort, chamomile, vervain
* **To aid in healing:** Angelica, cinnamon, burdock, lemon balm, garlic
* **For divination:** Orange, star anise, laurel leaves, nutmeg, coltsfoot
* **To stop gossip:** Clove, slippery elm
* **For protection:** Frankincense, agrimony, clover, fennel, lavender, mint.

Recurring dreams

These are dreams that seem to recur either over a series of nights or get replayed every once in a while. These dreams may be either pleasant or they can be nightmares. Regardless, it is important to focus on dreams that recur as they can have some important information that you need to take on board. Ask yourself why this dream keeps coming to your attention.

Start paying particular attention to this dream and don't be afraid to work with it. Write down as many of the details of the dream as you can remember. As with all dreams, the more attention you give them, the more answers you will receive.

This type of dream can also alert you to some past-life situations or traumas. Many cultures believe in reincarnation – the idea that our souls return to earth to inhabit different bodies in our search for perfection. The solution to a current life problem may well have its root in a past-life experience. Dream work is one of the best ways of accessing that information.

Discover your past lives through your dreams

Have you ever felt that you know about a place even though you have never been there? Or have you ever met a person and felt an unbelievable connection to them? This déjà vu phenomenon may actually indicate a past-life experience.

Our soul contains a blueprint – an awareness of what our life purpose is based on and experiences gathered during our previous lives. Before we come physically into being, our soul collects all the necessary memories and data to allow it to live with a particular purpose. When we are born, the soul brings the blueprint with it, seeking to fulfil its purpose.

The memory of our past lives and the lessons we need to learn this life time are encoded in this blueprint, and are just waiting for the right time, the right person or situation to arise to activate our learning processes. It is believed that we are experiencing another lifetime to resolve old karma as well as to experience a physical life with joy or pain. We have all had many lifetimes, and past-life awareness is only as useful as what you do with it.

If you want to connect with a past life to gain knowledge about present-life issues, you first need to list all the historical periods with which you feel you have an affinity. Are you drawn to Ancient Egypt or Rome, or to Native America?

Write down any feelings or thoughts you have about these times. You may also want to meditate on a selected period to see if any thoughts that flow about that time can help you with a current-life issue. To be more specific, do the following ritual to tap into the wisdom of the past.

Just before you retire for the night, do a short relaxation exercise or the ritual for body awareness earlier in the chapter. Open your heart energy by visualizing the area around your heart glowing with a beautiful soft green light. Feel the light becoming suffused with love and compassion.

Visualize yourself in a particular historical time that you feel a particular connection to. Make it feel as real as possible. Surround this image with your feelings of love and compassion and ask this energy what you most need to learn from this time. Alternatively you can ask a specific question, such as why you are suffering from a particular phobia or illness, as a trauma in your past life may be the cause. Request that you be given guidance on this question. Clear your mind and go to sleep.

Upon waking, write down any dreams, thoughts, feelings or impressions that came to you during the night. Do this exercise until you gain clarity around your question.

Global Godde

21st Century

Directory

Meditation, Chakras, Psychic Development and Healing

✴ The College of Psychic Studies
16 Queensberry Place
London SW7 2EB
Telephone 020 7589 3292
www.psychic-studies.org.uk

You can take a course in meditation here, attend a day workshop on your chakras, learn how to read the Tarot, or book a session with a healer or medium.

The college is near the Natural History Museum and South Kensington tube station, and has a bookshop, library and meditation room. For a booklet, send an SAE and you can find out what is on offer.

✴ The Spiritualist Association of Great Britain
33 Belgrave Square
London SWIX 8QB
Telephone 020 7235 3351
www.spiritualuk.com

This is the place to see some of the world's most famous mediums – like Gordon Smith – in action. You can also take meditation classes, and if you want to develop your psychic abilities, you can enrol in a course. Like the College of Psychic Studies, it's possible to become a member here and receive discounts.

There is a cafeteria here, and a library, and it's one of the most beautiful and best known spooky centres in Great Britain!

✴ The Edinburgh College of Parapsychology
2 Melville Street
Edinburgh
Scotland
EH3 7NS
Telephone 0131 220 1433
www.parapsychology.org.uk

J.K. Rowling lives a few miles away – could this be the inspiration for Hogwarts? It certainly has an incredible range of speakers, visiting psychics and gifted mediums. You can book a session here, or enrol in a long course, or just a weekend workshop. The library has an unbelievable 2000 books and if you become a member, you get borrowing rights. Some of the world's leading speakers make a point of stopping off here, but book early. Aura readings, meditation, reiki and shamanism were on the bill when we last looked.

Extraordinary stores

✳ **Body and Soul**
166 Bruntsfield Place
Edinburgh
Scotland
EH10 1ER
Telephone 0131 228 6906

Edinburgh's leading one-stop-shop for gorgeous Buddhist wall hangings, good quality amethysts, interesting and well-chosen books, nice post-cards and more.

After you've visited the Edinburgh College of Parapsychology, have a look here. It's tiny, but it's great.

✳ **Calmia**
52–54 Marylebone High Street
London W1U 5HR
Telephone 020 7224 3585
www.calmia.com

The health and beauty expert Josephine Fairley describes Calmia as the 21st century version of Space NK and we have to agree. Yoga mats, silk eye bags, herbal tea and inspiring books are laid out beautifully along with essential oils, incense and virtually all a goddess could want. Sit at the tea bar or check into the day spa, but we dare you to walk in here and emerge without spending your entire salary!

✳ **Feng Shui**
www.chienergy.co.uk

Simon Brown is our Global Goddess Guru when it comes to Feng Shui. He and his wife Dragana Brown (who co-wrote a macrobiotic cookbook with Boy George) have established a one-stop shop online for sorting out the chi in your new flat. You can also find Simon and friends at their new shop in London at 240 Kensington High Street – call 0207 371 6987.

✳ Hocus Pocus

38 Gardner Street
Brighton BN1 1UN
Telephone 01273 572212
www.hocuspocus.co.uk

If you are visiting Brighton, don't miss Hocus Pocus, hidden away in the Lanes near the station. There is a large magical oil and herb section which we haven't seen anywhere else, and a crammed fairy section. Some of the staff are Wiccans, we are told – which might explain why the magical book section is particularly well-stocked. This store gets crowded, but it has a bit of everything, and is very popular with young goth girls.

✳ Mysteries

9–11 Monmouth Street
Covent Garden
London WC2H 9DA
Telephone 020 7240 3688

Mysteries is one of this country's oldest and best-known spooky stores, with a huge selection of different tarot and oracle cards. They also stock New Age cassettes and videos, books and accessories for spells and witchcraft.

✳ L'Occitane

46 Buchanan Street
Glasgow
Scotland
G1 3JX
Telephone 0141 248 7940

9 The Market
Covent Garden
London
WC2E 8RB
Telephone 020 7379 6040
www.http://uk.loccitaneworld.com

We know there are loads of companies producing incense out there, from basic Nag Champa to extraordinary stuff which smells like bananas. We recommend L'Occitane because it makes incense, candles and room spray from pure ingredients in Provence, but also because the company has a sound ethical philosophy. For a start, they package their products with braille writing, so that blind customers can shop more easily. And they also work as co-producers with the women of the Burkina Faso village in Africa, so that their Shea Butter range benefits the community there. To find your nearest L'Occitane, visit their website, but we've listed two of the biggest here.

Astrology galore

* **The Astrology Shop**
  78 Neal Street
  Covent Garden
  London WC2H 9PA
  Telephone 020 7497 1001.
  www.astrology.co.uk

Barry Street is in charge at the Astrology Shop, which is close to some of London's most lethally tempting shoe shops, and just around the corner from the legendary Neal's Yard. Lots of people come here just to order a computer chart, which can be ready in just a few minutes – some of the world's leading astrologers have written personalized computer programs to calculate your past, present, future and personality – and all you need to do is bring in your birth details. There are books here too, and astrological paraphernalia.

* **Astrological Consultations**
  www.astroboogie.com

If you don't want a computer chart, you might want to book a private consultation with Global Goddess Guru Adam Smith, who is a regular columnist on Spirit magazine, and an occasional contributor to Jonathan Cainer's horoscope column in the *Daily Mirror*. Adam is based in north London and writes for several magazines overseas too. For more information, see his website.

* The British Astrological and Psychic Society

PO Box 363
Rochester
MEI 3DJ
www.baps.ws

This is one of the best places for an absolute astrological beginner to start. President Adam Fronteras is a gifted psychic and astrologer in his own right, and the bestselling Tarot writer Sasha Fenton is a longtime member. You can take classes by correspondence, so it's great if you live outside London. You can also book a psychic reading or an astrological consultation with any qualified BAPS members.

* Equinox

The Mill House
Santon
Isle of Man
IM4 1EX
Telephone 01624 827000
www.equinoxastrology.com

To order your personal horoscope, try Robert Currey's amazing mail-order service. Robert is an experienced astrologer and has produced a wide range of astrology charts to order, from personality profiles to future trend reports. A personal hand-drawn report or consultation would be more expensive, but these reasonably priced, computer-calculated charts are extremely accurate.

* The House of Astrology

9 Parliament Street
Temple Bar
Dublin 2
Ireland
Telephone 01 679 3404

Ireland's best-known shop for astrology – and also fine crystals, Native American rattles and dream catchers, Tibetan Buddhist statues, and more. There are Tarot readers and even aura photographers in residence, and of course you can get your chart done too. Ask here for a recommended clairvoyant – otherwise take your chances with the ten-quid Tarot readers in Temple Bar.

Don't miss

* **Alternatives**
  Alternatives
  St James Church
  197 Piccadilly
  London
  Telephone 020 7287 6711
  www.alternatives.org.uk

Alternatives is a floating organization based in beautiful St James Church, on Piccadilly. A colour magazine listing lectures, workshops and classes is published every few months, and you can hear about sacred sites, sacred space, self-healing, aura cleansing, sound therapy, planetary responsibility and peace activism (and that's just a conservative taster) on their website. Some of the most famous names in the new age come here to talk, but book early (and turn up early to hear them).

The best spooky bookstores

* **Watkins Books**
  19 Cecil Court
  Charing Cross Road
  London WC2N 4EZ
  Telephone 020 7836 2182
  www.watkinsbooks.com

Watkins is the oldest mind, body, spirit bookshop in the world. A psychic sits in the window, and on two levels you will find everything from secondhand tomes on astral travelling to bestselling new age fiction. Every topic in our book has its own shelf space in Watkins and the atmosphere is calm, unhurried and friendly. Don't forget the bargains on the ground floor! And when you're done, go to Watkins Esoteric Centre, a few doors up, which has flower essences, videos, Buddhist cards and wall hangings, incense, Tara statues and easily the biggest and best selection of crystals and Tarot cards in London.

* **The Green Buddha Bookshop**
  15 Bond Street
  Brighton
  BN1 1RD
  Telephone 01273 324 488

Brighton is often called the alternative capital of England, and this is the city's nicest, most interesting bookshop. As you might expect, the section on Buddhism is enormous, but you'll also find vegetarian cookbooks, relationship self-help tomes, meditation CDs, birthday cards, incense and crystals in here.

There is a permanent bargain section at the front which is always worth a look!

Cool compact discs

✳ **Jonathan Goldman**
Trance Tara
Spirit Music/Ambient
www.healingsounds.com

Jonathan is into sound healing, and he uses Tibetan singing bowls, bells, and chanting on this CD, which is a tribute to Tara, the Tibetan Goddess of Compassion and Protection. Side one invokes the Goddess, side two evokes the Goddess.

✳ **The Mind Body and Soul Series**
Meditation and Visualization
New World Music
www.newworldmusic.com

Composer Medwyn Goodall and healer and homeopath Cornelia Glynn have joined forces on this CD. The Mind Body and Soul Series also offers CDs to accompany aromatherapy, crystal work, Feng Shui, reiki, tarot, and yoga. Check out the website.

✳ **Nawang Khechog**
Quiet Mind
Sounds True

Nawang Khechog has dedicated this CD to the preservation of Tibetan culture and civilization. He was born in Tibet, where he learned to play the bamboo flute. He has worked with Kitaro, the Grammy-nominated musician. He has also played live with Paul Simon and Michael Stipe from REM. This is a really powerful CD and the flute playing is beautiful.

Goddess

Finally, here is a general website that offers a variety of products for your magical pursuits! Visit: www.goddess.com.

If you are wanting to explore ritual magic or the path of the ancient Goddess more fully, visit Starhawk, who is an author and spiritualist, at her website: www.starhawk.org.

Here's another site that is dedicated to bringing awareness of women's issues and all things Goddessy to the world. There are some quite interesting links worth exploring while you're there: www.goddess2000.org. The Religious Tolerance Group is an organization that works to dispel the myths around witchcraft and is an open forum including chatrooms for teenagers and others who wish to know the facts about Wicca and The Craft in relation to religion. Visit the website for more information.

The Religious Tolerance Group can be found at: www.religioustolerance.org.

And don't forget

You can always e-mail one of us (Jelena, Anthea or Jessica) at our website: www.21stcenturygoddess.net

Goddess Library

Margot Adler, *Drawing down the Moon*,
Beacon Press, Boston, 1981.

Judith Anodea and Selena Vega, *The Sevenfold Journey*,
The Crossing Press, Freedom, CA, USA, 1997.

Jennifer Barker-Woolger and Roger J. Woolger, *The Goddess Within*,
Random Century, London, 1990.

Catherine Basquali, *Catherine*,
Pan Macmillan, Australia, 2000.

Andrew Bell, *Creative Health*,
Benton Ross Publishers, New Zealand, 1989.

Robert E. Bell, *Women of Classical Mythology*,
ABC-CLIO Santa Barbara California, 1991.

William Bloom, *Working with Angels, Fairies and Nature Spirits*,
Piatkus Books, London, 1998.

Barbara Ann Brennan, *Light Emerging and Hands of Light*,
Bantam Books, NY, 1993.

Zsuzsanna E. Budapest, *The Goddess in the Office*,
HarperSanFrancisco, San Francisco, 1993.

Suzy Chiazzari, *The Complete Book of Colour*,
Element Books, Great Britain, 1998.

Cyndi Dale, *New Chakra Healing*,
Llewellyn Publications, USA, 1996.

J.E. Cirlot, *A Dictionary of Symbols*,
Routledge, London, 1971.

Amanda Cochrane and Clare G. Harvey, *The Encyclopaedia of Flower Remedies*, Thorsons, London, 1995.

Scott Cunningham, *The Complete Book of Incense, Oils and Brews*,
Llewellyn Publications, St Paul, Minnesota, USA, 1985.

Scott Cunningham, *Earth Magic*,
Llewellyn Publications, St Paul, Minnesota, USA, 1983.

Lucia Capacchione, *Visioning*,
Thorsons, London, 1999.

Irene Dalichow and Mike Booth, *Aura-Soma*,
Hay House, USA, 1996.

Marie Farquharson, *Natural Detox*,
Element Books, UK, 1999.

Shakti Gawain, *Creative Visualisation*,
Bantam Books, USA, 1982.

Shakti Gawain, *Living In The Light*,
Bantam Books, USA, 1993.

Judy Hall, *The Illustrated Guide to Crystals*,
Sterling Publishing Company, NY, 2000.

Louise L. Hay, *Heal Your Body*,
Eden Grove Editions, London, 1989.

Louise L. Hay, *You Can Heal Your Life*,
Eden Grove Editions, London, 1994.

Roni Jay, *The Book of Goddess*,
Barrons, USA, 2000.

Carl Jung, *Dreams*,
Ark Paperbacks, Great Britain, 1982.

Carl Jung, *Man and His Symbols*,
Aldus Books, London, 1964.

Leslie Kenton, *Rejuvenate Now*,
Vermilion, London, 1996.

Debbi Kempton-Smith, *Secrets from an Astrologer's Notebook*,
Topquark Press, New York, 1999.

Karen Kingston, *Clear Your Clutter with Feng Shui*,
Piatkus Books, London, 1998.

Denise Linn, *Sacred Space*,
Rider Books, London, 1995.

Anne McIntyre, *The Complete Floral Healer*,
Hodder and Stoughton, Australia 1996.

David A. Phillips, *Discovering the Inner Self*,
Gary Allen, Australia, 1996.

Christian Ratsch, *The Dictionary of Sacred and Magical Plants*,
ABC-CLIO, Santa Barbara, California, 1992.